Post-Classical Hollywood

Post-Classical Hollywood

Film Industry, Style and Ideology since 1945

Barry Langford

Edinburgh University Press

© Barry Langford, 2010

Edinburgh University Press Ltd
22 George Square, Edinburgh

www.euppublishing.com

Reprinted 2011

Typeset in Monotype Ehrhardt
by Servis Filmsetting Ltd, Stockport, Cheshire, and
printed and bound in Great Britain by
CPI Antony Rowe, Chippenham and Eastbourne

A CIP record for this book is available from the British Library

ISBN 978 0 7486 3857 4 (hardback)
ISBN 978 0 7486 3858 1 (paperback)

The right of Barry Langford
to be identified as author of this work
has been asserted in accordance with
the Copyright, Designs and Patents Act 1988.

Published with the support of the Edinburgh University Scholarly
Publishing Initiatives Fund.

Contents

Illustrations   vii

Acknowledgements   ix

Introduction   xi

Part I: Hollywood in Transition 1945–65   1

Introduction to Part I   3

1   The Autumn of the Patriarchs   11

The Biggest, the Best: 1946 (*The Best Years of Our Lives*)   41

2   The Communication of Ideas   45

The Biggest, the Best: 1955 (*Marty, Cinerama Holiday*)   69

3   Modernising Hollywood   73

Part II: Crisis and Renaissance 1966–81   97

Introduction to Part II   99

The Biggest, the Best: 1965 (*The Sound of Music*)   104

4   The Changing of the Guard   107

5   New Wave Hollywood   133

The Biggest, the Best: 1975 (*One Flew Over the Cuckoo's Nest, Jaws*)   154

6   Who Lost the Picture Show?   157

Part III: New Hollywood 1982–2006   181

Introduction to Part III   183

7   Corporate Hollywood   191

The Biggest, the Best: 1985 (*Out of Africa, Back to the Future*)   216

8   Culture Wars   219

The Biggest, the Best: 1995 (*Braveheart, Toy Story*)   241

9   Post-Classical Style?   245

The Biggest, the Best: 2005 (*Crash, Star Wars Episode III: Revenge of
   the Sith*)   265

Conclusion: 'Hollywood' Now   269

Appendix   285

Further Reading   287

Index   295

Illustrations

1   Looking ahead to an uncertain future: *The Best Years of Our Lives* (Goldwyn 1945). Reproduced courtesy of The Kobal Collection   12

2   The 'Hollywood Ten' and their families protest in vain against their prison sentences in 1947. Reproduced courtesy of The Kobal Collection   46

3   Publicity for *This Is Cinerama* (1953), the opening salvo of the widescreen era. Reproduced courtesy of The Kobal Collection   72

4   Hunt's Cinestage, Columbus, roadshow-era showcase. Reproduced courtesy of the Columbus Metropolitan Library Photo Collection   98

5   'Just drifting': Mike Nichols (standing, in sunglasses) directs Dustin Hoffman in *The Graduate* (Avco Embassy 1967). Reproduced courtesy of The Kobal Collection   108

6   'Sappy Endings': *New York, New York* (United Artists 1977). Reproduced courtesy of The Kobal Collection   132

7   *Jaws* (Universal 1975): the start of a new era. Reproduced courtesy of The Kobal Collection   155

8   Living up to a 'big rep': McCabe (Warren Beatty) plays the hero in Robert Altman's *McCabe & Mrs. Miller* (Warner Brothers 1971). Reproduced courtesy of The Kobal Collection   158

9   Marty McFly invents rock 'n' roll: *Back to the Future* (Universal 1985). Reproduced courtesy of The Kobal Collection   190

10 Making his mark on history: *Forrest Gump* (Paramount 1994). Reproduced courtesy of The Kobal Collection   220

11 'Welcome to Jurassic Park!' The digital sublime in *Jurassic Park* (Universal 1993). Reproduced courtesy of The Kobal Collection   244

12   *Crash* (Lionsgate 2005). Reproduced courtesy of The Kobal
     Collection   266
13   Hollywood's nightmare: pirated DVDs seized by police.
     Reproduced courtesy of The Kobal Collection   268

Acknowledgements

Numerous people have contributed, without necessarily always knowing it, to the development of the ideas that inform this book. My thanks to several generations of students on my Post-Classical Hollywood course at Royal Holloway, University of London, who have helped enormously, often by making me answer – and ask – questions I would not otherwise have considered. My colleagues in the Department of Media Arts at Royal Holloway have offered extremely helpful feedback and canny insights when various parts of this project have been presented at departmental research seminars. Dr Jacob Leigh read some chapters in draft form and responded in a characteristically helpful and constructive fashion. Part of Chapter 9 was presented as a paper at the 2007 Society for Cinema and Media Studies conference in Philadelphia; my thanks to the conference committee, to the British Academy for the award of an Overseas Conference Grant allowing me to make the trip, and to the audience at the Contemporary Filmmakers panel who responded in such stimulating and challenging ways to my thoughts on Steven Spielberg and the dialectic of spectacle.

The research and writing of the book were supported by the Faculty of Arts at Royal Holloway, which offered an invaluable period of sabbatical leave in 2007, and the Department of Media Arts, who funded a trip to gather research on moviegoing in Columbus, Ohio. In Columbus, my warmest thanks to Professor David Stebenne of the Department of History at The Ohio State University for his hospitality; and a particular thanks to David's graduate student Frank Blazich, who undertook vital long-distance research assistance at a late stage of drafting the book.

At Edinburgh University Press, Sarah Edwards saw the book through the commissioning stage, and Esmé Watson was helpful and – not least – patient as several deadlines came and went without the manuscript arriving. My thanks and I hope it was worth the wait.

A book such as this obviously owed an enormous debt to other scholars: in the case of Hollywood studies, foremost among these, inevitably, is David Bordwell, Kristin Thompson and Janet Staiger's pioneering *The Classical Hollywood Cinema*. It will be apparent from the following pages just how important I consider their work to be, even when I disagree with some of its conclusions. Obviously, wherever I have profited from their or other scholars' labours, the responsibility for any errors of emphasis or interpretation is entirely mine.

The final vote of thanks goes to my long-suffering family, who have coped with the colonisation of the kitchen (because it overlooks the garden) by papers, notes and books, and still more with my testing transformation into a recluse, and an often ill-natured one at that, throughout much of the summer of 2009. I hope my wife, Carole, and my son, Noah, know what their love and support means to me, though even from among the unduly large number of words in this book it is difficult to find the few simple words that can express just how much it does mean. This book is dedicated to Noah, who likes Hollywood movies and who can now retrieve his dad and once again whup him on Mario Karts to his heart's content.

Introduction

The Hollywood film industry compels and receives universal attention, and for obvious reasons: for most of the last 100 years, Hollywood has set the terms of global film culture, and while that pre-eminence has frequently been criticised it has – notwithstanding the many other worldwide centres of cinematic excellence, some of them extremely successful – yet to be seriously challenged. Indeed, as I will repeatedly have cause to note in this book, an important dimension of Hollywood's enduring success has been its facility in adopting and adapting the attributes and the technical and stylistic innovations of its competitors, from pre-World War I Italy and Scandinavia to Weimar Germany, through the European New Waves of the 1960s, and on to Bollywood and Hong Kong today.

Since the end of World War II above all, Hollywood has been without question the dominant global film industry. The seven decades since 1945 have certainly confronted American cinema with challenges and crises that could not easily have been – and were not – anticipated as the Hollywood studio system prepared in 1945 to enjoy the fruits of victory (Hollywood's own contribution to the war effort having enhanced its public profile and reputation). Notwithstanding these challenges, and the era-defining social, political and economic changes that gave rise to them, by the end of the so-called 'American century' Hollywood's worldwide dominance remained self-evident – indeed, in a largely borderless global economy the products of the American entertainment industry are more ubiquitous now than ever.

Yet today's 'Hollywood' – that is, the 'filmed entertainment' divisions of the transnational media conglomerates NewsCorp, Sony, Time Warner, Walt Disney, GE[1] and Viacom, alongside numerous 'mini-majors' and independent production companies of various kinds – and how it differs from the old studios of popular legend, remains obscure to most of its audience. This misunderstanding testifies partly to the confusing, ramified and multi-dimensional nature of the contemporary corporate American entertainment industry and partly to the enduring myth of the 'Hollywood studio', whose iconic brands (Warner Brothers, Paramount, Disney) remain part of the contemporary scene, though bar their names and common histories they share little with the vanished personal fiefdoms of the long-gone moguls. Partly, too, it reflects persistent assumptions that how movies are made – the industrial structures and business practices governing the decision to 'greenlight' any given picture – is less important than the creative impulses of visionary filmmakers, and certainly less interesting than the artistry of the films themselves. Over the last twenty-five years, such scholars as Thomas Schatz, Douglas Gomery, David Bordwell and many others working in the fields of film history, stylistic analysis and critical interpretation have demonstrated conclusively that the meanings and motives of Hollywood films cannot be adequately understood without systematic explication of the architecture of Hollywood: the dominant frameworks and conventions, the historical contexts and the governing attitudes which enable certain films to be successfully made and marketed, others to fail, and countless others never to reach the multiplex or to disappear into 'development hell'.

Equally, however, if film history is to be more than business history or the history of technology, the complex linkages between economics and film aesthetics need careful examination and analysis. So too does the question of how films make meanings for their audiences, in the shared context of their times – an understanding which has to move beyond unexamined auteurist assumptions as well as simplistic notions of how film 'reflects' social realities. The journey from *The Best Years of Our Lives* (Academy Award for Best Picture and top earner of 1946) to *The Dark Knight* (the top-grossing film of 2008, taking in more than half a billion dollars at the US domestic box office alone) is not a straightforward one. This book therefore combines analysis of the changing film industry with detailed discussion of both the principal stylistic characteristics and the ideological content of Hollywood motion pictures across their postwar history/histories.

As the title makes obvious, an overarching aim of the book is to elucidate in what fashion and to what extent films and filmmaking have moved away from the 'classical Hollywood cinema', as expounded in David Bordwell, Janet Staiger and Kristin Thompson's 1985 study with that title, itself now a classic and surely one of the most influential and agenda-setting works of recent scholarship in any field. As *The Classical Hollywood Cinema* acknowledges, the use of the term 'classical' to describe Hollywood filmmaking in the studio era probably originates in the French film theorist André Bazin's declaration in an essay of the early 1950s that by the outbreak of World War II the sound film in the USA (and France) 'had reached a level of classical perfection'. The films of William Wyler, John Ford and other studio filmmakers, Bazin wrote, brought cinema to 'its perfect balance, its ideal form of expression' through firmly established paradigms and protocols of genre, visual style and editing – 'a complete harmony of image and sound . . . In short, here are all the characteristics of a classical art'.[2]

Bazin was not concerned to specify or systematise the idea of the 'classical' cinema in more than a general way. In *The Classical Hollywood Cinema*, Bordwell, Staiger and Thompson set out to do just that. This book will explore in detail the paradigm of Hollywood practice they identify, but its general outlines – a stable temporal and spatial regime, achieved through adherence to continuity principles and a general though not absolute commitment to stylistic transparency, in the service of linear, character-centred narratives – are well known. The 'classicism' of this model of filmmaking consists in the classical Hollywood cinema's properties of 'decorum, proportion, formal harmony, respect for tradition, mimesis, self-effacing craftsmanship, and cool control of the viewer's response – canons which critics in any medium usually call "classical"'.[3] Determining the validity and the limitations of this model – developed over 500 double-columned pages with a hitherto unprecedented wealth of textual and documentary evidence, as well as a (somewhat controversial) 'unbiased sample' of 100 films produced between 1915 and 1960 – has set the agenda for how Hollywood style is discussed in historical contexts for the last twenty-five years.

Among the several vexed issues raised by *The Classical Hollywood Cinema*, one particular crux is the confusing question of 'classicism' as a stylistic, rather than a historical, category. That is, to what extent does the 'group style' of studio-era films – around the existence, if not the nature, of which there is a reasonable measure of scholarly consensus – actually display the decorous, proportional, etc. qualities identified by Bordwell, Staiger and Thompson as 'classical'? How 'classical', exactly, was 'classic Hollywood'? Various commentators have pointed out that 'classicism' hardly seems to cover the stylistic variety and at times sheer oddity of Hollywood films, which range from three-hour-plus Biblical epics to singing cowboys;[4] nor, in its emphasis on narrative as the 'ultimately determining instance' of film style, does this model seem fully to take account of the obvious appeal Hollywood films make through various kinds of visual spectacle.[5] All of these unresolved problems are naturally exacerbated when one comes to consider the – quite evidently very different – production contexts and practices of Hollywood since the end of the studio system, and the stylistic regimes that have emerged from them.

Since the 1970s the term 'post-classical Hollywood' has come into increasingly wide, though by no means consistent, critical usage to describe various aspects of this contemporary Hollywood cinema. Current scholarship approaches Hollywood from a wide variety of methodological and interpretative perspectives, and has identified numerous ways in which the making, marketing, form, content and reception of films have all changed significantly since the studio era. Yet critical consensus on 'post-classical Hollywood', its timeline, defining aspects, limits and prospects, remains obstinately unachieved. Both David Bordwell and Kristin Thompson in their recent work have argued against any sense of a decisive break in film style since 1960 (when *The Classical Hollywood Cinema* ends). Justin Wyatt and others, by contrast, argue that a fundamentally different political and aesthetic economy of moviemaking sets in around 1980. There is terminological confusion here too. Peter Krämer identifies the 'New Hollywood' – a term in general circulation, to describe Hollywood since the end of the old studio system, since at least 1957, and which overlaps with 'post-classical Hollywood' – specifically with the period 1967–77 (also known as the 'Hollywood Renaissance' or 'auteur renaissance'); Geoff King distinguishes two consecutive 'versions' of New Hollywood(s). Tom Schatz's New Hollywood is defined by the emergent hegemony of the blockbuster; Jim Hiller's, by the proliferation of production centres and sectors (mainstream, exploitation, independent, etc.).[6]

One aim of this book, therefore, is quite simply to elaborate, explain, and interrogate critically the various understandings of the 'post-classical' – its coherence, historical justification and relevance to our understanding of Hollywood filmmaking, historically and in the present. I will do this by charting the key critical debates alongside the histories they interpret, and offering my own account of the 'post-classical'.

I have chosen to approach Hollywood since 1945 chronologically. The postwar period as a whole is divided into three sections, from 1945 to 1965, 1966 to 1981 and 1982 to 2006. These divisions correspond in broad terms to the established periodisation of Hollywood historians: each focuses on a period delimited and defined by major shifts and/or historical watersheds. The first covers the two decades immediately following World War II, years in which the American film industry underwent major reorganisation following the Supreme Court's decision in *United States v. Paramount Pictures, Inc. et al.* that ended the vertically integrated studio system, and faced challenges from declining audiences and the rise of television. How Hollywood adapted to these changing circumstances, institutionally and stylistically, is the focus of this section. The second section covers the period in which, under continuing financial pressure, the studios first turned to a new generation of filmmakers to court younger audiences with, in part, more topical and unconventional styles and subject matter; but then, following the runaway success of *Jaws* and *Star Wars*, shifted again in the late 1970s, towards a more spectacular, action-oriented cinema of sensation and away from the (somewhat) more character-centred and (sometimes) challenging films of the 'Hollywood Renaissance'. The final section explores the Hollywood that emerged from these three postwar decades of upheaval and transitions, restabilised – but stabilised in new ways – by Hollywood's incorporation as one arm of a diversified and constantly expanding contemporary global media industry. A shorter final chapter, '"Hollywood" Now', brings the story up to date.

Each chronological period/section is subdivided into three chapters, each of which takes a different perspective on the whole of the period at hand. The first chapter in each section summarises and interprets the evolving history of the American film industry, its key personnel, its business models and institutional practices. The second considers Hollywood films in relation to their social, cultural and political contexts. The third considers the visual style, approaches to narrative and other stylistic elements most characteristic of the films of a specific period. This structure is intended to plot a clear pathway through the book and to enable direct comparisons across periods. The order reflects my own general belief that forms of creative cultural practice, and the nature and degree of artistic innovation, are strongly influenced by their economic and social contexts – though this is certainly not to say they are reducible to them.

The inclusion of a strand on social context and ideology clearly differentiates this book's approach from that of *The Classical Hollywood Cinema*, which explicitly brackets off any discussion of 'ethico-social-political norms'. I hope to show, by contrast, that the stories Hollywood films tell – the kinds of stories they *can* tell – are profoundly influenced by, and responsive to, both concrete historical issues and events (such as anti-communism or the Vietnam War and its aftermath) as well as the ideological currents that circulate around and through such events and supply the terms on which they are available to be understood. Because this obviously does not happen in an unmediated or straightforward fashion, these chapters will pay extensive attention to generic trends, using genre as a means of mediating the relationship between film and social, political and economic contexts. I have written elsewhere that genre study can offer 'a historically-grounded method of establishing "family resemblances" between films produced and released under widely differing circumstances, and of mediating the relationship between the mythologies of popular culture and social, political and economic contexts', and maintain that methodology here.[7] These chapters are intentionally placed between the industrial/historical and the stylistic/analytical chapters to make the point that film form is not, and cannot be, ideologically innocent. Only in the second section of the book, dealing with the period 1966–81, is this order reversed, with the chapter on form ('Hollywood New Wave') preceding that on ideology ('Who Lost the Picture Show?'). This is not supposed to indicate the primacy of form in the Hollywood Renaissance, but rather the reverse: to illustrate that in this period, there is an unusually self-conscious and clearly articulated 'politics of form' by which the range and nature of stylistic options and innovations is largely governed, but which also limits the capacity of these films to offer authentic ideological challenge.

Two other strands, also chronologically sequenced, are interwoven with these large historical blocks. Each historical section has an introduction reviewing the changes to the film industry as experienced 'on the ground', that is as cinemagoers and movie spectators (in the age of television, home video and digital download these are, of course, no longer the same thing) have encountered them during each of these periods. I do this by summarising the changes in film exhibition and consumption in one mid-size American city, Columbus, Ohio, from 1946 to the present. The choice of Columbus was governed by its size, its Midwest location, Ohio's reputation as a 'bellwether' state in electoral politics, and its own widely-recognised 'representative' qualities (which have long made it a favoured test market for new products), all of which make it arguably more illustrative of industry trends (which themselves are of course affected by social trends, such as the demise of the downtown picture palaces in favour of first duplex and triplex, and then multiplex cinemas in suburban shopping malls) than a 'world city' such as New York or Chicago. Of course every community is unique and affected by different factors, but as these analyses make clear, Columbus's experience of consuming Hollywood films could largely be replicated throughout the USA (and increasingly worldwide).

The remaining elements in the book are short sections, 'The Biggest, the Best', that take the temperature of Hollywood cinema at the midpoint of each decade covered by this book (starting in 1946, and then touching down at 1955, 1965, and so on) by discussing the top-earning/highest grossing film[8] and the winner of the Academy Award for the year's Best Picture. (For 1946 and 1965 these were the same film.) Neither of these milestones is intended as a straightforward criterion for estimating excellence or even 'popularity'. (We can know that more people saw one film than any other, but we cannot always be sure what they thought of it.) The Best Picture award, in particular, I take to reflect the industry's estimation of its own virtues and the preferred self-image Hollywood projects to the world. In some cases both films are discussed, in others one film receives a good deal more attention than the other (I am afraid I struggled to find much to say about *Braveheart*). These sections, interpolated over the course of the book, also allow for more close analysis of individual films than can always be included in the necessarily wider-ranging perspective of the main chapters.

The book's title delimits its coverage, so readers will find that apart from some discussion of some forms of independent production as it has intersected with and affected 'mainstream' Hollywood, this book does not cover documentary or experimental film, or explore anything like the full range of 'indie' and other semi-autonomous forms of narrative filmmaking. (For the latter, the reader is referred to excellent recent studies by Geoff King and Yannis Tzioumakis.)

NOTES ON STATISTICS

Except where otherwise noted, industry statistics (annual attendances, number of US cinemas, number of releases, etc.) are taken from the data collated in Joel Finler, *The Hollywood Story*, revised edition (London: Wallflower, 2003), pp. 356–81.

Box office returns as cited here are of two kinds: before 1981, the figures are for *rentals* (that is, the money returned to distributors by exhibitors after deducting their percentage of the box office takings and the 'house nut', the sum allocated for the theatre's own operating costs). Rentals were how *Variety* and other industry trade publications recorded box office performance through the late 1970s. Since the 1980s, the figure reported has been the *box office gross*, the total amount of money taken at the box office during a film's theatrical release. Chapters 1–6, therefore, use rentals; Chapters 7–10, box office gross. Except where otherwise noted, these figures are derived from the records in the 'Revenue Database' at www.boxofficereport.com and the 'Yearly Box Office Results' at www.boxofficemojo.com

NOTE ON REFERENCES

This book draws on a wide range of contemporary sources, primarily from trade and business press. These are fully cited in the endnotes to each chapter. A list of suggestions for Further Reading at the end of the book, organised according to chapter, is limited to secondary sources, many, but not all, directly cited in the text.

NOTES

1. Shortly before this book went to press, cable TV operator Comcast announced a deal with GE to acquire a majority stake in NBC Universal; with this deal the company rejoined the giant dedicated media conglomerates, having exited their ranks in 1995 when the former owners Matsushita sold the then Universal Studios to the Canadian liquor distributor Seagram (see Chapter 7).
2. André Bazin, 'The evolution of the language of cinema', [1950, 1952] in *What Is Cinema?* trans., ed. Hugh Gray (Berkeley: University of California Press, 1967), pp. 29–30.
3. David Bordwell, Janet Staiger and Kristin Thompson, *The Classical Hollywood Cinema: Film Style and Mode of Production to 1960* (London: Routledge, 1985), p. 5. (Hereafter *CHC*.)
4. My thanks to Lee Grieveson for this pithily made point.
5. See for instance Elizabeth Cowie, 'Storytelling: classical Hollywood cinema and classical narration', in Steve Neale and Murray Smith (eds), *Contemporary Hollywood Cinema* (London: Routledge, 1997), pp. 178–90.

6. Peter Krämer, *The New Hollywood: From* Bonnie and Clyde *to* Star Wars (London: Wallflower, 2005); Geoff King, *New Hollywood Cinema: An Introduction* (London: I. B. Tauris, 2001); Thomas Schatz, 'The New Hollywood', in Jim Collins, Hilary Radner and Ava Preacher Collins (eds), *Film Theory Goes to the Movies* (London: Routledge, 1993), pp. 8–36; Jim Hillier, *The New Hollywood* (London: Studio Vista, 1993).

7. Barry Langford, *Film Genre: Hollywood and Beyond* (Edinburgh: Edinburgh University Press, 2005), p. 3.

8. See the note on grosses and rentals.

PART I

Hollywood in Transition 1945–65

Introduction to Part I

Friday, 30 August 1946: the first peacetime summer in five years draws to a close and the long Labor Day holiday weekend beckons. Filmgoers strolling through downtown Columbus, Ohio, on this balmy Friday (temperatures approaching 74°F) faced a wide range of moviegoing choices typical of the nation as a whole. Columbus boasted four major first-run theatres, ornate 'picture palaces' constructed in the silent era, each capable of holding some 2,000 spectators, in a city with a population of just over 300,000).[1] As in all the principal urban markets in North America, these showcase cinemas were owned by one or other of the so-called 'Big Five' vertically integrated producer-distributor-exhibitors: in this case, the Broad and the Ohio were owned by Loew's (parent company of MGM), the Grand and the Palace (proudly promoted on its opening in November 1926 as 'One of the World's Most Beautiful Playhouses'[2]) by Radio-Keith-Orpheum (RKO). (The other members of the Big Five were Paramount, Warner Bros., and Twentieth Century-Fox.) Because the majors' theatre chains tended to be geographically concentrated, a pooling system enabled their theatres to receive new releases not only from their own companies but also from other Big Five studios who did not own theatres in that area, as well as – on slightly less favourable terms, although moviegoers would not be aware of this – from the 'Little Three' producer-distributors who owned no theatre chains of their own: Universal,[3] Columbia and United Artists.

Thus, on this late summer Friday, the Grand and Palace theatres proudly offered two major seasonal attractions released through RKO itself: *The Kid from Brooklyn*, a Technicolor comedy vehicle for new contract star Danny Kaye (held over for its '2nd Big Week!') and Alfred Hitchcock's latest romantic thriller, *Notorious!*, starring Cary Grant and Ingrid Bergman.[4] In fact, both films were RKO distributed but independently produced, from veteran freelancers Samuel Goldwyn and David O. Selznick, respectively, reflecting

RKO's relative weakness compared to the other majors in securing and retaining top-line contract talent; again, such contractual niceties passed by most casual moviegoers completely.

Loew's Broad, on the other hand, was showing a Twentieth Century-Fox production, the Jerome Kern-scored musical *Centennial Summer*, transferring down the street from the Ohio for a '2nd Overwhelmingly Wonderful Week!'; newly opened at the Ohio itself was Columbia's mid-budget Western *Renegades* (promoted to appeal across the gender divide with poster art featuring leading lady Evelyn Keyes holding both a six-shooter and a newborn baby).

Two of these films would feature in *Variety*'s list of the year's top-earning films: *Notorious* came in eighth and *The Kid From Brooklyn* sixteenth. All of these programmes bar *Notorious*, whose star appeal and commercial prospects were reflected in the decision to present it as a single feature, offered the standard supporting film to bulk out the evening's entertainment, often, as here, supplied by either Columbia or Universal, the most parsimonious studios: *The Kid From Brooklyn* was partnered with Universal's *Danger Woman*, *Centennial Summer* with Columbia's *The Unknown*, and *Renegades* with Columbia's *It's Great To Be Young*.[5]

There were four other theatres in the immediate downtown area, but these did not compete directly with the first-run houses: as again was the norm nationwide, such second-run theatres offered a mixture of genre B-movies from either the majors' own B production units or the 'Poverty Row' minor studios – such as Universal's *River Gang* and Republic's hoary (1941) *Death Valley Outlaws*, sharing a double bill at the Majestic – and major studio productions which had completed their profitable first-run engagements at studio-owned houses, such as Universal's *Patrick the Great* and Warners' *One More Tomorrow*. Beyond these downtown subsequent-run theatres were no fewer than forty-one other cinemas serving the city's outlying neighbourhoods ('nabes' in *Variety*-speak), providing, taken together with the downtown theatres, roughly one theatre for every 6,000 inhabitants. The nabes typically comprised a few individual 'mom and pop' theatres and – the majority – local and regional chains such as the Academy Theatres ('delux [*sic*] entertainment'), owners of six local cinemas, or Neth's, who ran another seven. In this segment of the exhibition business, unlike the cosy closed-shop of the first-run market, margins were tight and competition for sellable product was genuine and intense. (However, the smallest exhibitors persistently complained that the chains, who obviously generated more business, received preferential treatment from the big distributors.) As ever, the most attractive product was a major studio release, once 'cleared' by the majors' own distribution exchanges for second- and subsequent-run exhibitors, usually two or three months after completing their first runs. Independent exhibitors determined neither the timing nor in many cases the choice of their presentations, of necessity conforming to the studios' strictly worked out system of 'runs' and 'clearances' which siphoned a film down through the less profitable stages of its distribution in any given market over the course of many months, and frequently having to accept less desirable, low-grade studio pictures bundled in with the top-line A-picture attraction.

The reward for deferring the pleasure of seeing the latest release (to say nothing of foregoing the exotic splendours of the picture palaces themselves in favour of modest neighbourhood theatres) was a lower ticket price than was charged for admission downtown – sometimes far lower, depending on how late in a movie's progress through second-run and outlying theatres the moviegoer waited to see it. At these theatres at the end of August 1946 could be seen such studio hits from earlier that year as MGM's *The Green Years*, premiered in first run in April, and *The Postman Always Rings Twice*, which had opened in early May. (These two films would rank twelfth and twentieth, respectively, in the year-end round-up.) Given the nabes' low ticket prices and the relatively small catchments of subsequent-run theatres, a rapid turnover of attractions was a business necessity; films were rarely booked in for more than a few days, and audiences thus enjoyed the benefit of an enormous variety of programming, albeit some of it fairly long in the tooth. Across the city as a whole, including both main features and supporting pictures, in the single week beginning Thursday (changeover day at the first-run houses) 29 August 1946, Columbus moviegoers had a choice of well over 200 different films.

This profusion of picturegoing options testified to two unchallengeable facts: that 'going to the movies' remained in 1946, as it had been for the previous quarter-century and more, by far Americans' favourite leisure pastime; and that 1946 itself was the highpoint – as reflected in attendances, box office receipts and the major studios' corporate profits alike – of Hollywood's fortunes to date (and, as it would prove, for a very long time to come, inflation notwithstanding). More Americans bought more cinema tickets in 1946 than ever before or since: that year over 4 billion tickets were sold at US box offices, and the average American went to the movies over thirty times. Moviegoing accounted for almost 25 cents of every dollar Americans spent on recreation of all kinds, and more than 80 per cent of spectator expenditure (including theatre and sports). The studios boasted combined record profits of over $125 million.[6] The value of motion picture shares, which had tripled between 1940 and V-J Day, doubled again in the next ten months. The studios, several of which had teetered on the verge of financial collapse during the Depression years of the 1930s, thus embarked upon the postwar era in apparently rude financial health. Of course, not every picture was a classic: though popular at the time, today only film historians and cinephiles pay much attention to Paramount's *Blue Skies* (the year's fifth highest-grossing film), MGM's *Till the Clouds Roll By* (ranked ninth), or Fox's *Margie* (fourteenth). But then they did not all need to be classics: there were some 370 US-produced films released that year by the major and minor studios combined, more than one for every day of the year, and with audiences buoyant almost all of them had a guaranteed market.

Ten years later, the weather in Columbus was pretty much the same; but changes had begun to make themselves felt, here as across the country, in the way Americans watched movies, in which movies they watched and how often, and – though this was harder to quantify – in their relationship to, and their expectations of, the medium. The downtown first-run theatres remained. Following the Supreme Court's landmark 1948 decision in the antitrust case *United States* v. *Paramount Pictures, Inc. et al.* the Palace and Grand were no longer owned by RKO Pictures (which itself had just eighteen months to live) and Loew's, somewhat belatedly, was in the process of divorcing its production-distribution activities from its theatre chain, including the Ohio and Broad in Columbus.[7] But the studios still maintained cordial relations with their erstwhile exhibition arms' sibling companies and reserved top-of-the-line studio productions for exclusive runs at the downtown houses:[8] this week Warners' *Mister Roberts*, the year's top-grossing studio film (held over at the Grand for a fifth successive week), and *The McConnell Story*, MGM's Gene Kelly musical *It's Always Fair Weather*, and the enduringly popular Alfred Hitchcock's latest, *To Catch a Thief*. All were colour productions, the first three filmed in the hugely successfully CinemaScope widescreen process introduced by Fox in 1953 and *To Catch a Thief* in Paramount's own proprietary large-screen process VistaVision. One intriguing innovation in the exhibition sector was the advertisement of a live closed-circuit TV broadcast of Rocky Marciano's upcoming world heavyweight title fight against Archie Moore, showing on a reserved-seat basis at the Palace on 30 September – despite some previous disappointments, in the mid-fifties the industry continued to harbour hopes for 'theatre TV'. In general, however, little at the first-run theatres suggested an industry any less robust now than at the war's end. (Peer ahead one year, however, and more cracks are visible, even at this top end of the market, the Grand belying its name with a gutter-trawling double bill from exploitation quickie specialist AIP (American International Pictures), *Girls in Prison* and *Hot-Rod Girl*.)[9]

The second- and subsequent-run markets more obviously bore witness to an industry undergoing major change. Perhaps surprisingly, the overall number of cinemas in Columbus remained virtually unchanged at forty. However, fourteen of the city's neighbourhood 'four-wall' theatres had closed since 1946 (another two would go dark in the coming year). Three of the survivors were now courting a very specific niche audience as self-proclaimed 'Art Theaters': a category that at this stage denoted less a focus on highbrow or art house films than the promise of racier fare – often imported from socially more liberal Europe (hence the 'art' label, a defence against anticipated or real opposition from local bluenoses). The Bexley offered *The Young and the Damned* ('"Shocking!" – *N. Y. Times*'), the Indianola *Love Island* ('Throbbing Adventure and Blazing Lips!' starring 'Sultry' Eva Gabor, sister of the more notorious Zsa Zsa). The shortfall was made up by a category of theatre unknown in Columbus, though not elsewhere in the USA, in 1946: drive-ins, or in industry parlance 'ozoners'. Thirteen of these now operated in and around the city, offering an undemanding diet of Westerns at eight sites, family fare such as *Hans Christian Andersen* and Disney's animated 'Scope feature *Lady and the Tramp*, and exploitation fare aimed at the teen market: at the Riverside, a double bill of two Columbia B-movies, *It Came From Beneath the Sea* and *Creature with the Atom Brain*. Although the number of screens in Columbus remained stable, the variety of programming was reduced: some 110 different films – still a considerable number – were scheduled for the week beginning Thursday, 31 August. Arguably, tonal and generic as well as simple numeric variety was reduced; undoubtedly reflecting contemporary tastes but also the increasingly youthful profile of mid-fifties moviegoers, at least a third were Westerns and horror or science fiction films (the last a virtually non-existent genre before the dawn of the atomic age) aimed primarily at youthful moviegoers. The rise of drive-ins, which specialised in such fare, tilted the overall trend in this direction.

In none of these aspects was Columbus anything but typical of general trends industry-wide. Across the USA, for example, while the total number of cinemas had remained roughly stable throughout the preceding decade at just under 19,000, this headline figure masked the real story, that the burgeoning 'ozoners' (up from just 300 in 1946 to 4,600 in 1955, a fifteenfold increase) were making good the precipitous decline of more than 25 per cent (from 18,700 to just over 14,000) in four-wall theatres – the great majority of them, as in Columbus, subsequent-run houses in outlying neighbourhoods and rural areas.[10] (See Appendix: Figure 2.) The emergence of teenagers as a discrete and influential demographic – a 1955 survey conducted by ABC-Paramount Theatres reported that the 15–30 age group now supplied some 65 per cent of the movie audience – and the adjustment of production priorities to cater increasingly to juvenile tastes would come increasingly to dominate studio strategy in the years ahead.[11] The overall reduction in exhibited films reflected a sharp decline in the number of releases by the major studios as they consolidated their operations in the challenging business climate of the fifties, concentrating on fewer, mostly bigger pictures – in turn enabling the emergence of new outfits such as AIP to supply exhibitors with cheap, crowd-pleasing entertainment. The reason for the wave of closures of small theatres was equally plain: nationally, in 1955 US cinemas saw barely half as many admissions (just under 2.1 billion) as in 1946. Box office receipts were down too, from

$1.7 billion in 1946 to $1.3 billion in 1955, a 17 per cent reduction (inflation and higher ticket prices partly compensated for the lost millions of moviegoers). As industry spokesmen bullishly insisted throughout the decade, with some 50 million admissions every week, moviegoing remained by any measure Americans' most popular spectator amusement. But the industry's direction of travel, measured in traditional terms, was downwards nonetheless.

A major factor, of course – though not, as we shall see, the only one – was television, since 1949 as much a fact of daily life in Columbus, with its three network affiliates,[12] as in the more than 500 other markets which now boasted their own TV stations.[13] A glance at the schedules confirms that, at least as far as the majors were concerned, television in 1955 remained a major part of the industry's postwar problems, rather than – as it would soon become – the solution to them. The prime-time schedules were showcases for anthology drama series broadcast live from the networks' New York studios: in 1955, the episodic series that would soon overwhelm live drama were still second best, mostly corralled in early or late evening slots and produced not by the studios, whose high overheads and luxurious production schedules made it hard for them compete, but by pioneer telefilm companies such as Ziv (*Waterfront*, 10.30 p.m. Friday on NBC affiliate WBNS). As a secondary market for theatrical releases, television was still off-limits in 1955; with the majors refusing to license their film libraries to broadcasters, the networks padded out their late-night and afternoon schedules with older Poverty Row films such as Monogram's 1938 *Michael O'Halloran* (late Friday on NBC) or British imports such as Rank's *Latin Quarter* (1947, same time slot on ABC). However, the upstart medium's appeal to Hollywood talent (now largely liberated from the long-term studio contracts of the 1940s) was apparent at both ends of the Hollywood spectrum, whether in longtime B-movie heavy George Raft's turn upholding justice as Police Lt George Kirby in the filmed series *I'm the Law* on ABC, or the live *Ray Milland Show* on NBC. A sign of things to come, the latter was produced by Revue, the production arm of the dominant Hollywood talent agency MCA (Music Corporation of America), which by the early 1960s would not only come to dominate TV entertainment but, through its relationship and eventual ownership of Universal Pictures, would help transform Hollywood as a whole.[14]

Spool forward a further five years to 1960, and a measure of stabilisation seems to have set in. There were still forty theatres in Columbus, and the four first-run houses had been joined by the 1959 opening of Hunt's Cinestage (previously the Uptown) a little to the north of the traditional downtown district. Hunt's would henceforth be the preferred showcase for the 'roadshowed' (booked into long exclusive runs on a premium-priced, hard-ticket basis) historical epics and large-scale musicals that were Hollywood's current top-of-the-line product. In September 1960, almost a year after its release, Hunt's was still showing *Ben-Hur* (MGM 1959) in Technicolor and six-track stereo. There were seventeen nabes and fifteen drive-ins, but some of the fare on offer suggested that exhibitors faced impoverished choices: the Bexley was reduced to showing the cheap British series comedy *Carry On Nurse*. This reflected a downturn in domestic production, most marked at the top end of the market as the studios put an ever larger proportion of their production investment into fewer roadshow-style blockbusters: studio releases were down 15 per cent since 1955, from 215 to 184. Imported films – many of them, such as *Come Dance with Me* with Brigitte Bardot at the World, featuring Continental starlets in varying states of undress – had increased correspondingly. The roadshows relied on peeling Hollywood's traditional undifferentiated mass audience away from its TV sets and back into theatres for the big-screen experience. But elsewhere it became apparent that the underlying trend was in the opposite direction, towards the demographic fragmentation of audiences. The three films on widest release that week in September – Jerry Lewis, one of the few bankable new studio stars of the period, in *The Bellboy* (Paramount), at six theatres; Joseph E. Levine's dubbed Italian import *Hercules Unchained*, also at six; and Roger Corman's *House of Usher* for AIP, at seven – all appealed primarily to the youth market. More significant still was the 'For Adults Only' warning for *Elmer Gantry*, opening at the Ohio. Eight years before the age-based ratings system, this indicated that Hollywood recognised that the future lay in marketing movies effectively to particular niche audiences.[15]

It would be plausible enough to characterise this scene as one of inexorable decline, and several histories of postwar Hollywood do. Decline, however, is only one part of the big picture of Hollywood history in this period. The time-lapse sequence recorded here, with the city of Columbus as its lens, is accurate as far as it goes, using the health of the domestic theatrical market as the traditional barometer of the film industry's well-being. Yet like the image in a camera obscura, the picture is, though detailed, limited by what it cannot see and is in any case inverted, because, by the early 1960s, the fortunes of 'Hollywood' – which at the end of World War II denoted an industry equally involved in the production, distribution and exhibition of motion pictures – were for a number of reasons far less securely shackled to those of cinema owners and exhibitors than had once been the case, and thus at once both more volatile, more flexible and, potentially, more recuperable than the bleak view from Main Street might suggest.

In fact, if Main Street had by the early 1960s become an inadequate vantage point from which to estimate Hollywood's fortunes (and in reality the view from Wall Street had always been just as important), this in turn tells us something about the direction the film industry had started to take, and the kind of entertainment industry into which even at this early stage, and at this low ebb of its fortunes, Hollywood had begun to transform itself. In truth, by the mid-sixties a 'New Hollywood' had already been constituted by the many and far-reaching changes that had confronted the film industry since the end of World War II. More 'New Hollywoods' would be born in subsequent decades, of various kinds and longevity. But arguably the heaviest labour and the most significant metamorphosis from Old to New Hollywood had already taken place well before the dramatic upheavals of the late 1960s and 1970s. To understand this process, how it unfolded and what it entailed, we need first to return to Hollywood at the zenith of its fortunes – its 'high noon', in the words of film historian Thomas Cripps – and examine the delicate dynamic balance on which the enormous success of that system was, at least as it seemed in 1946, so securely founded.

NOTES

1. The 1940 US Census recorded the population of Columbus as 306,087. http://www.census.gov/population/www/documentation/twps0027/tab17.txt
2. Phil Sheridan, *Those Wonderful Old Downtown Theatres* (Columbus, OH: Sheridan, 1978), p. 47.
3. Universal had owned a small chain of theatres in the early 1930s but was forced to sell them in 1934 to stave off bankruptcy.
4. The exclamation point is usually omitted in critical discussions of the films but featured emphatically in promotional artwork.
5. *Columbus Dispatch*, 30 August 1946, pp. 17–18.
6. 'Hollywood shakes its slump', *Business Week*, 11 February 1950, p. 82.
7. On *Paramount*, see below, Chapter 1, pp. 17–21.
8. In traditional Old Hollywood style, some business relationships were thicker than water: when Twentieth Century-Fox set about complying with the Court ruling in *Paramount*, Spyros Skouras remained head of the production-distributor arm while his brother Charles took over the new Fox Theatres. In 1954 the Supreme Court rejected a suburban Baltimore exhibitor's complaint that the majors' continuing refusal to allow smaller outlying theatres access to first-run pictures constituted illegal restraint of trade. See 'Sherman Act redefinition', *Time*, 18 January 1954, p. 86.
9. *Columbus Citizen*, 2 September 1955 p. 9; *Columbus Dispatch*, 2 September 1956, p. 7.
10. *Motion Picture and Television Almanac* 1956; 'Cinema count', *Newsweek*, 18 October 1954, p. 100.
11. 'Bid for teens', *Business Week*, 14 May 1955, pp. 114–15.
12. WTVN switched to ABC from the collapsing Dumont network early in 1955.
13. The great majority of these opened after 1952, when the Federal Communications Commission (FCC) ended its four-year moratorium on new station licences.
14. *Columbus Dispatch*, 2 September 1955, p. 21B.
15. *Columbus Citizen-Journal*, 1 September 1960, p. 9.

CHAPTER I

The Autumn of the Patriarchs

As everyone knows – scholars, journalists, novelists, poets, pundits and most certainly filmmakers – 'Hollywood' is a myth. The subsumption of the American commercial film industry as a whole beneath the name of a Los Angeles suburb has in some measure always been simply a universally convenient shorthand that obscures a great deal of what it denotes. It is a metonym: the use of a part to designate a larger, and certainly in this case a much more complex, whole. In fact, the metonym is doubled, for just as 'Hollywood' blurs or brackets the relationship between what Leo Rosten called 'the movie colony' nestled amid the palm and orange groves of Southern California and its financial and strategic overseers in grimy Manhattan, so the equally conventional term 'studio' emphasises one, highly visible and glamorous, dimension of the motion picture industry over another. By design, the overwhelming focus of mainstream (though not business) media, cultural commentators and politicians – to say nothing of the self-generated torrent of publicity, fan literature and the like – throughout Hollywood's 'Golden Age' (1927–45) was always on the physical creation of movie narratives on studio lots and soundstages by writers, producers, directors, technicians, craft workers and of course stars, their creative energies all corralled and driven relentlessly onward by the cigar-chomping production head of popular legend, at the expense of other, more obscure industrial procedures that often took place far away from the shores of the Pacific. Yet these other activities – specifically the distribution and exhibition of motion pictures – were not only chronologically the senior elements in the evolution of the American film industry, they were the *raison d'être* of the entire system. If the studio lot was the shop floor of the 'dream factory', like any other factory its very existence depended in the first place on the strategies and decisions taken by accountants, lawyers and executive boards; its products in turn justified the considerable labour of their own creation not only, or indeed primarily, as expressions of creativity but to the degree they could be brought efficiently and profitably to market.

Looking ahead to an uncertain future: *The Best Years of Our Lives* (Goldwyn 1945).
Reproduced courtesy of The Kobal Collection

As this book will demonstrate, 'Hollywood' (and for that matter, Hollywood) changed profoundly over the sixty-five (and counting) years covered in these pages. In some ways the confusion of Hollywood the place and the Hollywood film industry has been clarified – for example, by the relocation of the studios' corporate headquarters from East Coast to West during the recessionary late 1960s and early 1970s; in some ways it has become more acute – for instance, the dismantling of the old centralised production machinery and its replacement by a ramified, globally dispersed congeries of interrelated and often short-lived freelance entities on the one hand and titanic diversified multimedia conglomerates on the other. To unpick this tangled skein we need not start from the very beginning, with the origins of the Hollywood film industry and the studio system; but we do need to understand the mature form of the organism whose ongoing evolution is this book's subject.

TIPPING THE BALANCE

By common consent, both critical and popular, America's entry into World War II found the studio system at its apogee. Fans and historians like to debate whether 1939 (the year of *Gone With the Wind, Stagecoach, Mr Smith Goes to Washington* and *The Wizard of Oz*), 1940 (*The Grapes of Wrath, Pinocchio, His Girl Friday, The Philadelphia Story*), or perhaps 1941 (*Citizen Kane, Sullivan's Travels, The Maltese Falcon, Sergeant York, How Green Was My Valley*) was 'Hollywood's greatest year'. Others would argue the case for 1946, the last real year of that older Hollywood, and the year this book's narrative begins. Adjudicating such arguments is hardly possible and anyway misses the point. Whatever one's preference, that list of titles – highly selective, omitting numerous other excellent pictures as well as many that were mediocre or worse – makes it clear that this was an industry capable of producing a rich stream of technically and artistically outstanding work that was also, despite the system's factory-like aspects, richly varied in tone and content. At the same time, these films all bore Hollywood's unmistakable stamp: they did not look or feel quite like the pictures of any other national cinema (though they drew for inspiration on many of them).

One, not entirely conventional, way to understand the studio system at its zenith is as a carefully balanced regulatory system. 'Regulation' in business generally means government-mandated controls on business practices; in this sense of the term, Hollywood at the end of World War II was very lightly regulated indeed. Yet a variety of forms of regulation, broadly conceived, both internal and external, played a vital role in sustaining the intricate and profitable mechanisms of the studio system. The most obvious and visible of these was the self-censorship of motion picture content though the industry-sponsored, arm's-length Production Code Administration (PCA), run since 1934 – when the largely ineffectual 'Hays Code' was revamped in the face of pressure from politicians and religious groups and given meaningful powers of enforcement – by Joseph Breen. The 'Breen Office' was anything but ineffectual. At every stage from the acquisition of a property (a novel or stage play) through to post-production, but above all during the screenwriting process, the PCA applied the rigorously conservative moral standards enshrined in the 1934 Code to the narrative content, dialogue, stated and implied attitudes and visuals of every picture distributed by a member of the Motion Picture Producers and Distributors of America (MPPDA). The studios for their part contracted to abide by the PCA's decisions and undertook neither to distribute nor, on behalf of their theatre chains, to exhibit any film distributed without a Code Seal of Approval. Self-regulation was motivated by concern to avoid regulation from outside – a very real prospect in both the early 1920s and the early 1930s. As odious as the Code's antediluvian positions on sexual and social relations may have been to many in the Hollywood creative community (it was antediluvian even by the standards of the 1930s, let alone the considerably altered American society emerging from World War II), nonetheless the Code achieved its primary goal for over a decade, which was to ensure the smooth running of the distribution of films to audiences, with minimal risk of interference from state or municipal censorship bodies.[1]

In a different sense, the effective regulation of output through the operations of an assembly line-like system of production, distribution and exhibition was central to the business model of the Big Five studios. The agreement (collaboratively between production head in Los Angeles and the studio's chief executive in New York, with the latter generally having the final say[2]) of an annual 'slate' of releases categorised by budget, from top–class 'prestige' pictures through mid-range 'programmers,' to B-films and series; the assignment of the creative responsibility for delivering the finished picture to a producer and thence to contracted, salaried studio personnel (writer(s), director, stars, cinematographer, production designer, all the way down to grips, electricians, set painters and carpenters); the production itself, filmed on the studio lot under the close supervision of the assigned producer, with rewrites, reshoots and cuts at his (and not the star's or director's, let alone screenwriter's) behest, typically with a careful eye on potential cost overruns; the distribution of the finished film, rolling out nationwide in carefully staged sequence over several months or more through the 'run clearance' system[3]; the ruthless manipulation of the studios' market advantage (secured through their domination of the first-run exhibition sector) to extract preferential terms from independent exhibitors wishing to screen studio films: this entire complex process, first synthesised by Adolph Zukor at Paramount in the late 1920s, entailed a careful regulation of investment and expenditure-limiting economies of scale to deliver a reliable flow of profits to the parent company and its shareholders in New York. Where this system had wavered, its problems were typically due to misguided corporate strategies (such as William Fox's over-expansion of his theatre chains in the Depression-ridden early 1930s) or inadequate leadership (as afflicted RKO, youngest and weakest of the Big Five, throughout the 1940s). The system itself was, if not foolproof, then certainly robust enough to survive all of the challenges (including the Great Depression) it had faced in its twenty-odd years of existence.

Another crucial dimension of the studio system was the careful regulation of labour relations, which operated both at the highly visible top end of the industry salary scale – the star system – and down through the ranks to the studio craft workers. The latter, though belatedly unionised in the 1930s partly as a consequence of Roosevelt's union-promoting National Recovery Administration (NRA) programmes, were under more or less constant pressure throughout the studio era, enduring among other woes the takeover of the principal craft union by mobsters who were bribed by studio bosses to impose sweetheart deals and wage restraint upon their members. Although Hollywood was one of the most thoroughly unionised sectors of American industry, its labour force, paradoxically, was always in an uneasy position, its hard-won gains never wholly assured in the face of the persistent hostility of Hollywood's capitalist establishment (Walt Disney was a persistent union antagonist throughout the 1940s).[4]

Stars, of course, enjoyed financial rewards beyond the dreams of set painters and make-up artists; but their fortunes were also precarious, at the mercy both of fickle public favour and of their employers' unremittingly instrumental perception of talent as a resource which the studios had bought and paid for and which they were entitled to exploit on their own terms. The studios set out to ensure a steady return on their considerable investment in their top name stars by applying identical strategies to those by which they managed their other personnel and their physical plant. Assigning staff writers to create scripts tailored to each leading man or lady's particular qualities and abilities, for example, ensured a steady throughput of star vehicles and avoided any costly periods of underemployment for their prize ponies. Star personae, once established, locked performers into generic paradigms from which they would sometimes struggle to break free – for example, the 'tough guy' roles which by the late 1930s James Cagney at Warners was chafing intensely against.

In fact the stars themselves, locked into seven-year contracts with no right to renegotiate terms however popular they became, for all the flattering glamour in which they were bathed by studio publicity machines had little control over the trajectory of their own careers: by mutual consent, MPPDA member studios did not poach each other's stars (hence stars were denied the opportunity to improve their contracts and working conditions by soliciting better offers elsewhere). Inter-studio loan-outs (usually from a larger to a smaller studio), conversely, were commonplace – as, for example, MGM's loan of Clark Gable and Claudette Colbert to Columbia in 1934 for Frank Capra's *It Happened One Night* (as it turned out, a multi-Oscar-winning major hit). Those stars bold enough to complain of substandard scripts or stereotyping found themselves subject to punitive treatment. In more extreme cases, stars who refused to accept a particular role could find themselves charged with breach of contract and suspended without pay – Bette Davis at Warner and David Niven, under contract to independent producer Samuel Goldwyn, both found themselves on the receiving end of such treatment. Such actors could easily acquire a reputation for being 'difficult' which could mar their prospects in what was to all intents and purposes a company town. In this as in other regards, even Hollywood aristocracy had to accept that they were looked on effectively as chattels by the real powers of the film business. (Such facts of Hollywood life naturally applied all the more to supporting players and extras. Hollywood actors had used their obvious leverage to unionise successfully through the Screen Actors' Guild in the mid-1930s, but the contract system still weighted the conditions of their labour heavily in the studios' favour.)

All of these practices, ideally arranged to the benefit of the studios – which is to say with an eye to what ultimately mattered, the bottom line – relied in the final analysis on the most fundamental, though unacknowledged, form of industry self-regulation, that is to say the relationship, to all intents and purposes a partnership, between the ostensibly competing companies who dominated the American film marketplace. Not for nothing has the classical Hollywood studio system been described as a 'mature oligopoly': that is, rule by a few (companies), the 'maturity' of the arrangement consisting precisely in the members' basically collaborative relations. Of course each studio set out to produce the most profitable pictures it could; but 'facts on the ground', such as the different strengths and geographical concentrations of the Big Five's exhibition arms (the oldest integrated company, Paramount, had by far the most theatres, while the much smaller size of Loew's/MGM's and RKO's chains, each barely a tenth of Paramount's, was partly compensated by their control of the lucrative New York market) promoted cooperative relations. During the war years in particular, pretty much everybody won, with even the traditionally weaker studios posting record results (Warner Bros., for example, saw profits rise from just $1.7 million in 1939 to $19.5 million in 1946).[5]

Above all, the collusive regulation of competitive relations between the major studios worked effectively to exclude new entrants to the market.[6] The studio system conceded a limited, and by the early 1940s growing, role to independent producers, especially the prestigious boutique outfits headed by former studio moguls like David O. Selznick and Samuel Goldwyn which produced a handful of high-class pictures each year (including some enormous popular and critical hits, most famously Selznick's *Gone with the Wind* in 1939), from which the studios in any case benefited by distributing;[7] but none of these – let alone the typically ephemeral production companies occasionally established by individual stars or directors, or the impoverished beneath-the-radar efforts of producers targeting the urban ethnic and 'race' (African American) markets – posed any threat to dominion by the majors.[8] The majors generally perceived a challenge to any one of them as a challenge to all – rightly, given the extent of their collusion on all aspects of industry practice. The MPPDA allowed the studios to come to common arrangements on a variety of industry issues in the guide of a 'trade association', thus circumventing antitrust laws. Two different, but representative, examples of collective wagon-circling under threat in the same year, 1941, were the combined majors' proposal to purchase (and destroy) the negative of *Citizen Kane* from RKO, under fire from press baron W. R. Hearst, scathingly portrayed in Orson Welles's film; and Twentieth Century-Fox chairman Joe Schenck (brother of Loew's chief executive Nicholas Schenck) 'taking the fall' and serving time for the mob/union payoffs of which all the studio leaders were equally guilty.[9]

This cooperative quasi-competition was the stable and profitable heart of the Hollywood film industry and fundamental to the self-regulated studio system from the start of the sound era until after the end of World War II. In the end, however, it was this same collusive architecture of Hollywood's political economy that proved its Achilles heel and, in hindsight, leveraged the restructuring of the industry as a whole. The decisive intervention of external regulation, in the shape of the Federal Government, revealed how delicate and fragile was the balance that the studio system in its brief heyday had achieved; and, logically, the dismantling of the system's economic foundations led in short order to the old Hollywood's wholesale supersession by the (first) New Hollywood. When after the war Truman's Justice Department renewed the antitrust suit first launched by the Roosevelt administration in 1938, the studios fought the court decisions against their interests all the way until they ran out of road in the Supreme Court. The decision the Court finally handed down in 1948 in *United States* v. *Paramount Pictures, Inc. et al.* – the famous 'Paramount Decree' – revisited and definitively resolved the question of whether the major studios constituted a 'trust' in the terms of US commercial law, that is, a cartel operating illegitimately to restrict market freedom in a given industry.

The Court found, to no one's surprise, that the studios were indeed a trust and acted decisively to remedy the situation, going far beyond the terms of the compromise consent decree by which the previous suit had been resolved in 1940 (revised in 1941). That decision had tried to settle disputes between theatre owners and the studios through arbitration, while eliminating some of the most egregious anti-competitive abuses in the terms on which exhibitors acquired studio product.[10] *Paramount*, by contrast, addressed the structural causes of exhibitors' complaints in the studios' monopoly control of the film business through the vertical integration of production, distribution and exhibition. The Court took a strong line and required the studios to divest themselves wholly of their exhibition interests (the theatre chains). They also prohibited the studios' predatory and unfair practices in dealing with independent exhibitors, such as blind- and block-booking (which compelled theatre owners to accept bulk consignments of inferior studio B-movies, often sight unseen, as the price of acquiring a hit A-picture).

This last ruling highlighted a striking aspect of the studio system. For years the majors had been turning out a torrent of product, much of it of frankly inferior quality. Yet it might be asked why the studios persisted in churning out such a large amount of substandard product? Why not concentrate on fewer, better, productions and save everyone the bother? The answer is that the system the studios had built led inevitably to over-production. The large overheads the majors incurred as they expanded (the size of the average workforce in the film industry increased fivefold between 1927 and 1937, years in which the size of studio lots also expanded greatly) prohibited extended periods of idleness. Only an almost constant stream of pictures could justify the sizeable investment in production facilities and contract personnel. In this sense the studios not only were, but needed to be, if not factories then at least factory-like. By the same token, it made sense to spread financial risk across as many productions as possible rather than betting the studio's fortunes on a few ultra-expensive releases.

Equally, however, the system only made sense, and could only sustain itself, in the artificial market environment the studios had themselves created. In effect, the studios could dump the results of their over-production on the market, confident that their monopoly control, combined with the ongoing demand for their premium product, ensured they would suffer no backlash. Audiences and exhibitors, after all, had nowhere else to go, or so it seemed. (Audiences, however, were not passive or uncritical dupes: a legislative initiative to ban double features in Illinois in 1938 – in reaction against the poor quality of supporting features – only narrowly failed to reach the statute books.)[11] Such a strategy meaningfully hedged against the inherently risky business of successfully anticipating and responding to changing public tastes – to the gratification of Wall Street, upon whose continuing support the studios, like any other big business, relied for investment and affordable credit. And it ensured that the public, who particularly during the war displayed an enthusiasm for moviegoing that seemed almost blind to considerations of quality, would continue to have their habit fed by a reliable supply of fresh (or at least new) films two or three times a week at their local theatres.

Theatrical exhibition was the heart of the old Hollywood; it was in every case the sector in which the founding generation of studio owners (Marcus Loew and Nick Schenck at MGM; Harry, Jack and Abe Warner; William Fox; Adolph Zukor at Paramount) had first entered the business back in the nickelodeon days at the start of the century. The original motivation for establishing their production arms (initially in New York and New Jersey, shifting to the West Coast in the mid-teens) was essentially to provide a reliable supply of suitable, marketable product for the expanding theatre chains each company controlled, and to make proper use of the national distribution systems they had established to deliver films and collect receipts from theatres. Key strategic corporate decisions – including the approval of annual production slates – were taken in New York, not in Hollywood. The vertically integrated system pioneered by Adolph Zukor at Famous Players (the precursor of Paramount) and subsequently adopted by all of the Big Five was predicated on a simple and obvious premise: money was made in the film business when audiences bought movie tickets; the greater your control of the exhibition sector, the greater your ability to maximise your share of box office revenues, both in the theatres you controlled directly and in the remainder who required your premium product to keep their own businesses on a paying basis. The majority decision in *Paramount* noted that while the Big Five owned, wholly or in partnership, around 20 per cent of all the nation's theatres, in America's ninety-two largest cities the Big Five controlled over 70 per cent of first-run theatres. (As we have seen, in Columbus – in 1946 the twenty-sixth largest US city – all four downtown first-run theatres were studio-owned.) The Big Five's domination of these metropolitan markets, by far the most profitable sector, through their chains of downtown picture palaces, enabled them both to cream off the revenues their A list pictures generated and to command premium rates and terms for allowing independent exhibitors access to such films in second and subsequent runs.[12]

Whereas in later years, as we shall see, new emergent ancillary markets would massively expand the studios' range of profit-taking opportunities, in the late 1940s these were all in Hollywood's future. The money to be made from motion pictures relied entirely, as it had done since the medium's earliest days, on distribution fees and box office receipts; and while overseas markets made a very significant contribution, domestic US first-run release was much the most important element, outstripping foreign sales by a ratio of around two to one. (Re-releases had limited value; some high-visibility individual pictures – such as *Gone With the Wind*, profitably re-released several times in the late 1940s and 1950s – and some categories of film – notably Disney's animated shorts and features, which had a self-renewing constituency of new child audiences every few years – could deliver repeat business over time, but in most other cases a film's value to a studio was pretty much exhausted once it had finished its initial run in theatres.)[13]

Exploiting this single profit window to the fullest degree was therefore the studios' paramount concern. To ensure that every film wrung the last possible cent from its markets entailed both the constant adjustment of 'rental' income (the percentage of box office receipts returned from theatres to distributors, using the Big Five's control of the first-run market as leverage) and the careful manipulation of a film's availability in different market segments over the course of its lifetime in active release, always with the aim of directing as large a proportion of audiences as possible to see the film at higher ticket prices in the earlier stages of its release in first-run (studio-dominated) theatres.[14] This latter strategy was the 'run clearance' system which saw studio films booked first into the studio's own downtown picture palaces – their most prestigious and profitable runs; they were then withdrawn from the market altogether for a predetermined period (usually several weeks) before their release to the second-run houses; and so on down through to the independent theatre chains and finally the individual 'mom-and-pop' theatres typically located in rural areas. A successful film's lifespan through the entire run clearance programme could easily take months, even up to a year. This process – which among other advantages to the studios reduced the need to strike expensive and quickly redundant multiple prints, since a given film would only ever be distributed to a limited number of cinemas at any one time[15] – could also be seen as a form of sophisticated regulation of the market.

LIFE AFTER *PARAMOUNT*: THE RISE OF THE INDEPENDENTS

The *Paramount* decision threw out virtually at a stroke the business model on which the majors' success had been founded. The case opened up the prospect of each film having to sell itself to exhibitors and audiences on its individual merits (or at least on the qualities which could be advertised through massively increased spending on marketing and publicity). The Court had also outlawed the sweetheart ('you scratch my back') deals whereby studio pictures gained preferential access to first-run theatres owned by other studios in markets where they themselves were weaker. This inevitably implied a much fiercer competition among the studios for market share – which of course was precisely the intention of the judgment. Finally, a very serious problem posed by divestment was the loss of the valuable real estate represented by the theatres, whose collateralisation against bank loans used for production finance gave the Big Five a crucial competitive advantage against smaller studios and independents.

Small wonder then that the studios dragged their heels on complying with the Court's demands for as long as possible (Loew's finally divorced its theatre chain from MGM only in 1957); nor that some of the old guard of studio leaders – men in any case of pensionable age by the mid-1950s – preferred comfortable retirement to the effort of equipping their companies for a new and uncertain business environment. Harry Warner, Nicholas Schenck at MGM, and Y. Frank Freeman, Barney Balaban's longtime head of production at Paramount, all stepped down from executive responsibility in the 1950s. Balaban himself and Spyros Skouras at Twentieth Century-Fox followed suit in the early 1960s. A more dismal fate awaited RKO, always the weakest of the Big Five, which following its takeover by Howard Hughes in 1948 and the loss of its theatre chain in 1950 (the first of the majors to comply with the Court ruling) stumbled through several years of drastically reduced output and disastrous losses before Hughes wound the company up and sold off its assets in 1957.

Still, although some textbooks maintain that the effect of the *Paramount* decision was immediate and dire,[16] in fact the direct impact of the judgment was necessarily limited. As already noted, it was the best part of a decade before the majors finally all exited the exhibition business as the Court directed

– an extended transition that reflects their collective attempts to find a new way of doing business before they turned their back forever on the old one. The larger problem was that *Paramount* was far from the only challenge confronting the studios in the postwar period. Industry revenues plummeted in the late 1940s: collective studio profits in 1948 were barely $50 million (a figure that included a $3.2 million loss at Universal, the first posted by any of the majors since 1940), down a whopping 60 per cent from 1946.[17] The combined balance sheet would dwindle further, to $30 million in 1950, prompting the financial press to diagnose movies as America's 'New Sick Industry'; but *Paramount* had little to do with any of this.[18] In fact, by 1948 the film business was already being buffeted by the first blasts of what would prove over the next few years a perfect economic storm. *Paramount* ensured it would be no passing squall.

The air started to leak from the industry's postwar balloon of confident prosperity when overseas revenues took a sudden and drastic downturn in the summer of 1947. Towards the war's end and in its immediate aftermath, Hollywood had profited immensely from its renewed access to continental European markets inaccessible during wartime. Four or more years' worth of American films, penetrating liberated Europe in the footsteps of the advancing Allies, were able to satisfy pent-up demand facing little or no competition from physically and morally prostrated domestic European film industries (this was particularly true of Germany, which before 1933 had boasted the best capitalised, most technically advanced and aesthetically ambitious world film industry outside Hollywood itself). However, European governments quickly fought back, alarmed at both the cultural and the commercial implications of Hollywood domination. In 1947 Britain, for whom Hollywood's hegemony (of 465 feature films shown in the UK in 1946, 328 were American imports) and the associated flight of dollar payments back to the USA exacerbated a catastrophic postwar balance of payments deficit, slapped a 75 per cent tax on foreign film earnings.[19] Other countries in Europe and Latin America followed, imposing punitive tariffs and quotas on US films and the dollars they repatriated.[20] Hollywood remittances from abroad accordingly dropped by some $50 million between 1946 and 1948, while motion picture company share values dropped accordingly.[21] To get around tariffs, the studios invested in a wide diversity of overseas operations, from Swedish shipbuilding to Italian marble and Finnish bibles – all imported to the USA and finally sold for dollars.[22]

At home, meanwhile, the falling arc of studio revenues met a rising curve of production costs. Peace put an end to the wartime culture of patriotic self-denial: wage claims and consumer demand alike accelerated out of fifteen years of Depression and war, generating a mutually reinforcing inflationary spiral that hit movie production along with every other sphere of the US economy. During the wartime movie boom, the negative cost of an average A production had already ballooned, nearly tripling from $304,000 in 1940 to $900,000 in

1946.[23] As the postwar chill set in, the studios publicly declared their intention to reduce production costs; but with salaries in a heavily unionised industry accounting on average for 85 per cent of a picture's negative cost, such savings proved easier to announce than to deliver. The rate of increase slowed, but production costs continued to rise; by 1950 the price of an A-picture had hit the $1 million mark and – with the move towards blockbuster production propelling costs upwards – continued to rise much faster than inflation, by about 50 per cent every five years for the next two decades.

Beyond all this, the inescapable bottom line – the perspective which magnified every other challenge the movie industry faced in the late 1940s – was that Hollywood's audience was rapidly shrinking. No sooner had the industry basked in its record 1946 receipts than a steep decline in attendances set in. Admissions tumbled 10 per cent in 1947 alone, and a further 18 per cent over the next three years. By 1950 over a billion moviegoers annually had been lost to theatres in just five years. (See Appendix: Figure 1.)

That attendances and revenues could not be sustained at wartime levels in itself came as little surprise. With many other spectator amusements, such as major league baseball, cancelled for the duration, an influx of labour to big cities (disproportionately dominated by studio-owned theatres) to man the war effort, and a public naturally eager to find both inspiration for and distraction from the stresses of conflict, wartime for Hollywood was an artificially benign business environment. The studios' corporate strategies during the wartime boom, retiring debt and strengthening their reserves of working capital, indicated a general recognition that the good times could not last indefinitely. But the extent and rate of the apparently bottomless drop into which attendances tumbled in the years from 1947 found the studios scrambling to understand what, it soon became apparent, was actually a tectonic shift in patterns of American leisure and entertainment that amounted to the wholesale abandonment by tens of millions of Americans of moviegoing as a habitual practice.

The dramatic social and demographic shifts of the postwar period (see Chapter 2) domesticated patterns of leisure consumption and expenditure in American life, diverted discretionary spending into consumer goods, discouraged large numbers of young newlyweds and first-time parents from developing the moviegoing habit, fragmented the traditional moviegoing family unit into demographic bands with increasingly diverse tastes and social practices, physically removed newly suburbanised spectators from the downtown areas in which the first-run houses were traditionally clustered, and ultimately left moviegoing the occasional pleasure of a constantly dwindling customer base, rather than the ubiquitous national pastime of previous decades. All this of course happened quite regardless of Supreme Court decisions.

In a radically more challenging business environment, the unmistakeable lesson of *Paramount* was that the studios had to overhaul their business practices root and branch. The old assembly-line model of studio film production had become unsustainable. What in the old days of monopolistic internal regulation were economies of scale now stood revealed as wasteful and inefficient. With the end of their armlock on exhibition, the studios lost their guaranteed market for every film. Unreformed, there was a real danger that the system would turn out a glut of films that quite simply no exhibitor wished to show, and which no one could any longer compel them to show – a problem dramatically evidenced in late 1948 when Warner Bros., faced with a growing backlog of unreleased features and an $11 million fall in profits year-on-year, shut down production for three months. Jack Warner spoke publicly merely of 'appraisal, analysis and planning for the future'[24] but the unmistakeable reality was the need for a radical reorientation of studio activities. *Paramount* issued in a period of reappraisal and restructuring across the industry. Strategies of adaptation varied from one company to another, but the 'survival two-step' was industry-wide: each major studio set themselves first to consolidate and cut costs before exploring where, in the transformed industry, the opportunities to actually make money were.

The obvious way to economise was to produce fewer films. This was indeed the logic of *Paramount*, which deprived the studios of their captive market for each and every release. But reduced production in turn dictated that the massive overheads incurred by the armies of contract personnel on virtually round-the-clock production shifts no longer made economic sense. As long as the studios remained in the business of actually producing pictures themselves it made sense to retain some craft and office staff on the studio lot to maintain capacity, but in reduced numbers and with some radical corporate surgery. Warner Bros.' outright elimination of its story department in spring 1951 was a dramatic example. Given the story department's crucial importance to the old studio system – finding and developing the material on which the entire production cycle relied – its dissolution implied not simply cutbacks in but a significant redirection of studio activity as a whole.

Warners' decision was itself both symptomatic of and a response to other moves already underway in that studio and throughout the industry. For while the studio, as a production facility, could still justify the cost of retaining a proportion of its studio workers as long as there was work to be done, the greater expense of keeping salaried talent on the traditional long-term contract was evidently obsolete. A Bogart, or Cooper, or Hepburn only paid their way as long as they were put to good use in two or three pictures a year. Without such a guaranteed throughput of product, stars (and this held equally good for other top-line talent, including directors, producers and writers) were on a week-to-week basis an unaffordable luxury: better to rent, lease or partner with them as needed and wanted on individual projects. The decade 1945–55 accordingly saw the total number of contract players at the major studios (apart from MGM) decrease from 804 to 209: in early 1953 *Newsweek* reported that Paramount had just twenty-six contract players, mostly low-salaried youngsters, and only three bona fide stars (Bob Hope, Bing Crosby, and William Holden).[25] At the same time, having drastically reduced their own production rosters, the studios needed additional independently produced films to maintain a full slate of releases. So began the shift towards a new industrial model, in which the old studios[26] came increasingly to function as financier–distributors to independent producers who in turn took on the lion's share of the creative work. Warners' abolition of its story department clearly signposted an anticipated future in which independents originated and developed material they then brought to the studios. (Over the same ten years, the total number of writers under contract at the majors dwindled from 490 to just sixty-seven.[27])

Such a shift was both in keeping with trends that had been underway since the earlier 1940s and readily coincided with the plans of top talent in the postwar period. MGM's windfall with Selznick's *Gone With the Wind* had persuaded the other majors to mitigate their historic coolness to independent productions. Arguably, the limitations on blind- and block-booking set by the interim antitrust consent decree in 1940 also helped prioritise the recruitment of top-line talent, rather than the studio 'brand' or house style, as a key marketing tool for promoting studio pictures to exhibitors.[28] Last and certainly not least, incorporation enabled top earners – who during the war faced marginal personal tax rates as high as 90 per cent – to have their income taxed not as salary but as capital gains, at a far lower rate. This stratagem saw stars such as James Cagney (with Cagney Productions, incorporated in 1941) set up financing/distribution deals, most often with either United Artists (which, lacking any production facilities of its own, had since its inception in 1919 specialised in distributing independent productions), the other two members of the non-vertically integrated 'Little Three' (Columbia and Universal), or with RKO, the most receptive of the Big Five – particularly after George Schaefer's arrival as president in 1938 from UA – to prestigious independent producer-directors such as Orson Welles and Alfred Hitchcock (*Notorious!*, it will be recalled, played the RKO Palace in Columbus as an RKO release). Thus by the late 1940s, just as the majors started to shift their production strategy, an embryonic infrastructure of independent production was in place. The enormous success of high-end postwar independent productions such as Goldwyn's *The Best Years of Our Lives* and Selznick's 'adult Western' melodrama *Duel in the Sun* (both 1946) spurred a boom in independent production companies of all kinds in this period.

But independence remained a risky business, particularly given ongoing increases in production costs, as even a major player like Selznick discovered, following the successive box office catastrophes of *The Paradine Case* (1947) and *Portrait of Jennie* (1948) which effectively ended his Hollywood career. Lacking the collateral and credit lines of the publicly traded majors, any independent was only as seaworthy as its last success or failure. As Stanley Kramer, one of the most successful postwar independents, observed in 1951 after *Cyrano de Bergerac*'s critical acclaim failed to reap comparable box office rewards, 'The independent producer can't afford what department stores call a loss leader. One of these will put him out of business'.[29] In 1947 Congressional tax reforms closed off the loopholes that had made independence such a lucrative proposition, and with bank credit now harder to secure in the industry-wide downturn, many independents either shut down altogether or sought the security of long-term financing arrangements with the majors, such as Frank Capra's Liberty Films at Paramount.

Such partnerships, however, threatened to compromise the other great attraction for top talent of independent production, beyond its financial incentives: the elusive prize of 'creative freedom'. Capra himself, following his move to Paramount – ostensibly as an 'in-house independent' – found the reality of the renewed constraints of studio control intolerable and within four years had effectively retired from filmmaking altogether. Capra's timing was singularly unfortunate: as the ripples of *Paramount* widened, the balance between independents and studios shifted definitively and Capra's own erstwhile partners in the (now defunct) Liberty, George Stevens and William Wyler, emerged as principal luminaries of the new dispensation.[30] During 1950–1, first the smaller companies – Columbia and some of the old Poverty Row studios – followed by Paramount, Warner Bros. and Twentieth Century-Fox all started to recruit independent producers. But the studios still preferred to keep as close a hold as possible over these semi-autonomous production units – in effect confining in-house independent producers' freedom of movement within bounds that could seem often little more expansive than those of the old 'producer unit' system.

It took a studio that in 1950 was not only industrially marginal but on the verge of bankruptcy to change things. United Artists was the studio that had done most to nurture and sustain independents throughout the studio era; ironically, however, owing to a poor recent track record and weak management, UA was at first poorly placed to capitalise on the independents' 'boom'. But following UA's takeover by Arthur Krim and Robert Benjamin in 1951,[31] UA once again took the lead by changing the terms of the relationship between studio (that is, financier/distributor) and creative talent. UA was prepared to concede much creative control to its chosen producers, subject only to initial story, cast and budget approval. (UA's lack of a backlot meant that production was in any case physically removed from studio oversight: whereas the majors, as noted above, tended to see independent production as a means to keep studio technical facilities in use and thus help pay for overheads, but also conveniently close at hand.) UA also offered producers a more attractive financial package at both the front (no administrative overhead) and back (reduced distribution fees) ends. In effect, UA rebranded itself as a supplier of services to filmmakers rather than an old-style hands-on producer; during the fifties UA would sponsor further downstream movie service providers and 'packagers' such as the Mirisch Corporation. Krim and Benjamin were naturally motivated not by idealism but by the urgent need to secure the struggling company a slice of the market for top talent. With this move not only did UA gain a competitive edge with the most ambitious independent filmmakers of the period such as Otto Preminger, but they established a new way of doing business in Hollywood, one the other studios would duly follow. Most persuasively of all, UA's example proved immensely profitable: having posted a loss of $200,000 in 1949, by 1959 the company was turning a profit of $4.1 million.[32]

The move towards independent production also tilted the Hollywood balance of power. The studios' emerging role as the godfathers to already gestating projects presupposed that someone – someone else, that is – had the wherewithal to oversee the early stages of development and bring the ready-to-go picture to the table. Yet while some independents – notably those created around leading stars such as Hecht-Hill-[Burt] Lancaster – had a measure of star power of their own, few independent producers were in a position to retain contracted talent even if they wished to. Moreover, as HHL's own boom-to-bust life cycle from 1954 to 1960 would demonstrate, the most successful independents were prone to the perils of unsustainable expansion: as former MGM production head Dore Schary pithily summarised it, 'this [kind of] 'independent' may turn into a major studio, with all the problems that drove people in the major studios to become independents'.[33] For their own part, the newly enfranchised actors, directors and writers were very conscious of the advantageous bargaining position they derived from their marketability.[34] But they were in the main ill-suited to exploit their situation to maximum advantage. Thus, almost inevitably, power in what was becoming a recognisably 'New Hollywood' increasingly devolved on to those who did have access to a range of talent and were skilled in the art of the deal. These were not the old-style prestige independents like Goldwyn, but newcomers – talent agencies. Specifically, one agency, MCA, and one pre-eminent and perspicacious agent above all, Lew Wasserman.

Wasserman, who ran MCA in partnership with its founder Jules Stein, had during the 1930s helped the agency achieve a virtual monopoly in the music industry, moving from representing individual musical performers to booking complete 'packages' of live entertainers of all kinds to venues and subsequently radio broadcasters. When MCA expanded rapidly into Hollywood in the early 1940s, principally by aggressively acquiring numerous smaller agencies, Wasserman quickly set about applying the same principles to the film industry, his company's newly ubiquitous reach earning it the half-admiring, half-fearful soubriquet 'The Octopus'. In the old Hollywood of long-term contracts and studio micromanagement of star profiles, the role of agents – widely despised as parasitic bottom-feeders – was strictly limited. In the new free-market Hollywood, by contrast, agents were enormously empowered, and MCA's control of so many key players by design increased that power exponentially. Even before the postwar downturn, Wasserman was promoting the advantages of independence and incorporation to his clients. Olivia de Havilland's successful lawsuit against her contract with Warner Bros. in 1943 had greatly enhanced the freedom and power of stars; at the same time, the studios' retrenchment made star power an even more crucial dimension for those films that did get made, and correspondingly empowered newly enfranchised freelance talent – and their agents – to drive hard bargains. Wasserman established himself as the new sheriff in town in 1950 by negotiating a historic profit-participation deal that secured MCA client James Stewart 50 per cent of the profits from the Universal Western *Winchester '73* – ultimately netting Stewart over $600,000.[35] Over the course of the 1950s, MCA consolidated its power, becoming a major player in the new telefilm market (see below). Its TV production requirements spurred MCA to acquire the 420-acre Universal City for $11.25 million in 1959; Universal as a result became briefly a tenant on its own lot, before Wasserman took the final step of acquiring the entire studio in 1962 and thus inaugurated the new era of Hollywood conglomeration (see Chapter 4).

Like UA's ascendancy, MCA's rise to prominence was emblematic of the postwar inversion of the old Hollywood class system. It was the smaller, nimbler minor studios – long accustomed to thinking on their feet and chiselling profits off tight margins – who set the tone in the 1950s alongside some established independent producers, above all Walt Disney. This was never truer than with the most important of all the post-*Paramount* developments, Hollywood's halting but ultimately unequivocal accommodation with television.

COMING TO TERMS WITH TELEVISION

Whether television should be seen as the cause of the dramatic drop-off in movie attendance in this period (and beyond), or simply as catalysing a trend that had already begun by the late 1940s, remains intensely controversial. Perhaps we can most productively think of television as the perfect evolutionary predator in the altered circumstances of the 1950s: that is, as the medium best adapted to profit from the environmental changes facing the entertainment industry at this time. As we shall see, those Hollywood studios that suffered the least from the universal downturn of the early 1950s were those that recognised the new business logic established by television's emergence and moved most quickly to establish relations of peaceful coexistence or cooperation with television. Those that viewed the new medium with hostility or pretended indifference, by contrast, could expect a much rockier passage ahead.

The truth was that the coincidence of *Paramount* and the novelty of real competition for the American entertainment dollar was a watershed in Hollywood history, marking the shift from the (theatrical) exhibition orientation that had characterised the industry's first half-century, and in which Hollywood itself had its roots, and towards a new reality driven by domestic, rather than theatrical, consumption. This was, however, by no means as self-evident in 1950 as it seems today, with the benefit of hindsight. Indeed, only a handful of far-sighted individual business leaders seem to have fully perceived the dimensions of the change at hand, and it was the organisations steered by men such as Walt Disney and Lew Wasserman which would set the pace in the decades to come.

In its broad outlines, the story of television's transformative impact on American entertainment is very well known. Television began its long march into America's living rooms soon after the war. Take-up was initially modest, with just 1 million sets sold by 1949 (though this figure certainly underestimates television's overall impact, with many sets located as crowd-pullers in neighbourhood bars and other communal gathering places). But the pace quickened rapidly, and growth soon became exponential: by 1954, 56 per cent of American households had acquired a TV. (See Appendix: Figure 3.) Television stations also multiplied, many of them affiliated to the three broadcast networks CBS, NBC and ABC.[36]

Its full impact may not have been not anticipated, yet television did not take the film industry by surprise. Given the cultural importance of radio, it was a fair bet that a domestic broadcast medium that could add pictures to radio's existing equation of immediacy and intimacy would be successful. In fact, Hollywood's early relationship with television resembled less the hostile rivalry of legend than that stock figure of silent comedy, the lummox – the shambling suitor, at a loss how to convert his admiration into marriage.[37] Initially, the major studios could not conceive of a profitable relationship to television outside the 'supply-side' strategies that had proved so successful in the foundational years of the movie industry: that is, controlling distribution and exhibition. The major studios' initial attempts to cut themselves a slice of the new pie, however, foundered in the tightened post-*Paramount* regulatory climate. Paramount's own attempted acquisition of TV stations in the late 1940s and Fox's proposed takeover of ABC both fell foul of the FCC. Other industry attempts early in the television era to co-opt the new medium – such as closed-circuit live broadcasts in theatres, or primitive versions of pay-TV

– failed for technical, aesthetic or social reasons. It was this frustration of their overtures, rather than systemic rivalry, that saw the Hollywood majors revert through the middle of the fifties to an uneasy cold war with television, typified by MGM's condescending rebuttal of NBC's overtures to explore a production partnership in 1950.[38]

In one area in particular, however, the studios were uniquely well placed to supply the networks with something they urgently needed: product. Fifties television is famous as a 'golden age' of broadcast drama, in the anthology series showcasing original work written and directed by such major talents as Rod Serling, Abby Mann, Paddy Chayefsky, Sidney Lumet, John Frankenheimer and many others (many of them important future Hollywood filmmakers). But these prestigious vehicles, performed and broadcast live from the networks' New York studios using Broadway and off-Broadway talent, were not the broadcasts by which fifties America came to set its collective watch and in front of which it would eat its frozen TV dinners. The shows that became synonymous with the era and which drew enormous weekly audiences and stratospheric advertiser rates were the generic comedies and dramas, typically starring second-string or superannuated Hollywood players in such time-honoured Hollywood B-formats as the police thriller and the Western. Although TV industry spokesmen deprecated Hollywood-originated telefilms as inferior fare compared to live performance, the commercial sponsors who underwrote early US television output recognised soon enough that a filmed half-hour programme would cost them a fraction of the same amount of live airtime. Moreover, the FCC's cessation of its four-year freeze on the issuance of new television licences in 1952 created a burgeoning demand for entertainment to fill airtime that the networks alone simply could not supply.

The emerging market for filmed TV sparked a short-lived boom in shoe-string start-up production companies from 1950 to 1952 that observers compared to the Gold Rush – or to the earliest, Keystone Kops years of the movie business itself. The vast majority of the speculative production undertaken in this period by fly-by-night companies in corner lots and converted garages throughout the LA region failed to find buyers and evaporated as quickly as it had sprung up, leaving – by one estimate in late 1952 – some two dozen 'solid' telefilm producers, including such old Hollywood hands as Hal Roach and Bing Crosby. But the market remained, and for companies that were sufficiently well capitalised and possessed the appropriate facilities, the estimated 1,500-plus hours of filmed entertainment (almost double Hollywood's combined yearly output of theatrical pictures) broadcast annually by the networks was an irresistible honeypot. As standards (and hence prices) of filmed television rose by the mid-fifties (allowing the studios, with their heavy fixed overheads, to compete more effectively in what was a high-volume, fast-paced, tight margin business quite different from their more leisurely traditional pace of theatrical production), the studios recognised that television could be a life-saver given the straitened circumstances of the theatrical market.[39]

It was members of the Little Three – who, lacking theatrical holdings, had always operated on a different business model as well as on far tighter margins than the fully vertically-integrated majors – that were quickest to anticipate and accommodate the new medium. The weakest of these, Universal – deeply in the red following a slew of expensive box office failures in the 1947–8 seasons – was the first to establish a television production subsidiary, but the most successful was Harry Cohn's Columbia, whose Screen Gems opened for business in summer 1949 under the management of Cohn's nephew Ralph. By mid-1952, when Screen Gems became the first major studio to announce a contract to produce a sponsored series of telefilms for network broadcast, Cohn established what would become Hollywood's standard model for profitable telefilm production: producing episodic series for a sponsor – in this first case, Ford Motors – or network at an initial loss (that is, the purchaser paid the studio below cost for the first-run rights to the show) but retaining resale rights for the series thereafter and looking to reap handsome dividends in the subsequent-run syndicated TV markets.

By the late 1950s, television production had firmly established itself at the centre of Hollywood production. The same studio lots that had all but fallen silent in the postwar downturn were once again occupied, producing filmed series – Screen Gems' productions were using one-third of Columbia's studio space – and both trade and mainstream press excitedly reported Hollywood's transformation into a television town and its value to the industry. New York-based live production was being phased out as the networks drew ever more heavily on the armies of talent available on the West Coast. Hollywood had come to dominate network broadcasting as the majors had dominated first-run exhibition, supplying 40 per cent of all network programming and 78 per cent of primetime schedules. TV production thus provided an important new revenue stream and kept Hollywood personnel in employment in lean times (albeit for all but a handful of household names less well-paid, and undeniably less glamorous and prestigious). This was indeed, as *Time* proclaimed in 1957, a 'New Hollywood'.[40]

Much TV production was in the hands of the companies who had got in early and weathered the industry's birthing pains, like Desi Arnaz and Lucille Ball's DesiLu, which employed more than 1,000 people to turn out *I Love Lucy* and fourteen other primetime shows with an annual turnover above $21 million. Having secured a unique waiver from the Justice Department allowing it simultaneously to represent talent and produce entertainment, MCA was also a major player through its TV subsidiary Revue Productions. But the studios were also heavily involved, with Columbia (where Screen Gems compensated for the feeble performance of the theatrical division and helped keep the company afloat throughout the late 1950s), Universal and Warners especially prominent. Republic, the Poverty Row producer celebrated for its series Westerns, converted itself into a dedicated television company. Even the studios that were slowest to move into TV production saw benefits: at MGM, TV revenues amounted to only 10 per cent of gross income in 1959 but accounted for over 40 per cent of profits.[41]

As Hollywood started to profit from television, its hostility to the desire of the TV stations to broadcast theatrical pictures also faded. The majors had all refused to sell or lease their libraries to TV through 1955, although the Poverty Row studios Republic and PRC had cashed in early.[42] That initial hostility had been driven by the violent opposition of exhibitors, fearful that the regular availability of moviegoers' favourite stars on free-to-air TV would devalue the theatrical experience and cause further attrition within their already thinned ranks. But once the studios had complied with *Paramount* they were no longer so responsive to the concerns of theatre owners. Predictably, it was the maverick Howard Hughes who as RKO owner broke the united front when he sold the studio's entire library outright to a middleman, C&C Television, for $15.2 million in 1955. That same year, Columbia marketed 104 of its pre-1948 titles direct to broadcasters through its own Screen Gems subsidiary. All of the majors shortly followed suit in a series of deals that generated total revenues of some $150 million between 1955 and 1960. The studios initially withheld movies produced since 1948, under continuing pressure from exhibitors – warning direly of 'a death blow to theaters'[43] – and also from the talent guilds, who eventually resorted to strike action to extract a new schedule of residual payments for the broadcasting of their work (unanticipated, hence not covered in traditional Hollywood contracts).[44] Once agreement had been reached with the unions, Fox moved to break the 1948 watershed with the broadcast of *How To Marry a Millionaire* (1953) on NBC in September 1961. Newer films naturally commanded a premium from the networks, for whom 'Saturday Night at the Movies' and similar showcase slots quickly became fixtures in the weekly schedules and shock troops in the ratings wars, and the ensuing windfall became a life-support system for the studios in the turbulent mid-sixties.

The Walt Disney Company established a different, but in the long run equally influential, model of collaboration with television. Long dissatisfied with the service his animated pictures had received from his distribution deal at RKO, with ambitious ventures like *Fantasia* (1940) underperforming at the box office, and still chafing from bitter disputes with craft unions in the early forties, by the start of the fifties Disney was less and less invested in his traditional role as a niche producer of theatrical family films. In 1954 Disney struck an innovative deal with ABC, the third television network, to co-produce and broadcast a new weekly anthology programme, to be entitled simply *Disneyland* – not coincidentally, also the name of Disney's personal obsession, the theme park currently under construction in Anaheim, California, on whose development viewers received regular updates during *Disneyland*'s first season and which ABC's money (giving the network a third share in the park) helped finance when Disney's own board were dubious. *Disneyland* built upon Disney's existing reputation as a provider of premium family entertainment to help create the first recognisably modern media 'brand', for which the show itself was effectively an hour-long weekly commercial. For the first time a media company's identity was systematically promoted and profitably reinforced across different 'platforms': the TV show, the theme park, theatrical production and the branded products associated with Disney's animated characters. The unexpected sensation of *Disneyland*'s three-part dramatisation of the life of frontiersman Davy Crockett generated a merchandising bonanza (and gave the decade one of its benchmark images, the coonskin cap adopted by small boys nationwide) and offered further proof of the benefits of synergy (a term not yet in general use). Other studios followed Disney's lead with such vehicles as 'Warner Bros. Presents', 'MGM Parade', and the like, aimed at promoting new studio releases, but they as yet lacked the other marketing avenues that made Disney's venture uniquely successful.[45]

By the end of the fifties, the movie and television industries had become inextricably linked. That the new medium providentially gave back in the form of ancillary revenues and new production opportunities what it took away at the theatrical box office was clear. One minor, but highly visible, symbol of the newly synergistic Hollywood was the circulation of properties between the two media, with successful network series and single plays such as *Dragnet*, *Twelve Angry Men* and *Marty*[46] remade as features, and studio classics such as Warners' *Casablanca*, *King's Row* and *Cheyenne* being adapted into episodic continuing series. What was perhaps less clear at the time – except to some far-sighted financial speculators, whose new interest in the sector helped movie stocks stage a sharp recovery in the early 1960s from the depressed levels at which they had mostly languished since *Paramount* – was the long-term logic of the move towards filmed programming. Syndicated programming and foreign sales markets provided an irrefutable economic argument for recyclable programming. As technologies evolved to make the prospect a commercial reality, the concept of an industry built on the repeated exploitation of the same product in a variety of different contexts would emerge in the age of pay cable and home video as the new paradigm for Hollywood as a whole.

'MAKE THEM BIG; SHOW THEM BIG; AND SELL THEM BIG':[47] BLOCKBUSTER LOGIC

Still, Hollywood in the fifties remained primarily a film business even if the rules of the game had shifted substantially. Revenues from television production and sales might offset losses elsewhere, the creative responsibility of filmmaking itself might be increasingly outsourced: releasing films that could retain or win back US moviegoers was still Hollywood's *raison d'être*. By 1953, it had become clear that the downturn in admissions was permanent and continuing, although the rate of decline may have started to slow slightly; there was a further 13 per cent decline in admissions (some 380 million lost spectators) from 1950 to 1953. Hopes at the start of the decade that demand for durable goods like cars and white goods would have been sated by the postwar binge – freeing up more spending power for non-durable items like movie tickets – proved unfounded as Americans inaugurated a new and apparently self-perpetuating culture of consumption, fuelled by advances in consumer technology and design, Madison Avenue advertising, peer pressure and built-in obsolescence. The studios at this stage had yet to clamber aboard the TV gravy train and still faced sharply declining profits. Although payrolls had been radically pruned, rosters of contract players reduced and economy drives (including executive pay-cuts) announced, the problem remained of what the public now sought or expected from their pictures, given the end of movies' monopoly on visual entertainment.

Routine programmers – shoddily made bottom-of-the-bill B-films – were increasingly redundant in the face of the glut of cheap filmed genre television series. In mid-1952, both Fox and Warners announced that they were dropping B-film production altogether.[48] But the surviving high-turnover neighbourhood exhibitors and the preferences of rural audiences continued to support modest Westerns and action pictures, and several studios, including Universal and Allied Artists (formerly Monogram), focused intensively on this market.[49] Meanwhile, the elusive 'good little picture', lower-budget films with a distinctive, compelling or unusual dimension (a 'gimmick') – including the suddenly popular science fiction film, or the rash of tough postwar *noir* thrillers – seemed to be faring well. And the retrenchment of the period 1948–52, including announcements of capped production costs by most studios, logically suggested a shift away from high-budget glamour towards more smaller-scale contemporary dramas and character-centred films (a turn many filmmakers would have welcomed).

Yet 'good little pictures' seemed unlikely to pay studio overheads. When studio bosses and theatre owners in this period repeatedly spoke of focusing on 'better' pictures, their operative notions of quality had little in common with the kind of realist, humanist cinema favoured by some filmmakers in the immediate postwar period, nor did they share the aspirations of some of the new independents to exploit the creative freedoms unleashed by the end of the old studio system. Industry analysis of the past few years' business pointed the studios in a different direction. Notwithstanding the overall downturn, since 1949 the yearly top-ranking films had not only outstripped their immediate competition but had posted record-breaking earnings. DeMille's *Samson and Delilah* set the benchmark in 1949 with rentals of $11.5 million (more than twice the second-placed picture, MGM's *Battleground*). MGM's *Quo Vadis* in 1951 and *The Greatest Show on Earth*, another DeMille extravaganza at Paramount the following year, repeated the trick. A glance at the coattails of these breakaway smashes showed a preponderance of films in a similar vein: *David and Bathsheba*, *The Snows of Kilimanjaro* (Fox), *King Solomon's Mines*, *Ivanhoe* (MGM) – high-budget spectaculars, strong on visual appeal and star power like the large-scale musicals *Showboat* and *An American In Paris* (both MGM) which were also strong draws in the same years. The studios interpreted these figures to mean that in an era of occasional rather than habitual filmgoing, the right kind of pictures, promoted properly, could transcend the medium to become exciting 'must-see' events commanding exceptional public interest. As expensive as such films were, their box office performance proffered a clear lesson: spend big to win big. And, in what was now a fiercely competitive and far from secure industry, this lesson was quickly learned.

The trend towards 'bigness' took another turn with the extraordinarily successful debut of the independently developed widescreen process Cinerama in September 1952 (see Chapter 3). While Cinerama's cumbersome production and exhibition requirements limited its market, its box office appeal indicated the public appetite for spectacular alternatives to television. The various widescreen and wide-gauge processes quickly introduced by the industry in Cinerama's wake – including CinemaScope, VistaVision, and Todd-AO – were not limited to epic or spectacular subject matter, but they obviously accommodated casts of thousands and showed off spectacular sets and vistas to best effect. The first CinemaScope picture, *The Robe* (Fox 1953), was the year's top-earning film and, like *Quo Vadis?*, an epic set in classical antiquity. In its wake would come many more large-format antiquarian hits with Roman (*Demetrius and the Gladiators*, Fox 1954; *Ben-Hur*, MGM 1959; *Spartacus*, U 1960), Egyptian (*The Egyptian*, Fox 1954; *Valley of the Kings*, MGM 1954), or Biblical (*The Ten Commandments*, Par 1956) settings, as well as sprawling musicals (*Seven Brides for Seven Brothers*, MGM 1954; *The King and I*, Fox 1954), war films (*Battle Cry*, WB 1955; *The Bridge on the River Kwai*, Col 1957), Westerns (*Gunfight at the OK Corral*, Par 1957; *The Alamo*, UA 1960) and indeed every genre and setting capable of expansion to blockbuster scale. Ballooning budgets included soaring prices for 'pre-sold' properties as the studios competed for bestsellers and Broadway hits, insurance against the greater risk blockbusters necessarily incurred: twenty of MGM's twenty-eight forthcoming pictures at the start of 1955 were based on classics or bestsellers.[50] The motion picture industry had, according to Jack Warner – historically one of the most cost-conscious studio chiefs – entered its 'Cadillac age'. 'Nothing', he added, 'is exorbitant if it is the right thing.'[51]

Early signs were that the logic behind the shift to ultra-high-budget pictures was sound. Before *The Robe*, perhaps 100 pictures in Hollywood history had returned over $5 million in rentals; just eighteen months later, another thirty films had done so.[52] Large-scale films had other financial advantages: costume epics could be filmed abroad, enabling studios to work around quota systems imposed by foreign governments to protect domestic film production, by investing in overseas production facilities and filming with local crews. Thus was born 'runaway' production, one of the most notable phenomena of the fifties and early sixties.

Foreign filming in fact offered multiple benefits. Locales such as Tobago, Burma or Central Africa, highlighted in *Heaven Knows, Mr Allison* (Fox 1957), *The Bridge on the River Kwai*, and *The Nun's Story* (WB, 1959) respectively, married well with movies' turn towards vivid and exotic locations and enhanced claims of authenticity – all combating television's monochrome domesticity while maximising the impact of new colour and widescreen processes. Runaway production also made sound business sense given the lower wages paid to often highly skilled technicians either on location or in well-specified rebuilt European studios such as London's Pinewood or Rome's Cinecittà.[53] At the same time, productions such as *Around the World in Eighty Days* (UA 1956), *Trapeze* (UA 1956), *The Pride and the Passion* (UA, 1957) and *El Cid* (AA 1961), showcasing international stars like Cantinflas, Gina Lollobrigida and Sophia Loren alongside European settings, maximised interest in the burgeoning European markets. The dramatic German-led European economic recovery of the fifties saw Hollywood's overseas revenues, even with currency controls and other barriers, soaring both in dollar terms (hitting a new high of $185 million in 1954) and as a proportion of gross receipts, rising from the prewar 33 per cent to 44 per cent or more by mid-decade.[54]

The big-picture trend matched other industry shifts. 'Bigger' films, for example, played well in the thriving drive-in sector (although musicals suffered from appalling sound reproduction). Furthermore, whatever the potential for social and political allegory concealed in ancient Rome or the frontier West, blockbusters suited a traumatised Hollywood's mood in the aftermath of the House Un-American Activities Committee (HUAC) witch-hunts: a wholesale retreat from social problem films and an emphatic turn towards escapist entertainment as far removed as possible from controversial contemporary social realities.[55] Nor did the rise of the blockbuster conflict with the shift towards independent production. In the studio era, ultra-high-budget productions had largely been the province of top-rank independents like Selznick while the studios persevered profitably with their variegated slates of prestige and routine films. Now, the studios formed ongoing partnerships with comparable specialists, tried and trusted to handle the mammoth logistical, artistic and financial demands of a blockbuster production, old studio hands such as Sam Spiegel (*The Bridge on the River Kwai*; *Lawrence of Arabia*, Col 1962) and Darryl Zanuck (*Island in the Sun*, Fox 1957; *The Longest Day*, Fox 1962), producer-directors such as DeMille, Otto Preminger (*Exodus*, US 1960) and Stanley Kramer (*The Pride and the Passion*; *Judgment at Nuremberg*, UA 1961; *It's a Mad, Mad, Mad, Mad World*, UA 1963), and producer-stars such as Kirk Douglas (Bryna Productions: *The Vikings*, UA 1958; *Spartacus*, U 1960). The blockbuster's typically extensive location shooting and runaway production anyhow pretty much mandated surrender of day-to-day studio oversight; in theory at least, an independent producer had every motivation to run a tight ship as his own fortunes were closely bound up with the production at hand. In reality, cost control was rarely that straightforward: the inherent unpredictabilities of location work (incompatible working practices, over-stretched lines of communication and supply, weather, tropical diseases) were particularly liable to slow production. Nor were producers – now themselves personally committed to the picture's creative vision – necessarily inclined to take management's side and crack the whip on talent. In practice, once principal shooting began a studio had very little power to curb or curtail the production: it had to ride the tiger.

Of course, this mattered less as long as blockbusters were making money. And the market for high-cost high earners seemed robust. By 1960, sixteen studio-distributed films (and another three Cinerama spectacles) had matched or surpassed the $11 million dollar benchmark set by *Samson and Delilah*. The trend accelerated (hastened by inflation) in the early sixties, with another twenty-three films earning above $11 million by 1965. The blockbuster was not of course the only game in town: but it was much the most visible, and in important ways characteristic, kind of Hollywood production in the late fifties. The blockbuster's preferred exhibition mode, roadshowing – indefinite engagements at a limited number of prestigious theatres (typically one per major market), with bookable seats at premium prices – provoked fierce bidding wars between exhibitors and compelled them to accept distributors' often eye-watering terms. If the film proved less of a draw than anticipated – as was the case with *Cleopatra*, provoking the owners of a Broadway theatre to sue Fox for lumbering them with 'an inferior attraction'[56] – the distributor stood to suffer less than the exhibitor. Hollywood's growing distance from the theatrical sector in which it had its origins was apparent. The antitrust suit brought against the majors by the small drive-in chain National Amusements in 1958 (for limiting access to first-run studio films) underlined the divide. (For his aggressive efforts, National Amusements president Sumner Redstone was rewarded with the presidency of the National Association of Theatre Owners; he would subsequently grow his company into cable giant Viacom and in 1994 buy Paramount.)[57]

By a neat irony, the metonymic simplification of the film industry as a whole into 'the studios' and the misleading elision of New York-based exhibition and distribution into Hollywood-centred production had, with the divestment of the majors' theatre chains, drawn closer to business reality. However, in a further twist the physical 'studio' itself had by the early sixties become an increasingly virtual entity, as following UA's lead the majors reconfigured their core business as the financing, servicing and distribution, rather than the hands-on production, of motion pictures. Throughout the 1950s, Hollywood grew less and less reliant on its erstwhile parent and principal focus, the domestic theatrical box office. In fact, this was perhaps the most unexpected outcome of 'Hollywood TV'. By the end of the 1950s, not only had the majors all divested themselves of their theatrical holdings, in line with the *Paramount* judgment, but as producer-distributors they were now increasingly invested in an industry whose success directly competed with, and even *threatened*, business at theatres. It seemed to prove that *Paramount*, far from killing the goose that laid the golden egg, had simply provoked the bird into laying not one, but several new eggs in new roosts. Not for the first time or for the last, out of acute economic necessity Hollywood had adapted, innovated and started to diversify.

NOTES

1. For more on the impact of the Production Code on motion picture content, and challenges to the Code in the postwar era, see Chapter 2.
2. Harry Cohn, president and production head of 'Little Three' studio Columbia, was the only executive in this period to combine the two roles.
3. See below, p. 19–20.
4. On Hollywood unions in this period, see Gerald Horne, *Class Struggle in Hollywood, 1930-1950: Moguls, Mobsters, Stars, Reds, and Trade Unionists* (Austin: University of Texas Press, 2001).
5. 'Hollywood is a little better off,' *Business Week*, 23 July 1949, p. 62.
6. Tino Balio has suggested, via a case study of Columbia Pictures' expansion strategies in the 1930s, that the 'mature oligopoly' orthodoxy needs adjusting to take into account smaller companies' ongoing efforts to establish themselves in the industry. See 'Columbia Pictures: the making of a motion picture major, 1930–1943,' in David Bordwell and Noel Carroll (eds), *Post-Theory: Reconstructing Film Studies* (Madison: University of Wisconsin Press, 1996), pp. 419–33.
7. Spectacularly in the case of *Gone With the Wind*, which not only helped Selznick International Pictures – uniquely in the studio era – post higher profits ($10 million) for 1940 than any major studio, but contributed nearly 50 per cent of that year's profits at its distributor MGM, second-placed with $8.7 million. (Selznick normally distributed his pictures through RKO: distributing *Gone. . .* was the price MGM extracted for the loan-out of its contract star Clark Gable to play Rhett Butler. See Douglas Gomery, *The Hollywood Studio System: A History* (London: BFI, 2005), p. 106.
8. Independent production in Hollywood is considered at greater length below. The efforts and travails of the 'race' market and its auteurs, notably Oscar Micheaux, have generated a considerable critical literature in recent years: see inter alia Donald Bogle, *Toms, Coons,*

Mulattoes, Mammies and Bucks: An Interpretive History of Blacks in American Films, 3rd ed. (Oxford: Roundhouse, 1994).

9. Thomas Schatz, *Boom and Bust: American Cinema in the 1940s* (Berkeley: University of California Press, 1997), pp. 33–4.

10. The terms of the 1940 compromise are clearly laid out in Richard B. Jewell, *The Golden Age of Cinema: Hollywood 1929–1945* (Oxford: Blackwell, 2007), pp. 79–80.

11. See Denise Mann, *Hollywood Independents: The Postwar Talent Takeover* (Minnesota: University of Minneapolis Press, 2008), p. 37.

12. The standard analysis of the *Paramount* decision is still Michael Conant, *Antitrust in the Motion Picture Industry: Economic and Legal Analysis* (Berkeley: University of California Press, 1960).

13. In fact, it was standard studio practice to sell off the negatives of older films for a token fee so they could be written off the company's inventory. With the arrival of television, the small distributors who had originally acquired these ancient pictures intending to squeeze a return out of obscure rural theatres and ten-cent urban 'grind houses' came into windfall profits. See Milton MacKaye, 'The big brawl: Hollywood *vs.* television', *Saturday Evening Post*, 26 January 1952, p. 121.

14. In modern business jargon, first-run audiences were 'high-value' consumers – prepared to pay premium rates for a first-class product (a first-run studio film at a downtown picture palace), and second- and subsequent-run moviegoers progressively 'lower value,' given the low rentals that accrued to the studios from these venues. For an application of this principle to the contemporary theatrical-to-home video release window, see Chapter 7, n. 41.

15. The average number of prints for a Big Five A-picture seems to have been around 200.

16. Jon Lewis, *American Film* (New York: Norton, 2007), p. 208.

17. 'Hollywood shakes its slump,' *Business Week*, 11 February 1950, p. 82.

18. 'Movies: new sick industry', *Business Week*, 25 November 1950, p. 26; 'Movies come out of the dog house', *Business Week*, 10 November 1951, p. 140.

19. 'U.S. exports: end of a boom', *Business Week*, 16 August 1947, p. 103.

20. Britain had previously imposed quotas on Hollywood imports in 1927.

21. 'Boxoffice pinch', *Business Week*, 4 October 1947, pp. 62–3.

22. See 'Hollywood's exports pay off', *Business Week*, 29 April 1950, pp. 113–14;

23. Schatz, *Boom and Bust*, p. 331.

24. Quoted in Christopher Anderson, *Hollywood TV: The Studio System in the 1950s* (Austin: University of Texas Press, 1994), p. 38.

25. 'How Hollywood hopes to hit comeback road', *Newsweek*, 12 January 1953, pp. 66–7.

26. In his study of American independent filmmaking, Yannis Tzioumakis refers to the majors in the post-*Paramount* period as 'ex-studios' to emphasise the change in industry relations.

27. Peter Lev, *The Fifties: Transforming The Screen 1950–1959* (Berkeley: University of California Press, 2003), p. 26.

28. See Yannis Tzioumakis, *American Independent Cinema* (Edinburgh: Edinburgh University Press, 2005), pp. 48–9.

29. Quoted in Tino Balio, *United Artists: The Company That Changed the Film Industry* (Madison: University of Wisconsin Press, 1987), p. 47.

30. For a full discussion of Capra and the demise of Liberty Films, see Schatz, *Boom and Bust*, pp. 347–52.

31. The terms of Krim and Benjamin's deal stated that, should UA turn a profit under their management in any one of their first three years in charge, they would acquire a

controlling 50 per cent of the company. The (somewhat fortuitous) instant success of Sam Spiegel's *The African Queen* and Stanley Kramer's *High Noon* – Krim and Benjamin had originated neither project – ensured this happened with their first year. The pair subsequently bought out UA's surviving founding partners, Charles Chaplin and Mary Pickford, in 1955 and 1956 respectively, and the following year floated the company on the New York Stock Exchange at an initial capitalisation of $14 million. See Balio, *United Artists*, Chapter 2.

32. Balio, *United Artists*, p. 92.
33. Dore Schary, 'Hollywood: fade out, fade in', *The Reporter*, 18 April 1957, pp. 20–4. For Hecht-Hill-Lancaster, see 'The Biggest, the Best: 1955', pp. 69–71.
34. This was especially true of leading men, in a period when as *Business Week* observed, 'top male actors with built-in box office appeal [were] scarcer than Confederate nickels'. 'Reviving Hollywood spirits', *Business Week*, 13 November 13 1954, pp. 116–18.
35. Balio, *United Artists*, p. 77, notes by comparison that Clark Gable never earned more than $300,000 a year in his heyday at MGM.
36. A short-lived fourth network, DuMont, ceased broadcasting in 1956.
37. The myth of Hollywood's hostility to television was of course a much better story, and probably suited both industries well enough in the early fifties. Thus in early 1951 the *Saturday Evening Post* ran a three-part series by Milton MacKaye, 'The big brawl: Hollywood vs. television' (19 January, p. 17 ff.; 26 January, p. 30 ff.; 2 February, p. 30 ff.). The first instalment claimed tremulously that 'Life in the shade of the Beverley Hill's palm trees today is lived dangerously and in an atmosphere of civil war. There are overtones in every cocktail party conversation of the tumbrel and the gibbet' (p. 17).
38. See Anderson, *Hollywood TV*, Chapter 2.
39. 'The movie makers look for gold on the TV screen', *Business Week*, 23 April 1955, pp. 154–6.
40. 'The new Hollywood', *Time*, 13 May 1957, pp. 44–5.
41. 'It's 'side' assets that count', *Business Week*, 17 September 1960, pp. 175–8.
42. UA's library had also become available in 1951 under the terms of a third-party deal to finance the studio's purchase of Krim and Benjamin's former company Eagle-Lion Pictures.
43. 'The vanishing moviegoer', *Time*, 10 February 1958, p. 100.
44. 'Hollywood: strike in a ghost town', *Time*, 21 March 1960, p. 72.
45. On Disney and *Disneyland*, see Anderson, *Hollywood TV*, pp. 133–55.
46. See 'The Biggest, the Best: 1955', p. 69.
47. 'Getting them back to the movies', *Business Week*, 22 October 1955, pp. 58–63.
48. 'Hollywood hope: extravaganzas and TV quickies', *Newsweek*, 16 June 1952, p. 72; 'End of 'B' films', *Newsweek*, 23 June 1952, p. 74.
49. Universal head Edward Muhl defended his company's against-the-grain strategy of churning out cheap pictures 'with Apache in the title' to the *New York Times Magazine*: 'Did they tell you at the other studios that the program picture is dead? We're still doing fine with it . . . We found out that people like pictures about Indians in Technicolor. So, they're getting them' (10 January 1954, p. 21ff; see also 'Movies' comeback', *Fortune* February 1955, p. 127ff.). But within 18 months Universal too was announcing a slate of high-budget productions.
50. 'Reviving Hollywood spirits', p. 117.
51. 'Getting them back to the movies', p. 60.
52. Freeman Lincoln, 'The comeback of the movies', *Fortune*, February 1955.

53. 'Rome's newly rebuilt Cinecittà studios', comments Drew Casper, 'became one of Hollywood's homes away from home' – and the training ground for later Italian directors such as Sergio Leone, whose 'Spaghetti Westerns' of the 1960s would have such a profound impact on the direction of that quintessentially American genre. *Postwar Hollywood, 1946-1962* (Oxford: Blackwell, 2007), p. 50; on Leone and Cinecittà, see Christopher Frayling, *Something To Do With Death* (London: Faber, 2000), pp. 64–79.

54. 'Reviving Hollywood spirits', p. 117.

55. On the witch-hunts and their consequences, see Chapter 2, p. 54ff.

56. See Sheldon Hall, 'Twentieth Century Fox in the 1960s', in Linda Ruth Williams and Michael Hammond (eds), *Contemporary American Cinema* (Maidenhead: McGraw-Hill, 2005), pp. 46–9.

57. Edward Jay Epstein, *The Big Picture: Money and Power in Hollywood* (New York: Random House, 2005), pp. 67–8.

The Biggest, the Best: 1946

Best Picture, Box Office No. 1: *The Best Years of Our Lives* (Samuel Goldwyn Productions)
D: William Wyler; **P:** Samuel Goldwyn; **W:** Robert Sherwood

If 1946 was indeed the highpoint of classic Hollywood, that judgement rests not only on the year's record-breaking annual revenues and domestic attendances, but also on the sheer quality of the year's releases. Memorable and timeless films included *Notorious*, one of Hitchcock's most accomplished blends of suspense and romance; another Selznick production, the epic – and epically steamy – Western *Duel In the Sun* ('Lust in the Dust'); Frank Capra's ambivalent fable of American individualism and community *It's a Wonderful Life*, featuring perhaps James Stewart's definitive performance (the film's lukewarm initial reception has, with television's help, long since yielded to classic status[1]); John Ford's archetypal Western *My Darling Clementine*, with Henry Fonda as Wyatt Earp; Howard Hawks's equally authoritative private-eye thriller *The Big Sleep*, whose bafflingly labyrinthine plot took second place to Humphrey Bogart and Lauren Bacall's combustible chemistry; the horror film *The Spiral Staircase*, stylishly directed by Robert Siodmak in the contemporary Gothic style that would become RKO's postwar trademark; and several dark melodramas that typified what some French (but not as yet American) film critics had already labelled *film noir*, including *The Postman Always Rings Twice*, Columbia's *Gilda*, and Universal's *The Killers*.

Yet neither audiences nor critics had any doubt which picture stood head and shoulders above its impressive competition. *The Best Years of Our Lives*, directed by William Wyler for veteran independent producer Samuel Goldwyn, was the year's biggest hit, returning record rentals of $11 million. A realist melodrama depicting the experience of returning servicemen and their families, powerful, touching and expertly crafted, the film clearly spoke directly to the experience of millions. Critical opinion was equally unanimous and as widely predicted the film cleaned up at that year's Academy Awards, winning Best Picture, Director, Actor (Fredric March), Screenplay and Supporting Actor (real-life veteran and double amputee Harold Russell).

The Best Years of Our Lives is both one of classic Hollywood's exemplary achievements and pregnant with possibilities of a new direction for postwar American cinema – notwithstanding the film's enormous success, a path ultimately not taken. In various ways Wyler – who had himself served over-seas in the war, flying with bomb crews to create the poetic documentary *Memphis Belle* and returning with his hearing permanently impaired – strove to extend mainstream Hollywood cinema beyond its self-imposed limitations of conventional form and content. The narrative structure of *Best Years*, for example, though never anything but organised, is unconventional in running three intersecting narrative lines throughout the film (and giving the film's two headline stars, March and Loy, in some ways the least dramatic of the three). Moreover, as each storyline follows the experiences of one of three newly demobilised servicemen (Army sergeant Al Stevenson, March; Air Force officer Fred Derry, Dana Andrews; and Navy engineer Homer Parrish, Russell, who has lost both hands) returning to their Midwest hometown, it becomes clear that these characters offer a cross-section of postwar American society. United by their wartime experiences, in peacetime they are divided by class, age and personality, though not always in predictable ways: the grizzled infantryman Al is an affluent banker, while sharp flyboy Fred is a former soda jerk from a railside shack.

Wyler's careful delineation of class distinctions (to which the three veterans themselves are indifferent) underscores the potential dangers if the solidarity fostered by the war effort collapses into renewed social divisions. In the opening scene, a flush businessman (a war profiteer?) pays excess baggage for his golf clubs as Fred struggles to find a flight home; later Al's boss pressures him to help the bank avoid its social obligations by refusing to co-sponsor GI loans. Late in the film, Homer is harangued by a loudmouthed rightist arguing that he and his dead shipmates were 'chumps' duped by 'Washington radicals' who suffered needlessly in the 'wrong war', a scene that extends this social consciousness into an explicit, and topical, politics. (*Best Years*' topicality is notable, with references to Hiroshima and radiation poisoning, the Bretton Woods economic summit, the GI Bill and postwar conglomeratisation, among others.) *Best Years* looks forward to some of the social problem films that would start to emerge in the next two to three years; but – partly because its subject matter is broader – it avoids the didactic tone that would date the anti-racism message film *Gentleman's Agreement*, the following year's Best Picture Academy Award winner, so badly.[2]

As Bazin discerned, the film finds an important formal corollary to its progressive democratic politics in Gregg Toland's trademark deep-focus camerawork, deployed far less ostentatiously here than in *Citizen Kane*.[3] Toland and Wyler allow scenes to unfold organically through staging in depth, often in long takes: the awkwardness of Al and Millie's first scene alone together unfolds over 100 stilted but unbroken seconds, and the crucial scene where Wilma undresses Homer, fully revealing his prostheses for the first and only time in the film, is almost a minute long. The viewer is invited to inhabit such scenes with the characters and explore the textures of personal and social relationships mapped out in them; in parallel to contemporary Italian neorealism, Wyler here abjures overly directive or emotionally manipulative cutting as if exemplifying Bazin's ethical prescriptions. At other times, the film visibly draws on wartime developments in documentary technique, as in the montage of vignettes of daily life in postwar Boone City[4] glimpsed by the returning vets through their taxi window (shot on the fly using a hidden camera).

Sexuality is another area *Best Years* treats with more sophistication than the Production Code encouraged. Al and Millie's household, in particular, is marked by an understated maturity in regard to sexual relations. An unexpressed yet tangible source of tension in Al and Millie's first scene alone together is the question of Al's fidelity while overseas (Millie's monogamy is apparently assumed): Al's reflex offer of a cigarette – forgetting Millie doesn't smoke – both symbolises the catching-up they have to do and suggests he may have performed this gesture many times for many other women in the past four years. But dancing at Butch's bar, husband and wife simultaneously acknowledge and defuse the issue by adroit role-playing: 'You remind me of my wife,' Al ventures drunkenly – but knowingly?; 'but let's talk not about her now,' replies Millie (still stone-cold sober) in character. Later, Al and Millie greet Peggy's declaration of intent to break up Fred's dysfunctional marriage not with horror or moralistic outrage but with concern, openness and understanding. The adulterous relationship itself is depicted in a notably matter-of-fact way (compare, for example, the histrionic *Now, Voyager*), reflecting the enhanced maturity the film both brings to and proposes for the social comprehension of adult emotional relationships.

Needless to say, *Best Years* is not a radical film (let alone a communist one): on the contrary, when Homer confronts the rightwing blowhard in the drugstore, having torn the Stars and Stripes pin from the fascist's lapel he later tenderly retrieves it and slips it into his breast pocket (next to his heart). Fred's proposal to Peggy, holding out the prospect ahead of hard graft and sacrifice, allegorises the task of building not only their, but America's future. Nonetheless, and despite its massive popularity, it came as no surprise that during the following year's HUAC investigations, the right-wing Motion Picture Alliance for the Preservation of American Ideals indicted *Best Years* as a film incorporating 'sizable doses of Communist propaganda'. By 1948 the *New Yorker* recorded Wyler himself commenting that in the changed political climate he could no longer have made *Best Years*.[5]

Best Years' box office record would eventually be overturned in 1949 by Cecil B. DeMille's Biblical epic *Samson and Delilah*. This bombastic blockbuster not only marked out the commercial and stylistic path Hollywood would follow for the next fifteen years. As a leading light of the Motion Picture Alliance, DeMille had promoted loyalty oaths as a prerequisite for Directors' Guild membership and had openly questioned the German-Jewish 'Vyler's Americanism. Ideologically, *Samson and Delilah* and the pious behemoths that followed in its wake were poles apart from the socially conscious, humanist Hollywood cinema Wyler had tried to create. It was thus no small irony that Wyler won his third Best Director Oscar – and once again broke box office records – with a film that seemed to epitomise the Hollywood epic, MGM's 1959 remake of *Ben-Hur*. Sarah Kozloff has identified anti-HUAC references smuggled into *Ben-Hur*: the necessity for such covert strategies in itself, however, testifies to the way in which Hollywood in the 1950s had turned its back on the progressive humanism so memorably embodied in *The Best Years of Our Lives*.

Notes

1. Interestingly, this process of reassessment was already underway as early as 1958, when James Stewart noted the film's growing appeal in a *New York Times Magazine* article about television screenings of theatrical films.
2. Although there are no speaking parts for black people in *Best Years*, Wyler makes a point of including African American extras in integrated groups at several points in the film, including a black serviceman in the opening scene.
3. The film testifies to the power of creative partnerships in Hollywood – Wyler had previously directed eight Goldwyn productions, while Toland shot a total of thirty-seven of Goldwyn's fifty-seven sound pictures and in turn worked with Wyler seven times before his premature death in 1948.
4. Goldwyn's publicity suggested that Cincinatti was the model for Boone City, but James I. Deutsch has proved fairly conclusively that Iowan MacKinlay Cantor's original blank-verse treatment, from which Robert Sherwood drew his

screenplay, was based on Des Moines. The taxi montage footage, in any case, was probably shot around Los Angeles. See '*The Best Years of Our Lives* and the Cincinatti story', *Historical Journal of Film, Radio and Television*, 2006; 26(2): 215–25.

5. Quoted in Thomas Schatz, *Boom and Bust: American Cinema in the 1940s* (Berkeley: University of California Press, 1997), p. 382.

CHAPTER 2

The Communication of Ideas

The conventional image of the USA from the end of World War II to President John F. Kennedy's assassination in November 1963, is of two febrile periods of heightened Cold War tensions, nuclear paranoia and domestic turbulence bookending a somnolent, self-satisfied and insular phase of conformity, commodity culture and conspicuous consumption. Two eventful Democratic administrations, Harry S. Truman (1945–52) and Kennedy (1960–63) bracketed the two ostensibly placid terms of Republican former Allied Supreme Commander Dwight D. Eisenhower, whose own buttoned-down, golfing, bridge-playing persona seemed to epitomise the suburbanised, conservative culture over which he presided. One could plot Hollywood's output in this period along a similar contour: first, a brief postwar period during which the cycles of social realist and *noir* films pushed boundaries of subject matter and style, all too soon stifled by a reactionary political climate; then a decade-long retreat to socially irrelevant spectacles like the epic and the musical, during which innovation was largely confined to the presentation and promotion of Hollywood films, using novel or updated technologies like 3-D, widescreen and colour to consolidate an idea of moviegoing as spectacular escapism;[1] eventually the first stirrings of a new, more artistically ambitious and daring cinema in which landmark auteur pictures such as Hitchcock's *Psycho* (Par 1960), Billy Wilder's *The Apartment* (UA 1960), John Frankenheimer's *The Manchurian Candidate* (UA 1962) and Stanley Kubrick's *Lolita* (MGM 1962) and *Dr Strangelove* (Col 1963) challenged, or indeed shattered, conventional constraints.

Inevitably, such a snapshot both contains a fair measure of truth, but is also a convenient caricature that misses or coarsens a great deal. Recent historians have stressed the Eisenhower era's pivotal, transformative role in modern American history and the currents of controversy and dissent that circulated through it, often suppressed but at other times highly visible. It is also worth

The 'Hollywood Ten' and their families protest in vain against their prison sentences in 1947. Reproduced courtesy of The Kobal Collection

stressing that the received view of Eisenhower's America as blandly material-istic and stiflingly conformist originated at the time and circulated widely, not only in self-identified dissident elements such as the East Coast intelligentsia or the beleaguered American left, but in bestselling works of cultural criticism that were in turn widely disseminated through the popular media – thence also informing the images of American society in many motion pictures of the period. The fifties were no more socially monolithic than any other period. Similarly, the perception of Hollywood's output in the fifties over-looks the ways in which, across numerous genres and in a variety of different ways, Hollywood films accommodated critical perspectives on contemporary American mores and social relations, while simultaneously expressing a range of responses to the Cold War in particular – running the gamut from phobic aggression to nuclear anxiety and even despair – none of which comfortably match the general account of the time as one of complacent insularity.

Undoubtedly, the ongoing industrial transformations discussed in the previous chapter contributed importantly to opening up a space for non-consensual perspectives in Hollywood pictures. The shift towards independ-ent production allowed filmmakers greater freedom to initiate projects outside the constraints of studio orthodoxies. For example, two of the best-known independents, Stanley Kramer and Hecht-Hill-Lancaster, never concealed their liberal inclinations and created timely films portraying ordinary blue-collar life (*Marty*, HHL/UA 1955) and youth subcultures (*The Wild One*, Kramer/Col 1953) or critiquing contemporary mass culture (*Sweet Smell of Success*, HHL/UA 1957), race relations (*The Defiant Ones*, Kramer/UA 1958), and the prospect of nuclear war (*On the Beach*, Kramer/UA 1959), among other topics. For their part, the studios were (in varying degrees, partly reflecting their degree of outsourced independent production – UA more so, as the previous list suggests, MGM much less) more receptive to potentially contentious material as part of their drive to differentiate theatrical releases from the bland fare of broadcast TV (especially the filmed series which, ironically, the studios themselves were by the late 1950s profitably producing in volume). From 1953 onwards most of the majors endured repeated skirmishes with the waning authority of the Production Code; though naturally motivated by commercial interests, these also reflected filmmakers' estimation of the shifts underway in broader public attitudes. These typically related to sexual morality, yet can nonetheless be seen as clearly 'political' in an expanded sense of the term.

No one (other than, as we shall see, HUAC) could seriously claim that Hollywood films were in any serious sense radical. Even those pictures, always a minority, which starting in the late fifties explicitly took on social and political issues – most notably racism – usually adopted cautiously liberal positions and often disguised their topical concerns in generic and/or period trappings. But the political consciousness of American movies was never fixed or completely monolithic and both expressed, and helped shape, the changing ideological field of American life.

POLITICS, HOLLYWOOD STYLE

Hollywood films are not political statements, they are commercial entertainment; unlike Western Union, as Samuel Goldwyn's famous aphorism reminds us, they are not designed to send messages but to earn a return on their considerable investment by selling as many tickets as possible to as wide an audience as possible. From before America's entry into World War I until the early 1950s, this was not simply industry orthodoxy: it was judicially codified fact, a judgment handed down from the highest court in the land. In its 1915 decision in *Mutual Film Company* v. *Industrial Commission of Ohio*, the US Supreme Court unanimously found film to be 'a business pure and simple, originated and conducted for profit, like other spectacles [e.g., fairgrounds and circuses], not to be regarded . . . as part of the press of a country or as organs of public opinion'. Amplifying this claim, the Court characterised movies as 'mere representations of events, of ideas and sentiments published and known'; hence, however, 'vivid, useful and entertaining', in the Court's own words, not entitled to the free speech protections extended by the First Amendment to the US Bill of Rights to the press, literature and other arts (including the theatre).

As Jon Lewis has argued, this judgment, which seemed to deny movies First Amendment protections on the grounds of a (barely testable) require-ment for the propagation of *original* ideas (not merely 'sentiments [previ-ously] published and known'), reflected establishment hostility to the new mass medium of film and anxieties about the movies' influence over their lower-class, often immigrant audiences. Which meant that *Mutual* v. *Ohio* was shot through with contradictions from the outset; asserting that film, a purely commercial proposition, was not a medium of ideas as the grounds for endorsing the State of Ohio's constitutional right to ban D. W. Griffith's *Birth of a Nation*, the Court ignored Ohio's stated rationale for the ban – the feared inflammatory effects of the racist ideology informing Griffith's masterpiece; that is, its ideas. Contrary to the Court's stated position, it was precisely the fear of movies' capacity to communicate (bad) opinions to (the wrong) people that made their control by social and judicial authority an imperative. The *Mutual* decision was consistent with contemporary efforts to regulate movies in the interests of social hygiene (for example, by policing building codes and safety regulations with uncommon rigour in working-class and immigrant neighbourhoods). Movies were implicated in politics from the outset, as *Birth of a Nation* illustrates perfectly: from the national black protests against the film, the NAACP emerged as the leading US civil rights organisation. At exactly the same time, the industry's enthusiastically interventionist line on World War I led to Hollywood's first partnership with Government in the wartime Committee on Public Information (predecessor of the next war's Office of War Information), which supported the export of Hollywood films in the interests of promoting 'the wholesome life of America'.[2]

The consequences of *Mutual* v. *Ohio* for the American film industry were profound and long-lasting. The Court's decision empowered not only state and municipal censorship boards but also the conservative religious and com-munity groups who exerted organised pressure upon them to ban 'subversive' or 'immoral' pictures. Film historian Garth Jowett has suggested that movies, as representatives of a modernising national culture contemporaneously reflected in the expansion of retail chains and the growing reach of the Federal Government, became a symbolic arena for traditional localist authority to take a stand. (Traditionalists' animosity towards Hollywood's Jewish leader-ship reinforced this dynamic.)[3] In *Mutual*'s wake, the often unpredictable and arbitrary actions of local censorship boards became a sufficiently serious commercial problem that when, in the early 1920s, the rape/murder trial of the popular silent comedian Roscoe 'Fatty' Arbuckle, the murder of director William Desmond Taylor and other lurid Hollywood scandals again inflamed public hostility towards the industry and the Hearst press began to call for federal censorship, the studios took action.

Setting up the Motion Pictures Producers and Distributors Association (MPPDA) as the industry's own regulatory body under the leadership of the impeccably sober Presbyterian (that is, visibly non-Jewish) former postmaster general Will Hays, who duly produced the first version of the famous 'Hays Code', was in the first place primarily a public relations gesture (as well as a means of corralling talent with contractual 'morality clauses'). In due course, however, Hays' deliberately ineffectual 'Don't's and Be Careful's' evolved into the Production Code proper; and when the widely publicised Payne Fund Studies (1929–32) examining movies' impact on children were followed by another outcry at the violence of the gangster cycle and the sexual sugges-tiveness of Mae West and Jean Harlow, under the leadership of conservative Catholic activist Joseph Breen the Production Code Administration began to enforce Code provisions rigorously. For the next two decades Hollywood pictures were locked into a moral schema that, as David Cook memorably describes it, was 'awesomely repressive, prohibiting the showing or mention-ing of almost everything germane to the situation of normal human adults'.[4]

The Code took its stand on questions of morality – as defined in the rigidly conservative terms of organisations such as the Catholic Legion of Decency, which throughout the Code's active lifetime exerted remarkable influence on PCA decisions. Political positions as such were not stipulated by the Code, but its reactionary stance on most aspects of American society ensured that in practice those few Hollywood films that took an explicit political stance did so, bar a few notable exceptions, within a very narrow ideological range. The PCA's official line, in any event, was that movies were entertainment, not vehicles for political pontification or controversy. The odyssey of the epony-mous film director hero in Preston Sturges' *Sullivan's Travels* (Par 1941), a celebrated studio picture that dealt directly with the question of film's social obligations, reached the same conclusion: the common man is best served by motion pictures that offer unpretentious escapist entertainment, not preachy politics (a lesson illustrated in the movie itself, perhaps appropriately, by a Mickey Mouse cartoon – Disney was noted for his antagonism to the unions).

Many filmmakers undoubtedly chafed at this straitjacket; independent pro-ducer Walter Wanger surely spoke for many when he protested in a 1939 letter to the *New York Times* that the PCA's 'formulated theory of pure entertain-ment [made] impossible the honest handling of important truths and ideas'.[5] Yet the Code should not simply be seen, in this context or in others, as a grim interloper infringing creative freedoms. The attitudes of liberal filmmakers such as Wanger were not those of studio bosses, among whom a vocal New

Deal progressive such as Darryl Zanuck, production head in the 1930s and 1940s at Warner and Fox (where he supervised production of John Ford's *The Grapes of Wrath* and *Tobacco Road*, both pictures proving lightning rods for conservative wrath throughout the 1940s[6]), was in a decided minority; staunch conservatives such as MGM's Louis B. Mayer and Irving Thalberg (who oversaw the studio-backed propaganda campaign that in 1934 helped defeat Sinclair Lewis's insurgent Democratic candidacy for the California governorship) were far more typical.

It was these men who paid Joe Breen's salary and the other costs of maintaining the Code apparatus; the PCA was part of the Hollywood system, not imposed from outside, and in his ideological proclivities as in his other duties Breen was serving the interests not only of conservative churchgoers but primarily of his employers. His own 'all-encompassing conservatism'[7] notwithstanding, Breen was not in the job of preventing motion pictures getting made; he was in the business of ensuring that, armed with the anticensorship prophylactic of a Code Seal of Approval, studio pictures could be profitably distributed and exhibited nationwide and indeed overseas. (Hence the Code provision urging 'sensitive' treatment of other national cultures; Breen strongly opposed the production of several prewar antifascist pictures such as Warners' *Confessions of a Nazi Spy*, ostensibly at least on commercial rather than ideological grounds.)

The economic calculus that informed production decisions was inherently conservative. Studio releases sought as wide an audience as possible, politics was divisive, and progressive political positions especially likely to antagonise the types who found their way on to local censorship boards. Films espousing civil rights for African Americans, for example (or for that matter which simply portrayed black Americans as rounded human beings), were almost certain to be barred from theatres in the segregated South. Politics was bad box office. Such considerations would always have discouraged expressions of radical sentiment, regardless of the personal politics of studio executives (which themselves were subject to change: Jack Warner, for example, who helped establish Warner Bros. as the most socially conscious major studio in the 1930s, after the war became an outspoken anti-communist). Hence the turbulent social and political realities of the Depression found only a hazy reflection in most studio pictures: even *The Grapes of Wrath* was watered down to highlight maternal sacrifice rather than workers' rage. Several of Frank Capra's late 1930s/early 1940s films, such as *Mr Smith Goes to Washington* (Col 1939) and *Meet John Doe* (Col 1941), addressed problems of American democracy, but did so in ways that carefully avoided identifying specific topical issues, proposed personal and individualist rather than collective or overtly political solutions, and always concluded in an affirmative tenor. A film that directly confronted modern mass society such as Chaplin's satirical *Modern Times* (UA

1936) – 'radical propaganda' according to PCA associate Martin Quigley – was possible precisely because Chaplin, as owner of his own studio, could exercise complete creative control.

The war both changed many filmmakers' sense of popular film's own vocation and highlighted the medium's enormous capacity for the communication of ideas, in important ways that all too soon would return to haunt the industry. The enthusiastic and effective deployment of motion pictures by the Soviet and Nazi states alike between the wars had already vividly demonstrated film's power as propaganda (as indeed, much closer to home, had the Sinclair campaign). In the USA (after initial reluctance), studio heads worked closely with the Washington Office of War Information (OWI) to ensure that studio pictures, from *Mrs Miniver* and *Bataan* to *Sherlock Holmes and the Voice of Terror*, toed a suitably patriotic line, while maintaining a balance between war-related output and a majority of more escapist fare. By almost every measurement, Hollywood had a 'good war', with many studio personnel seeing active service and others tirelessly touring to entertain servicemen and factory workers and promote war bonds, while OWI-sponsored productions such as Frank Capra's famous documentary series *Why We Fight* contributed importantly to public understanding of the conflict. The newly conceived mutual respect and partnership between government and industry persisted in various ways after the war, notably through the activities of the industry-sponsored Motion Picture Export Association (MPEA), which promoted studio pictures in overseas markets (provided, of course, they portrayed the USA in an appropriately positive light; throughout the 1950s, establishment organs such as Henry Luce's *Time* continued to complain that movies promoted an image of America that 'parades its vices, mutes its excellences'[8]).

Following World War II, Hollywood's institutions and methods, as well as Hollywood movies, would find themselves unexpectedly implicated in the major political and social concerns of the period. Anti-communism and Cold War paranoia; the slow thaw of the permafrost of American Puritanism and the emergence of a more socially tolerant, yet also more openly divided, society; the sudden onset of postwar consumer culture and its social and psychic consequences: the impact of all of these on Hollywood's political complexion and its ideological unconscious alike would be unpredictable but undeniable and profound.

CHANGING TIMES

For a significant minority of filmmakers, wartime experience convinced them that movies could and should improve on the deliberately escapist, socially irrelevant fare typical of the prewar studio system, and that motion pictures must contribute constructively to the creation of the postwar social order. The wartime combat film in particular had contributed to the emergence of a rein-vigorated realism in Hollywood films. The dominant tenor of the majority of wartime combat films was not gung-ho heroics but a hard-bitten, sometimes grim professionalism. Encouraged by the OWI to damp down unrealistic expectations of a quick, easy victory, the war was presented as a tough, often grimly attritional struggle against fierce, organised and ruthless enemies (in the case of the Japanese, often freighted with negative racial stereotyping). New technologies such as lightweight cameras took combat documentaries right to the front line and enabled filmmakers, including leading studio directors such as Wyler, George Stevens and John Huston, to bring modern warfare to the screen with unparalleled immediacy – sometimes more than military censors could stomach, as in Huston's *The Battle of San Pietro* (1945). Postwar combat films such as the hugely successful *Battleground* (MGM 1949) maintained this gritty, unglamourised approach.

In the immediate postwar period, however, with combat films on sabbati-cal from a war-weary public and amid widespread expectations that the age of the 'thinking picture', as diplomat James Shotwell put it, had at last arrived, the focus for socially conscious filmmakers shifted to serious dramas more relevant to the new challenges of 'winning the peace'. *New York Times* film critic Bosley Crowther approvingly noted, somewhat after the fact, 'pictures of greater substance and variety' and 'a new comprehension of the signifi-cance of the medium'.[9] Starting with *The Best Years of Our Lives*, a number of films used the figure of the returning veteran to highlight the persistent disparities between the values he had fought for and the society to which he returned. There followed a cycle of postwar social problem films dealing with, for example, domestic American racial discrimination: in 1947, *Gentlemen's Agreement* (Fox) and *Crossfire* (RKO) (both focusing on anti-Semitism), in 1949, *Pinky* (Fox), *Intruder in the Dust* (MGM), *Lost Boundaries* (UA) and Stanley Kramer's *Home of the Brave* (UA) (confronting white–black racism).

The tenor of the social problem film was generally positive about the prospects for reforming American institutions, if impatient for change. More critical perspectives on American life were being expressed through another generic paradigm, the crime melodrama, in what was emerging as its dominant postwar mode, that of *film noir*. *Noir* revisited the terrain of the classic gang-ster film and recast it in a mood of bleak, exhausted cynicism. The thrilling (if antisocial) dynamism of classic thirties gangsters like Tom Powers (James Cagney in *The Public Enemy*, WB 1930) or Tony Camonte (Paul Muni in *Scarface*, US 1932), virile, individualistic, ruthless and ambitious, gave way to tortuous narratives centring on small-time protagonists, accidental criminals or patsies driven by transgressive sexual desire (*Double Indemnity*, Par 1944), manipulation by others (*D.O.A.*, US 1950) or simple error (*Scarlet Street*,

U 1945), often decidedly fatalistic in the face of onrushing disaster (*Out of the Past*, RKO 1948).

Such films seemed to express some of the uncertainties and doubts of the immediate postwar period. The year 1946 saw a wave of industrial unrest as unions threw off wartime pay restraint and put in large wage claims. The new Truman administration dismayed many liberals by adopting increasingly conservative economic and fiscal policies while paying little more than lip service to civil rights. *Mildred Pierce* (WB 1945) appeared to reflect the gender strife generated by the unceremonious layoff of women war workers to accommodate returning servicemen. The latter was himself a subject of much anxious sociological speculation: would the violent, homosocial masculinity promoted by the war make the veteran a disruptive force in postwar political and social life, or could he accommodate himself to the conflicting demands of peacetime – domesticity, docility and social conformity? *The Best Years of Our Lives* offered one, optimistic answer; the *noir Crossfire*, with its murderously anti-Semitic vet, a different and darker one. A few *noirs* were quite explicitly political: in Abraham Polonsky's *Force of Evil* (starring the radically inclined John Garfield), two brothers' experiences at the hands of New York racketeers allegorise capitalism's inherently destructive nature. *Film noir* generally had little regard for the American Dream, films such as *Ace In the Hole* (Par 1950) portraying a Darwinian social environment of pitiless competition with almost as little solace for winners as losers. *Noir*'s jaundiced eye occasionally turned towards Hollywood itself: the characters of *Sunset Boulevard* (Par 1950) and *In a Lonely Place* (Col 1950), cast-offs from the Dream Factory, eked out their damaged lives in the shadowy margins of the endless Californian sunshine. Mostly low- to medium-budget, and comprising only a small proportion of Hollywood's total output in this period, *noir* nonetheless provides a tempting key to unlock the apparently monolithic edifice of Hollywood's confident American imaginary. *Noir* is the buried seam of doubt, neurosis and transgressive desire along which that monument can be split open.

Noirs – their critical dimension masked by genre – were produced by most studios; social realism clustered around sympathetic production heads such as Zanuck or were independently produced by filmmakers such as Wyler, George Stevens and Stanley Kramer. Several filmmakers associated with both trends, such as *Crossfire* producer and director Adrian Scott and Edward Dmytryk, had belonged to the community of (mostly) writers and producers who, motivated by the Depression and above all by the advance of fascism in Europe, either joined the Communist Party or, more often, participated in (Communist-sponsored) 'Popular Front' anti-fascist organisations and campaigns in the mid-to-late 1930s. Barely visible beyond the Hollywood Hills before the war (the 1939 German–Soviet Pact disillusioned many former Party members and fellow travellers alike), these groups were to become a central focus of postwar Hollywood politics. New Hollywood recruits with roots in New York's equally radical theatrical culture, such as Elia Kazan, director of *Gentleman's Agreement* and *Pinky* and co-founder of the Actors Studio, home to the influential 'Method' style of naturalistic performance, also made important contributions. The socially conscious Weimar German cinema exerted a posthumous influence through the important contributions to forties *noir* of émigré directors such as Billy Wilder (*Double Indemnity*; *Sunset Boulevard*), Fritz Lang (*The Woman in the Window*, U 1944; *Scarlet Street*) and Robert Siodmak (*The Killers*, U 1946; *Cry of the City*, Fox 1948; *Criss Cross*, U 1948). Unaligned progressive American directors such as Orson Welles (*The Lady From Shanghai*, Col 1948) and Nicholas Ray (*They Live By Night*, RKO 1948; *In a Lonely Place*) also found *noir* style congenial (indeed, the chiaroscuro effects, low-key lighting and Dutch angles of *Citizen Kane* made Welles one of *noir*'s godfathers).

The onset of the Cold War not only determined the course of American foreign policy for two generations, it chilled the cultural climate in every walk of American life. So central an institution as the cinema could never be, and was not, exempt. Even before Japan's surrender ended the war in August 1945, relations between the USA and the USSR had grown increasingly tense. Truman's hostility to Soviet ambitions for territorial domination in Central and Eastern Europe and his (largely, it seems, groundless) fears of Moscow-directed communist insurgencies in Western European nations led him to pronounce the Truman Doctrine – a forthright declaration of unstinting opposition to the advance of world communism, a struggle Truman presented to the American public as a necessary moral and ideological crusade, a stark antagonism of freedom and tyranny. As what Winston Churchill in March 1947[10] indelibly termed the 'Iron Curtain' divided Europe, with non-communist governments in Hungary and Czechoslovakia supplanted by Soviet puppet regimes, the confrontational rhetoric, military standoffs and proxy wars that would come to characterise the next four decades of the Cold War took shape, crystallising around events such as the year-long Berlin Airlift of 1948–9. The USSR's detonation of an atomic device and Communist victory in the Chinese civil war, both in 1949, confirmed the American perception of an ongoing struggle for global hegemony.

In domestic politics, anti-communism had quickly established itself as the keynote. Truman himself formally inaugurated the new Red Scare when he instituted a loyalty programme for Federal employees in March 1947. In so doing he effectively legitimised the political inquisitions of the next few years. It was in this climate that the reconstituted House Committee on Un-American Activities (HUAC) began its investigations into alleged communist influence in Hollywood, convened in a blaze of publicity in October that year. HUAC, which before World War II had lived a subterranean existence as a dumping-ground for monomaniacs and Southern anti-Semites, was invigorated by the paranoid Red-baiting atmosphere of the postwar years and, encouraged by the Motion Picture Alliance of rabidly anti-communist Hollywood personnel such as Cecil B. DeMille, quickly seized on Hollywood – home to sizeable communities of both liberals and Jews, although the two were by no means wholly synonymous – as a highly visible target for their activities.[11] The sorry charade that unfolded during the following weeks is well known: the playing-off of 'friendly' (anti-communist) witnesses such as studio heads Jack Warner, Louis B. Mayer and Walt Disney against the nineteen 'unfriendlies' (of whom only eleven testified before the Committee); the chaotic and farcical (but deadly serious) confrontations between the unfriendly witnesses and Committee chair J. Parnell Thomas as the witnesses rejected Thomas's questions ('Are you now or have you ever been . . .'), tried and failed to read prepared statements before being shouted down and in several cases forcibly removed from the hearings; and the subsequent conviction and imprisonment of the 'Hollywood Ten', including Dmytryk, Scott and screenwriters Dalton Trumbo, Ring Lardner, Jr, and John Howard Lawson, for contempt of Congress.[12]

The studios' response to the HUAC hearings was shameful, shambolic and opportunistic in equal measure. Initially inclined to dismiss the Committee, upon realising its seriousness the studios pursued a defensive and staunchly conservative line through their mouthpiece Eric Johnston, head of the newly constituted MPAA (successor to the MPPDA), paying lip service to constitutional freedoms but to all intents and purposes bowing to the Committee's onslaught, disavowing the Hollywood Ten and announcing the start of the notorious Hollywood blacklist – having declared on the record just days earlier they would do no such thing. Studio heads such as Warner, scarred by recent industrial disputes led by the left-leaning Conference of Studio Unions (CSU), also exploited the witch-hunts as a convenient means of intimidating union activists. Attempts by Hollywood liberals such as William Wyler, John Huston, Humphrey Bogart and Gene Kelly to defend the Ten and combat the witch-hunts through the Committee for the First Amendment rapidly collapsed under studio pressure.

The Red Scare intensified to a hysterical pitch in the early 1950s, inflamed by war against Communist North Korea (militarily supported by both Stalin and Mao) from 1950 to 1953, the passage of further repressive legislation at home effectively outlawing the Communist Party of the USA, the arrest and execution of 'atom spies' Julius and Ethel Rosenberg and the sudden rise to national prominence of the demagogic Wisconsin Senator Joseph McCarthy, armed with unsubstantiated but alarming claims of communist infiltration of US government, diplomatic, and military institutions. In Hollywood, as HUAC began a second round of hearings in spring 1951, any remaining opposition to the witch-hunts collapsed. The renewed hearings introduced the infamous ritual of 'naming names' (of suspected communists or fellow travellers) as the only acceptable means for a subpoenaed witness to clear his or her reputation before the Committee. Non-cooperative witnesses – even those who simply invoked their constitutional rights against self-incrimination by 'taking the Fifth' (Amendment) – were rendered unemployable as the blacklist became a Hollywood reality. The studios colluded with a congeries of shadowy groups abetted by J. Edgar Hoover's FBI who ferreted out suspected Commies and vetted potential blacklistees – exercising make-or-break power over the careers of individuals with no effective right of reply.

The crusade against communist influence in motion pictures was not confined to Government and industry elites in Washington and Hollywood. The fortunes of individual films in individual markets could be affected, as chapters of the American Legion and other conservative organisations threatened and in some cases carried out pickets and boycotts of questionable films. These did not even have to be discernibly un-American in themselves; as campaigns against the charming *Born Yesterday* (MGM 1950) – starring the suspiciously leftwing Judy Holliday – or Chaplin's wholly innocuous *Limelight* (UA 1952) proved, it was enough for (suspected) Reds simply to be prominently involved in the production.

Compared to *Paramount*, the strictly commercial impact of the witch-hunts was minor. But deep and enduring divisions in the filmmaking community and the blacklist destroyed many careers (and indeed lives) outright and stripped Hollywood of some of its most innovative writers, producers and directors for over a decade, at a time when the industry was in sore need of creative originality. More damagingly perhaps, the Committee's accusations of communist propagandising, however baseless, reawakened longstanding middle-American doubts about Hollywood's suspiciously cosmopolitan nature, at a time when motion pictures faced the first real challenge to their dominance of the American entertainment market.

The witch-hunts certainly left a lasting legacy in Hollywood: a climate of fear, and bitter enmity between those who chose, however reluctantly, to name names to the Committee (perhaps the most famous example is director Elia Kazan, who with fellow friendly witness Budd Schulberg went on to create the Academy Award-winning stoolpigeon's manifesto *On the Waterfront* in 1954), and those who refused to cooperate and suffered blacklisting as the consequence.[13] In addition to the original Hollywood Ten,[14] non-complying artists unsurprisingly included many of the prominent filmmakers who had contributed to the brief postwar shift towards social relevance as well as the *noir* cycle. Some of these found work in the UK and Europe, including Carl Foreman, the screenwriter of *High Noon* (UA 1952); Cy Endfield; Joseph Losey, who stayed in Europe, where he was directing *Stranger on the Prowl* for UA, rather than answer his HUAC subpoena (when released the film was credited to the pseudonymous 'Andrea Forzano'); and Jules Dassin, whose pioneering documentary thriller *The Naked City* (U 1948) returned Hollywood cameras to New York City locations for the first time since the silent era. Others such as Abraham Polonsky and Lillian Hellmann did not work again in Hollywood for almost twenty years. Writers were in many cases able to continue working using aliases (or 'fronts'), albeit at drastically reduced salaries: in years to come, this would lead to several cases of screenwriting Academy Awards being awarded to pseudonymously credited writers or 'fronts': twice to Dalton Trumbo (as Ian McLellan Hunter – a front– for William Wyler's *Roman Holiday* in 1953, and as Robert Rich – a pseudonym – for Irving Rapper's *The Brave One* in 1957), in 1958 to Nedrick Young (writing as 'Nathan E. Douglas') for Stanley Kramer's *The Defiant Ones*, and in 1957 to blacklistees Carl Forman and Michael Wilson for *The Bridge over the River Kwai* (the credited writer was the French – and exclusively Francophone – novelist Pierre Boulle). Not until 1960, when Otto Preminger and Kirk Douglas insisted Trumbo receive screen credit for *Exodus* and *Spartacus*, respectively, was the blacklist finally consigned to history.[15] The number of careers blighted or destroyed by the blacklist is hard to determine, but a 1956 report was clear that at least 212 individuals whose names had been circulated on various lists between 1951 and 1954 had been completely excluded from the industry; many more were touched and damaged by the witch-hunts.[16]

Harder to quantify but undeniable was the demoralisation of an already beleaguered industry and a visible retreat from the social realism of the postwar period. In the climate of hysterical anti-communism, publicly to adopt even the most mildly progressive positions – such as approval of the United Nations, let alone support for civil rights or peace campaigners – was liable to place one under suspicion of 'unAmericanism'. The MPEA exerted pressure to ensure that foreign markets would receive only favourable images of America through American movies. Oddly, *film noir*'s borderline nihilism and fascination with sexual psychopathology – which often blurred the economic and political critique at which it hinted – may have allowed it to persist into the determinedly optimistic early fifties, though here too there was a notable shift towards 'official' protagonists like policemen – albeit flawed, haunted ones – in films such as Lang's *The Big Heat* (Col 1953). This was consistent with a trend towards studies of extreme psychological states – for example, *A Place In the Sun* (Par 1951) and *A Streetcar Named Desire* (WB 1952) – which for some contemporary critics diverted social consciousness into introspection.[17]

By contrast, once Hollywood fell under political scrutiny in the late forties *noir*'s social realist cousin was quickly extirpated. Films such as Losey's *The Prowler* (1951) and Joseph L. Mankiewicz's *No Way Out* (1950) that engaged directly with issues such as class and race in a contemporary context were the last of their kind. The mid-1950s saw survivors of the postwar social problem film shift their focus away from the intractable racial schism towards more superficial and malleable topics such as juvenile delinquency in Stanley Kramer's *The Wild One* (UA 1954), Ray's *Rebel Without a Cause* (WB 1955) and *The Blackboard Jungle* (MGM 1955). Even as Rosa Parks refused to go to the back of the bus, inaugurating the decade-long struggle of the civil rights movement, racism as a subject in Hollywood film went underground, emerging in disguised form in Westerns such as *Broken Arrow* (Fox 1950), *Devil's Doorway* (MGM 1950), and *Apache* (US 1954) that treated Native Americans with unusual sympathy or – more rarely – examined the pathology of white race hatred, as in Ford's *The Searchers* (WB 1955). The era's defining genre, the Western was inevitably imprinted with its political context: *High Noon* was intended by Carl Foreman as an allegory of society's failure to stand up against McCarthyite bullies, and in turn received a conservative rebuttal in the form of Howard Hawks's *Rio Bravo* (WB 1959), in which John Wayne neither seeks nor needs any help to stand up for what's right. Like *noirs*, these films' generic trappings ensured their politics were rarely closely examined – or taken seriously – in the middlebrow culture of the time. (*The Searchers* was dismissed as juvenilia upon its first release and compared unfavourably to Ford's prewar work such as the stilted *The Informer*, RKO 1935.) Meanwhile any regret at Hollywood's wholesale retreat from social relevance may have been mitigated by its concurrent achievements in such eminently escapist genres as the musical, which in this period reached its peak in the series of films produced by the Arthur Freed unit at MGM, notably those starring Gene Kelly – himself an object of hostile HUAC scrutiny – including, of course, *Singin' in the Rain* (1952). Yet even here politics was never very far away: *An American In Paris* (MGM 1951), the story of an expatriate finding creative fulfilment in Europe, has been considered a blacklist-era parable.

From the other side of the political divide, there was a cycle of some forty anti-communist films in the late 1940s and early 1950s, but few of these – except Samuel Fuller's typically idiosyncratic *Pickup on South Street* (Fox 1953) – made much impact at the time and films like *I Married a Communist* (RKO 1950) and *My Son John* (Par 1952) all seem at best quaint, at worst ludicrous, today, vitiated by their inability or refusal to engage seriously with the ideology they purport to be opposing (Commies are bad guys, indistinguishable from Nazis five years earlier or innumerable Hollywood heavies before and after). Peter Lev has suggested that studios may have produced these films primarily for political reasons – as celluloid equivalents of loyalty oaths – and this seems plausible enough.[18] A much more lasting transcription of Cold War anxieties and phobias was the 1950s science fiction cycle, the genre's first significant appearance in American cinema and indeed, alongside *film noir*, the most enduring and influential genre to have emerged in the post-studio period, not least in its formative impact on a generation of future filmmakers growing up in the fifties on a diet of supersized irradiated insects and emotionless alien invaders.[19]

Fifties science fiction (SF) films, typically low-budget and lacking in stars, offered American cinema a means to explore, in particular, anxieties about the nuclear arms race that had been largely suppressed in official media. While the unrepresentative A-picture *The Day the Earth Stood Still* (Fox 1951) offered an equally atypically liberal message, urging united worldwide action to combat the menace of nuclear arms, a majority of the decade's SF movies – especially the alien invasion films, such as *Invaders From Mars* (Fox 1953), *This Island Earth* (U 1955) and *I Married a Monster From Outer Space* (Par 1958) – supported a straightforwardly anti-communist line. Both these films and the 'monster movies' that came to typify genre and era alike, of which the best known are the giant insect pictures *Them!* (WB 1954), *Tarantula* (U 1955) and the prehistoric/aquatic creature films *The Beast From 20,000 Fathoms* (WB 1953) and *It Came From Beneath the Sea* (AIP 1955), often promoted alliances between scientists, the military and private individuals combining to defeat the exotic menace. God was occasionally recruited too, as in the coda to *The War of the Worlds* (Par 1953). Aliens, like communists, appeared to have little motivation beyond innate hostility to human (equated with American) life, and peaceable coexistence was neither contemplated nor desired by either side.

Few American SF films of the time approach the haunted, reflective tone of the original Japanese *Gojira* (1954; successfully vulgarised into English by Embassy as *Godzilla*, 1956): exceptions include *The Incredible Shrinking Man* (U 1957), the non-nuclear prehistoric creature film *Creature From the Black Lagoon* (U 1954), and three films bracketing the decade that confronted the consequences of nuclear holocaust undisguised and found terrible beauty and pathos in scenes of post-apocalyptic desolation: *Five* (Col 1951), *The World, the Flesh and the Devil* (MGM 1959), and Stanley Kramer's sober, high-budget and star-studded *On the Beach*. However, the mere presentation, so insistently and in so many varied yet unmistakeable forms, of phobic fantasies of 'the end of the world as we know it' testified to a completely rational terror in the face of unthinkable devastation, which the official culture of the decade sought strenuously to deny or decry. In hindsight, it is not the often laughable giant praying mantises or rubber-suited Martians that are monstrous in fifties SF: it is the entirely serious and all too real – yet insane – Cold War culture they transparently allegorise. This insight – that nuclear war was paradoxically too horrifying to be approachable except through satire and burlesque – would a few years later motivate the ultimate nuclear nightmare movie, Stanley Kubrick's hilarious and terrifying *Dr Strangelove* (Col 1963).

'YOU'RE NEXT!': THE LONELY CROWD

The most enduring of all fifties SF pictures is, not coincidentally, the most ambiguous and interpretable of them all, Don Siegel's *Invasion of the Body Snatchers* (AA 1956). Returning to the small Californian community of Santa Mira after a sabbatical, Dr Miles Bennell (Kevin McCarthy) discovers that the townsfolk are systematically being replaced as they sleep by alien 'pods': physically identical replicas who preserve their host's memories but are devoid of emotion and substitute a relentless hive-mind for individual personality. Initially sceptical, as one by one his closest friends and even his lover Becky fall victim to the pods, Miles is reduced to a hysterical fugitive running down the freeway vainly trying to warn the drivers speeding obliviously by of their imminent peril – screaming at them (and directly into the camera at us) 'They're coming! You're next!'. Produced on a modest budget for Walter Wanger at Allied Artists (the old Poverty Row studio Monogram's new identity), *Body Snatchers* has transcended the constraints of its original historical and political moment and established itself as a potent pulp myth, mutable and adaptable to changing social and ideological contexts, as testified by three very different remakes in 1978, 1996 and 2007.[20]

The film is most readily and straightforwardly read as a Red Scare parable: emotionless, organised and relentless, colonising an unsuspecting and all-too-unprepared Main Street from within, the pods personify potent myths of communist infiltration. The reassuring frame narrative – in which Miles's apparently lunatic ravings are finally validated and the authorities (specifically, arch Red-hunters the FBI) are mobilised to tackle the alien threat – added after preview audiences found the bleak and uncompromising original ending too harrowing, certainly supports this interpretation. Siegel himself in later interviews encouraged a counter-reading of the film as an anti-McCarthyite statement on the lines of Arthur Miller's play *The Crucible* – the pods here representing the hysterical group-think and denunciations of the witch-hunts – but these claims may well reflect primarily an understandable desire to distance himself from a discredited political stance and recommend his film to the temper of more liberal times.

More persuasive, perhaps, is a reading of the film that sees it as a critique of social conformity. During the fifties American lifestyles, at work and in the home, underwent epochal change. In numbers as great as the mass immigration at the start of the century, millions of Americans moved from cramped rented apartments in metropolitan downtown areas to the suburban communities springing up nationwide, in search of cheap, spacious, owner-occupied accommodation in which to raise growing families spawned by the postwar baby boom. Thousands of miles of federally subsidised highway linked these sprawling housing tracts (where public transportation was largely non-existent) to shops, services and commercial centres, creating a unique, almost entirely automobile-dependent, culture. Suburban living, and the affluent, consumerist lifestyle of dishwashers, barbecues and this year's model of chrome-finned Chrysler or Buick with which it became synonymous, was increasingly supported by white-collar work in the burgeoning service economy: in sales, in government bureaucracies, marketing, insurance and clerical and middle-management occupations of all kinds.[21]

This novel 'affluent society' extended material comforts on a grander scale, to a larger proportion of the population, than ever before in any society. Yet by mid-decade some voices were identifying flaws in the new suburban American dream and argued that the price of all this material comfort was a marked erosion of American traditions of individualism and personal liberty. Sociologist David Riesman suggested that the pioneering, entrepreneurial, self-motivated 'inner-directed' American character was being supplanted by an 'outer-directed' personality who sought approval and direction from others. William Whyte famously characterised the white-collar worker as an 'organisation man', oriented less to his ostensible professional task than to mastering the intricacies of the modern bureaucratic environment in pursuit of self-advancement. The more radical C. Wright Mills pointed to the growing domination of the US economy by a few gigantic enterprises like General Motors, AT&T and IBM and the emergence of a 'power elite' detached from traditional structures of democratic accountability. For all of these writers, whose bestselling books spread their ideas far beyond academic circles, suburbia – natural habitat of the 'organisation man' – embodied these trends, with its artificial communities, frantic consumption, highly conformist lifestyles and rigid policing of sex and gender roles.[22]

Hollywood was naturally attuned to such accounts because the industry had already been so dramatically affected by the social changes they analysed. The new suburbs boasted few movie theatres: urban flight had put the first-run downtown theatres, so crucial to studio profits, at the wrong end of a long drive. Add the cost of gas, parking, dinner out and probably babysitting to (rising) ticket prices, and going to the movies became an expensive inconvenience many families felt they could do without; free-to-air entertainment on TV meant they could easily do so. Drive-ins and, by the early sixties, the first theatres located in or around the new shopping malls eased the pain somewhat, but soaring suburban real-estate values meant theatre-building was a costly speculation for exhibitors already hit hard by the postwar downturn. What was happening was no secret: a 1953 US Senate report observed that 'changes in our living habits threaten the closing of many theatres'.[23] But post-*Paramount* the studios were no longer in the exhibition business, and during the fifties they could only look on as their audience pool shrank.

From this perspective, the drone-like uniformity of the pods in *Invasion of the Body Snatchers* portrays not an impending peril but the existing reality of the Eisenhower era. A striking, and repeatedly stressed, problem Miles faces is the difficulty of establishing from their outward appearance and demeanour just who is, and who is not, a pod, suggesting perhaps that the bland conformity of the period had created a society which was already pod-like in many respects. The pods' symbolic assault on American life in such details as the abandoned roadside fruit stand – standing for the steamrollering of small business and private enterprise, foundational elements of the American Dream, beneath the relentless advance of corporate culture and groupthink – could stand equally well for either the triumph of communism or the demise of the 'inner-directed' man. The aliens' use of the newly created interstate freeway system to distribute pods nationwide further associates them with postwar modernisation and bureaucratisation.

Television's close identification with suburban domesticity may have encouraged movies to offer critiques of fifties complacency and conformity. In a rather surprising turnabout of public perception, brash, glitzy Hollywood gradually reconstituted its image into a bastion of high modernist culture, contrasted to the banal, lowest common denominator medium of network TV, portrayed as an emblem of suburban soul-death in such pictures as *All That Heaven Allows* (U 1955).[24] The television industry's propensity to manipulate and deceive its impressionable public was satirised, lightly in *Will Success Spoil Rock Hunter?* and scathingly in Kazan's *A Face in the Crowd* (WB 1957). *Rebel Without a Cause* portrayed family life in the suburbs as atomised and dysfunctional; *There's Always Tomorrow* (U 1956) belied its optimistic title, suggesting that in suburbia every tomorrow would turn out exactly like the day before, and the one before that. The 'organisation man' was anatomised in *The Man in the Grey Flannel Suit* (Fox 1958) and most memorably and damningly in Billy Wilder's bleak comedy *The Apartment* (UA 1960).

Hollywood's willingness (albeit in a minority of pictures) to criticise majoritarian American culture reflected not only that such attitudes had already, as we have seen, entered mainstream culture; they also testified to the industry's readiness, or for that matter need, to mark out a more distinctive cultural 'location' now that television had so clearly usurped movies' role in holding a reassuring mirror up to American life. As ever, there was an economic calculus behind such moves: market research indicated clearly that families and older people made up an increasingly smaller fraction of the audience. The kinds of controversial subject areas Hollywood was now starting to explore had proven marquee appeal to younger, better-educated moviegoers, who were starting to predominate. One thing, however, stood in the way: the Production Code, the self-regulatory apparatus the studios themselves sustained and paid for. Once a necessary evil, the Code now seemed increasingly a burden, pure and simple – it was no longer obvious that it was even necessary. Something would have to give.

CHALLENGING THE CODE

In 1952 the Supreme Court issued another ruling with far-reaching consequences for Hollywood, once again undermining a pillar of the old studio system. That *Joseph Burstyn, Inc.* v. *Wilson* related not to a Hollywood or even an American picture but to an Italian film, Roberto Rossellini's *The Miracle* (1951), imported for the small – but growing – US 'arthouse' market, was in itself a significant signpost to the ways in which aesthetic and cultural trends would come to have an impact on Hollywood in the later 1950s and 1960s. But the direct impact of the Court's decision was much closer to hand and immediately obvious. The Court found in favour of the independent distributor Joseph Burstyn and against the New York state censors who had impounded Rossellini's film on grounds of its alleged indecency (though clearly a fable, the film supposedly offended Christian sensibilities by portraying a possible virgin birth). The majority opinion written by Justice Tom Clark explicitly reversed the Court's prior judgment in *Mutual* v. *Ohio*, unequivocally declaring cinema 'an important medium for the communication of ideas', rejecting the notion that the commercial nature of the film industry denied it constitutional free speech protections (newspapers were also produced for profit), and striking down any censorship on religious grounds.

The *Miracle* judgment in some ways did no more than recognise formally what commentators and critics of cinema, both supportive and hostile, had been insisting for decades. Both Hollywood's alliance with government during World War II and for that matter the HUAC hearings testified to the movies' far-reaching potential influence – for good or ill – on audiences. But what it meant was that the commercial rationale underpinning the Production Code – that if Hollywood did not regulate its own content and by so doing protect its access to markets, others (local censorship boards) indifferent to the studios' bottom line would certainly do so – was blown away. Any attempt by a municipality or state to suppress a motion picture on grounds of its offensive content would henceforth be liable to justify that action against the Bill of Rights' absolute guarantee[25] on Americans' entitlement to express and consume ideas and opinions freely. Armed with these protections, novels and 'serious' theatre had for decades been exploring those areas of human experience – notably sex – which the Production Code and the Legion of Decency had policed out of existence in motion pictures. Suddenly the screen was free to do the same.

Yet the Production Code endured, albeit with progressively diminishing effectiveness, for another decade and a half before finally being replaced by the ratings system. Why did liberation from the Code not occur sooner? Recall that the Code was not the bridle – chafing on an industry eager for self-expression – that it was often painted. It was a means to the end of ensuring pictures whose content was as acceptable as possible, hence marketable, to the broad majority of American picturegoers. As screenwriter Robert Ardrey divulged, this made the PCA an exponent of not only Puritanism but of institutionalised hypocrisy: 'At conference after conference [Breen] sweated out with the rest of us means of breaking his own Code without avoiding its responsibility.'[26] The *Miracle* decision made the prospect of costly interference by local censors much less likely, but the spectre of government censorship was not exorcised at a stroke: Columbus citizens, for example, had to wait the best part of a year to be allowed to see Otto Preminger's mildly risqué sex comedy *The Moon Is Blue*, as UA (who had released the film without a Code Seal of Approval) fought the state censors all the way to the state Supreme Court, which eventually overturned the ban and in so doing reiterated film's entitlement to First Amendment protections. Throughout the mid-1950s, a steady stream of such decisions by both higher and lower courts firmly established the basis in case law against government censorship of movies.[27] However, at the MPAA concern persisted that judicial liberalism might run ahead either of popular opinion generally, or – more likely still – of other bodies of opinion consequential to the studios. The very reason that a conservative Catholic such as Joe Breen had been appointed to head the PCA was that Catholics formed one of the nation's most outspoken and well-organised communities, much more likely to be guided by ecclesiastical authority in their cultural consumption than by the Supreme Court. Hence keeping the Legion of Decency's Catholic activists sweet and avoiding a dreaded 'C' (for 'Condemned') rating remained a priority in 1952.

As the 1950s drew on, however, it became inescapably obvious that the Code's morality – antediluvian as it had been even in the 1930s – was no longer America's. Dr Alfred Kinsey's sensational 'Reports' on male and female sexuality in 1948 and 1953 inaugurated an ongoing and ever franker public discussion about sex in American society, including such previously taboo topics as premarital and extramarital sex and homosexuality. Kinsey's second report hit American newsstands the same year as the first issue of *Playboy*. Symbolically, the Food and Drug Administration rang in the new decade by approving the oral contraceptive pill. America was not yet a permissive society, but it was no longer a wholly puritanical one either.

Against this backdrop producers and industry spokesmen gradually acquired some backbone and became more forthright in their defence of movies' entitlement, even obligation, not to skirt the more controversial areas of human experience and social life. Articles appeared in the consumer press under the byline of studio chiefs such as MGM's Dore Schary urging greater parental discretion and selectivity in shielding children from 'unsuitable' films, rather than a return to the 'basic and uncomplicated' universally family-friendly pictures of earlier decades: 'A given movie cannot possibly be all things to all men . . . Forty-year-olds and eighty-year-olds [also] have a right to be entertained and stimulated and edified and moved.'[28] In 1954 the moderate Episcopalian Geoffrey Shurlock replaced Breen at head of the PCA and as one of his first acts eased a few minor Code provisions (in contrast, Breen had recently added abortion and narcotics to the Code's list of taboos); in 1956 the MPAA revised the Code further.

By then, however, the PCA was already under siege from a steady stream of studio-produced or -distributed pictures challenging basic Code provisions. Several of these originated with the thoroughly independent and unbiddable Otto Preminger: the salacious *The Moon Is Blue*, in which the forbidden word 'virgin' was uttered and which UA, exploiting a contractual loophole, released despite the film being refused a Seal by Breen (and receiving a hitherto calamitous 'C' for 'Condemned' rating by the Legion of Decency); *The Man with the Golden Arm* (US 1955), whose theme of drug addiction again denied it a Seal and which UA again released regardless; *Bonjour Tristesse* (Col 1958), an unblinking account of hedonistic promiscuity; *Anatomy of a Murder* (US 1959), whose dialogue discussed rape in unprecedented forensic detail; and *Advise and Consent* (Col 1962), which added scenes in a gay bar to Allen Drury's prize-winning novel about homosexuality in political life. MGM made some moralistic compromises in their 1956 adaptation of Maxwell Anderson's *Tea and Sympathy* and won a Seal despite the film's sympathetic treatment of homosexuality and adultery; Elia Kazan made none with his version of *Baby Doll* (WB 1956), Tennessee Williams's lurid tale of a Southern child bride, and received both a Seal and a 'C' from the Legion. By the late fifties, as the Supreme Court started overturning state bans on cheap 'nudie' films such as *The Garden of Eden* (1955), non-MPAA independent distributors successfully brought to US screens examples of the candid new European cinema such as *Lady Chatterly's Lover* (1957), . . . *And God Created Woman* (1958) and *Room At the Top* (1959), pneumatic starlets like Marilyn Monroe and her cartoon imitation Jayne Mansfield infused American movies with raw sexuality, and even the Legion of Decency liberalised, the Code was clearly becoming an embarrassing, irrelevant and – given the box office success of many of these 'controversial' films – money-losing antique.

The big-budget roadshow studio pictures – epics, musicals, action pictures and war films – remained stolidly family-friendly, pursuing the increasingly elusive mainstream audience. But the studios urgently needed to be able to pursue the growing market for unashamedly adult fare without having to keep even half an eye on a Code they now mostly disregarded whenever convenient. Following *Paramount*, theatre chains were no longer MPAA members or Code signatories and could screen what they wanted (and local audiences would tolerate). The year 1960 saw both *Elmer Gantry* (UA) and *Psycho* – whose Seals rendered frankly nonsensical the Code's proscription of violence and sexual aberration – advertised 'For Adults Only', anticipating the endgame for the PCA. At this stage, with the legal battleground shifting away from mainstream narrative film towards pornography and definitions of 'obscenity', even the Legion now supported the abandonment of content control and the introduction of a classification system based on age. As further taboos were broached – in 1962 Kubrick's adaptation of Nabokov's *Lolita* (MGM) earned a Seal; in 1965 the PCA (over Shurlock's objections) passed *The Pawnbroker* (AA), including a brief scene of frontal female nudity – a final revision of the Code in 1966 abandoned most of its remaining exclusions and introduced a new 'For Mature Audiences' label. This was no more than a holding manoeuvre until the MPAA, under new leadership, could introduce its new ratings system (see Chapter 4). After thirty-odd years, the Code was dead. Few mourned its passing, while many regretted the effort wasted in past battles; but the struggle to liberalise motion picture content was a key part of the battle to enable American movies, as 'an important medium for the communication of ideas', to speak directly to the experience of an ever more rapidly changing society.

NOTES

1. Discussed in Chapter 3.
2. Quoted in Thomas Cripps, *Hollywood's High Noon: Moviemaking and Society before Television* (Baltimore: Johns Hopkins University Press, 1997), p. 32.
3. Garth Jowett, 'A capacity for evil: the 1915 Supreme Court *Mutual* decision', *Historical Journal of Film, Radio and Television*, 1989; 9(1):59–78.
4. David A. Cook, *A History of Narrative Cinema*, 4th ed. (New York: Norton, 2004), p. 237. On the history of the PCA, see Thomas Doherty, *Hollywood's Censor: Joseph L. Breen and the Production Code Administration* (New York: Columbia University Press, 2007).
5. Jon Lewis, *Hollywood v. Hard Core: How the Struggle Over Censorship Saved the Modern Film Industry* (New York: New York University Press, 2000), p. 24.
6. Both films were singled out by MPAA head and industry mouthpiece Eric Johnston during the HUAC hearings as an example of films supposedly emphasising 'the seamy side of American life' which Hollywood would no longer produce. Thomas Schatz, *Boom and Bust: American Cinema in the 1940s* (Berkeley: University of California Press, 1997), p. 382. Johnston's comments were likely influenced by *Pravda*'s recent nomination of *Tobacco Road* as a rare example of 'progressive' Hollywood filmmaking. See *Time*, 26 May 1947, p. 32.
7. Cripps, *Hollywood's High Noon*, p. 83.
8. 'The image of the U.S.', *Time*, 12 September 1955, p. 26. (This column incidentally once again cited *The Grapes of Wrath* and *Tobacco Road* as icons of alleged Hollywood anti-

Americanism. So long after the fact, this might tend to suggest an actual dearth of such examples in the intervening fifteen years.)

9. Bosley Crowther, 'Accent on the downbeat', *New York Times Magazine*, 16 March 1952, p. 38.

10. With Truman sitting alongside him as the former British leader made his speech at Fulton in the President's home state of Missouri.

11. Congress had some form for ideologically motivated attacks on Hollywood: in the autumn of 1941, Senators Burton Wheeler (MT) and Gerald Nye (ND) had convened hearings on 'Jewish propaganda' in such 'war-mongering' pictures as Chaplin's *The Great Dictator* and Hitchcock's *Foreign Correspondent* (both 1940). They were seen off by a combination of former republican Presidential candidate Wendell Wilkie, hired by the MPPDA to defend the studios, their own crudely expressed gutter anti-Semitism, and the attack on Pearl Harbor which rendered the proceedings irrelevant.

12. The eleventh unfriendly witness, the German dramatist Bertolt Brecht, testified that he was not a communist and immediately left for Europe. On the witch-hunts and the blacklist generally, see Larry Ceplair and Steven Englund, *The Inquisition in Hollywood: Politics in the Film Community, 1930–1960* (Berkeley: University of California Press, 1983).

13. Perhaps the best example again concerns Kazan, whose award of an honorary Academy Award for lifetime achievement in 1999 reignited the bitterness of the HUAC years even among those who could have little memory of the events: well-known Hollywood left liberals in attendance such as Nick Nolte, Tim Robbins and Ed Harris ostentatiously refused to applaud Kazan's award. Former blacklistee Abraham Polonsky announced he intended to watch the ceremony for the first time in years – in hopes Kazan might be gunned down onstage.

14. Edward Dmytryk reversed his position and testified as a friendly witness in 1951.

15. A notable act of defiance on the part of prominent victims of the blacklist was the wholly independent non-Hollywood film *Salt of the Earth* (1953), a union drama based on real events (a strike by Mexican American zinc miners in New Mexico in 1950), scripted by Michael Wilson, produced by Paul Jarrico, directed by Herbert Biberman, with a cast including Will Geer – blacklistees all (Biberman was one of the Hollywood Ten). The production was continuously harassed by federal agencies including the FBI and INS and denied proper distribution. Today, however, it is widely regarded as a landmark in American political cinema. See James J. Lorence, *The Suppression of* Salt of the Earth: *How Hollywood, Big Labor, and Politicians Blacklisted a Movie in Cold War America* (Albuquerque: University of New Mexico Press, 1999).

16. 'Seeing Red in Hollywood', *Newsweek*, 9 July 1956, pp. 66–7.

17. Peter Lev, *The Fifties: Transforming The Screen 1950–1959* (Berkeley: University of California Press, 2003), pp. 73–4.

18. See Lev, *Transforming the Screen*, pp. 51–2.

19. For a discussion of SF and *noir* as 'post-classical' genres, see Barry Langford, *Film Genre: Hollywood and Beyond* (Edinburgh: Edinburgh University Press, 2005), pp. 182–232.

20. *Invasion of the Body Snatchers* (Philip Kaufman, UA 1978); *Body Snatchers* (Abel Ferrara, WB 1993); *The Invasion* (Oliver Hirschbiegel, WB 2007).

21. See James Patterson, *Grand Expectations: the United States, 1945–1974* (Oxford: Oxford University Press, 1996), pp. 133–62.

22. See Martin Halliwell, *American Culture in the 1950s* (Edinburgh: Edinburgh University Press, 2007).

23. 'Drive-ins steal the show', *Business Week*, 15 August 1953, p. 114.

24. This argument is developed in Christopher Anderson, *Hollywood TV: The Studio System in the 1950s* (Austin: University of Texas Press, 1994), Chapter 10; see also Denise Mann, *Hollywood Independents: The Postwar Talent Takeover* (Minnesota: University of Minneapolis Press, 2008).
25. Except in cases of provable sedition or obscenity.
26. 'Hollywood's fall into virtue', *The Reporter*, 21 February 1957, pp. 13–17.
27. 'The censors', *Time*, 25 July 1955, p. 86.
28. Dore Schary, 'Why we don't always make "family" movies', *Good Housekeeping*, September 1955, p. 44ff.

The Biggest, the Best: 1955

Best Picture: *Marty* (UA/Hecht-Lancaster)
D: Delbert Mann; **P:** Harold Hecht; **W:** Paddy Chayefsky
Box Office No. 1: *Cinerama Holiday* (Cinerama)
D: Robert L. Bendinck, Philippe de Lacy; **P:** Louis de Rochment

The Academy's choice of the independently-produced *Marty*, a classic 'sleeper', as 1955's Best Picture was both a surprise and something of an anomaly in the context of the 'Make 'Em Big' fifties. The tally of the decade's other winners was dominated by the extravagant spectacles that had come to dominate the major studios' output in the years after divorcement and the coming of television: *An American In Paris* (1951), *The Greatest Show on Earth* (1952), *Around the World in 80 Days* (1956), *Gigi* (1958), *Ben-Hur* (1959). Only 1954's Best Picture *On the Waterfront* shared any part of *Marty*'s contemporary blue-collar milieu; but in all other regards Elia Kazan and Budd Schulberg's histrionic witch-hunt allegory of stevedores, corruption and the informer as martyred Christ-figure, played to the Method hilt by powerhouse actors like Brando, Lee J. Cobb, Rod Steiger and Karl Malden, had little in common with screenwriter Paddy Chayefsky and director Delbert Mann's deliberately muted 'slice of life' vignette of a shy Bronx butcher (Ernest Borgnine) tentatively reaching out to an equally reserved schoolteacher, Clara (Betsy Blair). (Borgnine, Chayefsky and Mann also all won Oscars, putting *Marty* on level pegging with fifties big-hitters like *Waterfront*, *From Here to Eternity* (1953) and *The Bridge on the River Kwai* (1957).)

For that matter, *Marty* had just as few peers among the unsuccessful nominees either, likewise dominated by large-scale, big-budget releases from the major studios (who after all paid the Academy's bills), other than 1957's *Twelve Angry Men*. Both were independently produced for United Artists, *Marty* by Hecht-Hill-Lancaster, the production company established by Burt Lancaster and his agent Harold Hecht in 1953.[1] Most obviously, both were adapted from original teleplays first broadcast on NBC's anthology drama series 'Television Playhouse'. As we have seen in Chapter 1, the undisclosed story of fifties Hollywood was the film industry's gradual embrace of television's salvific potential as a secondary focus for production and employment and an invaluable ancillary market. However, transferring material directly from the small screen to theatres was a further innovation.

Aware that *Marty* would likely miss its audience were it perceived as simply a primped-up TV play, UA carefully built its profile as a home-grown art film instead, entering it in competition at Cannes (where it won the Grand Prix in May 1955) and exploiting the emerging art house circuit to 'platform' the film at a limited number of such theatres (such as the Sutton in New York). Once *Marty* won the Academy Award, UA opened the film wide to 500 theatres.[2] The strategy paid off. Admittedly, *Marty*'s $3 million rentals for UA failed to place it in the year's top twenty and lagged far behind the year's highest-earning domestically produced film *Cinerama Holiday*, the follow-up (three years later) to *This Is Cinerama*, offering the same essentially non-narrative, travelogue-like spectacle and almost as popular with audiences as the original (the top-earning studio film was John Ford's pedestrian but popular version of the Broadway hit naval comedy *Mister Roberts*, filmed in colour and 'Scope for Warner Bros. with an all-star cast including Henry Fonda, James Cagney, and Jack Lemmon in an Oscar-winning and career-making performance as Ensign Pulver). But as a return on a $343,000 production cost, *Marty*'s earnings were outstanding – in fact, record-breaking for the time – and indicated that there was after all an audience for the right 'good little picture' among those moviegoers sated with epics. In *Marty*'s wake UA successfully distributed other teleplay adaptations including Michael Myerberg's *Patterns* (1956), based on Rod Serling's teleplay 'Patterns of Power' and Reginald Rose's *Twelve Angry Men* (1957), Sidney Lumet's directorial debut.

Marty's success had several further consequences. The film's rentals and its Oscar success – Krim and Benjamin's first Best Picture since their somewhat fortuitous triumph with *The African Queen* in 1951 – put UA's model of creative partnership with independent producers firmly on Hollywood's radar. Numerous other stars followed Lancaster's lead, formed production companies and beat a path to UA's door, including Kirk Douglas, John Wayne, Gregory Peck and Robert Mitchum. But for Hecht-Lancaster itself – which became Hecht-Hill-Lancaster (HHL) with the addition of former story editor James Hill in 1956 – *Marty* proved a false dawn. HHL surged ahead on the back of its success, developing an ambitious and increasingly expensive slate of films that owed little to *Marty*'s 'small picture' aesthetic. HHL's trajectory epitomised the perils of success for independent producers: announcing a six-picture production slate, setting up European and Asian publicity operations as well as offices on both coasts, and running up a yearly overhead of $300,000, HHL expanded rapidly beyond its means. A series of offbeat pictures including Alexander MacKendrick's brilliant, corrosive *Sweet Smell of Success* (UA 1957) did not find an audience, and a belated shift to bigger productions with John Huston's *The Unforgiven* (UA 1960) failed to retrieve the company's position. HHL folded in February 1960. UA's stable of independents meanwhile increasingly promoted blockbusters, such as Douglas's *The Vikings* (1958), Otto Preminger's *Exodus* (1960) and *West Side Story* (1961), that were largely indistinguishable from the other major studios' releases. After his unlikely brush with stardom, Ernest Borgnine returned to the ranks as one of Hollywood's best-known character actors.

The 'small picture', however, was not dead. Some successful films of the early 1960s, such as Billy Wilder's *The Apartment* (UA 1960) and another teleplay adaptation, *Days of Wine and Roses* (WB 1962), shared some of *Marty*'s unillusioned eye for contemporary life, though in both cases with a sharper narrative and satirical edge. It would take the crisis of relevance, over-spending and over-production at the end of the next decade to make the industry look once again at the virtues of small-scale, character-based, narratively underdetermined pictures in vernacular contemporary American settings. John G. Avildsen's *Rocky* in particular would quite openly revisit *Marty*'s tongue-tied working-class milieu (both the title character's name and his employment as a meat-packer echo the earlier character). Yet *Rocky*'s 'small' story – overshadowed and forgotten amid the testosterone-fuelled uplift that propelled the film and its several, increasingly ludicrous, successors – would prove as much of a dead end as that of its predecessor.

Notes

1. Hecht and Lancaster set up Norma Productions in 1947.
2. Tino Balio, *United Artists: The Company That Changed the Film Industry* (Madison: University of Wisconsin Press, 1987), pp. 79–82, 146–7. UA's 'saturation' release of *Marty* is another reminder that Lew Wasserman's legendary distribution strategy for *Jaws* in fact had numerous precedents.

Publicity for *This Is Cinerama* (1953), the opening salvo of the widescreen era. Reproduced courtesy of The Kobal Collection

CHAPTER 3

Modernising Hollywood

At the end of World War II, Hollywood moviemaking was typified by a distinctive style that had, over some three decades, proven itself durable, efficient and trustworthy. The specific attributes of what film scholars subsequently came to call – with varying degrees of enthusiasm and consensus – 'the classical Hollywood style' were influenced both by the (evolving) structure of the film industry and by social and cultural factors dating back to the silent era. Its stylistic priorities were to communicate narrative information effectively and clearly, and as an aid thereto to maintain the coherence and legibility of onscreen time and space. A distinctive notion of 'realism' (we might rather say verisimilitude) was frequently invoked by filmmakers to benchmark their practice, but the essential purpose of the style, it hardly needs stating, was not aesthetic harmonisation but profit; this mode of narrative cinema had proven acceptable to audiences since the early silent era, but heterogenous elements, notably various kinds of spectacle, could be and were regularly accommodated. The Hollywood style was highly conventionalised and relied upon the combined efforts of numerous skilled craft workers, working according to well-established professional protocols in accomplishing a set of procedures repeatedly and to the same high level of technical competence. This was undertaken for the most part in an undemonstrative and indeed conservative way. The nature of the studio system promoted standardisation, a degree of routinisation and a minimum of fuss and elevated these qualities into an aesthetic in which practitioners took professional pride; however, it also offered considerable room for innovation, if rather less for experiment.

At the core of the classical Hollywood style was storytelling. American cinema's commitment to narrative predated California's ascendancy over other production centres and was closely related to the movies' swift rise (over little more than a decade from the first publicly projected motion pictures in 1896) from novelty status, through rivalry with other early-twentieth-century

'attractions' competing for the attention and custom of a cosmopolitan pro-
letariat in major urban manufacturing and commercial centres, to a clear
primacy among American leisure pastimes that would remain unchallenged
until the advent of television. Even the one-shot shorts of cinema's first decade
might be said to possess a rudimentary narrative dimension, but a shift towards
longer and more complex (integrated rather than simply linear) narratives can
be marked around 1906, coinciding with the nickelodeon theatre boom and
a correspondingly increased demand for films from exhibitors. To meet this
demand, distributors such as Adolph Zukor set up nationwide film exchanges
and at the same time established production facilities to ensure a reliable
supply of quality films to theatres. Most of these were fictional narratives,
replacing the vaudeville skits, newsreel-like 'scenics' and 'trick' films that had
hitherto predominated. Audience preference may have played some part in
this shift, but as film historian Robert Allen has argued, the need for a regular
output of films, produced under controlled conditions and at a supportable
cost, promoted the production of fiction films in purpose-built studios over
the difficulty and expense of recording inherently unpredictable real events.[1]
Thus was the studio born.

Specific approaches towards fashioning fictional narratives, supported by
practice and influential theory, were found readily to hand in the popular literary and theatrical culture of the time, including novels and short stories and
the diverse forms of the late-Victorian stage – melodramas, the 'well-made-
plays' of the bourgeois theatre, and short playlets (particularly well suited to
one-reel films). Film production companies increasingly drew their personnel
from these media (for example, D. W. Griffith) and by the early teens their
own well-established formulae and mores had imprinted themselves upon
American moviemaking. These included such normative concepts as unified
action and the streamlining of narrative events in service of such unity; clear
causal relations between narrative events; strongly-drawn, consistent characterisation; active, 'goal-oriented' protagonists and antagonists; a clear arc of
action rising to an effective climax; and a stated commitment to 'realism' –
though just what this meant was in practice very variable. Even Griffith's *Birth
of a Nation* (Mutual 1915) still incorporates decidedly non-classical elements
such as tableau-style re-enactments of Lee's surrender and other historical
landmarks, detached from the narrative involvement or perspective of the
dramatic protagonists.

Storytelling also proved the means for cinema to shake off its faintly
unrespectable fairground origins and attract a more socially diverse audience. Adopting the aesthetic proprieties of bourgeois literary and theatrical
forms – and in numerous instances from as early as 1903, literally adapting
celebrated Victorian novels and plays to the screen – gained cinema a portion
of the middlebrow critical esteem these media enjoyed. In this way movies

began to secure their initially marginal location in American cultural life and could better combat the constant assaults from censors, social reformers and reactionaries. (The sensibilities of some influential early American filmmakers, such as Griffith, were also firmly grounded in bourgeois culture, and in movies' appropriation of the latter's preferred forms of culture they recognised a means to redeem the somewhat dubious reputation of their trade and procure for it – and themselves – a measure of cultural legitimacy.)

With the emerging dominance of fictional narratives a distinct method of organising temporal and spatial relations also began to evolve. This was for the most part not inherited from theatre or literature but was in fact a response to the particular challenges of adapting story material from these media to the screen. Narratives of increasing length and complexity meant, in practical terms, an ever larger number of separate scenes and shots to be edited together coherently, the breakdown of individual spaces through editing (scene analysis) and the juxtaposition of several different spaces in the course of one narrative, and the need to communicate (if only in very broad brushstrokes) some aspects of character psychology. This in turn mandated methods that could organise narrative sequence and present and penetrate onscreen space so as guide the spectator effectively through the story.

Classical easel painting could supply some premises for blocking action in a two-dimensional medium and Victorian theatrical scenography contributed ideas of staging and performance. But from 1906 onwards movies came to be characterised by the further exploration and analysis of dramatic space in ways that differed from either the static tableaux of academic painting or (particularly important in the absence of speech) the presentational styles of Victorian theatre. With the shared aim of maintaining a 'continuity' of narrative consumption by the spectator, a variety of techniques came to distinguish and typify American moviemaking; and without subscribing to the traditional identification of D. W. Griffith as the 'father' of the continuity style, certainly by *The Birth of a Nation* at the latest the basic 'grammar' of the continuity style – the use of establishing shots, scene analysis, a variety of framings including the half-figure two-shot (the *plan américain*), cutting on action, preservation of screen direction and observance of the 180-degree 'rule', staging in depth, sculptural lighting, eyeline matches, point-of-view shots and shot-reverse shot sequences, etc. – was fully present. The result is that modern audiences tend to find the action (attitudes and ideology are quite another matter) of films from this period onwards far more comprehensible than that of films from the earlier period (1895 to c. 1905), whose typically static proscenium-like setup, single-shot scenes, decentered staging and lack of narrational tools often render them all but unintelligible. Developments in later decades – notably the coming of sound from 1927 – would significantly affect the ways this grammar was inflected (the balance between montage and camera movement as means of exploring pro-filmic space, for example) and would often add to it – the incorporation (appropriately adjusted) of techniques drawn first from European cinema, later from television, and later still from other global national cinemas such as Hong Kong and Bollywood. But its basic elements have persisted to the present day, and have indeed become the normative language of narrative film worldwide. How did this consolidation come about?

Well before World War I, the establishment of craft associations enabled cinematographers and other technical workers to share and compare professional practice and, through formal and informal personal contact, trade publications and apprenticeships, to disseminate and reinforce standard approaches. A proliferation of 'how-to' screenwriting handbooks and magazines in the early 1910s similarly ensured that aspirant scenarists tended to conform to established narrative and dramaturgical conventions. With the transformation of the motion picture business into a major cultural industry by the mid-teens, the adoption of Fordist techniques of mass production (albeit limited, since motion picture production relies on at least notional variety, however minimal, whereas mass-producing consumer durables such as cars demands exactly the opposite, standardised uniformity[2]) further consolidated these already well-established conventions into standard industry practice. At least as influential or more so was the influence of Taylorist[3] efficiency models, which as production operations expanded progressively divided and subdivided areas of creative and craft responsibility into smaller specialised units, working to the remit and under the supervision of a central production office (or from the mid-1920s, under the 'producer unit system', working for one of several producers answerable to an overall head of production).[4] Thus, whereas in the early teens director-producers controlled many or most aspects of production personally, by the end of the decade these functions – including scripting, casting, production design and costume, location scouting, scheduling, editing and, above all, budgeting – were taken over by specialists managed from the production office.

Within each emerging film production company – or 'studio' – continuity in working practices and techniques across pictures promoted efficiency while contracted personnel – from craft workers to key talent (writers, producers, directors, cinematographers) – working week-in, week-out on similar projects were bound to solve recurring problems in proven ways. Indeed, the characteristic solutions and techniques adopted by given groups of such workers could give rise over time to a recognisable 'house style' or 'look', which contributed to the major studios' brand identity.[5] However, the larger pool of shared professional knowledge, custom and training ensured a high degree of family resemblance between such house styles: these were inflections of standard practice, not wild divergence. From 1927, the Academy of Motion Picture Arts and Sciences served as an important clearinghouse for coordinating and standardising practice and integrating new techniques. Such institutions helped establish what David Bordwell, appropriating a term from art history, termed the 'group style' of Hollywood cinema.[6]

The Hollywood style was stable but never static: the very nature of creative work and the personnel Hollywood attracted, a range of influences from other media, and the contribution made by equipment manufacturers and suppliers actively striving for a competitive edge by improving cameras, lenses, film stock, lights, make-up and the like all ensured that new techniques and refinements on existing methods continued to develop throughout the period. Take for instance the vogue for deep-focus photography in the early 1940s. The pioneering work of cameraman Gregg Toland on such films as *Wuthering Heights* (Goldwyn 1939), which won Toland an Academy Award, and *The Long Voyage Home* (UA 1940) was made technically possible by the introduction of faster film stocks such as Eastman Kodak's Plus X; Toland's work was encouraged by Samuel Goldwyn's wish to differentiate his high-end independent productions; and of course Toland encountered an iconoclastic Hollywood outsider, theatre director Orson Welles, who encouraged him to push his deep-focus experiments to a startling apogee on Welles's debut film *Citizen Kane*. David Bordwell and Janet Staiger have suggested that innovation in Hollywood was driven by three factors: production efficiency, product differentiation and the adherence to generally-understood and accepted standards of quality. Within these parameters, narrative-centred continuity cinema was adjusted and refined by a variety of stylistic and technological advances throughout the studio era, notably the introduction of sound.

The baseline of Hollywood's technical expertise – which thanks to the heavily capitalised US film industry was already set higher than anywhere else in world cinema prior to World War II, except perhaps Weimar Germany – was also constantly refreshed by the adoption of technical advances (such as the Schufftan process for filming miniatures) as well as aesthetic innovations from elsewhere. Hollywood's international distribution network and commercial alliances (such as MGM and Paramount's bail-out of the leading German studio UFA in 1927) ensured that studio-era Hollywood was – stylistically at least – neither insular nor parochial. But European avant-garde techniques were typically 'tamed' and accommodated to Hollywood's established needs (though as Henry Jenkins points out, one should not understate the degree of adjustment and destabilisation involved in the 'adoption of alien aesthetic norms'[7]). The subjective camerawork of German films such as G. W. Pabst's *Der Letzte Mann* (*The Last Laugh*, 1925) – which became known in the trade as 'Ufa shots' – and even the montage techniques of 1920s Soviet cinema were normalised in this way. Short bursts of distorted imagery clearly marked as a character's dream, derangement or intoxication came to feature in Hollywood films from the late 1920s and enhanced interiority in characterisation. 'Montage sequences' meanwhile became such a standard Hollywood tool for compressing long periods of elapsed (narrative) time, repeated actions of a similar kind (a quick succession of bar and nightclub vignettes interspersed with neon signage to portray a bar crawl, as in *The Best Years of Our Lives*) or important contextual information (such as the flood of refugees out of Nazi-occupied Europe at the start of *Casablanca*), that studios created specialist units to produce them,[8] and in the 1970s reflexive films such as Martin Scorsese's *New York, New York* (UA 1977) would knowingly recreate them as nostalgic *hommages* to the classical style.

Did this smoothly-oiled, highly functional system allow any room for variation, at the level of either form or individual creativity? Hollywood's image as a factory tirelessly manufacturing debased imitations of authentic art, while systematically suppressing genuine artistry and individual creativity, took hold early in the studio era and never let go, fuelled by streams of anecdotage filtered in particular through the sensibilities of East Coast writers and European émigrés at once fascinated and appalled by their encounters with Hollywood.[9] The spectacular catastrophes that befell maverick visionaries such as Erich von Stroheim and Orson Welles at the hands of Machiavellian studio moguls like Irving Thalberg tended to confirm the impression that Hollywood's wealth and power were matched only by its relentless philistinism. But the shipwrecks suffered by von Stroheim and Welles are hard to disentangle from their confrontational personal styles and industry politicking (in both cases, it became advantageous to studio management to discipline, and be seen to be disciplining, troublesome non-conformists): it was not Naturalist approaches to narrative causality that did for von Stroheim at MGM (his profligacy and perceived immorality, on the other hand, certainly did), or stylised deep-focus camerawork, overlapping dialogue and non-linear narrative that soured RKO on Welles. Throughout the studio era, the established critical and commercial track records of individual directors such as Cecil B. DeMille at Paramount, King Vidor (who made the first all-black musical, *Hallelujah!*, at MGM in 1929), or John Ford at Fox and RKO afforded them greater creative input and control than the norm, up to and occasionally including final cut. Of course, these were all directors who felt no need to go beyond the broad parameters of the classical style.

So the question of the extent – and limits – of formal and stylistic deviation from classical norms is harder to answer. Bertolt Brecht's utter frustration when attempting to fashion *Hangmen Also Die* (UA 1943) after his theories of 'epic theatre' certainly suggests the system's strong resistance to a wholly different set of formal (and of course ideological) principles (that said, Brecht's experiences with the prewar German commercial film industry had been little more encouraging).[10] Yet one can certainly find examples of highly idiosyncratic and indeed self-advertising directorial style in the studio era that challenge simple notions either of a one-dimensional factory system indifferently trampling individual creativity or of any rigid policing of stylistic parameters. Nor were these necessarily industrially marginal: for example, the dreamlike rhapsodies Josef von Sternberg wove around Marlene Dietrich at Paramount in the mid-1930s (*The Scarlet Empress* (1934), *The Devil Is a Woman* (1935)). Still more uncategorisable, indeed bizarre, are the mass ceremonials barely disguised as dance numbers choreographed by Busby Berkeley at both Warners and MGM in the same decade (*Gold Diggers of* 1935). Both von Sternberg and Berkeley flaunt technical virtuosity as a spectacle in itself in ways that stretch claims about the transparency or unobtrusiveness of Hollywood style to, or beyond, breaking point. Such examples go beyond mere stylistic 'excess' – overstated *mise en scène* and heightened performances, of the kind often identified as textual markers of ideological stress in, for example, the fifties melodramas of Douglas Sirk – and seem to teeter on the verge of a genuinely alternative mode of film practice. Indeed, the affinities of some such works with prewar abstract and art cinema are now widely accepted.[11]

It has been argued that these apparent breaks with classical style, from within the heart of the system (both filmmakers honed and intensified their formal experiments on large-budget projects, for Big Five studios, over a number of pictures), are generically motivated: that is, the musical, the horror film – James Whale's *The Bride of Frankenstein* (U 1935) is also marked by wild and self-conscious visual stylisation – and, more debatably, the romantic costume drama are all in different ways exempt from at least some of the conventions of classical filmmaking, such as psychological realism, causality or visual restraint, and/or empowered to adopt devices from alternative film practices like the European avant-garde in an unusually direct way. But this seems rather to beg than to answer the question of how sustainable – let alone consistent – a concept the 'classical style' actually is: how expansive can a category become before it ceases to be taxonomically useful? Seemingly more persuasive is an argument that such manifest deviations from the classical style in studio-era films gain expressiveness from, precisely, their apparent contradiction of stylistic, institutional and immediate textual contexts; Berkeley's phantasmagoric dance numbers are offset against passages of backstage comedy-drama filmed in a wholly conventional, indeed banally functional, style. In other words, classical conventions function as a given or norm set against which such deviations acquire expressive (authorial) or – at least potentially – critical or subversive force. (As we shall see, the self-conscious exploitation of this dynamic became an important dimension of the critical cinema of the 'Hollywood Renaissance'.)

In fact, there is no need to set up a fundamentally false antinomy which either finds the very notion of a classical style to be vitiated or subverted by the presence of such 'unclassical' elements as reflexivity, spectacle, or ostentatiously virtuosic technique and other forms of stylistic 'excess', or alternatively insists that all of these elements are seamlessly recuperated and subordinated to the demands of classical narration. As Bordwell stresses at the start of *The Classical Hollywood Cinema*, the classical Hollywood style is an 'aesthetic norm': a stylistic paradigm whose relative stability at any given time does not exclude either evolution or challenge[12] (although in practice Bordwell tends to stress continuity a great deal more than change).

It is true that the default setting, so to speak, of classic Hollywood is narrative transparency. That is, not only do the devices of the continuity system convey the viewer through a constantly changing series of vantage points, from which he or she is always ideally situated to perceive, interpret and understand the evolving storyline, but furthermore, as wholly artificial as the camera's mobility and perspicacity clearly are, and as extraordinarily complex as this entire apparatus of narrative elucidation is, the viewer's awareness of these complex functions is consistently suppressed. This seems self-evident. Yet if this is a rule, there are a very large number of exceptions to it. Comedy, for example, is allowed in different ways to 'bare the apparatus', as when Oliver Hardy's frustrated gaze catches the camera's eye or when Bob Hope and Bing Crosby spot the Paramount mountain on the horizon in Paramount's *Road to Utopia* (1945). Intentionally or not, even the most 'integrated' of traditional musicals (*Singin' in the Rain* or *The Sound of Music*) cannot but draw attention in countless ways to the sheer artificiality of its mode of performance. In a very large number of films from the silent era onwards, too, the narrative slows or pauses to incorporate scenes of large-scale spectacle that are superfluous, at least in size and duration, in strictly narrative terms but which deliver considerable spectatorial pleasure and are also heavily promoted in marketing the film (the burning of Atlanta in *Gone With the Wind*, the filming of which became a media event in its own right, is a good example). The 'wow factor' produced by special effects sequences, a major dimension of the contemporary Hollywood action spectacle (see Chapter 9), can also be found in classic Hollywood: consider Kong's protracted and narratively redundant battle with the dinosaur in *King Kong* (RKO 1933). And so on.

The point is that 'classic *Hollywood*' placed a measurable, but not an absolute, premium on the integrative, hierarchical norms of the 'classical Hollywood *style*'. Why would they? Audiences might decry a slipshod or grossly implausible narrative (then again, they might not, as the enduring popularity of *The Big Sleep*, infamously incomprehensible even to its own scriptwriters, seems to testify); but they might also reject a picture that denied them the narratively extraneous pleasures it guaranteed generically (a musical without large-scale song and dance numbers, an epic where the camera abjures panoramic shots that take in scenery, monumental sets or a cast of thousands). Classic Hollywood's 'classicism' is a relative, not an absolute, qualified by a capacity for heterogeneity, variations and deviations of many kinds in many different contexts. It is not clear either that such heterogeneity is generically quarantined: the low-key lighting and other aspects of *film noir*'s menacing *mise en scène* were previously employed in some silent American thrillers but more notably in 1930s horror films (which in turn incorporated techniques from Weimar German cinema and French 'poetic realism'). But *film noir* is a notoriously fugitive genre (or mode), centring on crime thrillers but extending to costume melodramas (*Gaslight*, MGM 1944) and even Westerns (*Pursued*, WB 1947). How does generic motivation function here to inoculate narrative against form?

The point, perhaps, is the unexceptionable one that the Hollywood style evolved alongside the system that begot it, and its classicism was – thoroughly in the American vein – a matter of pragmatism as much as, or more than, principle.[13] David Bordwell's tendentious assertion that signifying practices trumped commercial considerations is not born out by the evidence: between the introduction of sound (driven by the attempts of two minor companies, Warner Bros. and Fox, to crack the majors' monopolistic market position) and the investment in new production and exhibition technologies 25 years later, motivated by the crisis of the early fifties (see below), few if any stylistic changes incurred major expense on the studios' part. The dramatic lighting effects of *film noir*, the most notable deviation from the classical style in the immediate postwar period, among other virtues made thrifty use of limited resources (following *Citizen Kane*, which used pools of darkness to suggest Xanadu's cavernous expanses and emotional emptiness – but also to avoid building sets the budget didn't allow for).[14] The system's tolerance of deviance was indeed strictly limited: *The Devil Is a Woman* was a commercial failure and Sternberg's career nosedived thereafter; Busby Berkeley's excesses were tamed following his move to MGM in 1939; von Stroheim's and Welles's purgatories are well-known. The list goes on. But the commitment to one way of viewing and showing the world was also provisional. Under sufficient pressure, it could, and did, change.

'THE NEW DIMENSIONAL MARVEL'

For about two years starting in late 1952, discussion of 'the future of movies' in the trade and mainstream press alike was dominated by the advent of 'dimensional' pictures – a term which rather indiscriminately embraced, successively, Cinerama, stereoscopic 3-D, anamorphic (CinemaScope), and non-anamorphic (VistaVision) widescreen processes. Because all of these technologies enormously expanded the visual[15] sensorium and enhanced depth perception in the projected image (or claimed to), they were often lumped together in ways that testify both to the success of promotional publicity and to the hopeless confusion of non-specialist reporters.[16] No one was in any doubt about the principal motivation for this sudden rush to innovate moviegoing – the postwar downturn and above all the imperative of competing effectively with television. Nonetheless, there was much talk of the 'revolutionary' nature of these various formats – seen as competitors, though with hindsight it appears that each engaged medium and spectator alike in significantly different ways – and frequent comparisons to the conversion to sound a quarter-century earlier.

As Richard Maltby and others have pointed out, one clear lesson to be derived from the story of the various attempts to enhance the audiovisual experience of moviegoing in the early 1950s is the fallaciousness of techno-logical determinism (the belief that technological or scientific progress dictates changes in social or economic institutions).[17] In almost every instance, the cinematic technologies trialled in this period predated their adoption by film-makers, sometimes considerably. The principles of stereoscopic 3-D – using the tinted cardboard spectacles which, adorning beaming fifties audiences, would create one of the era's iconic images of uncritical consumerist stupe-faction – had been firmly established in the 1930s (MGM indeed won an Oscar in 1936 for its 3-D 'Audioskopic' shorts, but afterwards abandoned the format, correctly believing that audiences would come to find the spectacles too intrusive). Anamorphic widescreen (in which a specially designed lens on a standard 35mm camera 'squeezes' an image horizontally during filming and a compensating lens on the projector 'stretches' it out again for exhibition) had been patented by the French cameraman Henri Chrétien in the 1920s. Cinerama, the baby of the bunch, and also the first to the fifties market, was the only technique developed wholly independently of the commercial film industry. Inventor Fred Waller developed the process from his own experi-ments before the war, during it as a Defence Department contractor – when he developed a widescreen device for gunnery training – and in the late forties when he received support from private investors including the Rockefellers and Time, Inc.

The wild success during 1952 of first Cinerama's largely autonomous launch and next independent producer Arch Oboler's unveiling of *Bwana Devil* in 'Natural Vision' 3-D undoubtedly motivated the studios to dust down their own alternatives. Cinerama used an array of three interlocked cameras to produce an image that, when projected in specially outfitted theatres on to a screen curving through 150 degrees, was more than twice the width of the squareish 'Academy ratio' image in which Hollywood films had been made throughout the sound era.[18] *This Is Cinerama*, a non-narrative travelogue-like feature, premiered at the 1,300-seat Broadway Theatre in New York and ran continuously, three performances daily, for the next two years at prices of up to $2.80 a seat (more than double the normal price for a first-run picture on Broadway).[19] *Bwana Devil* survived a critical mauling and, picked up and distributed nationwide by UA, reaped grosses eventually nearing $4 million.[20] Oboler's entrepreneurial venture inspired all the majors to take up the (non-proprietary) stereoscopic process for what proved to be a short-lived 3-D novelty boom that fizzled out within barely a year – many 'dimensional' productions ended up being screened 'flat'.

Twentieth Century-Fox's purchase of the rights to Chrétien's Hypergonar anamorphic system for the first time threw the weight of a major studio behind a 'dimensional' process. Fox's commitment to CinemaScope – Spyros Skouras announced in 1953 that all Fox pictures would be produced in the new format with its spectacular 2.66:1 aspect ratio[21] – and the system's considerable cost advantages over Cinerama, as well as its obviously greater suitability for the kinds of narrative filmmaking the studios supported, all contributed to making 'Scope the most widely used of the fifties widescreen processes, notwithstanding its initial technical problems, later partly rectified (such as the warping of horizontal elements and the tendency of faces to bulge in close-up – 'Scope mumps'). Fox's first 'Scope picture, *The Robe*, opened to much fanfare in September 1953 and was outstandingly successful, the first top-grossing Fox release in over a decade, earning almost half as much again as the runner-up, Columbia's *From Here To Eternity*. Other studios licensed 'Scope from Fox and by mid-decade some 38 per cent of domestic productions were appearing in anamorphic formats.[22] 'Scope briefly seemed the answer to Hollywood's prayers: 'AreYou Equipped for CinemaScoprosperity?' asked ads in the trade press.

The prevailing assumption early on in the widescreen era was that the expanded visual field necessitated slower cutting rates to avoid overloading audiences.[23] Some theorists – notably André Bazin – suggested that formats such as 'Scope significantly shifted the traditional Hollywood style away from dependence on montage towards longer takes and thus enhanced realism,[24] and also 'activated' spectators by requiring greater attention and discrimination in discerning and interpreting relevant narrative and situational details within the expanse of the widescreen frame.[25] David Bordwell was retrospectively dismissive of such claims, arguing – in the first instance of a position he would maintain to the present day in relation to other apparent modifications of the classical style – that Hollywood's adoption of widescreen was 'but another instance of trended change, a new set of stylistic devices brought into line with the classical schemata'.[26]

Bordwell accepted, for example, that some early 'Scope films tended to have longer takes than Academy-ratio pictures of the same time (by some four to seven seconds) but calculated that by the end of the fifties the average shot length (ASL) of widescreen films had reduced to the same length as their standard-aspect peers. He also argued that even the slight lengthening of widescreen takes bore minimal formal consequences – precisely because, here as elsewhere, the motivation for such deviations from or adjustments to Hollywood stylistic norms was cinematographers' and directors' concern to ensure the continuing lucidity of classically organised narratives; in this case, doubting the capacity of audiences to absorb the increased amount of visual information in a 'Scope frame at conventionally faster cutting rates. Similarly, while in other cinematic discourses (such as those of the European New Waves and some Japanese directors), the 'Scope frame enabled an active play with cinematic space and what Jacques Rivette hailed as 'compositional violations',[27] Hollywood characteristically recontained widescreen's transformative or disruptive potential within the paradigms and practices of the classical style.

That widescreen's modifications of classical conventions were for the most part contained by Hollywood's ongoing commitments to narrative-centred moviemaking should come as little surprise. Fox had after all devised CinemaScope specifically in order to exploit the appetite tapped by 3-D and Cinerama for an enhanced moviegoing sensorium, but to do so without – as those technologies seemed to do – displacing Hollywood's traditional strengths in delivering audiences the satisfactions of compelling fictional narratives for a more 'attraction'-like experience.[28] However, it is interesting to note the extent to which, when first introduced, 'Scope relied quite openly on an updated aesthetic of attraction in which 'realism' appeared as the combined achievement of technological innovation and modernised representational conventions. Somewhat characteristically, Bordwell's account of widescreen's impact on classical style simply elides the question of how audiences were interpellated as participants in fashioning understandings of 'Scope and its rivals. The spectator, in fact, figures in Bordwell's work as a largely notional presence: (in relation to the exploration of depth in some 'Scope films) 'the spectator had to be alert for slight changes'.[29] But was the spectator alert? And in what ways was such alertness, or other new or modified 'dimensions' of spectatorship, inculcated or promoted? How, in other words, was the style of *watching* films, the condition of viewing – and not that of the sovereign text alone – 'adjusted' by the advent of widescreen? This, arguably, was one of the most notable 'dimensions' of the film image's overhauling in the early fifties.

As noted, the classical Hollywood cinema generally de-emphasised style and technology in favour of content. Trade publications such as *American Cinematographer* and non-specialist magazines such as *Amateur Photographer* of course made details of production technology readily available to connoisseurs and 'buffs' as well as professionals. Some of this behind-the-scenes detail would also form part of the general flow of supplementary information supplied to exhibitors and local press for distribution and marketing purposes. Rarely, however, did presentational techniques form a major, let alone the central, part of a film's promotion. Still more rarely was the audience invited to consider themselves in any relation to the film at hand except as breathlessly empathetic onlookers and vicarious protagonists. Take as an example the quarter-page print ad for Columbia's Western *Renegades*, opening at Loew's Ohio Theater in Columbus in the autumn of 1946 – the text supplementing the artwork (tightly bodiced contract starlet Evelyn Keyes, brandishing a revolver, flanked by gunmen and outlaws on horseback while, in a smaller image, she cradles a newborn) announces in the usual verbless telegraphese 'A Dangerous Woman . . . Desperate Men . . . defying bullet and noose for love and loot!'[30]

The poster art distributed nationwide in support of Fox's historic first CinemaScope production *The Robe* in the autumn of 1953 makes for a striking contrast. Over the course of the week prior to its Columbus debut at the Loew's Broad, a series of half-page ads in the local press advertised the film as, effectively, a spectacular demonstration of the new process – ubiquitously and confusingly plugged in an unsubtle jab at the fast-fading 3-D fad as 'The New Dimensional Photographic Marvel You See Without Glasses!'. In every ad the trademark bowed CinemaScope logo took equal billing with the film – in type the same size as, or larger than, the title, which was forced into the top left corner of the artwork. (The film's notional stars, Richard Burton, Jean Simmons and Victor Mature, were reduced to the small print.) In one particularly striking ad, running on the eve of the film's premiere, the poster art is rendered as the actual 'Scope image, projected on to an exaggeratedly curved screen before rows of spectators in a darkened theatre. A dotted outline on the screen purports to show the meagre dimensions of the old Academy Ratio – and it is surely no accident that the old format seems able to contain only facial close-ups while the enormous new expanses to either side teem with fighting legionaries, Imperial armies, and dancing handmaidens. A text box keyed to numbered points on the image explains the key points of the new process – the anamorphic lens, the location of stereophonic speakers, the 'curved Miracle Mirror Screen' – lending the ad the tenor of a technical specification. The film's strapline – again reproduced across the print campaign – proclaims 'The Greatest Story of Love, Faith and Overwhelming Spectacle!', further blurring the line between narrative content and spectacular mode of presentation.

Key to the promotional campaign was the explicit interpellation of the audience as sophisticated spectators, able to undertake informed comparisons of 'Scope and not only 'Natural Vision' 3-D but the square format and 'flat ordinary screen' of every previous film. The ad discussed above goes further, incorporating the act of moviegoing into the artwork and rendering *The Robe* not as an immersive narrative but as a projected image (on whose 'infinite depth and life-like reality [*sic*]' the companion text, perhaps paradoxically, insists. Television goes conspicuously unmentioned – perhaps the contrast is too obvious to be worth stating (this was in any case Hollywood's phase of lofty indifference to the interloper).

Arguably, throughout Hollywood history key moments of technological innovation and transition have permitted and legitimated some relaxation of the generally well-policed 'fourth wall' between spectator and text, the most famous example of course being Al Jolson's direct to camera 'You ain't seen nuthin' yet!' in the first feature-length 'talkie', *The Jazz Singer* (WB 1927). Although the classical setting (and leaden gravitas) of *The Robe* closed off much opportunity for reflexive commentary, the film's opening credits were introduced by the parting of an on-screen velvet curtain, a gesture that emphasised at once the pious epic's 'seriousness' and the showy theatricality of its mode of presentation. The poster art discussed above also featured an interesting, subliminally directive motif. The faces of the three principals imprisoned within the puny Academy-ratio frame were all tilted upwards, eyes uplifted as if in awe, their gaze seemingly directed towards the film's title – and the wondrous process with which it shared equal billing. As we shall see, this subtly didactic touch, in which the characters' attitude of amazement acts as a kind of surrogate and guide for the spectator's desired response to the film's own technological achievement, would reappear later in the history of movie technology.[31]

But the assumed rationale for abandoning the living-room for the theatre is anything but naïve awe: on the contrary, 'Scope's debut solicited an informed and almost detached appreciation of its own merits, grounded in (pseudo-) technical outreach and an appeal to a completely embodied spectator. It opened up at least the possibility of a future Hollywood cinema where contemplation of technological achievement in the service of visual spectacle could be as much a part of the moviegoing experience as the traditional focus on (ostensibly) character-driven narrative. This promise would be intermittently realised in some widescreen films over the next two decades, perhaps most notably in the elaborate, extended, narrative-light and largely character-free special effects fugues of Stanley Kubrick's *2001: A Space Odyssey* (MGM 1968).

As it proved, the most extravagant and baroque exploitations of 'Scope were to be undertaken by independent US filmmakers such as Sam Fuller (*Forty Guns*, *China Gate*, both 1957), and especially by Sergio Leone and other Italian directors of the 1960s who made widescreen extreme close-ups of flinty stares beneath broad-brimmed hats synonymous with the retooled Western. Nor was CinemaScope the sole technique for extending the film image during this decade. Among its most notable rivals was Paramount's VistaVision (the cineaste's choice of fifties widescreen processes), which ran a standard 35mm filmstrip sideways through the camera gate, delivering an image with a 1.85:1 aspect ratio image that was also notably sharper and more detailed than either the Academy ratio or 'Scope. Though lacking 'Scope's extravagant dimensions, VistaVision also avoided its technical problems; its downside was cost[32] and Paramount discontinued the process in the early sixties (by which time, however, Panavision's anamorphic lenses had established 1.85 as the new standard ratio). Still more sumptuous were the levels of detail and brilliance achieved by Todd-AO, the 70mm process developed by independent producer Michael Todd, earning a Best Cinematography Oscar for *Around the World In Eighty Days* (UA 1956) and remaining a luxury option for road-showed super-spectacles such as *South Pacific* (Magna 1958) and *Cleopatra* (Fox 1963) into the 1960s.

But 'Scope in particular contributed to the gradual alloying of the recessive, understated style of classic Hollywood with more clearly modernist tendencies. Of course, in the rush to 'Scope following the blockbuster success of *The Robe*, the process and the viewing experience was normalised by usage. The emphasis in publicity on the technical aspects of the process was not repeated for subsequent releases; most fifties widescreen films, as already noted, strove to limit and contain rather than to accentuate 'Scope's disruptive potential. Yet the format remained a sufficiently notable transformation of the screen to provoke occasional reflexive satiric commentary: two well-known examples are the opening of Frank Tashlin's *The Girl Can't Help It*, where the proportions of the pneumatic Jayne Mansfield cue a joke about the 'Scope ratio, and *Silk Stockings* (1957), in which Fred Astaire and Janis Paige sing the praises of 'Glorious Technicolor, Breathtaking CinemaScope, and Stereophonic Sound' to each other from the margins of the 'Scope frame, separated at opposite ends of a ludicrously long conference table.

Less ostentatious but more intriguing were the ways in which widescreen formats enabled some directors to mobilise screen space to thematic, editorialising or ironic purpose in a highly self-conscious way. In a recent essay, David Bordwell has offered a more nuanced and detailed analysis of 'Scope's stylistic impact, still maintaining that 'norms of earlier decades were not so much overthrown as adjusted' but acknowledging to a greater degree the presence of non-classical elements such as 'graphic gamesmanship' and concluding that – at least in the hands of the most ambitious and imaginative filmmakers of the time – widescreen yielded 'uniquely valuable results'.[33] Alongside certain necessary adjustments to the staging and blocking conventions that had come to the fore in deep-focus-dominated forties Hollywood – replacing the latter's recessional compositions, as seen in *The Best Years of Our Lives*, with 'clothes-line' staging that arranged characters horizontally to colonise the 'Scope screen's enormous width – Bordwell notes how for certain directors, including George Cukor (*A Star Is Born*, MGM 1954) and Joshua Logan (*Picnic*, Col 1955), widescreen's intimidating uninhabited spaces could be embraced and actively exploited rather than (as in many cases) feared and simply packed with inert decor and distracting irrelevant detail.

One of the best-known early 'Scope films is Nicholas Ray's study of juvenile delinquency *Rebel Without a Cause*, the film that turned the doomed James Dean into an enduring icon and placed teenagers' inarticulate desperation and rage for the first time at the centre of a major studio picture. Alongside its topical and commercial mobilisation of teen sexuality and suburban *anomie* (but not rock 'n' roll, whose importance – unlike another 1955 release, *The Blackboard Jungle* – Ray and screenwriter Stewart Stern apparently missed), Ray uses the 'Scope frame to accentuate and intensify key elements. In the knife fight outside the planetarium, for example, Jim Stark's vulnerability and sense of deracination are intensified by his isolation in the centre of the frame, trapped by a guardrail, against a hazy backdrop of the indifferent expanse of suburban Los Angeles. Key confrontations between Jim and his parents are played out across the width of the entire screen, with sharply delineated vertical and diagonal elements – stair rails and banisters – drawing the spectator's attention to the gulf between them and the symbolically imprisoning aspects of the family house. Nor is Ray immune to the sheer visual pleasure to be derived from 'Scope's capacity for striking graphic arrangements, most famously in the shot of Judy (Natalie Wood) at the start of the 'chickie run', brilliantly illuminated by the headlights of the roadsters roaring past her on either side down the perspectival diagonals of the frame.

OVERWHELMING SPECTACLE

CinemaScope, VistaVision and Todd-AO – like 3-D and indeed colour – are perhaps most readily understood as shifting the balance between narrative and spectacle. And here too, while there is no wholesale abandonment of classical norms, there seems to be a meaningful adjustment of priorities. Once 'Scope and Cinerama upped the ante, other pictures had to announce their own non-televisual bigness or risk being left behind: 'It's Immense!' trumpeted the print ads for the (non-widescreen) Doris Day musical *Calamity Jane* (WB 1953) as *The Robe* opened down the block. Our contemporary sense of Hollywood as synonymous with extravagant large-scale spectacle in fact owes a great deal to the legacy of the early postwar period and obscures the fact that for the most part the studio system steered clear of ostentatious visual display as an end in itself.

Pre-classical cinema, certainly, heavily exploited the appeal of visual spectacle. Tom Gunning has argued that early cinema relied on an 'aesthetic of astonishment' to capture and retain its audience; initially the spectacle of movement itself, and subsequently the development of 'trick' films and the emergence of genres such as 'scenics' and historical re-enactments, recommended themselves to audiences on their ability to display and reveal novel, striking or exotic vistas and tableaux. The de-emphasisation of individuated character and plot in this earliest period of cinema history maintained a constant sense of the spectator as an embodied presence whose attention needed to be explicitly solicited and sustained by the film text. Early cinema's mode of spectatorial address echoed the carnival 'attraction' or the vaudeville 'turn', and before the age of purpose-built cinemas films might often be viewed as touring exhibitions in temporary auditoriums; short films themselves might comprise merely one 'turn' in a variety bill, alternating with stage acts and musical numbers. Even once the shift to fictional narrative was underway after 1907–8 (see above), the principle of the marvellous remained central, and early multi-reel films remained highly reliant on spectacle, whether understood as scenic views, exciting action sequences such as Mack Sennett's hair-raising chases, or increasingly elaborate special effects sequences such as the eruption of Mount Etna at the opening of the Italian epic *Cabiria* (1913).

With the transition to feature films – itself motivated by the need to compete with imported extravaganzas such as *Cabiria* and *Quo Vadis?* (1914) – character-driven narrative acquired its enduring centrality and spectacle began to be more cautiously deployed. Notably, *Intolerance* (1917), Griffith's follow-up to *Birth of a Nation*, both exploits visual spectacle on a scale of stupefying lavishness in its Babylon sequences and is also among the most thoroughly unclassical of all American silent films in its narrative organisation, unfolding four concurrent but entirely distinct storylines, separated by vast stretches of time and space and connected only through the abstract notion of intolerance and injustice. The film's complexities defeated audiences and the experiment was not repeated. In the aesthetic economy of the studio era, spectacle came to play a carefully rationed role.

Of course large-scale filmmaking, or 'superspecials', persisted through the studio era across genres and studios alike, including Westerns (*Cimarron*, RKO 1930) and costume adventures (*The Adventures of Robin Hood*, WB 1935; *Mutiny on the Bounty*, MGM 1935). Busby Berkeley's jaw-dropping 'mass ornament' dance spectacles, as noted, require a category all their own. But in general the 'wow' factor played only a limited role and the 'casts of thousands' of such late silent-era spectacles as *Ben-Hur* (MGM 1925) and *The Ten Commandments* (Par 1925) were left behind. The system of routinised production, the balanced release slate, and all-but-guaranteed audiences and revenues, rendered spectacle in most cases surplus to studio requirements; studio profits relied on a steady return across the full range of releases, not on the breakaway box office performance of any individual film. Even though *Gone With the Wind* remains the (inflation-adjusted) most successful film of all time and has become synonymous in collective memory with classic Hollywood at its zenith, it was of course independently produced and, as one of just three pictures Selznick International released that year, its need for product differentiation was exponentially higher than any product of the studio assembly line.

The restrictions set on blind- and block-booking by the 1940 interim consent decree in the *Paramount* suit required the studios to front-load pictures with more marketable elements and, as budgets rapidly increased through the early forties, so did the emphasis on the uniquely appealing and eye-catching properties of individual releases (whether piling on the star power in *Grand Hotel* fashion, or adding *outré* spectacular elements such as the giant squid in DeMille's *Reap the Wild Wind* (Par 1944)). Technicolor was also deployed for visual appeal, although as several historians have noted there was disagreement in the industry (and indeed between producers and technicians and executives at the Technicolor Corporation) about whether three-strip Technicolor should be regarded as a device to accentuate visual spectacle (as most obviously in *The Wizard of Oz* (MGM 1939), where colour is reserved for Oz and thus functions within a strictly and explicitly fantasy register) or as enhancing cinematic 'realism'. For as long as Technicolor's cumbersome and expensive additive process monopolised colour production, however, colour was bound to be perceived by audiences as a 'special feature' and was marketed as such.[34]

Interestingly, the introduction of inexpensive monopak EastmanColor in 1949 and the ensuing sharp increase in colour production in the early fifties, bound up as it was with the general spectacularisation of the film image at this time, did not in itself fundamentally undermine colour's qualities of 'special-ness'. Fifties colour pictures are typified on the one hand by an emphasis on brilliantly exotic vistas, often widescreen, in genres ranging from the Western (*Shane*, MGM 1951) to the epic (*Exodus*, UA 1960) and of course the musical (*It's Always Fair Weather*, MGM 1955). On the other hand, colour could be deployed to ironic (as in Douglas Sirk's ostensibly formulaic melodramas) or symbolic (Ray's use of red in *Rebel Without a Cause* to link his protago-nists and identify their commonalties: Judy's lipstick, Jim's jacket) purpose. Monochrome remained the first choice for 'realistic' genres such as the police procedural and the social realist drama (*Twelve Angry Men*, UA 1957; *To Kill a Mockingbird*, U 1962).

The use of colour in the fifties once again illustrates how impossible it is to extricate questions of form and style from ideological as well as industrial contexts: once colour production became the industry norm in the mid-1960s (following television's conversion to colour[35]), the ability to use colour in emphatic, non-naturalistic ways was significantly reduced. Like the intro-duction of widescreen, colour indicates the ways in which, in a new context of moviegoing as special event rather than everyday pastime, technological and stylistic changes combined to draw attention to the materiality of the medium in ways that were significantly different from, if not incompatible with, classical Hollywood practice. This entailed a changing relationship to the spectator, who to an increasing degree became a presence consciously evoked, addressed and activated by the film text itself. In the late fifties and early sixties, some directors used this more forceful, even aggressive, relationship to the spectator, in conjunction with changed standards of onscreen propriety as the Production Code eased its grip, in startling new ways.

EXCESS, INSTABILITY AND THE EMERGENCE OF THE DIRECTOR

Linda Williams has argued that from the early 1960s Hollywood film increasingly abandoned its traditionally solicitous regard for the security of audiences' narrative, cognitive and sensory experience and began to subject them to 'a sort of sado-masochistic roller-coaster ride' whose pleasure lay, precisely, in 'the refusal completely to re-establish equilibrium'.[36] Appropriately, she dates the trend from the release of *Psycho*; for Hitchcock had throughout the fifties been preparing the way for a more confrontational aesthetic. The climax of *Rear Window* (Par 1952) blinds the audience with white light as the wheelchair-bound hero fends off the murderer advancing towards him across a darkened room. *Vertigo* (Par 1958) employs the famous 'inverse zoom', distorting onscreen space to communicate the subjective experience of Scotty's agoraphobic panic. Most infamously *Psycho* itself, not content simply to kill off its star without warning after 30 minutes, in the shower scene literally rips Marion Crane, the screen, [37] audience expectations and the sedate conventions of Hollywood montage to shreds. Richard Maltby credits this sequence with fashioning a new dimension of 'unsafe space' in Hollywood film.[38] Maltby's principal interest is with the literally unsafe spaces increasingly encountered in horror films after *Psycho*, where areas 'just offscreen' – diegetically located, that is, yet out of sight of protagonist and audience alike – shimmer with potential threat. In Williams's broader view, however, *Psycho* can also be seen to inaugurate a new relationship between filmmaker and audience where the old proprieties no longer apply – where filmgoing itself becomes worryingly yet excitingly 'unsafe'.

Psycho's notorious manipulations and infringements of narrative decency – cheating us at every stage of the information we need to be able to anticipate the final revelation of Norman's psychosis and denying us any secure narrative perspective, were as dramatic and game-changing as the film's visual assault: they altered audiences' assumptions of what they can reasonably expect Hollywood films to do, or not to do, *to them*. The year 1960 was not exactly Year Zero: *Psycho* was building on experiments with obsessive, 'borderline' protagonists during the fifties, particularly notable in Nicholas Ray's *noir*-inflected melodramas (*In a Lonely Place*; *On Dangerous Ground*, RKO 1951; *Bigger Than Life*, Fox 1956) and in the James Stewart/Anthony Mann Westerns cycle (*Winchester 73*; *Bend of the River*, U 1952; *The Naked Spur*, MGM 1953); note also *The Searchers*. The heroes of all of these were driven by inner demons to act in ways that either countered star personae or pushed non-conformist qualities to alienated extremes and threatened to undermine the audience's assumed sympathies.

Narrative gamesmanship was taken a step further in Fritz Lang's *Beyond a Reasonable Doubt* (RKO 1956). A novelist proposes to expose the fallibility of the judicial system. He manufactures circumstantial evidence to frame himself for a murder; once he is convicted a magazine editor will reveal the subterfuge. But the editor is killed in a car accident and the novelist is condemned on the evidence he himself has fabricated. At the eleventh hour his fiancée (the dead editor's daughter) discovers the exonerating evidence that saves him from the gas chamber. However, a final (and completely unheralded) twist reveals that the novelist is guilty after all – his muckraking crusade has all been an elaborate ploy to enable him to escape suspicion while he eliminates an unwanted skeleton in his closet. This sensational reversal owes something to the macabre twists of contemporary 'horror comix', which drew congressional censure in 1954; Lang, however, intensifies the effect by an obstinately unremarkable, matter-of-fact style – anticipating Hitchcock's strategy in the sections of *Psycho* that take place away from the Bates Motel.[39] *Psycho* itself would put this style out of fashion, as revealed by the contrast between Lang's film and Sam Fuller's hysterical *mise en scène* in tackling somewhat similar narrative material in *Shock Corridor* (Allied Artists 1963).

Other examples of the creeping destabilisation of the visual field in the early sixties include John Frankenheimer's hallucinatory 360-degree pans in the brainwashing sequences of *The Manchurian Candidate* (UA 1962), and a variety of devices in Sidney Lumet's films of the period: the searching, bleached-out close-ups of President Henry Fonda agonising the ethics of nuclear confrontation in *Fail-Safe* (Col 1964), the grotesquely distorting effects of extreme wide-angle lenses in the inverted moral environment of *The Hill* (MGM 1965), and the jagged associative montage of *The Pawnbroker*. The ultimate classicist, John Ford's late Western *The Man Who Shot Liberty Valance* (Par 1962) produced a different kind of estrangement, perhaps intentionally, through its apparently perverse insistence on filming some key exterior scenes on all-too-obvious studio sets. (The equally obvious painted backcloths of Hitchcock's *Marnie* (U 1964) have a similarly mannerist feel.) With *Dr Strangelove*, meanwhile, Stanley Kubrick refined his distinctive mature style of entirely non-identificatory narrative. Finally, on the very cusp of a dynamic new phase in Hollywood's industrial and aesthetic practices alike, Arthur Penn's *Mickey One* (Col 1965) was in some ways – even more than his far more celebrated next film, *Bonnie and Clyde* (WB 1967) – the American film most thoroughly imbued with the stylistic lexicon of the early French New Wave.

In the early sixties, these non-conformist stylistic practices remained visible exceptions to generally more conventional rules. Yet even Hollywood's ostensibly most traditional products – the stolid, four-square roadshowed epics and blockbusters of the early sixties – in some measure embodied the changes that, as we have seen, adjusted and reshaped classical paradigms in the postwar period. The way had been cleared for a period of rapid, striking and far-reaching change.

NOTES

1. David Bordwell, Janet Staiger and Kristin Thompson, *The Classical Hollywood Cinema: Film Style and Mode of Production to* 1960 (London: Routledge, 1985), p. 116. (Hereafter *CHC*.)
2. For this reason, Janet Staiger adopts from Marx the phrase 'serial manufacture' – rather than 'mass production' – to describe Hollywood's mode of production. *CHC*, p. 92.
3. After Frederick Winslow Taylor, whose turn-of-the-century studies of business output exerted enormous influence on American business organisation throughout the early twentieth century.
4. The best-known example is the '[Alan] Freed Unit' at MGM which from the early 1940s to the late 1950s to produced a stream of classic musicals including *Meet Me in St Louis* (1944), *The Pirate* (1948), *An American in Paris, Singin' in the Rain* (1952), *The Band Wagon* (1953), and many others.
5. Kristin Thompson records that during the 1930s film laboratories at some of the major studios manipulated exposures during processing to try to obtain a characteristic studio 'look'. *CHC*, p. 286.
6. *CHC*, p. 4.
7. Henry Jenkins, 'Historical poetics', in Joanne Hollows and Mark Jancovich (eds), *Approaches to Popular Film* (Manchester: Manchester University Press, 1995), p. 114.
8. *Casablanca*'s montages were created by the Warners montage unit headed by Don Siegel – later an significant action director whose films include *Invasion of the Body Snatchers*, *Dirty Harry* (WB 1971) and John Wayne's final film, *The Shootist* (Par 1976).
9. The most fully elaborated example of this revulsion is of course T. W. Adorno and Max Horkheimer's excoriating account of the 'culture industry' in *Dialectic of Enlightenment* (1947), trans. J. W. Seabury (New York: Continuum, 1973).
10. Brecht's ordeal working on *Hangmen Also Die* – for which he was ultimately denied screen credit by the WGA – is recorded in James K. Lyon, *Bertolt Brecht in America* (Princeton: Princeton University Press, 1980). Brecht's own reflections on the commercialisation of *The Threepenny Opera* in Pabst's 1930 film can be found in 'The Threepenny lawsuit', in Marc Silberman (ed.), *Brecht on Film and Radio* (London: Methuen, 2001).
11. Berkeley's dance sequences are now regularly excerpted and included in programmes of American surrealist and avant-garde film.

12. *CHC*, pp. 4–6. Bordwell derives the concept of the aesthetic norm from the work of the art historian Jan Mukařovský.
13. I am referring here to philosophical pragmatism, the dominant American philosophical school of the first half of the twentieth century, associated most closely with C. S. Peirce and John Dewey; in such works as *Consequences of Pragmatism* and *Contigency, Irony and Solidarity*, Richard Rorty argues that pragmatism constitutes a recognisably and characteristically American philosophical mode.
14. See Robert M. Carringer, *The Making of Citizen Kane*, revised edn (Berkeley: University of California Press, 1996), pp. 135–42.
15. And in the case of CinemaScope, at least in its optimal installations, also the auditory experience, with the introduction of magnetic stereophonic soundtracks.
16. See for example the accounts of Fox's unveiling of CinemaScope in early 1953: 'Technically, Cinemascope falls somewhere between Cinerama and the stereo-type systems such as Natural Vision. But the end product is in the Cinerama class, where the third-dimension effect is accomplished by illusion, and without glasses' ('Fox's Moves . . .', *Business Week*, 7 February 1953, p. 27); '[Fox] is converting its entire film output immediately to a three-dimensional color process called Cinemascope' ('Cinemascope upcoming', *Newsweek*, 9 February 1953, p. 61) – this last doubly inaccurate as not only was 'Scope not three dimensional, it was also unrelated to colour processing (numerous 'Scope films would be eventually made in black and white).
17. Richard Maltby, *Hollywood Cinema*, 2nd edn (Oxford: Blackwell, 2003), pp. 251–8).
18. The aspect ratio (width to height) of the Academy format was 1.37:1, that of a Cinerama film, 2.8:1.
19. 'Third dimension: new bait for movie box offices', *Business Week*, 8 November 1952, pp. 132–7; 'Cinerama: a Wall Street hit?', same issue, pp. 171–2.
20. See Peter Lev, *The Fifties: Transforming The Screen 1950–1959* (Berkeley: University of California Press, 2003), pp. 109–10.
21. The width of the 'Scope frame diminished to 2.55:1 as Fox introduced optical (rather than magnetic) audio tracks in a concession to exhibitors reluctant to invest in stereo equipment.
22. Joel Finler, *The Hollywood Story*, revised edn (London: Wallflower, 2003), p. 372.
23. Bosley Crowther, 'Picture of Hollywood in the depths', *New York Times Magazine*, 14 June 1953, p. 17ff.
24. See André Bazin, 'Will CinemaScope save the film industry?' [1953], *Film-Philosophy*, 2002; 6(2). Available online: http://www.film-philosophy.com/vol6-2002/n2bazin
25. Charles Barr, 'CinemaScope: before and after', *Film Quarterly*, 1956; 16(4):4–24.
26. *CHC*, p. 361.
27. Quoted in *CHC*, p. 363.
28. On the 'aesthetic of attractions' see below, p. 247ff.
29. *CHC*, p. 320.
30. *Columbus Citizen-Journal*, Saturday 1 September 1946, p. 7.
31. See Chapter 9.
32. VistaVision required a specially adapted camera and, because it exposed a larger frame area (eight sprocket holes rather than the standard four), used twice the amount of film.
33. David Bordwell, 'CinemaScope: The Modern Miracle You See Without Glasses', *Poetics of Cinema* (New York: Routledge, 2008), pp. 281–325.
34. See Gorham Kindem, 'Hollywood's conversion to color: the technical, economic and aesthetic factors', in Gorham Kindem (ed.), *The American Movie Industry: The Business of Motion Pictures* (Carbondale, IL: Southern Illinois University Press, 1982), pp. 146–58.

35. Itself expedited by the broadcast of post-1948 studio films, many of them in colour, from 1961.
36. Linda Williams, 'Sex and sensation', in Geoffrey Nowell-Smith (ed.), *The Oxford History of World Cinema* (Oxford: Oxford University Press, 1996), p. 493.
37. Hitchcock's own description of the murder: 'An impression of a knife slashing, as if tearing at the very screen, ripping the film'. See Steven Rebello, *Alfred Hitchcock and the making of Psycho* (London: Marion Boyars, 1990), p. 134.
38. Maltby, *Hollywood Cinema*, 2nd edn, pp. 354–6.
39. Hitchcock used members of the crew from MCA-Revue's branded television anthology series *Alfred Hitchcock Presents* to shoot *Psycho* cheaply in a monochrome telefilm style far removed from the high-end gloss of his previous film, *North by Northwest* (MGM 1959).

PART II

Crisis and Renaissance 1966–81

Hunt's Cinestage, Columbus, roadshow-era showcase. Reproduced courtesy of the Columbus Metropolitan Library Photo Collection

Introduction to Part II

By the second half of the 1960s, as measured from movies shown in downtown Columbus, decline was harder and harder to disguise. The old downtown theatre district had started to fall into decay; while on Labor Day, 1965, the modish comedy *What's New Pussycat?* and the Cinerama Western *The Hallelujah Trail*, both United Artists releases, continued long runs at the Ohio and Grand, respectively, the closure of the Broad in March 1961 had reduced the old picture palaces to just three. In early 1969 both the Ohio and the Grand would fall dark – the Ohio would only narrowly escape the developers' wrecking ball – leaving only the Palace open for business for the holiday weekend in 1970.[1] (Of the subsequent-run downtown theatres, only the Southern remained, supplying a diet of mostly exploitation fare: in 1970, an AIP biker double-bill of *Hell's Angels on Wheels* and *The Wild Angels*, two 1967 pictures re-released to cash in on the success of *Easy Rider*.) The Palace's programme at the start of September 1970 also testified to changes in the social and demographic constituency of movies and of downtown Columbus alike: Melvin van Peebles's R-rated pre-blaxploitation racial satire *Watermelon Man* (Col), with a midnight show on Saturdays (next up was UA's *They Call Me Mister Tibbs* with Sidney Poitier, follow-up to the popular *In the Heat of the Night*).

Elsewhere, just fourteen nabes survived in 1965 alongside the drive-ins, which still remained although their heyday had by now passed. The 'art theaters' of the mid-fifties had bifurcated, into recognisable art house screens on the one hand, offering current fare such as *Zorba the Greek* alongside revivals of Bergman's *Wild Strawberries*, and on the other the new phenomenon of 'adults only' theatres such as the renamed Linden Follies, now showing *Blondes in Bondage* and *The Flesh Is Weak* (a decade earlier, as simply the Linden, it had been showing Disney's *Long John Silver*). A low-level skirmishing had begun between these new adult theatres and the city's recently-constituted Motion

Picture Review Board that would continue into the next decade, with the exhibitors gradually gaining the upper hand.[2] Across the board, in fact, and not only in the grind houses, the dissipation of the traditional family audience was visible both in the 'Mature Audiences Only' warning attached to *What's New Pussycat?* and the Columbus *Dispatch*'s 'Family Features: A Guide for Parents' (subdivided into 'Entire Family', 'Teens', and 'Mature Teens'). In earlier decades, with the firm hold of the Production Code ensuring the moral standards of mainstream motion pictures, such recommendations and caveats would have been wholly redundant. Here at ground level was a de facto classification system well ahead of the MPAA ratings, in 1965 still three years away. As before, the weighting of films exhibited in the remaining neighbourhood theatres and drive-ins towards low-budget genre films testified to the dominance of patrons under twenty-five among the rump of habitual moviegoers. This had its own drawbacks: it was reported that a 'near-riot' by teens attending a horror double-bill in February 1965 caused nearly $200 worth of damage to the Eastern Theater on East Main Street.[3] The reduction of audience choice also continued to outpace the loss of screens: excluding the adult theatres, Columbus moviegoers had just fifty-five films to choose between in the coming week. On the other hand – as had not been the case in 1946 and to a very limited degree in 1955 – they did have the option of staying home and choosing among numerous theatrical films on broadcast television. As discussed in Chapter 1, once the studios resolved their dispute with the actors' union over residual payments, licensing their libraries of post-1948 films became an important and regular revenue stream. Movies now not only padded out afternoon and late-night schedules but drew large audiences to prime-time slots with showcase presentations of recent(-ish) releases such as Kirk Douglas's epic *The Vikings* (UA 1958), at 9 p.m. Sunday on ABC.

As might be expected of a town chosen so frequently (on account of its representative qualities) as a test market for consumer goods that it was known as 'Test City USA', Columbus continued to keep pace with changes nationwide.[4] The penetration of the American heartland by art house cinemas exhibiting both international films and homegrown independent productions – traditionally confined to the largest metropolitan markets – and adult theatres in both cases reflected a changing society, with more permissive attitudes to sexual morality and a greater intellectual curiosity fuelled by the burgeoning student population. High-school and college-age audiences now provided one of the few stable and consistent segments of Hollywood's ever shrinking market: from 1965 to 1966, annual admissions would dip below 1 billion for the first time since World War I. US theatres were now selling barely a quarter as many tickets as in 1946. Yearly box office receipts had slumped below the symbolic $1 billion mark as long ago as 1958 and had broadly flatlined since, largely thanks to inflation: the figure for 1965 was a weedy $922 million. The drive-in boom had peaked midway through the previous decade and, with outdoor theatre numbers themselves now starting to decline while the loss of four-wall cinemas continued apace (down a further 5,000 (35 per cent) on ten years ago), the overall downturn was stark: there were 5,300 fewer cinemas in the USA at the end of 1965 than in 1955. Nationally as locally, the blockbuster success of a few lavish traditional family features such as *The Sound of Music* could not allay the general picture of an industry in difficulties.

In most respects, bar the symbolic loss of the downtown theatres, the picture had changed little by 1970. One small difference was, however, significant: the *Columbus Dispatch* now included in its 'Downtown' theatre listings not only the two remaining theatres in the city's traditional downtown, but all nine theatres within the city limits of old Columbus, thus redesignating such former nabes as the University and Town and Country. This reflected the undeniable shift of cultural and economic gravity away from downtown and indeed the old city altogether. The city's focus for major first-run showcases had in 1965 already shifted yet further uptown, past Hunt's Cinestage (in 1965 showing *My Fair Lady* for a ninth consecutive month, in 1970 *Patton*) and out to the edge of the suburbs, where in 1965 the season's runaway hit, Fox's *The Sound of Music*, was enjoying an exclusive run at the area's first shopping-mall theatre, the Northland. (Following the exhibition orthodoxy of the period, such blockbuster releases were 'roadshowed' – exclusively booked at large modern theatres on an advance-booking, reserved-seat (and of course premium price) basis echoing the Broadway theatre from which most road-showed musicals were themselves derived.[5]) It would be these suburban areas that drove the gradual revival of moviegoing in Columbus, as elsewhere in the country.

By 1975, downtown was little more than an afterthought, the Palace showing the throwaway Spaghetti-style Western *Take a Hard Ride*, the Southern eking out the dregs of the blaxploitation and kung fu cycles with a double bill of *The Candy Tangerine Man* and the parodically titled *Kung Fu Mama*. Within a year the Palace would finally have closed its doors while the Southern ground out a familiar-sounding menu of *Jive Turkey* (another self-parodying genre title) and *Charley One-Eye*. As was the case nationwide, Columbus's downtown had fallen into a sharp decline as residents abandoned cramped apartments for roomier suburban homes, businesses also relocated to new quarters in suburban commercial and light-industrial parks, and the service industries that relied on them – restaurants, hotels and of course theatres – closed their doors. Many classic landmark buildings fell victim to the wrecking ball in Columbus and countless other American cities during the 1960s, making way for parking lots and office buildings with little thought given to preservation of the historic urban fabric. The small hotels and rooming houses, a feature of the American cityscape familiar from countless *noirs* and B-movies, were also torn down, in many cases turning their low-income residents out onto the street and creating the problems of homelessness that would be such a visible symbol of the crisis in America's inner cities in the late seventies and eighties (for example, in the opening credits of *Trading Places* (Par 1983)).

In other ways, however, moviegoing – and movie-viewing – in 'Test City USA' was ahead of the national curve in the early 1970s. In 1974–5 the total number of US cinemas reached its all-time low of 13,200. The following year saw a slight expansion, with 200 more theatres. The number of screens, however – broken out as a separate figure for the first time in 1974 – increased at three times this rate. (See Appendix: Figure 2.) The era of the multi-screen theatre, which over the next two decades would transform US moviegoing, had arrived, and Columbus was in at the creation. In early 1971 Centro Cinemas signed up as Columbus franchisees for Jerry Lewis Cinemas, comparatively small (200–350-seat) storefront theatres that seemed to have more in common with the old nickelodeons than with the contemporary multiplex. Nonetheless, these 'mini-cinemas' marked a new phase in the exhibition sector's efforts to come to terms with its radically altered market. 'The big, "white elephant" film houses – the old palaces – have had it', explained Centro's spokesman.[6] Although mini-theatres were stillborn, by 1975 a new trend was clearly visible. For the first time since 1946, the number of screens in Columbus had increased from a decade earlier, despite the 1972 closure of Hunt's Cinestage and its subsequent demolition. In the city's expanding and increasingly afflu-ent suburbs, new double- or triple-screen theatres had opened up (the Loew's Arlington and Morse, the Raintree III, the Graceland Shopping Center, the three-screen Forum and so on) to bring the total number of available indoor screens in Greater Columbus to thirty-eight. These new theatres offered car-reliant patrons easy access by road and ample parking, and were located in or close to consumer hubs such as shopping malls.

Columbus was also the chosen location of Warner Communications's first experiment in interactive television. By the mid-seventies Warner president Steve Ross had begun aggressively acquiring local cable systems, convinced that on-demand direct-to-home delivery of movies would open up a vast new market for Warner Bros. films. For the most part, cable television at this stage simply ensured that viewers could view outlying and independent stations, mostly confined to the inferior UHF spectrum, interference free (there were three such stations in the Columbus market). Cable TV channels as such were few and far between. But in 1977, in partnership with American Express Warner trialled Qube Television in Columbus, allowing viewers to order movies using their remote controls. While Ross was mistaken in believing that consumers would prefer such systems to what he saw as the cumbersome and inconvenient business of renting videotapes (another nascent but soon to explode source of ancillary revenues in the late 1970s), both the technologies pioneered in Columbus and the growing integration of different delivery mechanisms – here, cable television – under the same corporate ownership would become prominent features of the new movie market that emerged in the early 1980s.[7]

NOTES

1. 'Save Ohio Committee to attempt purchase', *Columbus Dispatch*, 24 March 1969, p. A1.
2. See 'Board finds only "trashy" movies', *Columbus Dispatch*, 8 April 1962, p. A7; 'City censors inactive', *Columbus Dispatch*, 9 October 1970, p. A1.
3. 'Second teen fracas broken up in theater', *Columbus Dispatch*, 1 March 1965, p. A17. Perhaps surprisingly, the films provoking the alleged unrest were two mild-mannered British imports from Hammer Studios, including the positively soporific *The Gorgon*; perhaps the teens' agitation was simple boredom. The film's star, the impeccably courteous Peter Cushing, would in any event have been mortified to learn that he had been the cause of riotous assembly.
4. Ed Lentz, *Columbus: The Story of a City* (Charlestown, SC: Arcadia, 2003), p. 138.
5. On roadshows and *The Sound of Music*, see 'The Biggest, the Best: 1965,' p. 104.
6. 'Local group acquires franchise for 20 mini-theaters', *Columbus Dispatch*, 12 February 1971, p. 11B. See also 'The movie theatre gets cut to size', *Business Week*, 14 March 1970, p. 29.
7. Edward Jay Epstein, *The Big Picture: Money and Power in Hollywood* (New York: Random House, 2005), pp. 45–6.

The Biggest, the Best: 1965

Best Picture, Box Office No. 1: *The Sound of Music* (Twentieth Century-Fox)
D, P: Robert Wise; **W:** Ernest Lehman

By the early 1960s, there were some worrying signs that Hollywood's road-show era was heading for a pile-up. Spiralling production costs were extending studios' risk to the point where even a high-earning film might turn only a small profit, while complex profit-sharing deals with key talent also cut into studio margins. UA, for example, cleared just $1.25 million on *It's a Mad, Mad, Mad, Mad World*'s $26 million gross.[1] Then there were the outright failures: every studio suffered expensive disappointments, and these started to grow in both scale and number by the turn of the decade. It became more and more apparent that the 'special occasion' moviegoers and family audiences who were the roadshow pictures' primary market would not change their twice- or three-times-yearly filmgoing habit simply because more 'big' films were being made and released; they would continue to pick and choose, while each blockbuster crowding the market eroded the 'event' quality of roadshows as a whole. MGM's $19 million remake of *Mutiny on the Bounty* lost the studio $12 million in 1962. Paramount's *The Fall of the Roman Empire* cost $20 million and earned less than $5 million. UA's epic life of Christ *The Greatest Story Ever Told*, originally budgeted at $7.4 million in 1962, finally reached screens three years later at three times the cost and grossed just $12.1 million; the studio ended up writing off 60 per cent of the film.[2] The studios' potentially catastrophic direction of travel became luminously apparent when Fox's notorious *Cleopatra*, the top earner of 1963, nonetheless – because of the bloated production's estimated $44 million cost – struggled to recoup its costs.

Cleopatra's protracted and chaotic production provided the backdrop to a boardroom shake-up at Fox that saw Darryl Zanuck return to the company as president, ousting another veteran, Spyros Skouras, and his twenty-seven-year-old son, Richard, appointed head of production. Zanuck Jr., however, tied his colours firmly to the roadshow mast, releasing six such pictures – runaway productions all – in 1965–6 at a combined cost of $55 million, the first being Richard Rodgers and Oscar Hammerstein's *The Sound of Music*, the latest in a long line of large-scale sixties musicals based on long-running Broadway hits.[3] The picture was not universally regarded as a sure-fire hit: Billy Wilder, whom Zanuck originally approached to produce and direct the film (surely a most unlikely choice), backed away after deciding the plot-line was 'too gooey'. Thus *The Sound of Music* became something of an acid test for the new Zanuck regime.

The rest, of course, is history. The film's critical reception was indifferent, but the audience response – buoyed, as Sheldon Hall has shown, by Fox's canny marketing campaign which kept ticket prices relatively low for a roadshow attraction – was sensational. *The Sound of Music* broke domestic and overseas box office records, returning $80 million in domestic rentals alone – twice as much as *My Fair Lady*. The film also unveiled the phenomenon of repeat viewing that would become a notable feature of the next blockbuster era, starting with *Star Wars* in 1977; it became clear that some viewers were returning to see the film several times, as if hungry for the communal experience of release and uplift it offered. By the time the Academy Awards rolled around the following spring (the ceremony, broadcast for the first time in colour that year, having now taken on its own familiar blockbuster proportions), the result was almost a foregone conclusion, only MGM's *Doctor Zhivago* offering serious competition.

Yet for all its record-setting success, *The Sound of Music*'s long-term significance was that, however unwittingly, it almost helped destroy Hollywood. Unsurprisingly, in its wake the studios pursued the – as it proved, chimerical – prize of the breakaway family hit with a string of blockbuster musicals and other extravagant spectacles. Fox led the way: 'The public will go in great numbers and pay stiff prices for pictures they want to see', declared Zanuck bullishly, buoyed by success.[4] The rest of his 1965–6 roadshow slate, including *The Bible – In the Beginning*, failed to live up to expectations, but it was the enormous losses of the next few years, inaugurated by Fox's own *Doctor Dolittle* (1967; cost: $17 million; domestic rentals: $6.2 million) which really threw the studio, and most of the rest of the industry, into a tailspin. Odd near-successes like *Hello Dolly* (whose own high budgets meant their cost-to-earnings ratio remained low) could not offset an apparently endless series of large-scale flops including *Chitty Chitty Bang Bang* (UA 1967; $16m/$7.1m.), *Star!* (Fox 1968; $14.2m/$4.5m), *Battle of Britain* (UA 1969; $12m/$2.5m), and *Gaily Gaily* (Par 1969; $9m/$1m). This run of flops continued through the end of the decade; the industry's roadshow habit seemed impossible to break. Appropriately enough an MGM executive used the language of addiction to describe the studios' losing run pursuit of the big score:

> Everybody acted as if there were some God of the movies who would periodically come down and save people from their follies by giving them a big hit. All they had to do was churn out movies and wait for the big smash that would make them well.[5]

A chastened Richard D. Zanuck – whose own career at Fox, as well as his relationship with his father, was a casualty of the crisis he had invited[6] – observed with hindsight that *The Sound of Music* 'was the worst thing that could have happened to us or the industry. We all tried to copy the picture, to make big musical smashes, and we all made costly flops'.[7] It was a signal irony of Hollywood history that this most wholesome and traditional of Hollywood entertainments should have made a very different kind of cinema not only possible, but necessary. The Academy's final Best Picture selection of the 1960s was *Midnight Cowboy*, the X-rated story of a homeless male hustler, shot on the lurid and sleazy streets of Times Square – a very long way from 'Edelweiss'.

Notes

1. Tino Balio, *United Artists: The Company That Changed the Film Industry* (Madison: University of Wisconsin Press, 1987), p. 146.
2. Balio, *United Artists*, pp. 133–46.
3. Sheldon Hall, 'Twentieth Century Fox in the 1960s', in Linda Ruth Williams and Michael Hammond (eds), *Contemporary American Cinema* (Maidenhead: McGraw-Hill, 2005), pp. 46–9.

4. 'Son of Zanuck stars at Twentieth Century', *Business Week*, 14 September 1968, pp. 76–8.
5. 'Making the movies into a business', *Business Week*, 23 June 1973, pp. 116–25.
6. 'M*A*S*H*E*D', *Time*, 11 January 1971, pp. 71–2.
7. 'New kind of movie shakes Hollywood', *Business Week*, 3 January 1970, pp. 40–5.

CHAPTER 4

The Changing of the Guard

In 1965 the film industry stood on the threshold of yet more far-reaching changes. Some of these bore directly on outdated industry practices and could have been foreseen; others related to seismic cultural shifts that Hollywood was as slow to recognise as the rest of America. In any event, in the mid-1960s Hollywood seemed more becalmed than in crisis. The new post-*Paramount* order had established itself; the studios were not generally in financial meltdown, although much was staked on each year's crop of big road-showed blockbusters; the influx of TV talent – most recently Sam Peckinpah, whose second film *Ride the High Country* (MGM 1962), a luminous elegiac Western, announced the arrival of a major talent – proved there was life yet in the Hollywood hills. Yet overall there was little sense of dynamism or innovation. The films of the European New Waves were causing enormous excitement at festivals and art houses, but how such radical departures from convention could be imported into the American commercial film industry was unclear.

The facts of postwar life remained unchanged. Audiences continued to shrink: the last decade had seen admissions halve again and in 1966 annual attendances would dip for the first time below the symbolically important 1 billion mark. Movies had lost three-quarters of their audience in just 20 years and had still not touched bottom. Movies continued to be America's favourite single spectator pastime, outstripping theatre and professional sports, but by mid-decade this statistic too was reaching a symbolic tipping-point: in 1966–7, for the first time since records began, movies attracted less than half of American spectator expenditure. All of the studios (except Disney, which throughout the early 1960s continued to dominate the family market with animated features such as 101 *Dalmatians* (1961) and live-action family films such as *Swiss Family Robinson* (1960), capping this with the vastly successful *Mary Poppins*, the top-grossing film of 1964) persisted in the strategy with

'Just drifting': Mike Nichols (standing, in sunglasses) directs Dustin Hoffman in *The Graduate* (Avco Embassy 1967). Reproduced courtesy of The Kobal Collection

which they had weathered the fifties: reduced production, mostly partnering with independents, and a heavy reliance on roadshowed blockbusters, both historical epics and Broadway musicals. The total number of films released by the seven majors fell by 22 per cent (from 184 to 144) between 1960 and 1964, with Fox (from forty-nine to just eighteen in the catastrophic aftermath of *Cleopatra*) and Columbia (thirty-five to nineteen) showing particularly sharp cutbacks. Of these, moreover, just 119 were produced by US companies (the majors and their independent partners) and sixty-five were imported, mostly from Britain. There were in any case far fewer cinemas to screen the films the studios did make: the total number of US theatres was approaching its all-time low of just over 13,000 (down from nearly 19,000 in 1946) as the fifties drive-in boom began to wane. Unsurprisingly, the film industry had lost a quarter of its workforce (some 60,000 employees) in the postwar period.

Television meanwhile was no longer the upstart newcomer but a ubiquitous presence in American culture and economy, and a crucial financial lifeline for the struggling Hollywood behemoths. From the boom in network TV sales of theatrical releases vital revenues flowed into studio coffers. All of the studios also supported TV production arms, but to the old majors these remained, despite their contribution to the balance sheets, ugly ducklings – unfortunate necessities lacking the prestige of the theatrical divisions, to be tolerated rather than championed. The trend continued that during the fifties had seen the smaller studios such as Columbia and United Artists, unencumbered by the expectations and traditions of the old majors, move quickest to grasp the opportunities for ancillary revenues offered by the new medium. Disney (which in 1955 added the iconic *Mickey Mouse Club* to the ongoing *Disneyland*, with even greater success) and Columbia (whose Screen Gems TV production-distribution division accounted for some 40 per cent of the company's annual revenues in the early 1960s) surged ahead while lumbering behemoths such as MGM floundered for direction.

Most successful of all was the new entity MCA-Universal, formed in 1962 when, under pressure from the Kennedy Justice Department, MCA president Lew Wasserman divested his company of its original talent agency business (now a minor part of his empire) and added Universal-International Pictures[1] to the 400-acre Universal City backlot MCA had acquired in 1959. Under Wasserman MCA-Universal became the first true media conglomerate, whose massively successful television production arm (MCA's Revue Productions had by some estimates grown to produce 60 per cent of all network filmed programming by 1960) to all intents and purposes subsidised its struggling theatrical division through the first half of the decade as Wasserman reorganised and renovated the company. In 1964 Wasserman followed Disney's lead beyond film into the wider and immensely lucrative leisure field, opening the Universal Studios Tour, which in time would rival Disneyland itself as a tourist attraction. The following year MCA produced the first feature-length made-for-TV movie, instantly creating a profitable new market for modestly budgeted studio product tailor-made for the small screen.[2] Throughout the coming decade, Wasserman would drive forward the expansion, innovation and diversification of the media – no longer simply the movie – business. The challenge MCA's competitors faced was whether they could find ways (and leaders) to match him. As it proved, they would not be drawn from Hollywood's dwindling gene pool; Wasserman's success had drawn Hollywood to the attention of an altogether bigger class of shark.[3]

THE NEW SHERIFFS

In the early 1960s, although a majority of Hollywood's founding fathers and golden age moguls had died or retired, most of the big studios remained 'in the family', under the control of their hand-picked successors or colleagues. Some famous aging titans still remained: Jack Warner (who had replaced his elder brother Harry as studio president during an acrimonious battle for control of the company in 1956), Barney Balaban at Paramount, and of course Walt Disney. Fox saw the comeback of a legendary mogul when Spyros Skouras, president and CEO of Fox since 1944,[4] in 1962 gave way to former production chief Darryl Zanuck, returning to the company after a six-year absence. Market observers did not fail to note that, Disney aside, it was the two companies which had fallen into entirely new hands – Universal and UA – that seemed hardiest and healthiest. And they drew the obvious conclusions: new ownership and management could turn the ailing Hollywood behemoths into profitable modern businesses.

The studios had long been publicly traded, hence like other companies answerable to variety of individual and institutional shareholders. But until the mid-1960s control of a studio had never passed altogether outside of the entertainment community (UA's Krim and Benjamin were experienced entertainment lawyers who had previously headed the minor studio Eagle-Lion; Lew Wasserman was of course the ultimate industry insider; even Howard Hughes had a long if chequered relationship with Hollywood dating back to the early sound era). This all changed when in October 1966 Charles Bluhdorn's industrial conglomerate Gulf and Western Industries, Inc. (Gulf + Western) bought Paramount for $144 million, setting off a wave of such buyouts; by the end of the decade only Columbia, Disney and Fox would remain independent companies.

Paramount's absorption into Bluhdorn's sprawling empire suddenly put it on the cutting edge of mid-1960s American business practice. Gulf + Western was a paradigmatic example of the new diversified conglomerate: a corporate entity whose strength was founded not in its narrow concentration of activity on one specialist field, but exactly the opposite – by operating in a large number of essentially unrelated but complementary areas of business and industry, thus profiting from market trends and cycles in one aspect of the business while hedging against under-performance in others. From very modest origins in 1958, in less than a decade Gulf + Western's assets – which at the time of the Paramount takeover included interests in natural gas, mining, agriculture, construction, defence contracting, paper products and auto parts, as well real estate and financial services – had increased from just $12 million to more than $2 billion.[5]

Bluhdorn was attracted to the idea of acquiring a Hollywood studio partly for hard-headed business reasons: the studios' film libraries represented a valuable asset in terms of future TV sales, while the box office success of some early sixties roadshow spectaculars promised (chimerically, as things turned out) growing profits ahead. Movie stocks were also undervalued in the mid-sixties, having yet to recover fully from the slump in their valuations during the fifties. With just one top five release since 1960, and that hardly a blockbuster (*The Carpetbaggers*, earning $15.5m in 1964),[6] and a board whose average age was over seventy, Paramount was an obvious target for takeover and rejuvenation. Also, rather like the jowly congressmen of HUAC twenty years earlier, besuited businessmen in the affluent but (in this pre-1980s era) unglamorous and anonymous environs of Wall Street were far from immune to the attractions of bathing in the reflected glow of the world's most glamorous industry.[7]

It was less clear whether Bluhdorn had the prescience in 1966 to realise that acquiring a movie studio would give his company a strategic advantage in the rapid evolution the US economy was already undergoing. American white-collar workers had outnumbered blue-collar workers since 1956: the US had become the world's first 'post-industrial' economy. The Paramount takeover was a first step towards what was not yet called the information economy – the intangible world of ideas, images, knowledge and the systems to deliver them which over the next thirty years would transform American business even as the 'old economy' activities in which Gulf + Western were in 1966 so heavily invested continued to decline in both value and importance.

One man who certainly did recognise this was Steven Ross, head of Kinney National Services, which in early 1969 beat off competition from another conglomerate, Commonwealth United, to become the owner of Warner Bros.-Seven Arts (as Warners had been renamed following its merger with the far smaller but much more dynamic Canadian film distribution company Seven Arts in 1967).[8] Originating in 1897 as a New York funeral parlour, by 1969 Kinney was not only America's largest operator of parking lots but also boasted (alongside florist shops, contract cleaners and banking) a growing entertainment empire that included a sports licensing arm, publishing and ownership of the lens manufacturer Panavision. The Kinney/Warners takeover would join MCA's earlier acquisition of Universal as an enduringly successful venture, in large part because in coming years Steve Ross would press forward with the business logic Wasserman had already understood in 1962.[9] (Gulf + Western/Paramount would ultimately follow a similar route but took longer to arrive at its destination, possibly owing to Bluhdorn's own domineering and somewhat pigheaded personality.)

In the late 1960s, as the film industry's fortunes took a sudden and drastic turn for the worse, the strength of their other commercial and industrial holdings would sustain the floundering movie companies; then, as industrial economies across the developed world entered a period of long-term decline and structural change kicked off by the 1973 oil crisis, these companies would progressively divest themselves of their outdated and now burdensome and unproductive holdings and smoothly accelerate into the new economic era. By 1973, Paramount (flush with the success of *The Godfather*) had become Gulf + Western's second most profitable division.[10] As 'diversification' yielded to 'synergy' as buzzwords of the moment among business theorists and strategists, they would emerge retooled and rebranded as a new species, the dedicated media conglomerate, tightly focused on the business of media and information in all its varieties. All eyes were on the still-untapped market for domestic consumption of movies not through network broadcasts but direct to the consumer, either through subscription services or on one of the new consumable media such as videocassette. From 1969 Ross set about divesting Kinney of its non-media businesses, raising $500 million in working capital and in 1972 naming his reorganised company Warner Communications; throughout the mid-seventies Warner acquired pay-TV cable systems. Following Bluhdorn's death in 1983 and Martin Davis' taking of the corporate helm, Gulf + Western finally mutated into Paramount Communications in 1987, by which time the synergistic vision pursued by Wasserman and Ross had become the industry norm. What some mid-sixties observers took for little more than a trophy, a glittering but impractical adornment to hardly productive businesses, would now become the motor of their enormously enhanced prosperity.

Not every sixties conglomerate takeover was successful or even beneficial. Having acquired United Artists in 1967, the financial services and insurance conglomerate Transamerica Corporation did little to refashion its core existing business in the image of its new one. In the long term – especially once Krim and Benjamin's relationship with Transamerica soured in the early 1970s, leading to their departure to form a new studio, Orion, in 1978 – this would leave UA orphaned by its unsympathetic corporate parent, with ultimately fatal consequences for the company founded by Chaplin, Pickford, Fairbanks and Griffith in 1919.

A different but also dismal fate awaited MGM, whose embroilment in the sixties takeover frenzy previewed one of the least attractive new American business trends, asset stripping. In summer 1969, MGM suffered the predatory attentions of Kirk Kerkorian, a Las Vegas-based casino and airline mogul. Kerkorian's sudden interest was merely the latest chapter in an all-but-unending succession of battles for control of the company since the mid-fifties. A listless box office performance since 1956, when longtime Loew's president Nick Schenck stepped down, had kept MGM perpetually in play on Wall Street. Some stability had beckoned in 1967 when the distillers Seagram (with support from Time Inc.) had moved to take the largest (though not a controlling) share in MGM. Since then, the studio had been badly hit by the late-sixties roadshow slump and its stock had almost halved in value when Kerkorian made his move. Though strongly resisted by MGM management, a labyrinthine series of financing deals gave Kerkorian the purchasing power he needed to take control in October 1969.[11] No sooner had he done so than – facing losses of over $35 million that year – Kerkorian shut down production on most of MGM's slate for 1970. Under MGM's abrasive new president, former television executive James Aubrey, 5,000 staff were axed over the next three years, the studio's 176-acre backlot was sold off to property developers and, most visibly – and with crushing symbolism for those with a nostalgic attachment to the old Hollywood – the studio's entire inventory of props and equipment, from lights and cameras to Ben-Hur's chariot and the Time Machine, was sold off at public auction. Aubrey also fired some 40 per cent of MGM's staff. While Aubrey made noises about producing cheap, topical pictures for the youth audience, the only remaining profitable arm of Hollywood's erstwhile most iconic studio was its small TV division, a specialist in daytime soaps and late-night genre cheapies.[12] Over the next few years, Aubrey acquired a reputation as a wrecker of creative projects (most infamously Sam Peckinpah's *Pat Garrett and Billy the Kid*, MGM 1973) on a scale to match his corporate vandalism.

Kerkorian meanwhile disposed of most of whatever assets remained on MGM's books. As became evident, his prime motivation in acquiring the studio had been to use the MGM name and logo to brand his new Las Vegas hotel; he held onto MGM's valuable back catalogue but he had little interest in running a company actively making new movies. One of the most mercurial and perplexing figures in contemporary Hollywood, Kerkorian's unpredictable moves kept him a gadfly on the flanks of the emerging New Hollywood leviathans into the twenty-first century, and continued to second-guess industry analysts – but ensured that as a major studio, MGM became little more than a fond memory.[13]

'DICTATORSHIP BY YOUTH'

Once in charge at Paramount, Bluhdorn lost no time hiring a new production head, the freelance producer and sometime bit-part Hollywood actor Robert Evans, who in his turn headhunted the twenty-nine-year-old Stanley Jaffe from Warners. The untested, high-maintenance Evans was only the most eye-catching of a wave of younger executives taking charge in Hollywood, including Ted Ashley at Steve Ross's new-look Warner Bros., and twenty-seven-year-old Richard Zanuck, who had taken over production at Fox upon his father's appointment as president. All had the same urgent brief: find an audience, and give that audience whatever it wanted.

Their freedom of manoeuvre in doing so was enormously eased by another new hire, former Presidential advisor and confidant Jack Valenti, appointed MPAA head in 1966 and tasked, as his first order of business, to retire the antiquated and increasingly irrelevant Production Code. As soon as Valenti took office he undertook a wholesale revision of the Code that effectively stripped it of any meaningful authority. In 1968 he scrapped the Code and its mechanisms of pre-production script approval, replacing it with a ratings system that classified films as released on an age-appropriate basis.[14] The initial ratings were G (general audiences), M (mature audiences), R (restricted; under sixteens must be accompanied by an adult) and X (over sixteen only). In 1969 the age threshold on R and X was raised to seventeen, and the following year M became GP and later PG (parental guidance). (The X rating – not copyrighted by the MPAA – was appropriated by hardcore pornography and became effectively off-limits to mainstream releases.) This move was vital in sanctioning the kinds of decidedly family-unfriendly films towards which Hollywood under its new masters was quickly moving at the end of the 1960s.

Many of the new managers had not apprenticed in the movie business, though some had worked as agents or television executives; they were unashamed to present themselves in conscious contrast to the old moguls – whom they openly derided as profligate and inefficient – as 'more interested in making profits than in making movies'.[15] They were unimpressed by the 'mystique' around moviemaking, which they suspected of being largely a smokescreen to conceal Hollywood's sloppy working practices from proper financial scrutiny. It was no coincidence that vampiric grey-suited money men started to appear incongruously in action films of the period, typically sucking the life-blood from the body of the Westerner (*The Professionals*, Col 1966) or the old-school gangster (*Point Blank*, MGM 1967; *Bring Me the Head of Alfredo Garcia*, MGM 1974).

And yet these outsiders and bean-counters presided, as it proved, over a period of remarkable vitality and creativity in Hollywood filmmaking, one moreover in which creative risk-taking was permissible, even encouraged, and – on occasion – rewarded in ways that would have been unthinkable under the 'undisciplined' studio system. The late 1960s to early 1970s was a period when self-styled mavericks and visionaries dominated moviemaking and the 'steady pair of hands' – the equivalents of Lewis Milestone or Michael Curtiz, the reliable contract directors of old – became decidedly unfashionable. What accounts for this apparent paradox?

The key lay in the perilous financial position that quickly confronted the new studio heads as they took occupancy of their corner offices in the late sixties. Moviegoing was more and more an occasional pastime (at best) for most Americans, accounting for barely three cents in every recreational dollar; only the inflationary effects of the Vietnam War kept gross receipts rising feebly. The life-supporting faucet of network TV revenue was staunched in 1968 when the networks (having acquired more pictures than they could show) suddenly cut back sharply on buying theatrical releases for broadcast. Studio fortunes were even menaced, perversely, by success. The perception of an industry upswing in 1967 encouraged new companies such as CBS and National General to enter theatrical production; the upshot was escalating production costs (as more money chased a fixed roster of bankable talent) and over-production. The shift towards roadshows had seen the annual number of US-produced releases tumble to around 150 in the early 1960s (down from well over 300 a decade earlier). In 1967–8 this rose to almost 180. But the market could no longer support that level of production. By 1969, of the eight major producer-distributors only Disney, Columbia and MCA-Universal were not in the red; between them, the majors recorded losses of $200 million. The non-conglomeratised Fox was especially vulnerable and teetered on the verge of bankruptcy. That year inventories of unshown films had reached $1.2 billion – about three years' worth of production.[16] Studio executives worried, moreover, that many of these films might prove obsolete in a market suddenly chilling to old-style Hollywood entertainment.

Having made a virtue of their indifference to Hollywood tradition, the new studio regimes were unabashed at the prospect of trying new ways of making movies (and hence money). They could hardly have failed to discern the clear pattern emerging from among the many box office losers and few winners of the later 1960s. Amid the wreckage of roadshowed flops such as *Dr Dolittle* and the rest, the impressive returns of two films stood out: the top-grossing film of 1967, *The Graduate* (Avco-Embassy 1967; cost: $3 million, domestic rentals: $49 million) and *Bonnie and Clyde* (Warner 1967; $3m/$24.1m). Several films in 1968–9 indicated a clear trend: *Bob & Carol & Ted & Alice* (Col 1968; $2m/$14.6m), *Goodbye, Columbus* (Col 1969; $1.5m/$10.5m), *Easy Rider* (Raybert/Columbia 1969; $0.6m/$19.1m) and *Midnight Cowboy* (UA 1969; $3.2m/$20.3m). Although only the independently produced negative pickup *Easy Rider* could be classed as low-budget, the rest were all produced on average or below-average budgets. None showed a rate of return much less than 7:1 (far higher for *The Graduate* and *Easy Rider*). Bar *Bonnie and Clyde* (whose director Arthur Penn's first film was *The Left-Handed Gun* at Warner in 1959), all had younger or first-time directors and starred younger, largely unfamiliar actors. All focused on contemporary American life (again *Bonnie and Clyde* was the exception, although it could be argued that the film used its Depression-era setting to explore aspects of contemporary American society) and furthermore many concentrated on its subcultural margins – drifters, bums, bikers, criminals, drop-outs. All enthusiastically exploited the end of the Production Code by portraying sexuality (including homosexuality, partner-swapping, prostitution, sexual relations between generations and abortion) and criminal violence in unprecedentedly graphic ways (*Midnight Cowboy* was rated 'X' on its initial release). A masculinist bias was also evident in the increasing tendency of hit films to focus not on traditional heterosexual romance but on male friendships and partnerships (often, as in *Butch Cassidy* and *Midnight Cowboy*, with the homosocial dimension barely suppressed). Above all, the protagonists of none of these films were much over thirty. (As if to drive the lesson home, Franco Zeffirelli's lush version of *Romeo and Juliet*, accurately casting the doomed lovers as teens, ranked fifth in 1968 with rentals of $17.5 million.)

As Peter Krämer and Steve Neale have pointed out, it was by no means the case that the market for traditional family films had dried up altogether:[17] as proved by strong performances during 1968–9 by *Funny Girl* (Col 1968; cost: $14.1 million – including a record-breaking $1.6 million marketing campaign;[18] domestic rentals: $26.3 million), *Oliver!* (Col 1968; $10m/$16.8m) and Disney's *The Love Bug*, the second highest-grossing film of 1969 ($5m/$23.1m). But for most of these films the ratio of earnings to cost was far lower. As had been increasingly the case in the later roadshow era – most infamously with *Cleopatra* – only the rare breakaway hits could find a large enough audience to justify their price tags. The trend as well as the windfall profits was clearly with the films whose strongest appeal, equally obviously, was to younger audiences – further corroboration being the unexpected appeal of Stanley Kubrick's philosophical science fiction film *2001: A Space Odyssey* ($11m/$24.1m) to hippie 'heads' (Metro's marketers quickly retooled it as 'the ultimate trip'). A famous and widely-circulated *Time* cover article in December 1967 distilled the intoxicating essence of a (at this point still embryonic) 'New American Cinema: Violence . . . Sex . . . Art'.[19] The new studio bosses duly took note, ushering in what *Variety* described in typically hyperbolic fashion in early 1970 as 'Dictatorship By Youth'.

Several surveys conducted around this time would also have affected studio thinking, as market research started to play a significant part in Hollywood forward planning for the first time. A 1972 MPAA survey indicated that people aged eleven to thirty, although they constituted only 39 per cent of the US population, made up 73 per cent of the theatrical audience. Within that audience segment, the same trends applied as across the population: regular moviegoers were far more likely to be college-educated, in higher income brackets, and male. Older people from low-income and blue collar backgrounds were the least likely to go to the movies at all.[20] This profile also coincided with opinion surveys of the same period showing that college-educated Americans under twenty-five typically held far more sceptical or even hostile views towards authority – including government, law enforcement and the military – and more liberal attitudes on sex, race and gender equality. (Daily headlines and TV news bulletins throughout the late 1960s and early 1970s would obviously have indicated much the same thing.)[21] The inescapable conclusion was that the majority moviegoing audience was lining up to see films that seemed more in tune with their own worldview and values, and rejecting those that persisted in propounding the perspectives of their parents' generation. While the latter could still be attracted to theatres for occasional standout productions offering more traditional, family-friendly appeal – outstanding examples in the early 1970s would include *Love Story* (Par 1970; ranked first for its year with rentals of $48.7m), *Airport* (Univ 1970; second/$45.2m), and *Fiddler on the Roof* (Fox 1971; first/$38.3m) – the over-production of roadshow pictures in the late 1960s had proven that a surfeit of such vehicles would not succeed in persuading this audience back into habitual moviegoing. Having so many 'event' movies to choose from devalued the roadshow currency.

The studios' parlous financial position made retrenchment a necessity. Further bellyflopping would-be blockbusters in the 1969–70 season such as Paramount's three strike-outs *Darling Lili* (cost $22m, rentals $3.5m), *On a Clear Day You Can See Forever* ($10m/$5.3m) and *The Molly Maguires* ($11m/$1m) confirmed that the roadshow era was over. Having read these runes, production heads started to search for new young filmmakers who could repeat the success of Arthur Penn, Mike Nichols and the rest. Between 1970 and 1973 directors such as Bob Rafelson (*Five Easy Pieces*, Col 1970), Hal Ashby (*The Landlord*, UA 1970), George Lucas (*THX 1138*, WB 1970), Peter Bogdanovich (*The Last Picture Show*, Col 1971), Philip Kaufman (*The Great Northfield Minnesota Raid*, U 1971), Robert Benton (*Bad Company*, Par 1972), Martin Scorsese (*Mean Streets*, WB 1973), Steven Spielberg (*The Sugarland Express*, U 1973), Terence Malick (*Badlands*, WB 1973), and Michael Cimino (*Thunderbolt and Lightfoot*, UA 1973) made their first studio-distributed pictures. Several other directors with previous industry experience in other areas also made their directorial debuts around this time, including choreographer Bob Fosse (*Sweet Charity*, U 1969), screenwriter Woody Allen (*Take the Money and Run*, UA 1969), and producer Alan J. Pakula (*The Sterile Cuckoo*, Par 1969). Such untried talent, beyond their notional ability to connect with the target youth audience, had the important additional advantage of being inexpensive. Echoing the early post-*Paramount* austerity, most of the studios announced stringent budget limitations in 1970–1, aiming to spend no more than $2–3 million per picture. The younger directors' character-centred films, shot on domestic locations with equally affordable young performers, suited the studios' temporarily tightened belts. 'You don't have to spend a lot of money to make a meaningful story', declared Stanley Jaffe in a typical public statement.[22]

Not that spending big was wholly out of fashion: those directors credited with the breakaway youth-oriented hits of the previous two years got larger budgets and virtual carte blanche, resulting in some serious let-downs such as Nichols's *Catch-22* (Fox 1970; cost $18 million, rentals $12.2 million). Several older and/or more experienced, but hitherto commercially unsuccessful directors, like Penn with the right 'feel', were also able to capitalise on the mood of the times, sometimes very profitably (Robert Altman, *M*A*S*H*, Fox 1970, $3.5m/$37.7m; William Friedkin, *The French Connection*, Fox 1970, $1.8m/$26.3m; Alan J. Pakula, *Klute*, WB 1971, $2.5m/$7m; Sam Peckinpah, *The Getaway*, National General/WB 1972, $3.3m/$18.4m). In 1972, the astonishing success of Francis Ford Coppola's *The Godfather* ($7m/$86m) not only single-handedly redeemed Bluhdorn and Evans's dismal track record but made Coppola and his long-harboured dream of creating a filmmaking atelier, American Zoetrope, the highly visible public (and enthusiastically self-publicising) face of the new cadre of American cineastes. Coppola and his colleagues vocally espoused the cause of the *auteur*, the filmmaker as autonomous artist rather than studio journeyman.

For perhaps five years, it made good business sense to indulge these idealistic claims, and to allow such filmmakers a degree of creative autonomy and freedom from studio oversight that would have been unthinkable in the old Hollywood. Youth-oriented and/or auteurist production companies were embraced at the majors: *Easy Rider* producers BBS at Columbia; Coppola's Zoetrope at Warner; The Directors' Company (Bogdanovich, Friedkin, and Coppola again) at Paramount. As veteran screenwriter Robert Ardrey wrote in a different historical context, it was 'an ideal time to make a film. No one quite knew who owned the studio, no one quite knew what pictures were being made, and no one, therefore, was in a position to intervene'.[23] And Richard Maltby has pointed out that between 1971 and 1975 – the new cinema's peak years – tax shelters originally introduced by the Nixon administration following successful industry lobbying after the 1969–71 slump encouraged outside investment in production financing, while also making investors less focused on the bottom line. The critically lauded, but mostly commercially unsuccessful, early seventies peak of directors such as Altman and Peckinpah likely owed much to this temporarily more forgiving fiscal environment.[24] Out of such conjunctures was born the 'Hollywood Renaissance' of myth and legend.

The late sixties would probably have seen an influx of new talent into Hollywood even had times been less turbulent. Just as the era of the old moguls had passed, similarly the generation of directors that had dominated Hollywood filmmaking in the studio era and the roadshow years had by 1970 largely run its course. Such major filmmakers as John Ford, Howard Hawks, George Cukor, William Wyler, David Lean, Joseph L. Mankiewicz, Otto Preminger, Billy Wilder, Stanley Kramer, Vincente Minnelli, Alfred Hitchcock, Fred Zinneman and Robert Wise had all reached or were approaching the end of their long careers. While several would continue to make films into the 1970s, including some commercial successes (Hitchcock's *Family Plot*, U 1976; Wise's *Star Trek: The Motion Picture*, Par 1979), their best years were behind them. The mid-1960s already had a distinctly transitional flavour as a new cohort of directors, many trained in television, started to make an impact, including John Frankenheimer (*The Manchurian Candidate*; *Seven Days in May*, Seven Arts 1964), the prolific Sidney Lumet (*12 Angry Men*, Col 1957; *Fail-Safe*; *The Pawnbroker*), Blake Edwards (*Breakfast at Tiffany's*, Par 1961; *Days of Wine and Roses*, WB 1962), Franklin J. Schaffner (*The Best Man*, UA 1964; *Planet of the Apes*, Fox 1968), and Norman Jewison (*The Russians Are Coming, The Russians Are Coming*, UA 1966; *In the Heat of the Night*,

UA 1967). Other TV- and theatre-schooled directors would a few years later themselves become strongly identified with the Hollywood Renaissance, most notably Altman (whose career took off with *M*A*S*H*) and Peckinpah, whose *The Wild Bunch* (WB 1969) had more in common with *Psycho* than with *Bonnie and Clyde* in associating a new, visceral era of screen violence with the most radical montage practice since Eisenstein.

The core Renaissance filmmakers came from diverse backgrounds. Alongside the older Penn, Altman and Peckinpah – all born in the 1920s – the best-known were all in their twenties or early thirties at the end of the 1960s. Only a few were film school graduates, including Coppola (UCLA), George Lucas (USC), Martin Scorsese (NYU), and the writer-directors John Milius (UCLA) and Paul Schrader (*Taxi Driver*, Col 1976). Peter Bogdanovich followed the *Cahiers du Cinéma* route into filmmaking, starting his career as a film critic, while Steven Spielberg was a wunderkind director in broadcast TV from 1969 to 1972. Dennis Hopper was a Method actor, a lesser contemporary of Brando and Dean (and a supporting player in *Rebel Without a Cause*). European émigrés gave the Renaissance an international flavour: the Polish-Jewish Holocaust survivor Roman Polanski (*Rosemary's Baby*, Par 1968; *Chinatown*, Par 1974), the Czech Milos Forman, a refugee from the Prague Spring of 1968 (*One Flew Over the Cuckoo's Nest*, UA 1975), and the Britons John Schlesinger (*Midnight Cowboy*) and John Boorman (*Point Blank*; *Deliverance*, WB 1972). The last all cut their teeth in their various national New Waves, but several of the native-born directors had served apprenticeships grinding out cheap exploitation quickies for Roger Corman at AIP, including Coppola (*Dementia 13*, 1963), Scorsese (*Boxcar Bertha*, 1970), and Bogdanovich (who uniquely managed with his seven-day shoot and borrowed star, Boris Karloff, to produce a genuinely disturbing and original contemporary horror film, *Targets* (1968) that owed nothing to Corman's Gothic kitsch).

Out of the Renaissance new stars were born, many somewhat unconventional by traditional studio charm-school standards: Elliott Gould, Donald Sutherland, Jack Nicholson, Robert Duvall. Some were unmistakably ethnic, again countering old Hollywood's homogenising tendencies: Italian-Americans Al Pacino and Robert deNiro, Jewish-Americans Dustin Hoffman, Barbra Streisand, Mel Brooks, Gene Wilder, and actor-writer-director Woody Allen (most black actors aside from Sidney Poitier, a star since the fifties, struggled to break out of the 'blaxploitation' ghetto; see below). In this period character actors such as George C. Scott or Gene Hackman could headline a picture in their own right (winning Oscars in successive years 1970–1, for *Patton* and *The French Connection*, respectively). Of course there continued to be a place for conventionally attractive leading men and ladies, but the most important male stars – Steve McQueen, Clint Eastwood, Warren Beatty, even Robert Redford, all of whom took a hands-on roles as producers or producer-directors of most of their films – seemed content to present less ingratiating screen personae than Cary Grant or Henry Fonda. This was an era of few major female stars and it is noticeable that those few who did emerge, such as Streisand and Jane Fonda, did so by establishing tough, 'ballsy' public images and were also unafraid to appear unsympathetic both on and off screen.

The new filmmakers delivered the goods, though as it turned out not through the 'youth-oriented' films of 1969–70, which produced only one major hit, the documentary of *Woodstock* (WB 1970); but that was just as obviously a one-off – its longer-term significance was the chart-topping synergistic relationship of the film and the (Warner label) soundtrack album.[25] After 1970 few Hollywood films, and none by major Renaissance directors, directly portrayed the counterculture (which by the early 1970s was in any case ebbing and mutating), although some Westerns such as *Kid Blue* (Fox 1973) and Peckinpah's *Pat Garrett and Billy the Kid* (MGM 1973) clearly allegorised contemporary youth–Establishment conflicts. Many of the films that became synonymous with the auteur-led New American Cinema dealt either with aspects of contemporary middle-class or working-class American life; still more worked within genre frameworks, either traditional genres such as the Western and the police procedural or newer modes such as the road movie and a revitalised *noir* (or neo-*noir*), establishing their auteurist credentials by the revisionist spin they put upon these familiar forms (see Chapter 6).

NEW FRONTIERS

Alongside the vaunted emergence of an American art cinema, however, a less heralded but ultimately more influential trend was also taking shape: the shift away from traditional genres and towards both the forms and the associated practices of exploitation film. A comparison of the top twenty box office hits of 1961–4 and 1971–4 reveals a decline in the popularity of tried and trusted genres, including not only musicals (from thirteen to six – including such untraditional latter-day entries as *Cabaret*, *Lady Sings the Blues*, and the MGM compilation *That's Entertainment!*) but also romantic comedy (from nine to two), melodramas (from eight to four) and of course family films (from eleven to six, all Disney). Vanished altogether were the war/combat film (five in 1961–4) and the historical epic (eight). On the rise were police procedural thrillers (none in the early sixties, eight in the seventies), gangster films (from one – the joky Rat Pack vehicle *Robin and the Seven Hoods* – to five, or six if one counts *The Sting*), science fiction (one marginal entry, *Dr Strangelove*, to five), horror (one, *The Birds*, to three), detective thrillers (none to four), and, perhaps surprisingly, Westerns (three to five).[26] Alongside these long-standing but newly ascendant types in the early seventies were some wholly novel genres. One of these (blaxploitation, three entries) was a low-budget genre, the other (the disaster film, five) very expensive; both, however, marked a trend towards exploitation cinema. (So too did hardcore pornography, by no means a new genre, of course, but one that had never previously troubled *Variety*'s record keepers; a brief porno vogue in 1972–3 saw two X-rated films, *Deep Throat* and *The Devil in Miss Jones*, ranked number 7 and number 11 in successive years.)

This summary reveals a historic shift away from American cinema's chosen path since 1915, when Griffith's *The Birth of a Nation* consciously aimed to steer the young medium away from its carnivalesque origins towards the respectability of the legitimate theatre, substituting – more accurately, mitigating – spectacle with story, sensation with character, and brawling topicality with historical sobriety. Not coincidentally, the only deviations of note from this house-trained cinema were the gangster films and sex comedies of the 'pre-Code' early 1930s – another period when, hit by the Depression, over-extension in their theatre chains and the costs of the conversion to sound, several studios were in major financial difficulties. The troubled early seventies similarly saw studio resources diverted away from those genres that had traditionally commanded both large audiences and critical respect, such as historical drama and large-scale musicals, and investing in others which had generally been the province of B movies and the exploitation sector. The most obvious examples are horror and science fiction, with two X-rated examples released by Warners standing out, one in each genre: *The Exorcist* (WB 1973, capitalising on the earlier success of *Rosemary's Baby* (Par 1968)) and *A Clockwork Orange* (WB 1971).

Very clear too is the gender trend towards the genres historically favoured by male moviegoers over women – including even the Western, which other evidence might lead one to expect to see in decline at this time.[27] It is worth pointing out that all of the genres on the upswing in this period routinely feature acts of violence – indeed both the Western and the horror film, in different ways, might be said to be about violence – and of the thirty-seven films cited here (excluding the two porn films), twenty-four were rated 'R' or 'X'.[28] Sexual content figures much less prominently in this group of films: only seven feature significant nudity, for example (although sexual violence was a disturbing presence in several films, particularly of course *A Clockwork Orange*). Finally, the decline of musicals, epics and war films, combined with a move away from runaway production towards domestic location filming and an overall lowering of budgets, shifted Hollywood films away from exotic foreign settings and subjects and multi-national casts towards a much more distinctively contemporary and American focus (Peter Krämer has suggested this may reflect a backlash against overseas entanglements in the wake of Vietnam[29]).

In short, Hollywood's output in the early seventies was starting to resemble the staple programming of the drive-in and the grindhouse – which also of course appealed strongly to the youth audience whose custom the studios were so earnestly soliciting. This audience, however, if as a whole differentiated from the less reliable older adult market for more traditional films, was itself heterogeneous, divided by region, education and above all race. Awareness of the potential market significance of these divisions gave rise to one of the most notable and highly visible cycles of the early 1970s, blaxploitation.[30] The intensive production of over a hundred black-themed action films, sparked by the success of *Cotton Comes to Harlem* (UA 1970), the independently produced, uncompromising and thoroughly inflammatory *Sweet Sweetback's Baaadasssss Song* (Yeah 1971) and *Shaft* (MGM 1971), was of course partly a function of the centrality of race to American political culture in the late sixties and early seventies, and more specifically to pressure from civil rights groups for Hollywood to improve its lamentable record of both portraying and employing African Americans. However, it was also a recognition on the studios' part of the economic importance of black urban moviegoers (especially young males), by the late 1960s the core audience in many markets at the remaining first-run inner-city theatres. While many blaxploitation pictures were independently made, it is often hard to find much to distinguish between studio-released films and those from traditional exploitation companies; almost all had low budgets, featured a repertory company of black action stars such as Jim Brown and Pam Grier, relied on strongly generic narratives set in the crime- and drug-ridden black ghettoes of major US cities, and portrayed strongly individualistic – but also non-political – black heroes fending off 'The Man', who took the form of authoritarian figures (police, corrupt officials, gang bosses) both black and white.[31]

Dollar-for-dollar, during its brief lifespan the blaxploitation cycle was enormously profitable. Its decline after 1975 may have resulted from the studios' realisation that the black inner-city audience could be drawn equally to the non-black-themed action films it started to produce in the wake of *Jaws*, which could be expected to out-perform the latter in mostly white suburban markets. Blaxploitation's success confirmed existing trends towards high-impact action- and sensation-oriented genres such as horror, gangster and police films. All these genres, blaxploitation not least, have been the subject of ongoing ideological analysis – often discovering a contradictory blend of progressive and reactionary elements reflecting the confused and volatile mood of the Nixon and Ford years (see Chapter 6). In any case, Hollywood's move towards exploitation had an inbuilt logic extending beyond generic form or content to its core business of distributing, and in particular promoting, its films.

Kevin Heffernan's research has established that black inner-city audiences were in the mid-1960s also the principal targets of certain marketing techniques – wide opening on a regional and citywide basis accompanied by saturation TV, radio and print advertising to clearly defined audience demographics – used by independent and exploitation distributors of low-budget horror films. Such techniques prioritised 'marketability' – the technique of opening a film in as many venues as possible simultaneously, with a barrage of high-impact print and spot TV advertising – over 'playability' (a film's ability to expand its audience week-on-week through favourable critical reception and word of mouth). Exploitation films depended on high-intensity advertising to instil curiosity and short-term demand; once word got out about the generally mediocre (or worse) quality of the picture itself, it was time to move on to the next market. Such techniques had occasionally been adopted by the major studios, for example for *The Carpetbaggers* (Par 1964), or where the profile of studio product was similar to exploitation films (a fifties creature feature such as Warners' *Them!* or a pop spin-off such as The Beatles' *A Hard Day's Night* (UA 1964), both released 'wide'), but in the trade they were generally tainted by association with the exploitation quickies' 'get out of town fast' tactics for hard-selling dross. In the post-*Paramount* era, the majors mostly replaced the old run-clearance system with a broader two-tier release strategy of 'platforming' films in first-run houses followed by a rolling wider release to suburban and outlying theatres over weeks and months. As the studios closed in on traditional exploitation territory, however, the latter's marketing paradigm was widely adopted and adjusted to the marketing and promotion of major studio films.

The new tactics started to make their presence felt as early as 1971 with *The Godfather*, which Paramount released in 355 theatres. *The Godfather* heralded Hollywood's future: the lavish, large-scale treatment of genre material traditionally identified with cheaper productions. *The Exorcist* moved the affinity several significant steps closer, generically (horror was a good deal more 'unrespectable' still than crime); stylistically (the film's barrage of obscenity and transgressive imagery was unprecedented for a studio release); and commercially (Warner not only released the film wide but 'four-walled' it, renting theatres outright for the duration of the film's run and claiming 100 per cent of the box-office take, a tactic borrowed directly from Tom Laughlin's immensely successful promotion of his hippie-vigilante flick *Billy Jack* in 1971).[32] *Billy Jack*'s exploitation of television spot advertising probably also influenced Lew Wasserman's legendary promotional campaign for *Jaws* in 1975, whose colossal success naturally codified Hollywood-style exploitation as the new orthodoxy.[33] Notwithstanding the roadshow era's 'sell them big' mantra, until the seventies Hollywood marketing had not progressed much beyond traditional ballyhooing. After *Jaws*, Hollywood (like many other industries) raised marketing to the status of a science, if not a religion: the industry's total promotional outlay rose 350 per cent from around $200 million in 1970 to over $700 million in 1980, with TV advertising (less than 10 per cent in 1970) now accounting for almost 30 per cent of that spending. Average marketing costs per picture rose from $680,000 in 1970 to $3 million in 1980, but this tells only part of the story: for the biggest blockbusters publicity budgets regularly exceeded production costs. *Alien* (Fox 1979) cost $10.8 million to make, but $15.7 million to advertise.[34]

The studios incurred significant additional costs from the number of prints required for saturation booking, which continued to trend upwards. By the early 1980s simultaneous opening on over 1000 screens was not unusual: in 1981, *Superman II* opened on 1,397 screens; the following year *Star Trek II: the Wrath of Khan* debuted on 1,621. This was in turn made possible by the long-awaited upswing in domestic exhibition. Starting in the late 1960s, new companies such as General Cinema and American Multi-Cinema (AMC) had begun constructing new multiplex cinemas in suburban shopping malls, finally severing Hollywood's reliance on the old inner-city picture palaces, many of which were (as in Columbus) now in disrepair or being demolished. Thus while between 1974 and 1980 the number of US *cinemas* remained stable at a postwar low of just over 13,000, in the same period more than 3,000 additional *screens* were added, almost all small-medium multiplex auditoria in the profitable suburban markets, just as the studios shifted to a policy of wide release. From 1980 the rate of increase picked up even more sharply.[35] Meanwhile, annual attendances at last bottomed out at 820 million in 1971 and by the early 1980s were approaching 1.2 billion, levels not seen since the early 1960s. (See Appendix.)

Increased studio spending, drawing a line under the economy drive of the early 1970s, was motivated by the prospect of enormous, indeed unprecedented, returns. Over the course of the decade, first *Love Story*, which returned rentals of $50 million to Paramount in 1971, then successively *The Godfather* ($87m), *The Exorcist* ($89m), *Jaws* ($129m) and then of course *Star Wars* (Fox 1977, $167m) all dramatically raised the bar of box office success. In so doing, they affected industry thinking in three particularly important ways. Firstly, such hits exerted an absolute domination over their competition, earning perhaps twice as much as the films placed second or third that year. Successes such as these could single-handedly sustain a studio's yearly operations, underwriting less profitable and loss-making releases. 'If you have your *Godfather*', observed *Godfather*-less Columbia's Leo Jaffe in 1973, 'you can do no wrong'.[36] The annual quest for such 'tentpole' pictures became a marked feature of studio filmmaking as the decade drew on. Second, *Jaws* and *Star Wars* in particular exponentially expanded the familiar postwar concept of an 'event' movie to an inescapable trans-media presence, something like a ubiquitous nationwide obsession. Audiences, it appeared, eagerly wished to participate – often repeatedly – in the 'experience' these ineffable phenomena offered. Of course, gold-plated guarantees of such transcendent success were hard to come by: the utterly unexpected supremacy of *Star Wars*, widely perceived as more or less George Lucas's folly right up to its release, was famously a case in point. Many of the biggest properties of the 1970s, however, were both pre-sold and cross-promoted: production of *Love Story*, *The Godfather* and *Jaws* was in each case already underway before the bestselling novels were published, and the publicity campaigns for the latter primed audiences.[37] Many also boasted what would come to be known as a 'high concept', an easy-to-grasp – and promote – premise ('a giant shark terrorises a New England tourist resort'): other major late-seventies/early-eighties hits such as Warner's big budget *Superman* (1979, $83m), the rock 'n' roll musical *Grease* (Par 1979, $96.3m) and the Spielberg–Lucas collaboration *Raiders of the Lost Ark* (Par 1981, $115.6m) were similarly conceived. While there was no way to ensure a game-changing success such as *Star Wars*, massive promotional campaigns aimed at making the 'brand identity' of each new product unmissable and inescapable offered as good a chance as any. Finally, the post-*Jaws* mega-hits were alike in one other conspicuous regard: none were promoted on the basis of art or auteurism.

EXIT THE AUTEURS

Chapter 7 will examine in greater detail the long-term consequences of the historic success of *Jaws* and, especially, *Star Wars* that allowed the full realisation of the synergistic visions of Lew Wasserman and Steve Ross (and those that followed in their footsteps in the 1980s). A more immediate effect was the demise of the auteur-oriented filmmaking of the Hollywood Renaissance. Even this did not occur overnight, however, and the cause–effect process was perhaps less straightforward than some accounts suggest. The responsibility for the much-lamented downfall of an American art cinema fell not only on the 'suits' – who would in time-honoured fashion take the fall – but on the Hollywood auteurs themselves.

By 1977, there were hints that the creative energies fuelling the Renaissance were starting to ebb. The previous four years (1973–6) had seen a mutually beneficial partnership between the majors and the auteur generation of directors. Of course not every such picture was a success, but of the forty films in the top ten during these years more than half could plausibly be classified as Renaissance, including such breakout hits as *The Exorcist*, *American Graffiti* (U 1973; third/$55.1m), *One Flew Over the Cuckoo's Nest* (UA 1975; second/$60m), *A Star Is Born* (WB 1976; second/$37.1m) and of course *Jaws*. As already noted, old Hollywood was not dead and gone. The most consistent challenge to the youth-oriented trend came from the series of disaster films following on from the success of *Airport* in 1970: in this four-year period *The Towering Inferno* (Fox/WB 1974; first/$48.9m), *Earthquake* (U 1974; fourth/$35.9m), *Airport 1975* (U 1974 (oddly); seventh/$25.3m) and *King Kong* (Par 1976; third/$37m) were all profitable examples of these expensively-mounted, star-studded, family-friendly action spectaculars, all anonymously directed by safe pairs of veteran hands.[38] Handsome costume dramas of different types set between the two world wars – *The Sting* (U 1973; second/$78.2m), *The Way We Were* (Col 1973; fifth/$22.5m), *Murder on the Orient Express* (Par 1974; tenth/$19.1m), *Funny Lady* (Col 1975; eighth/$19.3m) also did surprisingly well.

In 1977, however, there was a discernible shift in audience taste and/or the Renaissance filmmakers' finger on the public pulse. Although all three of the year's runaway successes, *Star Wars*, *Close Encounters of the Third Kind*, and *Saturday Night Fever* ($210m, $78m, $74m, respectively), could certainly be classed as New Hollywood films, as discussed elsewhere the fantasy orientation of the first two marks a move away from the social consciousness of many Renaissance films earlier in the decade,[39] while the gritty blue-collar setting and social commentary of *Saturday Night Fever* was generally overlooked in the disco fever the film ignited and the synergistic success of its soundtrack album.[40] Beneath these the year's top ten bore a distinctly more conservative flavour, including screwball comedies (*The Goodbye Girl*, MGM/WB, fifth/$42m), redneck farce (*Smokey and the Bandit*, U, fourth/$59m), seaborne adventure (*The Deep*, Col, seventh/$31m), a Bond film and, following up on *Midway* (U 1976; tenth/$21.6m), the first traditional World War II combat film to dent the top ten since *The Dirty Dozen* (MGM 1967), Richard Attenborough's mammoth recreation of the battle of Arnhem, *A Bridge Too Far* (UA, tenth/$21m). Such a line-up seemed to confirm hints from the previous year's resuscitation of the sports film (*Rocky*, UA, first/$56.5m; *The Bad News Bears*, Par, seventh/$24.9m) and the glossy adventure-romance (*Silver Streak*, Fox, fourth/$30m) that the wind was changing. Few of the major hits of 1978 – apart from possibly the sleeper *Cheech and Chong's Up In Smoke* (Par, ninth/$28.3m) – could unproblematically be set alongside the Renaissance films either. They included *Grease* (Par, first/$96.3m; the first traditional musical to top the annual chart in seven years), *Superman* (WB, second/$83m; another major step down the juvenile path blazed by *Star Wars*), a successful example of a new 1970s trend, the numbered sequel (*Jaws 2*, U, fifth/$50.4m), two more profitable ventures into redneck comedy (*Every Which Way But Loose*, WB, fourth/$52m; *Hooper*, WB, seventh/$35m), further evidence of a revival in two romantic comedies from Paramount (*Heaven Can Wait*, sixth/$49.4m; *Foul Play*, tenth/$27.5m) and even a non-musical Broadway stage adaptation (*California Suite*, Col, eighth/$28.4m), the first top-ten film of this kind since *The Odd Couple* a decade earlier (and from the same dramatist,

Neil Simon). The third-placed film, the gross-out comedy *Animal House* (U, $70.9m) combined aspects of *M*A*S*H* and *American Graffiti* and was certainly youth oriented, but directed itself firmly toward adolescent vulgarity rather than student revolt, an increasingly distant memory by 1978. According to Paramount chairman Barry Diller, Hollywood had made 'a decision to get into pictures that made people feel good'. *Time* applauded the industry's emergence from 'ten years of soul-searching, issue-oriented movies'.[41]

While the winds changed, the auteurs were busy on a series of visionary disasters that would help seal their fate. An early omen of the possible consequences of untrammelled auteurism had been Dennis Hopper's follow-up to *Easy Rider*, *The Last Movie*, which disappeared in a Peruvian haze of acid and expensive improvisation. Hopper did not work again as a director in the USA for seventeen years. But his folly (which only cost Universal $1 million) was dwarfed by the colossal blow-outs of his peers later in the decade. Between 1977 and 1981, some of the most talismanic directors of the seventies generation turned in films that sought to paint highly personal visions on the largest possible canvas, in an unprecedented blend of auteur principles and old-style Hollywood extravagance. The saga of the ultimate runaway production, Francis Coppola's Vietnam epic *Apocalypse Now*, a fifteen-month shoot (including a five-month shutdown following hurricane damage) in the Philippines which cost Coppola his marriage, one leading actor and much of his personal fortune, became a media story in its own right and eventually cost United Artists some $32 million. UA also picked up the tab for Martin Scorsese's $14 million deconstruction of the backstage musical *New York, New York* while at Fox, Bob Fosse spent $13 million on another modernist musical, the black semi-autobiographical comedy *All That Jazz*, complete with scenes of open-heart surgery. Steven Spielberg, untouchable after *Jaws* and *Close Encounters*, proceeded to blow $35 million of Universal and Columbia's money on the supersized wartime farce *1941*. William Friedkin followed up *The Exorcist* with *Sorcerer*, a remake of the French classic *The Wages of Fear*, another tortuous location shoot that cost Fox $22 million.

Apocalypse Now was a gamble that paid off, or at least paid for itself, ultimately returning $37.8 million to UA;[42] *New York, New York*, however, turned in just $6 million. *1941*'s $23.3 million rental was respectable enough – but not when set against mammoth costs; a similar reckoning could be made of *All That Jazz* at $20 million. *Sorcerer*, meanwhile, was (perhaps appropriately) an outright car-wreck, earning just $6 million. Of these films, all except perhaps *1941* were shot through with the pessimism and cynicism that had so marked the decade but which *Star Wars* and *Close Encounters* had suddenly made unfashionable. Pessimism and cynicism – not to mention fatalism and a radical revisionist class perspective on American history – were present in spades in UA's strike-out third, and hugest, auteurist catastrophe in 1980,

Michael Cimino's *Heaven's Gate*. An out-of-control production driven by a mania for historical authenticity and artistic freedom, combined with a complete indifference to cost control, drove the budget towards a rumoured $40 million; equal indifference to narrative and characterisation, plus a media backlash against 'directors' cinema' epitomised by *New York Times* critic Vincent Canby's irresistibly quotable judgment of the film as 'an unqualified disaster', ensured the film had minimal prospects of making much of it back. *Heaven's Gate* was withdrawn from distribution (poisoning relations with exhibitors) and hastily recut,[43] but it took just $1.5 million and its failure ultimately persuaded Transamerica to offload the loss-making studio into the black hole of Kirk Kerkorian-owned MGM for $380 million.[44] Ironically, the same promise of creative freedom which had allowed UA to transform the ossified conventions of studio filmmaking in the 1950s seemed to have mutated and devoured the company three decades later.[45]

Critical opinion was divided on these films at the time; several, notably *New York, New York*, *All That Jazz* and indeed *Heaven's Gate*, are today regarded as among the most significant films of the period. But they were manifestly out of temper with the changing times. The last hurrah of late-seventies large-scale personal cinema, Warren Beatty's *Reds*, a $35 million biopic of journalist John Reed, a founder of the American Communist Party, returned Paramount $22 million in 1981, and earned Oscars for Vittorio Storaro's exquisite photography and for Beatty himself; but aesthetically it was as hopelessly out of place in a top ten list headed by *Raiders of the Lost Ark*, *Superman II* and *Arthur* as its politics were in the first year of Ronald Reagan's presidency.

The end of Hollywood's short-lived 'auteur era' was not simply – as self-serving studio publicity and a compliant media insisted – a question of mammoth egos, poor discipline and quixotic projects on the part of directors who had come to believe their own publicity. Enormous budgets and colossal overspends remained regular features of Hollywood practice: in 1979, for example, *Star Trek: the Motion Picture*, originally budgeted at $15 million, eventually cost Paramount $42 million; Warner ended up spending $55 million on *Superman*. The difference, of course, was that such fantasy blockbusters were following in *Star Wars*' footsteps to (as it seemed) virtually limitless profits, massively enhanced by the prospect of revenues from tie-in promotions and merchandising. By a neat irony, the runaway successes delivered by Renaissance directors – *The Exorcist*, *Jaws*, *Star Wars* – were films of a new kind that firmly closed the window for creative experimentation that had briefly opened at the start of the decade.

New York, New York and *Reds*, by contrast, had little teen appeal and offered little opportunity for comic books, action figures, product placement or sequels. As *Heaven's Gate* had demonstrated, such films involved an unacceptable level of risk that could threaten the viability of an entire company.

The new high-concept blockbusters, by contrast, however wildly expensive, represented what Justin Wyatt calls a 'safe risk': prime commodities on which investors, exhibitors and commercial partners all looked favourably, covering a good deal of production and promotional expenditure before the film was even released (typically on highly preferential terms). They were, in Fox production head Alan Ladd, Jr's words, 'broad-based, through-the-roof movies which kids will go to see two or three times'.[46] And they were unmistakably Hollywood's future.

NOTES

1. As Universal had been renamed following the merger with Leo Spitz and William Goetz's International Pictures in 1946.
2. 'Television: nonmovie movies', *Time*, 13 January 1965, p. 66.
3. 'Hollywood: a new kind of king', *Time*, 1 January 1965, pp. 50–1.
4. Skouras had taken charge of Fox in 1942 following Joe Schenck's conviction in the union bribery scandal (see above, p. 16) and production chief Darryl Zanuck's enlistment in the Army; former Republican presidential candidate Wendell Wilkie was the firm's titular head and public face until his premature death two years later, when Skouras took full charge.
5. On Gulf + Western, see 'Corporations: living on breakdowns', *Time*, 8 October 1965, pp. 98–100; on conglomeration generally, see 'The conglomerates' war to reshape industry', *Time*, 7 March 1969, pp. 75–80.
6. With the terms of Alfred Hitchcock's deal making *Psycho* (second-placed in 1960 with $11.2m) more profitable for MCA than its titular distributor, Paramount's losing streak arguably dated back even further, to its palmy mid-fifties days when *White Christmas* and *The Ten Commandments* topped the charts in successive years.
7. The *Paramount* takeover is detailed in Bernard F. Dick, *Engulfed: The Death of Paramount Pictures and the Birth of Corporate Hollywood* (Lexington: University Press of Kentucky, 2001), pp. 85–108.
8. 'Movies get new moguls', *Business Week*, 8 February 1969, pp. 29–30.
9. On the transformation of Warner, see Robert Gustafson, 'What's happening to our pix biz? From Warner Bros. to Warner Communications, Inc.', in Tino Balio (ed.), *The American Film Industry*, 2nd edn (Madison: Wisconsin University Press, 1985), pp. 574–86.
10. 'Conglomerates: *Godfather*'s godfather', *Time*, 15 May 1972, p. 79.
11. 'New showdown looms at MGM', *Business Week*, 2 August 1969, pp. 66–8; 'Eurodollars finance the new MGM drama', *Business Week*, 16 August 1969, pp. 41–2.
12. 'MGM is cutting more than film', *Business Week*, 9 May 1970, p. 23.
13. 'MGM fades fast from the screen', *Business Week*, 22 September 1973, pp. 23–4. The whole saga is well told in Peter Bart, *Fade Out: The Calamitous Final Days of MGM* (New York: William Morrow, 1990).
14. In 1991 a new rating, NC-17, was introduced to try to accommodate non-pornographic adult content, but, faced with resistance from exhibitors and print media (who largely refused to carry advertising for NC-17 rated films), few distributors were prepared to risk

the scarlet letters. Most directors were in any event contractually required to deliver an R-rated cut. See Jon Lewis, *Hollywood v. Hard Core: How the Struggle Over Censorship Saved the Modern Film Industry* (New York: New York University Press, 2000), pp. 296–9.

15. 'Making the movies into a business', *Business Week*, 23 June 1973, pp. 116–25.

16. *Ibid.*

17. See Peter Krämer, *The New Hollywood: From* Bonnie and Clyde *to* Star Wars (London: Wallflower, 2005) pp. 58–66; Steve Neale, '"The Last Good Time We Ever Had?": revising the Hollywood Renaissance', in Linda Ruth Williams and Michael Hammond (eds), *Contemporary American Cinema* (Maidenhead: McGraw-Hill, 2005), pp. 90–108.

18. See 'Building a dowry for *Funny Girl*', *Business Week*, 28 September 1968, pp. 82–4.

19. *Time*, 6 December 1967.

20. See Garth Jowett, *Film: The Democratic Art* (Boston: Little, Brown, 1976), pp. 485–7.

21. A number of such surveys are usefully summarised and discussed in Krämer, *New Hollywood*, pp. 68–78.

22. 'New kind of movie shakes Hollywood', *Business Week*, 3 January 1970, pp. 40–5.

23. Robert Ardrey, 'What happened to Hollywood?' *The Reporter*, 24 January 1957, pp. 19–22.

24. Richard Maltby, *Hollywood Cinema*, 2nd edn (Oxford: Blackwell, 2003), pp. 179–80. See also 'Cinematic shelter', *Time*, 19 January 1976, pp. 56–7.

25. For a discussion of countercultural reactions to the 1969–70 cycle, see Aniko Bodroghkozy, 'Reel revolutionaries: an examination of Hollywood's cycle of 1960s youth rebellion films', *Cinema Journal*, 2002; 41(3):38–58.

26. These categories are purely indicative and for clarity's sake allocate each film to one genre only (thus *West Side Story* and *Fiddler on the Roof* are classified only as musicals, not as melodramas, *Mary Poppins* as a family film rather than a musical, and so on). I have argued elsewhere that melodrama is as much a mode as it is a conventional genre and informs Hollywood cinema generally, especially the contemporary action film: see Barry Langford, *Film Genre: Hollywood and Beyond* (Edinburgh: Edinburgh University Press, 2005), especially Chapters 2, 10.

27. See the next chapter for a discussion of the importance of the Western as a vehicle for ideological critique.

28. Both *The Exorcist* and *A Clockwork Orange* were subsequently reclassified R.

29. Krämer, *New Hollywood*, p. 73.

30. The term itself was coined by black activist Junius Griffin in 1972 and was intended derogatorily.

31. On the complex politics of blaxploitation, see William R. Grant, 'The political economy of blaxploitation', in William R. Grant (ed.), *Post-soul Black Cinema: Discontinuities, Innovations, and Breakpoints, 1970–1995* (New York: Routledge, 2004).

32. Laughlin repurchased *Billy Jack* from Warner after the studio failed to promote the film successfully and distributed it himself through the National Student Film Corporation. 'Four-walling' was challenged by theatre owners as contrary to the *Paramount* judgment (because it combined distribution and exhibition, albeit on a temporary basis), and the tactic was prohibited by the Court in 1976. See Justin Wyatt, *High Concept: Movies and Marketing in Hollywood* (Austin: University of Texas Press, 1994), pp. 110–11.

33. On the legend of *Jaws*, see 'The Biggest, the Best: 1975', pp. 154–6.

34. See David A. Cook, 'Appendix 8: Marketing Expenses for Major Releases, 1970–1980', in *Lost Illusions: American Cinema in the Shadow of Watergate and Vietnam* (Berkeley: University of California Press, 2000), p. 493.

35. On the multiplex boom, see introduction to Part 3, pp. 183–9.
36. 'Making the movies into a business', *Business Week*, 23 June 1973, p. 123.
37. *Love Story* was in fact Erich Segal's novelisation of his own screenplay, published shortly before the film was released. Paramount subsidised Mario Puzo's completion of *The Godfather*.
38. *Jaws* also has elements of the disaster film in its first half, with the scenes of panicked bathers fleeing the water.
39. See Chapter 8.
40. And the film's street language and sexual frankness, which earned it an R rating and hence excluded a good proportion of its teen audience, were subsequently trimmed allowing the film to be re-released as a PG.
41. 'Show business: Hollywood's hottest summer', *Time*, 21 August 1978, p. 68.
42. 'A bet on *Apocalypse* starts to pay off', *Business Week*, 11 June 1979, p. 42.
43. '*Heaven's Gate* leaves theatre owners fuming', *Business Week*, 8 December 1980, pp. 29–30.
44. 'MGM's gamble on UA gets riskier by the day', *Business Week*, 28 September 1981, pp. 36–7.
45. 'Transamerica: a new prosperity grounded in financial services' and 'How UA became a grade B film company', *Business Week*, 22 June 1981, pp. 34–5.
46. 'Is Hollywood making the right kind of film?', *Business Week*, 27 October 1980, p. 62.

'Sappy Endings': *New York, New York* (United Artists 1977). Reproduced courtesy of The Kobal Collection

CHAPTER 5

New Wave Hollywood

Around thirty minutes into *The Graduate*, 1967's top-grossing film, shortly after Benjamin Braddock's (Dustin Hoffman) first sexual encounter with the predatory Mrs Robinson (Anne Bancroft), director Mike Nichols introduces an effectively self-contained six-minute sequence intended to communicate Ben's state of lassitude and alienation. An abstract pattern of light and colour resolves itself into the play of sunlight on the water of Ben's parents' swimming pool, and we cross-fade into a wordless montage scored to the melancholy commentary of two Simon and Garfunkel songs, 'The Sound of Silence' and 'Tuesday, Come She Will'. We see Ben and Mrs Robinson together directly before or after having sex in a variety of soulless hotel rooms, the meaninglessness of their encounters underscored by their blank gazes and lack of communication. These vignettes are intercut with scenes of Ben moping around the pool, the same affectless torpor distancing him from his surroundings here too. Nichols exploits continuity editing conventions to deliberately confuse spatial relations: Ben opens the door to the pool house and via a match cut walks straight into the room where Mrs Robinson awaits him half-dressed on the bed. Eyeline matches and cuts on action are used to collapse the physically separate domestic/parental and worldly/erotic spaces into one continuum of isolation and dysfunctional personal relationships.

Although these scenes all obviously take place after Ben and Mrs Robinson first have sex, temporal relations – how many days or weeks are being summarised, whether the events occur in the order depicted onscreen – are left purposely undefined. Indeed, it is possible we should understand the entire montage as a transcription of Ben's mindscape as he reveries about his own life. At the end of the sequence, the music fades as Ben heaves himself up out of the pool onto a floating inflatable – 'lands' atop Mrs Robinson, breathing hard as he climaxes – but then looks over his shoulder (Mrs Robinson still beneath him) as if in response to his father's offscreen query: 'Ben, what are you doing?'. Next a shot of Mr Braddock looming over the camera, backlit by the California noonday sun (the lens flares slightly), marks this as Benjamin's point of view; cut to a reverse shot of Ben on the inflatable, shielding his eyes with his hand: 'I'd say I'm just . . . drifting'.

This sequence, in the film that – along with *Bonnie and Clyde* – kicked off a decade of stylistic experimentation in Hollywood, in many ways encapsulates late-1960s American cinema's absorption of stylistic techniques associated with the early-sixties European New Waves and the international art cinema of the previous decade. Disjunctive or associative editing, often geared to communicating subjectivity; a privileging of mood and character over tightly plotted action; the 'dialectical' juxtaposition of image and of non-synchronous or non-diegetic sound and music; destabilisation of the secure spatial environments that typified most classic Hollywood films; episodic, ambiguous, unresolved and/or temporally complex, non-linear narratives, sometimes combined with a flaunting (and hence questioning) of narrative agency itself; at the level of content, an embrace of hitherto taboo subjects and of modishly candid and/or confrontational attitudes towards sex, violence and (in some cases) aspects of dominant American ideology; 'uncertain, counter-cultural and marginal protagonists, whose goals were often relatively ill-defined and ultimately unattained'[1]: such modernist devices, which collectively heightened the self-consciousness and reflexivity of many Hollywood films, promoted understandings of film as a medium of personal artistic expression and social comment, and in so doing ran directly counter to the orthodoxies of stylistic understatement and conventionality that typified the classical Hollywood style, all became widespread in the late 1960s and early 1970s.

These devices were by no means ubiquitous, any more than all early sixties French cinema was part of the *Nouvelle Vague*: the top-grossing films of 1968 and 1970 were the wholly conventional *Funny Girl* and *Airport*. Even where they were present, in the hands of filmmakers as different as, say, Peter Bogdanovich and Dennis Hopper they ran the gamut of restraint and radicalism, from the stylistic diffidence of *The Last Picture Show* to the wholesale deconstruction of stylistic conventions and hegemonic ideologies in *The Last Movie*. Nonetheless, the dissemination of such devices, which could be found in only a handful of pre-1965 Hollywood films, was widespread and marked a clear shift of emphasis, if not an outright change of direction. Having said that, we have also seen that the classical Hollywood style itself was never completely fixed but was, rather, flexible, adaptive, integrative and inherently syncretic. So did Hollywood's New Wave amount to anything more than the latest synthesising adjustment of the classical paradigm – 'trended change', as Bordwell prefers? Did the decade of the Hollywood Renaissance see anything more than, in Robert Ray's words, 'superficial stylistic exuberance, leaving Classic

Hollywood's paradigms fundamentally untouched'[2] – the adoption of a set of eye-catching stylistic tics that added to the lexicon of Hollywood cinema but left its grammar fundamentally unaffected?

In *The Classical Hollywood Cinema* Bordwell analyses a celebrated seventies Hollywood auteur film, Francis Ford Coppola's *The Conversation* (UA/The Directors' Company 1974) with the aim of demonstrating that Renaissance Hollywood filmmaking remains basically stylistically conservative and in thrall to genre, qualities that severely constrain its ability to challenge classical norms. Contrasting Coppola's film – the story of Harry Caul (Gene Hackman), a surveillance expert whose inferences about his latest assignment (inferences the audience is directed to share, but which later prove disastrously misguided) lead him to abandon his professional and personal detachment and to attempt to change the perceived course of events, with catastrophic consequences – with Michelangelo Antonioni's *Blow-Up* (MGM 1966), a European art film which clearly influenced it, it is argued that the latter's constitutive and abiding ambiguities and ellipses become in Coppola's hands the enigma devices of a slightly unconventional detective thriller whose resolution grounds *The Conversation* in the security of genre and hence more generally of the classical cinema.

Whereas in *Blow-Up* we are never made privy to the motives, methods or consequences of the conspiracy that the protagonist (perhaps) stumbles upon, or even assured that a conspiracy actually exists independent of his perception of it, in *The Conversation* these relationships are all finally clarified by means of a very striking and foregrounded narrative reversal. Harry realises that a key recorded phrase ('he'd kill us if he got the chance'), apparently indicating a young couple's fear of violence on the part of the woman's husband, is in fact a justification for the adulterous lovers' plan to murder the husband and in so doing take control of a large corporation ('he'd kill *us* if he got the chance'). The climactic moment at which this reversal occurs is unconventional for Hollywood, as it reveals that an apparently established 'objective' narrative fact (Harry has listened to the recording in the presence of others) has actually been filtered through Harry's subjective perception all along (specifically his unexpiated guilt at an earlier episode of passive complicity in an act of violence). In this way the narrative authority accorded to the detective protagonist by generic convention is withdrawn, or at least compromised. Moreover, a degree of formal contradiction is introduced by the revelation of the narrative's unsuspected unreliability. Having shared in Harry's misprision, we are forced like him to reflect on the unexamined assumptions that govern our habitual processes of interpretation – whose obvious reflexive relevance to the ways of making meaning in and of motion pictures are underscored throughout *The Conversation* by the camera's identification with intrusive surveillance apparatus (especially in the opening and final scenes).

Yet as Colin MacCabe argues in another context, the contradiction thus introduced into the classical text is quickly resolved in favour of a larger, non-contradictory reality: the surveillance expert was mistaken and indeed, like Oedipus, the first literary detective, reaches the recognition of his error through his own efforts, though too late to avoid suffering the consequences (he falls victim to the real conspiracy).[3] Thus *The Conversation*, according to Bordwell, illustrates the claim that sixties and seventies Hollywood's selective borrowings from European art film should be seen as simply another instance of the process of 'stylistic assimilation' which allowed Hollywood in the twenties and thirties to absorb, adapt and ultimately accommodate devices from German Expressionism and Soviet montage – hence demonstrating not rupture but rather 'the persistence of a mode of film practice'.[4] One wonders to what extent this conclusion is predetermined. Bordwell's account of seventies Hollywood is shot through – oddly, given that the earlier assimilation of prewar avant-garde techniques has been presented not as parasitic but if anything as rather creditable – with implicitly derogatory or at best diminutive rhetoric such as 'rehashes', 'imitating', 'derivative', 'borrowings' and 'pastiche'; these terms all colour the account of what might just as reasonably be called simply 'influence' (itself, as Harold Bloom has argued, an indispensable prerequisite of creative originality[5]).

Such language perhaps betrays a governing assumption: so committed is *The Classical Hollywood Cinema* to its 'strong' model of Hollywood narrative film that any adjustment of that model by elements from a different one can only be seen as inorganic and cosmetic. Since Hollywood film is, and remains by definition, classical, and since the classical, also by definition, excludes the alternative practices represented by the art cinema, Hollywood film can only allow for 'weak', non-disruptive and hence ultimately superficial approximations of the latter. Or might it be that the differential assessments of the adoption of art film elements in studio-era and Renaissance Hollywood, effectively delegitimating the latter, in fact testifies to its more fundamental challenge?

No one could dispute that New Wave techniques were indeed often incorporated and turned, in time-honoured fashion, to Hollywood purposes. Take, for example, the jump cut,[6] Jean-Luc Godard's trademark from *Breathless* (1960) onwards. For Godard, the highly visibly dissection of discontinuous time and/or space draws the viewer's attention to the constructedness of the image, among other purposes. The pre-credits sequence of the James Bond film *On Her Majesty's Secret Service* (Peter Hunt, UA 1969), by contrast, uses unremarked jump cuts to energise a violent fistfight. The bicycling sequence in *Butch Cassidy and the Sundance Kid* (George Roy Hill, Fox 1969) pastiches Truffaut's *Jules et Jim* (1963) and renders it saccharine by the soundtrack overlay of Burt Bacharach's 'Raindrops Keep Falling On My Head'. Equally, the 'mainstreaming' of disruptive devices can be tracked over time. At the start of Martin Scorsese's *Mean Streets*, as Charlie (Harvey Keitel) lies down on his bed three rapid cuts – Charlie's movement overlapping, minutely but perceptibly, each time – bring us successively closer to his face, synchronised to the snare drum salute that opens the Ronettes' 'Be My Baby'. This striking effect, writes Robert Kolker, 'generates a nervous and purposeless energy' that sets the film's tone, 'makes us uneasy, and does not permit rest'.[7] A decade later, in Steven Spielberg's *E.T.* (U 1982), however, when Elliott sees the troopers barring his escape with ET, Spielberg repeats the triple cut-in, but here to maximise the impact of a critical narrative juncture (exhilaratingly resolved when ET reveals his telekinetic powers for the first time and levitates Elliott's bike over the roadblock).

But one can also readily find examples where comparable effects are not only not naturalised but foregrounded, and not only in an obvious auteur film such as *Mean Streets*. Two early seventies examples demonstrate that 'New Wave' style penetrated well beyond the critical modernism of Altman, Penn and their peers. Don Medford's *The Hunting Party* (MGM 1971), an unapologetically exploitative and derivative spaghetti-style Western, opens with a close-up of a cow having its throat (really) slit – intercut with a non-contiguous scene of Candice Bergen being brutally sexually violated by Gene Hackman. Both images supply crude shock value, especially as opening scenes (there are no conventional establishing shots, a point I will return to later) and their juxtaposition offers a fairly crude analogy of woman as brutalised livestock or chattel. The point, however, is that such didactic, sub-Eisensteinian montage has become a stylistic given in an unhailed genre film from a minor director. However unsubtle, Medford's montage establishes in a highly unclassical way an externally located editorialising, commentative presence that works through form to comment on narrative content.

The Getaway (First National 1972), though directed by one of the most important Renaissance filmmakers, Sam Peckinpah, is generally reckoned a minor work, his slickest and most unapologetically commercial venture. Yet the first eight minutes of this crowd-pleasing heist thriller intercut no fewer than seven discontinuous spaces illustrating the corrosive monotony of prison life as experienced by Doc (Steve McQueen). Six elements in the montage, their precise temporal relations unclear, show Doc in various different prison environs – the workshop, the yard, clearing brush, the showers, playing chess and alone in his cell, the spaces linked by an oppressive sound overlay of guards barking orders; the seventh, erratically and briefly interpolated in hard-to-read close-ups, are erotic memory images of Doc and his wife Carol (Ali McGraw). As Doc's rage and frustration build, all of these different image-tracks are cut together with increasing rapidity, to almost impressionistic effect. All of this is further interfered with by the opening credits, appearing as title cards over freeze-frames (Peckinpah's signature style from *The Wild Bunch*). The last of these, 'Directed by Sam Peckinpah', stamps an auteurist signature on the sequence as a whole.

Rather than belabouring the question of continuity and/or change in Hollywood film practice, we might simply note that by 1971–2 overtly disruptive modernistic techniques such as these had become part of the toolbox for mainstream genre films. Yet just a few years earlier, *The Pawnbroker*'s associative montage had been sufficiently unusual to draw considerable comment. How had this rapid expansion of stylistic options come about? The most obvious answer is that American filmmakers in the 1960s were naturally aware of, interested in and keen to try out techniques they encountered in the films of their foreign contemporaries.

As previously noted, such alertness to innovative practice was no less true of their studio–era predecessors. The institutions of influence had changed, however, and with them also changed governing assumptions about how, or to what extent, innovation should be domesticated and absorbed into standard Hollywood practice. Even as the regular moviegoing audience diminished in the 1950s, a widening awareness of and interest in other European and global cinemas had contributed to a marked expansion of American film culture. As observed in Columbus, for independent neighbourhood exhibitors faced with rapidly dwindling audiences, art films were an alternative to exploitation or skinflicks. The number and reach of independent imported film distributors steadily increased from the early fifties. An art house conversion was not an option for theatres in hick towns of the sort depicted in Peter Bogdanovich's *The Last Picture Show* (Col/BBS 1971); elsewhere, however, the massive postwar expansion of higher education meant that most medium-size and bigger cities had large student populations to support non-traditional programming. The success of art cinemas led to them becoming known in industry jargon as 'sure seaters' – that is, they were sure to fill their seats. The number of first-run art house theatres in the USA climbed from around eighty in 1950 to 450 in 1963.[8] Repertory houses also appeared, showing revivals of prewar European – and sometimes also Hollywood – films.

Universities themselves supported film societies, while a small but growing number started running film criticism and appreciation courses. There were, of course, also well-established graduate film schools, notably in New York (NYU) and LA (USC, UCLA). Despite the latter's proximity to Hollywood, film school had never traditionally offered a pathway into commercial filmmaking. The LA schools mostly trained industrial filmmakers; NYU was identified with documentary and other independent filmmaking. In the studio era, the career ladder for aspiring Hollywood directors was usually to start out by assisting on established filmmakers' productions, moving on to apprentice on B movies, before being entrusted with bigger and more prestigious projects. The collapse of the studio system kicked this ladder away – the studio's reduced slates of increasingly expensive films required experienced, trustworthy and bankable talent, not novices. Hence the development of new routes into Hollywood filmmaking. One such was television: and if the brisk, no-nonsense techniques of television production, in which such Renaissance directors as Peckinpah, Altman, Spielberg and Hal Ashby had all worked extensively, seemed to have little in common with the expansive creative visions these directors developed in the 1970s, nonetheless the abandonment of the harmonious aesthetic to which much classical filmmaking aspired was probably encouraged by the experience of storytelling in a necessarily functional way.

From the mid-sixties, however, the major film schools also became a means for ambitious young filmmakers to get access to equipment, production skills – and ideas. These included a highly developed sense of film history and the intoxicatingly powerful conception of film as art, rather than commodity, and of the filmmaker – specifically the director – as artist. During the 1960s this vision of cinema as an artistic vocation was reinforced by the powerful appeal of auteurism, imported, adapted and Americanised from the fifties *Cahiers du Cinéma* writers – among them Truffaut, Godard, Chabrol and other core *Nouvelle Vague* filmmakers – by US critics such as Andrew Sarris. The expanding film culture meant that such attitudes were no longer the preserve of an intellectual elite, but were more widely shared among audiences and discussed in the print press. The growth of film festivals also heightened public awareness of alternatives to Hollywood cinema, most importantly the New York International Film Festival, established in 1963 and the focus of a *Time* cover story that year on the new 'religion of film'.[9] From the early 1960s, the expanding international festival circuit started to showcase the work of a new generation of independent US filmmakers such as John Cassavetes (*Shadows*, 1959), Sidney Meyers (*The Savage Eye*, 1959) and Shirley Clarke (*The Cool World*, 1963).

Of particular relevance for the future trajectory of the Renaissance directors was Sarris's claim that auteurism was forged, precisely, through the creative tension between individualist filmmakers and the constraints of a commercially oriented industry: hence his veneration of studio-era directors such as Hawks.[10] The auteur critics' canonisation of studio filmmakers alongside Continental masters such as Dreyer and Renoir encouraged the Hollywood New Wave to interrogate, rather than to break with, the classical Hollywood cinema. In professional terms, it predisposed them to find ways to work within the commercial mainstream, rather than outside it like the early sixties independent directors. The extent to which post-studio-era Hollywood was amenable to auteurist imprinting would be crucial to their success or failure.

Aesthetically, too, as the next chapter will explore further, an ongoing dialogue with classic Hollywood was one – perhaps the – indispensable common element among all the Renaissance filmmakers. Far more than the *Nouvelle Vague* (whose love–hate relationship with Hollywood was triangulated by their own Oedipal antagonism towards the '*cinéma du papa*', the hidebound, middlebrow literary French cinema of the previous generation), the incorporation of a diversity of non-traditional devices into the films of the Hollywood Renaissance testifies to the impulse to challenge, qualify, revise – but only in very rare cases to reject outright – their own cinematic and cultural patrimony. In a wholly unintended side-effect of Hollywood's postwar adjustment, their sense of this legacy was heightened by television's emergence as an informal, round–the–clock national *cinémathèque*. The constant, unheralded rotation of the studios' back catalogues – particularly the older films that filled out afternoon and late-night schedules in syndication on local stations, 'unreel[ing] with the steady persistence of an arterial throb' as *Time* evocatively put it – gave 'movie brats' such as Spielberg, Scorsese and De Palma a comprehensive education in the filmmaking traditions they would inherit and, in their different ways, also strive to transcend.[11]

Perhaps then, rather than despising the New Wave inflections of the Hollywood Renaissance as ersatz, it might be more profitable to see how innovations to the classical style enabled the 'auteur generation' to differentiate themselves from their cinematic patrimony, and to what degree these adjustments left a permanent imprint on the Hollywood style. It was established in Chapter 3 that a particular system of temporal and spatial organisation in the service of character-centred narrative was central (though not absolutely) to the classical Hollywood cinema. We can therefore proceed by examining how the Hollywood Renaissance reordered cinematic time and space before moving on to consider whether, and how, such adjustments shift predominant narrative paradigms.

TIME AND SPACE

As a time-based medium, narrative film is perhaps more centrally defined by its mode of temporal organisation than by any other single element. Alan Resnais' interplay of past, present, and (possible) futures in *Muriel* (Fr 1963) and *La Guerre est Finie* (Fr 1966), for example, are not 'simply' modernist complications of conventional linear narrative: they are the means through which Resnais articulates his principal concern, which is not storytelling but the nature of subjecthood and the means (formal, social and ideological) whereby it is constituted (questions that ally Resnais to the preoccupations of both European modernism and Western Marxism). Because neither the broader intellectual culture, the institutions of the American film industry, nor their personal inclinations or education prompted any of the major Renaissance directors towards similar enquiries, it is unsurprising that insofar as they treat time in sometimes strikingly different ways than most studio-era films, they are nonetheless also at variance with Resnais or Chris Marker. Broadly speaking, beyond flashy self-advertising technique for technique's sake, examples of which certainly abound (for example, Richard Lester's *Petulia*, WB 1968),[12] untraditional temporalities in Renaissance-era cinema are more likely to aim for pathos, sometimes irony, and occasionally detached judgment – or alternatively for a visceral transformation of the spectator's inhabitation of the immediate moment, most notably in Peckinpah's action sequences – than for philosophical ambiguity. All of these qualities might well be regarded as thoroughly American; yet that does not mean they cannot also be unclassical.

Resnais' critical-modernist narrative complexity is in any case only one aspect of the production and experience of film time. The rate at which narrative and visual information is presented to the spectator also importantly defines the experience of cinematic temporality. Figures for average shot lengths (ASLs) during the Renaissance period suggest that the shaping of film time through editing became a more noticeable feature of Hollywood cinema in the Renaissance years. That is, the majority of studio-era films (from 1930 through the mid-fifties) had ASLs of somewhere between eight and twelve seconds. This was not especially dependent on genre – *Gone With the Wind*'s ASL was around ten seconds, that of *Bringing Up Baby* (RKO 1938) around nine – nor on whether the film was oriented towards dialogue or action: perhaps surprisingly, the snappy repartee of *The Big Sleep* clocked in at 11.2 seconds. As noted in Chapter 3, ASLs seemed to lengthen slightly during the early widescreen/roadshow era, but there was no evolutionary rupture: *Ben-Hur*'s ASL was 8.1 seconds. One had to venture away from Hollywood to find, for example, the rapid montage of Welles's *Othello* (ASL 5.1 seconds, partly driven by circumstance[13]). Long takes were also a feature of the deep-focus-dominated late forties and early fifties: Wyler, Preminger and Billy Wilder's films all featured notably longer than average takes and ASLs.[14] From the late 1960s on, as the research of David Bordwell and Barry Salt has established, the range of ASLs in Hollywood films widens: in other words, both longer and discernibly faster cutting starts to feature.[15] Numerous films now possessed ASLs of 4–6 seconds, including, for example, not only Bob Rafelson's zany collage *Head* (Col 1968, 2.7 seconds), or *Easy Rider*, with its acid-trip sequence and proto-music video style (5.8 seconds), or Robert Aldrich's brutally fast-paced *The Dirty Dozen* (US 1967, 3.5 seconds), but Penn's ostensibly understated *Alice's Restaurant* (UA 1969, 3.1 seconds). On the other hand, other directors' persistence with long takes, such as Polanski's *Chinatown* (Par 1974, 14 seconds) and Woody Allen's *Manhattan* (UA 1979, 17.6 seconds) stood out in relief in this accelerated context. Both extremes, and the visible differences between them, worked to heighten spectators' awareness of the ways in which the viewing experience is constructed and of the stylistic signature of the individual director (and editor).

Of course, it was in particular sequences – not in statistical abstractions – that audiences most dramatically experienced stylistic developments in Hollywood cinema. Dede Allen's eye-catching editing of Bonnie and Clyde's death scene in 1967 demonstrated the stunning impact of rapidly-edited action sequences. Two years later, Peckinpah's *The Wild Bunch* took things much further, as is strikingly illustrated by a comparison of the film's famous closing gun battle at Aqua Verde with a very similar sequence of large-scale combat at the climax of Robert Aldrich's *Vera Cruz* (UA 1954), an earlier Western dealing with American interlopers in the Mexican Revolution. In 133 seconds Aldrich cuts seventy-eight times (giving an average shot length for the sequence of 1.7 seconds – itself exceptionally rapid for the period). In 135 seconds of *The Wild Bunch* (the entire Aqua Verde sequence, from Pike's first shot to the guns falling silent, lasts 4 minutes and 20 seconds) we have 291 cuts – an average shot length of 0.46 seconds, in other words about 11 frames of film (of course some shots are held longer and others shorter still). The numbers, however, hardly communicate the sheer stylistic radicalism of Peckinpah's (and cameraman Lucien Ballard and editor Lou Lombardo's) montage technique, for which Kurosawa's *Seven Samurai* (Jap 1959) offers the only, limited, antecedent, and which constitute arguably the most dramatic innovations in montage cinema since Eisenstein. These nearly 300 shots (*The Wild Bunch* in total has 3,642 shots, at a time when the industry average was around 700) intercut slow-motion and normal-speed footage (with an action and its consequences – the throwing of a grenade in normal time and the bodies thrown into the air by the detonation on slow motion, for example – consequently unfolding in discontinuous temporal relation), rapid zooms and whip-pans, wide shots and extreme close-ups of faces of men, women, children, shouting, snarling, crying, screaming in agony. Individual slow-motion shots both accentuate the impact of bullets on flesh – with Peckinpah's pioneering use of squibs simulating gouts of spurting blood and gobbets of meat – and simultaneously transform the carnage into a perverse ballet, with bodies fishtailing upwards into the air, as if defying gravity in the instant of death, or spiralling gymnastically down to the ground. The sequence as a whole discharges a barrage of visual information, thrusting the spectator into a sensory battleground as frenetic as the battle on the ground in Aqua Verde.

In *The Wild Bunch*, temporal distortion is indissociably bound up with a reorganisation of spatial relationships: destabilised (extended and dissected) time shapes dislocated (decentred, dynamised) screen space. A sequence from *The Getaway* illustrates the relationship in a more meditative tenor. After Doc has been released from jail – because Carol has slept with a corrupt local politician – the couple wander in the summer sunshine alongside a public bathing lake, set apart from the bathers in their street clothes and estranged from one another by Carol's infidelity. Doc gazes at the lake and sees himself and Carol diving in, fully clothed, their intimacy and their pleasure in one another restored. We take this imagery as pastoral romantic fantasy, until Doc sets off towards the water's edge undoing his tie – whereupon a cut to the soaked pair arriving at their apartment reinscribes the images as predictive of Doc's (now fulfilled) wish/intention. Peckinpah's use of an eyeline match to allow Doc's gaze, impossibly, to fall upon his own image in a space that is at once both physically present (but in the immediate future) and in his mind's eye, at once exploits and undermines classical continuity protocols.

From the outset, in fact, the Hollywood Renaissance had announced itself by the disruption of fundamental continuity conventions. *Bonnie and Clyde* opens, famously, on a close-up of Bonnie's red lips: the sequence that follows communicates her edginess and frustration through jump cuts and unexpected camera angles. The omission of an establishing shot denies the audience the spatial security – and thus the interpretative confidence – to which classic Hollywood had accustomed them. *Mean Streets*, similarly, opens close on Charlie wandering through his darkened apartment in his underwear. The camera tracks him as he moves purposelessly around. There is no dialogue to explicate setting or narrative context (in fact, this scene is dissociated from any specific temporal/causal relationship to the ensuing, itself episodic, narrative) and the only soundtrack is traffic noise from the New York streets outside. How the scene relates to the preceding voiceover (Scorsese's voice over a darkened screen: 'You don't make up for your sins in church. You do it on the streets. You do it at home. The rest is bullshit and you know it.') is just as unclear. *Apocalypse Now* starts with a series of almost abstract but disturbing images (Captain Willard's (Martin Sheen) upturned face, helicopter propeller blades slicing past the camera in slow-motion, a jungle landscape erupting in flames).

The openings of both *The Godfather* and *A Clockwork Orange* abjure conventional establishing shots for tight close-ups of faces – Alex's unblinking, provocative gaze in *A Clockwork Orange* seems to issue an especially unsettling challenge to the spectator – and then track back to reveal social contexts that are themselves visually disorienting, though in quite different ways: the intense chiaroscuro and pools of Stygian darkness in which cinematographer Gordon Willis sculpts Don Corleone's study, 'violat[ing] the rules of classical Hollywood cinematography',[16] and the futuristic, abstract, pornographic dreamscape of the Korova Milkbar. Perhaps the period's most considered subversion of the establishing shot is *The Conversation*, which begins with what appears to be a conventional, scene-setting high-angle shot of San Francisco's Ghirardelli Square – only for the camera's relentless slow zoom-in to reveal that this is anything but a 'neutral' perspective: in fact, this is the viewpoint of a surveillance camera whose scrutiny of the adulterous couple inaugurates the film's conspiracy narrative. The abolition of the 'innocent' transparency of the camera's gaze extends the narrative of the moral bankruptcy and futility of Harry Caul's posture of professional detachment to a broader critique of recording and reproduction. The first shot is echoed by the last, in which the camera's blank gaze as it surveys Harry in his wrecked apartment, panning mechanically back and forth like a security camera, is evacuated of any sense moral or ethical responsibility.

The Conversation challenges the assumption that any point of view can ever be anything but deeply implicated in the social relations it represents, and from which it sees. Numerous other Renaissance films explore similar themes, either compromising the objectivity of the omniscient narration like *The Conversation*, portraying a world literally steeped in the hallucinatory colours and skewed perspectives of psychosis like Scorsese's *Taxi Driver* (Col 1976), or conversely withholding intimacy and ready access to protagonists' subjectivity at moments when we are most fully primed to expect it. At the conclusion of Bob Rafelson's *Five Easy Pieces* (Col/BBS 1970) the protagonist abandons his girlfriend and hitches a ride on a truck headed for Alaska, but all this plays out without significant dialogue, and mostly in long- and medium-shot, rendering the character's inner life as opaque to us as it remains to him. At the other end of the decade, the extensive deployment of a subjective camera in William Friedkin's *Cruising* (Lorimar 1980) implicates its audience in the growing identity crisis of its protagonist – a New York cop working undercover in search of a serial killer stalking the leather bars and clubs of Greenwich Village, whose presumptively hetero-normative sexuality and subjecthood are progressively destabilised as he is drawn deeper into his role. We share the cop's perspective as he cruises the bars, looking and being looked at in return, his/our point of view poised uncertainly between the generically conventional (investigation and forensic enquiry in the search for a killer) and the highly unconventional (a direct, and explicitly and aggressively sexual, gay male gaze).

Several films use reflexive imagery – reflecting or distorting surfaces, cameras, films-within-the-film – to point up the inadequacy of the insights and perspectives available to their protagonists, and by extension the spectator. The conspiracy thrillers and revisionist *noirs* of the mid-1970s are a particularly rich seam of such devices; in genres predicated on investigation and illumination they insistently portray deceit – including self-deceit – and error. The labyrinthine and self-consumingly circular plot of Arthur Penn's *Night Moves* (WB 1975) unfolds through prisms, smudged windows, screens and the murky depths of the Pacific. The film's private eye protagonist ends the film literally adrift, viewed with calm compassion from a high angle as, immobilised by a gunshot wound, he circles helplessly in the middle of the ocean aboard a yacht called *Point of View*. *The Parallax View* (named for the differential perspectives of camera viewfinder and lens) shares with *The Conversation* a focus on questions of perception and narrative authority, and like *Night Moves* is organised thematically around a frequently ironic treatment of insight and blindness ('views'). Throughout the film, characters are viewed indistinctly, concealed behind barriers, or obscured from view, notably in the opening assassination sequence filmed through a blood-smeared plate-glass window. The film's formal reflexivity is highlighted by a somewhat non-identificatory protagonist, and a cool, slightly abstract formalism that promotes intellectual engagement over emotional involvement. The climax ironically reverses traditional tropes of illumination and insight when the hero, realising too late he has been set up by the organisation he has attempted to infiltrate, the sinister Parallax Corporation, tries to escape by running towards a brilliantly lit doorway – whence steps his own assassin; and in an ironic coda the film cuts to the crepuscular ignorance (or complicity) of a Warren Commission-style enquiry that studiously refutes any suggestion of conspiracy.

Some of the techniques most strongly associated with the Renaissance, including the increased use of hand-held cameras and the extensive use of the telephoto, or zoom, lens – the latter a particular trademark of Robert Altman – testify to the effect of the 'Direct Cinema' documentary filmmakers of the early 1960s (D. A. Pennebaker, the Maysles Brothers). Some of these techniques had of necessity been used during the filming of documentaries in World War II, including by such studio directors as John Huston (whose *Battle of San Pietro* features extensive handheld camerawork), but rarely found a place in postwar studio films, though they were taken up in TV news and drama, where several notable telephoto exponents, including Altman and Peckinpah, began their careers. The short-lived fashion for split-screen techniques (in *The Boston Strangler* (Fox 1968, Richard Fleischer) and *The Thomas Crown Affair* (Par 1969, Norman Jewison)) also drew partly on television style but was rarely used as a tool of radical montage: rather, it seemed to extend further the interest in abstract graphic forms displayed by some CinemaScope filmmakers and drew attention to the screen as a two-dimensional surface for the presentation of information, rather than a space of depth and plastic forms. *Head* offered a different example of 'graphic' style in movies, this time drawing its inspiration from the depthless brilliance of Pop Art. Again, it appeared that the context of the times at the turn of the 1970s was more receptive to deviations from established practice and convention.

As such examples indicate, the spatial security and stability of classical Hollywood were often qualified or compromised in this period by innovative cinematographic techniques that interfered with the transparency and legibility of the image and/or drew attention to their own technical accomplishment. Crucially, the new directors allied themselves with a new generation of cinematographers who all but monopolised the landmark films of the Renaissance era, including Gordon Willis (*The Godfather*, *The Godfather*, *Part II*, *All the President's Men* (WB 1976, Alan J. Pakula), *Annie Hall* (UA 1976, Woody Allen), *Manhattan*); the Hungarian émigrés Vilmos Zsigmond (*McCabe & Mrs. Miller*, *Deliverance* (WB 1972, John Boorman)), *The Long Goodbye* (UA 1973, Robert Altman), *Close Encounters of the Third Kind*, *The Deer Hunter* (EMI 1978, Michael Cimino), *Heaven's Gate*) and Laszlo Kovacs (*Easy Rider*, *Five Easy Pieces*, *The King of Marvin Gardens* (Col/BBS 1972, Bob Rafelson), *Shampoo* (Col 1975, Hal Ashby), *New York, New York*);[17] Haskell Wexler (*American Graffiti*,[18] *Bound for Glory* (UA 1976), *Coming Home* (UA 1978)); Michael Chapman (*Taxi Driver*, *Invasion of the Body Snatchers* (UA 1978, Philip Kaufman), *Raging Bull* (UA 1980, Martin Scorsese)). These cameramen were not only aware of the European New Waves: in some cases, such as the French Nestor Almendros (*Days of Heaven*, Par 1978, Terence Malick) and Italian Vittorio Storaro (*Apocalypse Now*, *Reds*), they had contributed to it. They were also enthused by the technological innovations that dramatically affected the ways films could be made and how they looked. These included fast lenses and film stocks – allowing for natural-light and low-light filming; new camera technologies such as the Steadicam; and the zoom (or telephoto) lens, whose widespread use became one of the period's visual hallmarks.

Like their directors, Renaissance-era cinematographers were not constrained by traditional concerns for technical 'correctness' or propriety in achieving artistic and expressive effects. Famously, Laszlo Kovacs's deliberate inclusion of lens flare – starbursts in the image caused by the scattering of light across the reflective surfaces of the lens, traditionally regarded simply as an error by professional cinematographers – in *Easy Rider* as part of the film's free-wheeling quasi-*verité* feeling, mandated a move away from the refinement and polish of classical cinematography. In both *Godfathers* Gordon Willis 'pushed' the film stock – that is, underexposed it during shooting and overexposed it to compensate in processing – to create areas of morally impenetrable blackness for the film's interiors. Michael Chapman also 'pushed' the film for the night-time environments of *Taxi Driver* and *Invasion of the Body Snatchers*. The advent of the Steadicam, first used commercially by Haskell Wexler on Hal Ashby's *Bound for Glory*, enabled ever more elaborate, vibration-free travelling shots and reached a memorable apotheosis in John Alcott's work on Kubrick's *The Shining* (WB 1980).[19]

Some of these new techniques and technologies, notably overuse of both the zoom (especially very rapid zooms into and out of faces) and rack-focus composition – in both cases probably impelled by the idea of reflecting the unpredictably kinetic energy of youth culture – quickly became visual clichés. At other times, however, they enabled quite subtle manipulations of filmic space to accentuate dramatic or conceptual elements. Bruce Surtees's use of the long lens to make it appear that Ben is running in place as he rushes to Elaine's wedding at the climax of *The Graduate* is one well-known example. Another, both more subtle and more experimental, is Vilmos Zsigmond's constantly moving, pan-and-zoom photography for Altman's *The Long Goodbye*: here the persistent instability of the image track informs us, long before Elliott Gould's shambling Philip Marlowe realises it, of the evasiveness that pervades the film's account of Southern California.

NARRATIVE

From the perspective of *The Classical Hollywood Cinema*, the critical and subversive potential of the kinds of devices and techniques discussed in the previous section are strictly delimited, if not by their basically cosmetic nature, then by the Hollywood cinema's ongoing commitment to character-centred narrative whose premises have been adjusted, but never fundamentally challenged. Most of the examples cited above can be related fairly clearly to narrative or theme. *Easy Rider*'s lens flare captures the improvisational feeling of life on the road; the edgy, jumpy openings of *Bonnie and Clyde* and *Mean Streets* reflect their protagonists' unsettled states of minds; the visual interference of *The Parallax View* and *Night Moves* reflects the films' opaque, conspiratorial worlds; and so on.

Elsewhere, the case is less obvious. The extensive use of the moving camera, for example, perhaps most notably in the films of Martin Scorsese and Brian De Palma, might be considered forms of stylistic 'excess', compared at least to the general restraint of classical Hollywood. In *Mean Streets* (photographed by Kent Wakeford), both the track through the bar introducing us to Charlie's environment and the party scene where a camera strapped to the drunken Charlie's body vividly communicates his growing disorientation and loss of motor control, could be seen – their extreme self-consciousness notwithstanding – as serving narrative and characterisation. By contrast, when Wakeford's camera hurtles after the characters during the pool hall brawl, this seems more an ebullient effusion of 'pure' style detached from specific narrative purpose. The arabesques performed by Zsigmond's camera in De Palma's Hitchcock pastiche *Obsession* (Col 1974) are also difficult to justify on purely functional grounds. Peckinpah's montage technique produces a rhapsody of violence that reshapes our experience of the action – it is not an expression of the state of mind of any of its brutal characters.

It seems then that there remains a visible tension between the centripetal impulse to account for and incorporate stylistic innovation in traditional narrative terms, and a countervailing centrifugal tendency to push further towards or beyond the limits of convention. It is striking, for example, how little

Renaissance directors drew on one readily available form of 'vernacular modernism'[20] within the Hollywood tradition, that of *film noir*. *Noir*'s use of flashbacks (the proto-noir *Citizen Kane*; *Out of the Past*; *Sunset Boulevard*, narrated by a corpse; etc.) played with time to highlight subjectivity and unreliability in narrative form to a limited degree that was unfamiliar – in the context of the studio era's general narrative transparency – yet by the late sixties no longer (if it ever had been) radically incompatible with Hollywood norms. *Noir* (or neo-*noir*) was also centrally important to New Hollywood genre revisionism.[21] Yet *noir*'s hallmark, subjective flashbacks, were not a notable feature of the period. Although some early seventies films, including *Slaughterhouse Five* (U 1972, George Roy Hill) and Altman's *Images* (Hemdale 1972), partly motivated their fragmentation of narrative temporality in their protagonists' mental states, in general (consistent with the examples from *The Hunting Party* and *The Getaway* cited above) temporal manipulation and fragmentation is modernistically dissociated from individual (diegetic) perspectives and introduced as a purely textual function whose affective charge is experienced by the spectator rather than the character. In *Easy Rider*, for example, the half-glimpsed flash-forward to Wyatt's bike flying through the air may or may not be Wyatt's premonition of his own death; stylistically, in any event, the interpolated images are consistent with the film's technique of interleaving the end of one scene with the start of the next, a device that subtly disorientates the security of linear narrative. By intercutting the nearly real-time story of the dance marathon with stylised flash-forwards to the hero's trial for the heroine's murder, *They Shoot Horses Don't They?* (UA 1969, Sydney Pollack) further intensifies the story's despairing quality.

As David Bordwell notes, such devices are notable for announcing 'an overt narration . . . some narrating process outside the characters' world'.[22] Some major Renaissance films establish linkages across large spans of time to open up critical perspectives on the action that are unavailable, or only partly or fleetingly perceived, by the characters themselves. The opening of Peckinpah's *Pat Garrett and Billy the Kid* explores the unavoidable ethical implication of past and present, intercutting Garrett's assassination in 1909 by agents of the Santa Fe Ring with the younger Garrett's arrival at Fort Sumner twenty-eight years earlier to warn his former comrade Billy that he has changed sides and Billy must quit the territory. Matching cuts (and sound overlays) interweave the shots blowing the aged Garrett off his buggy with Billy and his gang firing at chickens for target practice, making it appear as if it is Billy who is gunning Garrett down from the past – a reversal of what (as Peckinpah assumes) we all know to be historical fact (Garrett ends up killing Billy), yet at a moral and ethical level no more than the truth. The mocking laughter from the past that accompanies Garrett's body hitting the ground in the opening montage establishes the central irony of the film: as Garrett acknowledges near the end of the film, when having at last gunned down Billy he blasts his own image in a mirror, in killing Billy he has killed himself.

Whereas in *Pat Garrett* the ironic juxtaposition of past and present is confined to the opening and closing scenes, *The Godfather, Part II*, almost uniquely in Hollywood cinema (Bordwell suggests *Intolerance* as a comparison), is entirely structured around large-scale narrative counterpoint. Throughout the film the young Vito Corleone's rise to power in pre-World War I New York is juxtaposed with his son Michael's ramified, corporate criminal empire in the 1950s. Neither timeline really signifies without the other: the film's meaning arises precisely from the juxtaposition, the contrast and the ironic/melancholic disjunction of past (brutal but dynamic, unified, and motivated by an unequivocal, even primitive, commitment to family) and present (entropic, alienated and destructive of all human relationships, including family). Michael seems increasingly aware of the costs of his chosen path (though unable or unwilling to change it), but the dual time-scheme offers a further perspective unavailable to any of the characters, emerging as it were from the space 'between' the two temporalities – that Michael has not, as he fears, simply betrayed his father's legacy, but rather that the inherently destructive nature of American capitalism, veiled by the heroic nostalgia in which Vito's timeline is clad, has made Michael's corruption – so to speak 'always already' – inevitable.

The following chapter will look in more detail at some other ways in which Renaissance-era narratives deviate from classic Hollywood conventions, such as the unmotivated (or demotivated) protagonist and the marked trend towards ambiguous and/or downbeat endings. And no discussion of challenges to narrative convention in this period could fail to mention Stanley Kubrick, who, while not generally regarded as part of the Renaissance (set apart both by age and geography – Kubrick was based in England from the early 1960s), pursued throughout the 1970s the most radical departures of any American filmmaker: dispensing with character-centred narrative altogether in the virtually abstract *2001: A Space Odyssey*; compelling audience identification with an unrepentant sociopath (but still the closest available impersonation of a human being) in *A Clockwork Orange*; and in both *Barry Lyndon* and *The Shining* subjecting an essentially passive protagonist to the sadistic manipulations of an unnamed, yet incontrovertible and coercive, agency that can be identified as an embodiment of narrative structure itself.

THE CONTENT OF FORM

In trying to estimate the significance and extent of the challenge seventies Hollywood offered to the classical style, one important point to make is that narrative – on whose 'ultimately determining' role in classical film Bordwell places such emphasis – is a highly elastic term. Outside of experimental cinema and video art, very few films and vanishingly few feature films can confidently be described as 'non-narrative'. Many films often categorised as 'abstract' – for example, the 'city symphonies' of the 1920s, such as Walter Ruttman's *Berlin, the Symphony of a Great City* – display a narrative structure (a day in the life of Weimar Berlin, divided into four 'acts') which may be fairly rudimentary but is nonetheless crucial in guiding the audience's understanding of what they are watching. Of course some films – such as Dziga Vertov's *Man With a Movie Camera* (USSR 1929), or the projects Jean-Luc Godard undertook in the early 1970s as part of the Dziga Vertov collective – abjure storytelling as a political gesture; then again there are others – Patrick Keilor's meditative reflections on contemporary Britain *London* (GB 1995) and *Robinson in Space* (GB 1997) come to mind – where fragments of narrative tease the audience with hints of a larger picture into which they never cohere. Certainly, however, narrative is a fundamental dimension both of the international art cinema of Fellini, Bergman, Kurosawa, Visconti, etc., and indeed of most European New Wave filmmakers including Godard himself until 1967. What differentiates these films from classic Hollywood is not the presence or absence of narrative as a fundamental 'ground', but the extent to which assumptions about narrative *form* and *direction* shape the architecture of the film as a whole.

In fact, Bordwell and his co-writers know this very well, and their arguments therefore have a tinge of bad faith about them. A revealing aside claims that in seventies Hollywood, 'classical film style and codified genres swallow up art-film borrowings, taming the (*already limited*) disruptiveness of the art cinema'.[23] Assuming that 'disruption' here means 'challenge to discursive conventions' (and not the mobilisation of political consciousness, on which count Eric Johnston's favourites *The Grapes of Wrath* and *Tobacco Road* have as good a claim as most art films), this comment confirms that in Bordwell's view the resistance offered by art cinema to norms of style, genre and narrative are perhaps questions of degree rather than of kind. When Bordwell writes of the inconsistent attitudes and motivations, the self-questioning and undefined objectives of characters in films such as Fellini's *La Dolce Vita* (It 1960) or Bergman's *Wild Strawberries* (Swe 1957), notes the absence of clear choices/ turning points and the 'drifting, episodic quality' such elements lend to many art film narratives, and contrasts these to the 'clear-cut traits and objectives' of Hollywood film, his argument certainly holds good for *Casablanca* or for that matter *Jaws* – but what about *Five Easy Pieces* or *Pat Garrett and Billy the Kid*, to which all of the above 'art film' attributes could reasonably be applied? Conversely, how well do such claims illuminate a classic art film such as *The Seventh Seal* (Swe 1956)? The dilemmas and choices facing Bergman's Knight may be highly metaphysical by contrast with the Wild Bunch's desire for 'one last big score' but they are neither undefined nor inconsistent. It is undeniably true that, as Geoff King pointed out, few if any Hollywood films allow for the narratively unanchored ruminations on politics, economics and sexuality of, say, Godard's *Deux ou Trois Choses que Je Sais d'Elle* (1965), still less the didactic Marxist polemics of *La Chinoise* (1967).[24] However, there are Hollywood protagonists whose goal-oriented behaviour is foregrounded to the point of parody – such as Walker in *Point Blank*, whose obstinate determination to retrieve the loot stolen from him by his partner and cheating wife is the object of perplexed comment by pretty much everyone else in the film.

Once sees how quickly discussion of the stylistic attributes of Hollywood Renaissance films bleeds into consideration of narrative content, and beyond that to larger questions of ideology. When, starting in the late sixties, critics such as Pauline Kael and Roger Ebert and academic commentators such as Thomas Elsaesser first outlined the lineaments of a contemporary 'New Hollywood' or 'new American cinema', it was the transformation of narrative on which they laid greatest emphasis. They identified the emergence of looser narrative forms such as the road movie and a partial prioritisation of mood over story, the decline of the heroic individual protagonist in the face of a pervasive sense of the futility of traditional goal-oriented action, and a consequent tendency towards existential self-assertion through acts of motiveless violence, as key elements in this cinema.[25] According to Roger Ebert in a contemporary review, for example, the narrative indeterminacy of *Five Easy Pieces* 'doesn't matter much. What matters is the character during the time covered by the film'[26] – a claim that could apply equally well to Rafelson's follow-up *The King of Marvin Gardens* (Col 1972) or Altman's *Three Women*.

Although it relates film style in minute and copiously documented detail to industry practice (and applies Marxist economics to analyse the evolving studio system), *The Classical Hollywood Cinema* brackets off larger social, cultural and political contexts almost entirely. In his later study of Hollywood, indeed, Bordwell explicitly teases culturally oriented analyses of Hollywood for their 'immediate impulse to look for some broad cultural change as the trigger' for stylistic change in favour of 'more proximate [i.e., intra-Hollywood] causes'.[27] Kristin Thompson has named this critical practice 'neo-formalism'.[28] But it should be plain by now that the picture of the challenge to classical style offered by the Hollywood Renaissance cannot be limited to questions of 'how' without also asking 'why?' In Chapter 4 we have seen how the condition of the film industry in the late 1960s opened up a window of opportunity for the 'movie generation' of filmmakers. Contemporary commentators, however, were equally clear that the transformed American cinema was bound up with a particular politics: a radical scepticism about traditional American values. In the studio era, learning the formal and narrative conventions that regulated Hollywood films was a symbolic point of entry into

American civic identity. Its strongly individualised narrative focus, emphatically linear storylines, and typically positive and culturally affirmative resolutions, confirmed the providential lineaments of the American imaginary. By contrast, the modish left-liberal-cynical politics of Altman's *Nashville* (Par 1976) found formal expression in a destabilisation of the visual focus and a displacement of the traditional heroic individual protagonist and the vertical organization he authorised in favour of a polyvocal, multi-stranded lateral narrative from which is solicited the spectator's participation, not merely her acceptance. Indeed, one of the most significant features of the period – which distinguishes it from the modes of Hollywood cinema that preceded and followed it – is the extent to which form and narrative, answering to a specific and intense moment of industrial and social crisis, are consciously mobilised as tools of ideological critique. The next chapter will therefore examine the ways in which the formal innovations most characteristic of the Hollywood New Wave articulate critical (if often contradictory) stances on American society in a period of acute crisis, and on film's role in that society.

NOTES

1. Murray Smith, 'Theses on the philosophy of Hollywood history', in Steve Neale and Murray Smith (eds), *Contemporary Hollywood Cinema* (London: Routledge, 1998), p. 10.
2. Robert B. Ray, *A Certain Tendency of the Hollywood Cinema, 1930–1980* (Princeton: Princeton University Press, 1985), p. 287.
3. See Colin MacCabe, 'Realism and the cinema: notes on some Brechtian theses', *Screen* 1974; 15:7–27.
4. David Bordwell, Janet Staiger and Kristin Thompson, *The Classical Hollywood Cinema: Film Style and Mode of Production to 1960* (London: Routledge, 1985), pp. 372–7. (Hereafter *CHC*.)
5. Harold Bloom, *The Anxiety of Influence: A Theory of Poetry*, 2nd edn (New York: Oxford University Press, 1997).
6. Jump cut: sequential shots where the camera moves in space but not in time or vice versa, creating discontinuity.
7. Robert Kolker, *A Cinema of Loneliness: Penn, Stone, Kubrick, Scorsese, Spielberg, Altman*, 3rd edn (Oxford: Oxford University Press, 2000), p. 186.
8. Barbara Wilinsky, *Sure Seaters: The Emergence of Art House Cinema* (Minneapolis: University of Minnesota Press, 2001), p. 2.
9. 'A religion of film', *Time*, 20 September 1963, pp. 78–82 [cover story].
10. Andrew Sarris, *The American Cinema: Directors and Directions, 1929–1968* (Chicago: University of Chicago Press, 1985).
11. 'The Late Show as history', *Time*, 28 June 1968, pp. 76–8.
12. An obvious recent example would be Quentin Tarantino's deft but entirely superficial jostling of time-schemes in *Pulp Fiction* (Miramax 1994).
13. Welles's difficulties funding the production meant that *Othello* was filmed in a variety of different locations over a considerable period of time – shot-reverse shot patterns in the same scene might mask a gap of hundreds of miles and several months between shots.

14. Unless otherwise noted, the data for ASLs is derived from the Cinemetrics database at www.cinemetrics.lv

15. See David Bordwell, *The Way Hollywood Tells It* (Berkeley: University of California Press, 2005); Barry Salt, *Film Style: History and Analysis*, 2nd edn (London: Starword, 1992).

16. David A. Cook, *Lost Illusions: American Cinema in the Shadow of Watergate and Vietnam* (Berkeley: University of California Press, 2000), p. 359.

17. Both Zsigmond and Kovacs were refugees from the Hungarian uprising of 1956.

18. Wexler was credited as 'photographic consultant' on *American Graffiti*.

19. For a detailed discussion of the careers and techniques of the principal cinematographers of the period, see Dennis Schaefer and Larry Salvato, *Masters of Light: Conversations with Contemporary Cinematographers* (Berkeley: University of California Press, 1984).

20. The term is coined by Miriam Hansen in 'The mass production of the senses: classical cinema as vernacular modernism', *Modernism/Modernity* 1999; 6(2):59–77.

21. See Chapter 6, p. 169.

22. Bordwell, *The Way Hollywood Tells It*, p. 89.

23. *CHC*, p. 375, emphasis added.

24. King usefully contrasts Godard's famous zoom into a cup of coffee with Scorsese's 'quotation' of the shot – a fizzing glass of Alka-Seltzer – in *Taxi Driver*, pointing out both the brevity of the latter and its incorporation into Travis Bickle's mindscape.

25. See Thomas Elsaesser, 'The pathos of failure: American films in the 1970s: notes on the unmotivated hero', in Thomas Elsaesser and Andrew Horwath (eds), *The Last Great American Picture Show: The New Hollywood of the 1970s* (Amsterdam: Amsterdam University Press, 2004). These and other contemporary discussions of the Hollywood Renaissance as a post-classical cinema are summarised in Peter Krämer, 'Post-classical Hollywood', in John Hill and Pamela Church Gibson (eds), *The Oxford Guide to Film Studies* (Oxford: Oxford University Press, 1998), pp. 289–309.

26. Roger Ebert, *Chicago Sun-Times*, 1 January 1970, p. C3.

27. Bordwell, *The Way Hollywood Tells It*, p. 73.

28. See Kristin Thompson, *Breaking the Glass Armor: Neoformalist Film Analysis* (Princeton: Princeton University Press, 1988).

The Biggest, The Best: 1975

Best Picture: *One Flew Over the Cuckoo's Nest* (United Artists/Fantasy Films)
D: Milos Forman; **P:** Michael Douglas, Saul Zaentz; **W:** Lawrence Haubman, Bo Goldman (based on the novel by Ken Kesey)
Box Office No. 1: *Jaws* (Universal)
D: Steven Spielberg; **P:** Richard Zanuck and David Brown; **W:** Carl Gottlieb, Peter Benchley and Mario Puzo (based on the novel by Peter Benchley)

Important watersheds are often more visible in history's rear-view mirror. Looking back on 1975 at that year's end, it might well have seemed that the artistic and commercial ascendancy of the Hollywood Renaissance was more assured than ever. The annual box office top ten boasted perhaps the most quintessentially New Cinema line-up of the whole decade: two rock musicals (Fox's *The Rocky Horror Picture Show* and Columbia's *Tommy*), Warner's transgender heist movie *Dog Day Afternoon*, Columbia's political sex comedy *Shampoo* and the Paramount conspiracy thriller *Three Days of the Condor*. The year's second-placed film, Czech director Milos Forman's adaptation of Ken Kesey's anti-authoritarian countercultural classic *One Flew Over the Cuckoo's Nest*, went on to win all five major Academy Awards (Picture, Director, Actor, Actress, and Adapted Screenplay) the following March – the first time since *It Happened One Night* in 1934.

But from today's vantage point, the success and significance of all these films – even *Cuckoo's Nest* – are overshadowed by the year's runaway number one, Steven Spielberg's *Jaws*. Not that anyone was in any doubt in 1975 that *Jaws*' unprecedented success (Spielberg's film was officially declared the all-time top-grossing film in December) was a potentially game-changing milestone. 1975 was indeed, as *Time* put it, 'The Year of the Shark'. Yet what was less immediately apparent, maybe, was what now seems most obvious of all: that *Jaws* had ushered in a new blockbuster aesthetics and economics that would shortly close down the room for creative manoeuvre in which the artistically and politically challenging films of the Hollywood Renaissance had briefly flourished.

This was probably because *Jaws* at the time seemed very much part of the Hollywood revolution, rather than its gravedigger. As was also true of *American Graffiti* (U 1973), the earlier breakout hit of George Lucas – with whom Spielberg's name and career would afterwards come to be conjoined in many critical accounts – *Jaws* seemed a good deal more progressive than it does with benefit of hindsight.[1] The film's story of a venal small-town establishment covering up the deadly attacks of a rogue shark[2] to protect their commercial interests echoed – albeit, as Mark Shiel says, in 'a very dilute residue'[3] – contemporary anti-authoritarian conspiracy films and satires such as *Network*. Furthermore, everyone agreed, then as now, that technically and stylistically the film was a *tour de force* that announced the arrival of a major directorial talent.

Today – especially in light of Spielberg's obsessive focus on the defence and reconstitution of the nuclear family throughout his subsequent films – *Jaws*' reauthorisation of a conservatively conceived middle-class patriarchal

Jaws (Universal 1975): the start of a new era. Reproduced courtesy of The Kobal Collection

masculinity, embodied by father, husband and lawman Chief Brody (Roy Scheider), seems very much more apparent and has been particularly effectively anatomised by Robert Kolker.[4] (By the same token, Ken Kesey protested the way that *Cuckoo's Nest* had softened his novel's corrosive allegory of an oppressive and exclusionary American society into a populist, *Cool Hand Luke*-style fable of individualist rebellion.) We can also recognise *Jaws'* affinities with the immensely popular, ideologically conservative contemporary disaster film and (more distantly) vigilante/rogue cop movies.

Nonetheless, it is the commercial dimensions of *Jaws'* success that have secured its place in film history: not simply its record-breaking returns, which – expanding the reach of the decade's earlier, R-rated smashes *The Exorcist* and *The Godfather* to the lucrative juvenile/family audience – massively upped the ante for a major hit, but the publicity campaign masterminded with military precision by MCA president Lew Wasserman that maximised *Jaws*-awareness and paved the way for the contemporary Hollywood model of blockbuster film as multimedia phenomenon. Many aspects of Wasserman's release strategy for *Jaws*, and the $1.8 million marketing campaign that supported it, have entered industry lore as game-changing innovations: the intensely marketed 'pre-sold' property, the summer opening (traditionally a dead spot in the studios' release schedules), saturation booking in 500 theatres, and the use of spot advertising on network TV (and even a colour spread in *TV Guide*) to drive awareness of and interest in the picture to fever pitch ahead of its opening weekend.[5]

Perhaps inevitably, the Wasserman/*Jaws* myth has recently been subject to a certain amount of historical revisionism.[6] The summer season had in fact first taken on added importance in Hollywood's release schedules as far back as the early 1950s, when the popularity of drive-ins increased attendance in the warmer months, traditionally the doldrums for theatre operators. In response, the studios adjusted their distribution practices, booking big-budget spectacles such as Paramount's *The Greatest Show on Earth* 'wide', by the standards of the time (into seven Los Angeles theatres, including four suburban drive-ins, rather than the customary two downtown houses).[7] Wasserman's fabled innovation of TV spot advertising also drew on both recent (*Billy Jack*) and much older precedents: as early as 1955, industry surveys had proven television's effectiveness compared to print ads in drawing audiences to new releases.[8] As for the 'pre-sold' property, the enhanced value of high-profile acquisitions from Broadway and the bestseller lists had been recognised throughout the post-*Paramount* era, as had the mutually beneficial cross-promotion of novel and movie.[9] Nonetheless, the *Jaws* campaign brought together all these tactics into an eye-catching strategic synthesis and exploited them to the maximum. The way Universal turned the box office success of their film into a story in its own right – taking out a front-page ad in *Daily Variety* to trumpet its then-record opening weekend takings – also inaugurated the intense scrutiny and handicapping of box office prospects that today attends every major release.[10]

Notes

1. On *American Graffiti* and the Hollywood Renaissance, see Barry Langford, '*American Graffiti*', in Mandy Merck (ed.), *America First: Naming the Nation in American Film* (London: Routledge, 2007), pp. 157–76.
2. Modelled, *Jaws* author Peter Benchley grandly claimed, on Ibsen's *An Enemy of the People*.
3. Mark Shiel, 'American cinema, 1970–75', in Linda Ruth Williams and Michael Hammond (eds), *Contemporary American Cinema* (Maidenhead: McGraw-Hill, 2005), p. 153.
4. Robert Kolker, *A Cinema of Loneliness: Penn, Stone, Kubrick, Scorsese, Spielberg, Altman*, 3rd edn (New York: Oxford University Press, 2000), pp. 290–305.
5. See for instance 'Movies take to TV to lure the fans', *Business Week*, 3 March 1975, pp. 34–8; Douglas Gomery, *The Hollywood Studio System: A History* (London: BFI, 2005), pp. 213–15.
6. See Dade Hayes and Jonathon Bing, *Open Wide: How Hollywood Box Office Became a National Obsession* (New York: Miramax, 2004), pp. 156–60.
7. 'How Hollywood hopes to hit comeback road', *Newsweek*, 12 January 1953, pp. 66–7.
8. 'Change of heart', *Time*, 28 February 1955, p. 84.
9. See 'Getting them back to the movies', *Business Week*, 22 October 1955, p. 60: 'Hollywood is buying more pre-tested and pre-sold properties'.
10. See Elizabeth Guider, '*Jaws* phenom took bite of history', *Variety*, 11 June 2006. Online: http://www.variety.com/index.asp?layout=variety100&content=jump&jump=article&articleID=VR1117944996&category=1930

CHAPTER 6

Who Lost the Picture Show?

I 968 was a year in which America appeared almost to be coming apart. In January, TV news footage from Vietnam of hand-to-hand combat between US forces and Communist Viet Cong within the US embassy compound in Saigon and streetfighting in cities throughout South Vietnam shocked Americans who had believed the repeated promises of President Lyndon Johnson and his military commander in Indochina, William Westmoreland, that victory was at hand. The Tet Offensive (in strictly military terms a major setback) was a huge propaganda triumph for the North Vietnamese and con-tributed to a hardening of opinion against the conflict among middle Americans and the liberal establishment, if only because the war seemed manifestly unwinnable. Meanwhile antiwar protest on US campuses continued to inten-sify. Violent battles between student protestors and police became an increas-ingly familiar sight. The student left's increasing radicalism was matched by the growing militancy of the civil rights movement, now increasingly turning away from Martin Luther King's philosophy of principled non-violence and towards the more confrontational attitudes of black nationalism, personified in the slogan of the martyred Malcolm X: 'by any means necessary'. The two crusades – antiwar and anti-racism – were profoundly connected.

It was a year in which dramatic and tragic events followed hard upon one another in an almost apocalyptic spiral. With the Tet Offensive still raging, Johnson lost the New Hampshire presidential primary to Senator Eugene McCarthy, running on an antiwar platform – an almost unprecedented humiliation for a sitting president. On 31 March, Johnson, a haggard shadow of the man who four years earlier had proclaimed the Great Society, a pro-gramme of far-reaching liberal reforms intended to complete Roosevelt's New Deal, announced without warning that he would not run for re-election in November. Three days later Martin Luther King, whose own liberation poli-tics had expanded and radicalised since 1966 to incorporate both antiwar and

Living up to a 'big rep': McCabe (Warren Beatty) plays the hero in Robert Altman's *McCabe & Mrs. Miller* (Warner Brothers 1971). Reproduced courtesy of The Kobal Collection

anti-poverty campaigns, was shot dead in Memphis, where he had journeyed to support striking sanitation workers. King's murder provoked insurrections in the overcrowded black ghettoes in over 100 American cities. US soldiers were sent into action in the nation's capital and elsewhere to 'pacify' their fellow citizens even as their comrades (among whom poor African Americans numbered disproportionately) were trying and failing to 'win the hearts and minds' of the Vietnamese. Briefly, it seemed that the insurgent presidential candidacy of John Kennedy's younger brother Robert would take up King's mantle. Kennedy embodied the promise that the American political system, shaken to its core by its recent traumas, could yet harness the hopes and fulfil the aspirations of millions of poor, black and Hispanic Americans and end the violence in Vietnam. But just moments after claiming victory in the California primary in June – and with it, almost certainly, the party nomination – Kennedy, who on the night of King's murder, quoting Aeschylus, had urged reconciliation to a multiracial crowd in Indianapolis, was himself shot and killed.

The murders of King and Kennedy seemed to symbolise America's rage turned against itself. The year's convulsive rage peaked in pitched battles – televised live, as the battered protestors tauntingly chanted, to a watching world – between excluded antiwar activists and the brutal Chicago police outside the Democratic Convention in July. That November the veteran anticommunist and political manipulator Richard 'Tricky Dick' Nixon won the presidency for the Republicans on the promise of a 'secret plan' to end the war. Nixon's plan, it turned out in subsequent months, was to try to bomb the North Vietnamese to the conference table, futilely if murderously raining unprecedented amounts of munitions on the small peasant nation and recklessly extending the conflict to neighbouring neutral Laos and Cambodia – actions which provoked a crescendo of rage in the antiwar movement and led to six unarmed student protestors being shot dead by uniformed National Guardsmen at Kent State and Jackson State universities in April 1970.

Little of this turmoil, which led numerous commentators to speculate seriously about the possibility of outright social implosion, revolution and/or anarchy in the USA, could have been guessed at from the major Hollywood releases of the fateful year 1968. The year's top-earning film, *Funny Girl*, led a posse of Hollywood Establishment vehicles doggedly pursued the dwindling family audience, high-budget period musicals such as *Star!*, *Oliver!* (Col) and *Chitty Chitty, Bang Bang* (UA), and costume dramas such as *The Lion in Winter* (Embassy) and *The Fox* (WB). At that year's Academy Awards – postponed for two days following King's assassination – the 1967 Best Picture Oscar went to the liberal *In the Heat of the Night*, but its integrationist message now seemed instantly dated by the ongoing racial violence on US streets. (*Oliver!* would win Best Picture for 1968.) War itself took a mostly nostalgic form in rip-roaring if ultra-violent (on the model of the previous year's smash success *The Dirty Dozen*) World War II adventures such as UA's *The Devil's Brigade* – Hollywood acknowledged Vietnam only in John Wayne's self-produced *The Green Berets*, an unremittingly conservative and parodically gung-ho film which blames the US media's failure to 'tell the real story' for undermining America's noble mission in Indochina. Although commercially successful, ranking eleventh in the year's box office (indicating that by no means all of American society agreed with the antiwar movement), *The Green Berets* was dismissed by mainstream critics and greeted with predictable contempt and hostility by the left.

One distinct, if reactionary, trace of contemporary events might be discerned in the year's crop of violent contemporary *policiers* – Warner's *Bullitt*, Universal's *Madigan* and *Coogan's Bluff*, and Fox's *The Detective* – all focusing

on the struggle of lone lawmen to promote a conservative and fiercely individualist version of law and order in the face of burgeoning criminality, a
corrupt or impotent establishment, and a decadent and indifferent culture.
Such films looked forward to the vigilante and extra-legal crime dramas of the
early seventies which similarly pitted anti-heroic loners against urban devi-
ants, parasites and vermin: *The French Connection*, Warner's *Dirty Harry* and
its sequels *Magnum Force* (1973) and *The Enforcer* (1978), and *Death Wish* (Par
1974). The presence in the year's top ten of non-traditional genres such as
science fiction, with Kubrick's *2001:A Space Odyssey* (a major youth hit) and
Planet of the Apes, and horror, with Polanski's *Rosemary's Baby*, also hinted
that business was not quite as usual. In general, however, the majors effectively
abdicated responsibility for reflecting or responding to the engulfing turmoil
– despite the success with youth audiences of *The Graduate* and *Bonnie and
Clyde* the previous year – to independent producers, notably those producing
exploitation films for the youth market. AIP's *Psych-Out* and *Wild in the Streets*
and ABC/Cinerama's adaptation of Terry Southern's *Candy* luridly explored
the 'hippie' counterculture.

Perhaps the sheer extremity and volatility of the events of 1968 closed
down the creative space necessary for their translation into popular narrative.
Certainly, in the following two years, in the wake of *Easy Rider* numerous
campus rebellion and other youth-themed pictures came tumbling forth, but
apart from *Woodstock*, *Alice's Restaurant*, Haskell Wexler's *Medium Cool* (Par
1969), Antonioni's *Zabriskie Point* and John G. Avildsen's rabble-rousing *Joe*,
most of the overtly topical films released, such as a cycle of campus protest
pictures including veteran Stanley Kramer's *RPM** (Col 1970), were derided
by their target audience as the transparent, mealy-mouthed exploitations of
the counterculture by 'straights'. The almost universal failure of these films
to find their mark ensured that by late 1971 topical and political subjects
had once again retreated from view (although some youth-oriented 'lifestyle'
films from *Five Easy Pieces* to *Such Good Friends* (Par 1971) and *The Christian
Licorice Store* (National General 1971)[1] continued to feature). Blaxploitation
(which took off in 1971) of course addressed itself to post-civil rights African-
American urban audiences, but its tales of gang warfare, drug dealers, pimps
and super-spades typically paid only lip service (if that) to contemporary black
political concerns.

In fact, Hollywood *circa* 1970 found itself in something of a crux. In
Chapter 4 we saw how the structural upheavals in the film industry in the
late 1960s compelled Hollywood to attend more closely to the energies of a
turbulent American society than at any time since the demise of the studio
system. The stolidly affirmative Americanism that dominated the transitional
(late studio) era had proved unsustainable in the face of Vietnam, Watts and
the cycle of political assassinations. Just as the Beats' subterranean cultural

resistance to the culture of consumerism, conformity and Cold War erupted on to Main Street with the sixties New Left and the counterculture, so the dissident strains of both gritty realism and modernist experimentation in late fifties and early sixties Hollywood cinema went mainstream. Changing audience patterns – particularly the need to appeal to the youth market – encouraged studio executives to commission projects that seemed to take up fashionable critical attitudes towards 'Establishment' values and mores. As several commentators noted, the cinema's substitution by television as the preferred mirror of 'mainstream' American values – in Steve Neale's words, 'the main vector of ideology in the mass media' – both enabled and necessitated movies to adopt more marginal and controversial positions.[2] The CARA ratings system encouraged Hollywood to differentiate theatrical from television product through ever larger doses of graphic sex and violence: this in itself was no guarantee of progressive politics (as Peckinpah's *Straw Dogs* (UA 1971) vividly demonstrated), but it ensured that movies, unlike the anodyne fantasyland of network TV, at least swam in the same increasingly turbulent waters as the rest of the nation.

Yet although they kept their hair fashionably long, abjured suits and ties and usually wore beards, the Renaissance filmmakers generally had little personal connection to the counterculture or the New Left. (They had, after all, chosen to work in the world's most intensively commercialised film industry, hardly an incubator of radicalism.) There were some exceptions: Brian De Palma was involved with the New York underground, chronicled in his early independent Filmways productions *Greetings* (1968) and *Hi Mom!* (1970); both Peter Fonda and Dennis Hopper were fixtures on the West Coast 'scene'; BBS co-founder Bert Schneider was a prominent supporter of the Back Panthers; cinematographer Haskell Wexler's committed radicalism extended to secretly filming a documentary with the urban guerrillas of the illegal Weather Underground.[3] Sometimes these links were hard to distinguish from what journalist Tom Wolfe memorably called 'radical chic' – such as actor Jon Voigt loaning his San Francisco houseboat to Weather Underground fugitives. A very small number of Renaissance filmmakers at least partly shared the New Left's excoriating vision of Nixon-era America, while a somewhat larger number felt a measure of affinity with some – usually the more sybaritic or broadly 'cultural' (as opposed to 'political') aspects – of the youth counterculture. But few of their films dealt directly with hippies, drop-outs or student revolutionaries. The socially marginal protagonists of films such as *Midnight Cowboy, Five Easy Pieces, The Panic in Needle Park* (Fox 1971), *Klute, Steelyard Blues* (WB 1972), *Cisco Pike* (Col 1972), *Thieves Like Us* (UA 1974) or *Taxi Driver* were often older, more likely to be apolitical and isolated than part of any movement, their rejection of mainstream culture typically expressed through criminality, substance abuse or violence rather than protest.

All of which made a little-noticed 1968 AIP film a good deal more significant than it might have seemed at the time. The debut picture of Roger Corman protégé Peter Bogdanovich, *Targets* adroitly set the imaginary terrors of old Hollywood (personified by Boris Karloff, effectively playing himself as a courtly, ageing Golden Age horror legend) against the contemporary and highly topical horror of a psychopathic ex-Marine sniper. In retrospect, *Targets* can be seen as an early example of the critical interrogation of classic Hollywood tropes – a technique that would come to define the Hollywood Renaissance. Its conclusion, in which Karloff successfully faces down and disarms the gunman at a drive-in (showing Corman's *The Horror*, with whose left-over crew and shooting time Bogdanovich made his own picture), epitomised a new self-consciousness about the cultural role of cinema. Although *Targets* suggested a more idealised or even naively optimistic attitude towards the redemptive capacity of movies than most later Renaissance films, it previewed the principal tactic employed by the 'film generation' to engage with contemporary society and politics.

Over the coming decade, a small number of notable films would try to address directly some of the topical events and issues that continued to trouble American self-confidence and social cohesion, including police corruption (*Serpico*, Par 1973), the possible conspiracy to assassinate John Kennedy (*Executive Action*, EA Enterprises 1973), the secretive and even criminal activities of large corporations (*The Formula*, MGM 1975), the empty hedonism of the 'swinging' sixties (*Shampoo*, Col 1975), media manipulation (*Network*, MGM 1976), and of course Watergate (*All the President's Men*, WB 1976), which capped and summed up what historian John Morton Blum called America's 'years of discord.'[4] A far greater number, however, used political symbolism and allegory and formal methods that reflexively interrogated both the values of straight America and the ways in which those values had hitherto been seamlessly transmitted by Hollywood cinema. In a decade when, seeking some measurable security at a time of audience volatility and industrial certainty, Hollywood returned to regular genre production for the first time since the studio era, both the emergence of new genres such as the conspiracy film and the road movie, and the self-conscious revision and updating of traditional genres – above all the Western – also played a central role.

POLITICS, BY ANY OTHER NAME: GENRE REVISIONISM AND ALLUSIONISM

The directors with the most open affinity with the era's radicalism were all older: Arthur Penn (whose leftist politics dated back to the McCarthy era), the radical libertarian Sam Peckinpah and Robert Altman, whose unclassifiable yet unmistakeably left attitudes informed such films as *McCabe & Mrs. Miller*, *Nashville*, and *Buffalo Bill and the Indians*. Throughout the decade all these directors made predominantly genre films: all three made Westerns; Penn and Altman both directed private eye neo-*noirs* (*Night Moves* and *The Long Goodbye*), Altman and Peckinpah war films (*M*A*S*H* and *Cross of Iron* (EMI 1977)) and gangster films (*Thieves Like Us* and *The Getaway*), and Altman also made musicals (*Nashville* and *Popeye*). Apart from Peckinpah's late, marginal road movie *Convoy* (EMI 1978), none concerned themselves much with the newer genres. However, they turned these traditional genres to decidedly non-traditional ends, bending if not breaking generic conventions and inverting genre forms to comment on their own structures and motivations.

The Western, to which these three directors all turned in the early seventies, best illustrates their critical engagement with classical genres, typifying the critical strategies of the Renaissance as a whole. Its resurgence in the seventies (after a long and fairly continuous period of declining production and box office returns since the late 1950s) was directly lined to the genre's capacity to articulate critical positions in a particularly obvious way. As Jack Nachbar writes, 'the subject matter of Westerns has usually been the historical West after 1850, but the real emotional and ideological subject matter has invariably been the issues of the era in which the films were released', and so it was in the 1970s.[5] Westerns have long been seen as a kind of master key to unlocking and understanding the most basic elements of American identity. 'Westerns appeal so much to us [i.e., Americans]', according to Joan Mellen, 'because they are explorations of who we are, dramas in which America's soul, the national identity, hangs in the balance.'[6] Additionally, the Western's unusual degree of iconographic and thematic consistency and its uniquely specific social, historical, and geographic locus (North America west of the Mississippi, between the end of the Civil War and US entry into World War I) – the same factors that have always recommended the Western as a model for genre theorists – also made it peculiarly suitable for revisionist treatment. Interference in the narrative paradigms and iconography of the Western was exceptionally visible and its bearing on an ideological perspective – the myths of white settlement, 'manifest destiny' and American exceptionalism – equally legible.

Of the three directors, Peckinpah's association with the Western was much the strongest – in fact, all but two of his nine theatrical features from 1961 to 1973 were Westerns, and Peckinpah would become almost as closely identified with the genre as John Ford himself. He also displays the most serious, though radically unconventional, investment in the genre's rituals and mythologies: rather like his anti-hero Pat Garrett, his assassination of those forms might be characterised as both ruthless and regretful. Peckinpah's Westerns of 1969–73, *The Wild Bunch*, *The Ballad of Cable Hogue* (WB 1970) and *Pat Garrett and Billy the Kid*, are all 'end of the line' Westerns, like his earlier, eulogistic *Ride the High Country* (MGM 1962) and with *Junior Bonner* (ABC 1971) as a less tragic modern pendant. In these films Peckinpah explored the West's shrinking horizons and the Westerner's few remaining options in an era when, as Pike Bishop (William Holden), leader of the Bunch, memorably observes, 'We've got to think beyond our guns. Them days are closing fast.' Peckinpah's protagonists typically find themselves unable or unwilling to adapt to the new times, but equally unable to hold back the inexorable pace of social change. As Douglas Pye has commented, their 'range of action [is] finally limited in some cases to a choice of how to die' – as at the climaxes of *Ride the High Country* and, above all, the notorious bloodbath in which the Wild Bunch finally immolate themselves (and several score Mexican soldiers and camp followers).[7]

Although Peckinpah, unlike Penn and Altman, takes the supposed honour as well as the mythic status of the Western seriously, at the same time such ideals are repeatedly violated by his protagonists in the face of pitiless realities. Peckinpah's protagonists are mostly as brutal and unprincipled as circumstances require them to be (unlike the courtly outlaws of the contemporaneous and thematically similar but infinitely less challenging – and much more popular – *Butch Cassidy and the Sundance Kid*). The most they have going for them is that however compromised and violent, they are – perhaps – less venal, exploitative and hypocritical than their 'legitimate' opponents. Tellingly, the Bunch make their final stand in 1913, against symbols of a technological modernity compared with whose industrial killing practices their own brutality seems merely the violent child's play depicted in the film's viscerally upsetting opening sequence (children torturing insects). A Prussian military advisor and a Maxim gun both foretell the imminent mechanised mass slaughter of World War I, by entering which conflict, the fundamental violence of American ideology would be exported into world affairs. A continuum is thus created between the brutality of the frontier and the Vietnam War, whose escalating bloody barbarism Peckinpah explicitly intended *The Wild Bunch*'s unprecedented ferocity to invoke (the Bunch make their first entrance disguised as a US army detail).[8]

Penn's mock-epic *Little Big Man* has no interest in eulogising the passing of the West. Instead, it turns the genre's traditional values on their head to portray western expansion not as manifest destiny but as premeditated genocide. Over the course of the film's rambling, picaresque narrative its bi-cultural protagonist (a white man raised by Cheyenne Indians) shuttles between a white settler society rendered as corrupt, repressive, materialistic and life-denying and an indigenous culture portrayed as generous, grounded and humane. Whereas the contemporary reference of *The Wild Bunch* was indirect and associative, *Little Big Man*'s allegorisation of contemporary politics is intentionally hard to miss. In their environmentalism, their communal society, and their essential pacifism the Cheyenne are obviously identified with the counterculture; as victims of genocidal imperialism and advanced military technology they stand for the peasants of North Vietnam. Like another 1970 'Vietnam Western' *Soldier Blue* (Embassy), the film centres on a bloody massacre of unarmed Indian villagers that quite explicitly evokes the My Lai massacre of March 1968[9] and other atrocities committed by US troops in Vietnam. Both films go far beyond the 'pro-Indian' Westerns of the early 1950s and subsequently (including Ford's own proto-revisionist *Cheyenne Autumn* (WB 1964)) in inverting the traditional coding of Indians as the heathen 'other': here it is whites generally, and the US armed forces in particular, who are portrayed as barbarous savages (the troopers in *Soldier Blue* emit Indian-style war-whoops as they gleefully pillage, rape and murder).

Finally, Altman's take on the Western in *McCabe & Mrs. Miller* also critiques the myth of the frontier, but through detached irony rather than outrage or inversion. Set in a non-canonical wintry Pacific Northwest, the film tells a classically structured story of a lone horseman riding into a frontier town – in fact, barely more than a collection of jerry-built shacks. However, although upon his arrival John McCabe (Warren Beatty) is quickly identified as legendary gunfighter 'Pudgy' McCabe, in reality he is neither a gunslinger (like Shane), nor a lawman (like Wyatt Earp), nor is he a prospector, though this is a mining town: if 'Pudgy' ever really existed outside of his 'big rep', this isn't the guy. The soundtrack accompaniment of howling winds and Leonard Cohen's anachronistic, allusive folk songs ('he was just some Joseph looking for a manger . . .') adds to the distance from the generic tropes that are simultaneously invoked and denied. This McCabe is a businessman, and a distinctively unheroic one: his entrepreneurial vision is to open a brothel to cater to the growing settlement, and he is unable even to succeed at that until the English madam Mrs Miller (Julie Christie) becomes his partner (only in business, not, though McCabe wishes it were so, in love: as the ampersand in the title suggests, the classic Hollywood heterosexual romance is also among the targets of Altman's irony).

McCabe is finally forced – or as Altman plainly sees it, conned – into living up to the 'big rep' he has fostered when, his head filled with half-baked, second-hand sentimental notions of heroic individualism straight out of *Young Mr Lincoln*, he faces down a hit squad sent by a mining conglomerate whose buyout offer he has rashly rejected. In a sequence that ironically replays *High Noon* McCabe defeats his three opponents, but the townsfolk for whose 'freedom' he believes he is fighting never even notice: as the mortally wounded McCabe dies alone in the snow on the outskirts of town they are busy firefighting at the church they barely attend – their efforts, like McCabe's sacrifice, are unexamined, gestural, pointless.

McCabe & Mrs. Miller's key intertext is Ford's classic 'town-taming' Western *My Darling Clementine*, whose church dedication scene is one of the genre's great landmarks of progressive optimism (the name of the muddy ramshackle settlement in Altman's film is Presbyterian Church). As Western cattleman/lawman Wyatt Earp and Boston teacher Clementine awkwardly sashay around the impromptu dancefloor, Monument Valley behind and the Stars and Stripes fluttering gaily overhead, what Jim Kitses identified as the genre's 'structuring antinomies' – civilisation and wilderness, nature and culture, individual and community, etc. – are at once crystallised and annealed.[10] In *McCabe & Mrs. Miller* all of the principles in whose name Ford's heroes act are revealed as fatuous or simply lies. The church, as noted, is an empty symbol that mockingly points up the absence of the community it supposedly unites; the business know-how of the Cockney brothel keeper Mrs Miller parodies Clementine's Eastern refinement; McCabe's sacrifice, heroic as it may be, is futile: no one pays any attention and the mining company will, presumably, send in another set of goons the next week. (Peckinpah also takes on Ford when a temperance parade singing Ford's favourite hymn, 'Gather at the River' – sung at the church dedication in *My Darling Clementine* – is blown apart in the crossfire of the opening massacre in *The Wild Bunch*.)

In what proved the Western's last major flowering, with some three dozen released between 1969 and 1975, others followed one or other of these approaches alongside a few traditional Westerns, mostly starring John Wayne. Michael Winner's *Chato's Land* (UA 1971) and Robert Aldrich's *Ulzana's Raid* (U 1972) were among other 'Vietnam Westerns' of the early seventies. Peckinpah-esque eulogy-assaults on the traditional Western included Frank Perry's *Doc* (UA 1971), Clint Eastwood's *The Outlaw, Josey Wales* (WB 1975), Andrew V. McLaglen's *The Last Hard Men* (Fox 1976) and Walter Hill's *The Long Riders* (UA 1980). Deheroicized, ironic portrayals of the West abounded, including Philip Kaufman's *The Great Northfield, Minnesota Raid* (U 1971), Blake Edwards' *Wild Rovers* (UA 1971), Dick Richards' *The Culpepper Cattle Company* (Fox 1972), and Robert Benton's *Bad Company* (Par 1972). Penn and Altman each made a late, cruelly demystified and unpopular contribution to the cycle, *The Missouri Breaks* (UA 1975) and *Buffalo Bill and the Indians* (De Laurentiis 1976). *Heaven's Gate* took something from each strain and made the genre untouchable for most of the eighties.

All of these Westerns relied heavily on the visible evocation and 'refunctioning' of iconographic and narrative conventions, whether hard-wired into generic architecture (as in the portrayal of American Indians), or through more specific allusions to individual films and filmmakers (such as the ubiquitous references to Ford). John Wayne's own final Western, *The Shootist* (Par 1976), in which Wayne plays an ageing gunfighter dying of cancer (like Wayne himself), opens with a montage of shots from Wayne's own silent and series Westerns that supposedly summarises the character's career but obviously invoke Wayne's own, and through it the entire history of the Western.

Such explicit references to other films are the most visible form of the larger practice of allusion, one of seventies Hollywood's most characteristic devices, first analysed by Noel Carroll.[11] Alongside extensive genre revisionism, parodies (the decade's dominant comic mode – notably Mel Brooks's *Blazing Saddles* (WB 1973) and *Young Frankenstein* (Fox 1974)), and pastiches (including feature length in-jokes such as the imitation musical/boxing movie double-bill *Movie Movie* (ITC 1978)), this allusionism manifested itself in dialogue, *mise en scène* (theatre marquees, marquee cards and posters) and direct quotations from old movies (often motivated by characters going to the movies and watching television broadcasts of theatrical films). A mid-decade cycle of caustic Hollywood-on-Hollywood satires, including James Ivory's *The Wild Party* (AIP 1974), John Schlesinger's *The Day of the Locust* (Par 1975), John Byrum's *Inserts* (UA 1975), Howard Zieff's *Hearts of the West* (MGM 1975) and Elia Kazan's *The Last Tycoon* (Par 1976), as well as Bogdanovich's affectionate comedy of early cinema days *Nickelodeon* (Col 1976), underlined the trend.

As Carroll notes, none of this would have been possible without the heightened general levels of film literacy, part of the expansion of film culture in the USA discussed in the previous chapter, which enabled seventies filmmakers to add emotional and historical resonance to their work by drawing on a framework of film-historical reference they could assume their audience shared. Sometimes such allusions functioned to purely nostalgic or playful effect (such as the use of the early-1930s Universal leader to open *The Sting* (U 1973)). Yet many instances of allusion had a critical dimension in keeping with the politics of the Hollywood Renaissance – as well as its limitations.

One critical dimension of such *hommages* – hinted at in revisionist Westerns like *McCabe* but more obvious in genre films set in modern times or in the 'Golden Age' thirties or forties themselves – is the uselessness of classic Hollywood solutions to contemporary crises of personal and social relationships. Robert Towne's screenplay for the key neo-*noir Chinatown* quite explicitly conceived private eye Jake Gittes as modelling himself on Hollywood tough guy heroes, in his style of dress as well as his laconic, wisecracking manner. A conspiracy more engulfing and impenetrable than anything his moviegoing could have prepared him to deal with gives the lie to his surface smarts and exposes his powerlessness. In a more stylised vein, in *New York, New York* – a film that operates principally as an extended intertextual commentary on the sugarcoated myths of forties romantic musical comedies – Jimmy Doyle watches a silent, rapt dance routine between a sailor and his girl against a stylised backdrop of the El-train. The dancers have stepped directly out of Stanley Donen's *On the Town* (MGM 1948), whose 'New York, New York (It's a Wonderful Town)' number lends Scorsese's film its own title. But Jimmy, who is pacing the Manhattan streets in the small hours of VJ Day only because he has not managed to get himself laid, belongs to a different and more intractable reality than his cheerfully two-dimensional celluloid counterparts, and the scene exists to make that disjunction apparent: as the couple dance silently off into the night, Jimmy turns back without comment or evident reaction to his more complex professional and emotional environment. Scorsese's *Alice Doesn't Live Here Anymore* (WB 1974) opens with what are presumably the adult Alice's idealised memories of her own childhood, staged and shot in super-saturated Technicolor in the style of *The Wizard of Oz*. To judge from the set, however, it is *Kansas* (which in the original of course is monochrome) and not Oz that Alice remembers this way – which makes her the victim, so to speak, of a double disconnection from reality and the adjustment she has to make over the course of the film accordingly more painful. (The film's final shot of Alice and her son struggling along a drab roadside is a disenchanted version of the Yellow Brick Road.) Towards the end of *Taxi Driver* (partly a reworking of *The Searchers*, like screenwriter Paul Schrader's own later *Hardcore* (Col 1979)), as Scorsese's camera tracks through the gruesome aftermath of Travis Bickle's would-be heroic massacre, it catches a graffito, John Ford's nickname 'Pappy', scrawled in blood. This bloody shambles, it seems, is the legacy of Hollywood's myths of regeneration through violence.[12]

Hollywood Renaissance filmmaking often acquired a political dimension, almost in spite of itself. Peter Bogdanovich, for example, was avowedly apolitical and in *What's Up, Doc?* (WB 1972) produced a happy and entirely uncritical tribute to classic thirties screwball comedies. At the same time, however, it was not only the familiar traditions and types of Hollywood genres, but their changing social function and their imbrication in the lived and imagined realities of American communities, that animated his creative sensibility. Thus, through the device of the doomed movie house in *The Last Picture Show*, a film that works both as a disillusioned modern Western and as a layered, multi-referential critique of the national mythology proffered by the classic Western, Bogdanovich explores the movies' constitutive role in the ideology to which his doomed characters half-consciously subscribe, and the disabling consequences when the connection between that ideology and the reality it aims to underwrite is severed by changing social and economic realities. At the start of *The Last Picture Show*, necking with his drab girlfriend at the movies, Sonny (Timothy Bottoms) seeks romantic inspiration from the image of the young Elizabeth Taylor in *Father of the Bride* (MGM 1950). The moment is at once comic, ironic and at least potentially critical – is it Hollywood's fault or Sonny's that nothing in his life will ever live up to Hollywood's radiant myths? Near the end of the film, Sonny and his estranged high-school buddy Duane (Jeff Bridges), who is about to depart for the Korean War, attend the eponymous final show at the town's movie theatre, doomed to closure by the death of its owner. No fanfare accompanies the theatre's passing: the two young men are almost the only audience for a showing of Howard Hawks's *Red River* (UA 1948), the cattle drive sequence ('Let's take 'em to Missouri, Matt!') from which is excerpted by Bogdanovich, and when it's all over they wander out as indifferently as they entered. Deracinated modernity, manifest in the film's dysfunctional relationships, has according to Bogdanovich lost its capacity for the productive appropriation of popular myths.

Sometimes characters themselves make such allusions and in so doing realise the disconnection of Hollywood ideal and reality. In dealing with his desire for Diane Keaton, his best friend's wife, Woody Allen in *Play It Again, Sam* (Par 1972) has to get beyond the advice offered him by Bogart's shade that 'I never met a dame who didn't understand a slap in the mouth or a slug from a .45'. More painfully, in Penn's *Night Moves*, the cuckolded Harry Moseby is taunted by his wife's (crippled) lover with his impotence compared to his celluloid avatars: 'Go on, Harry, take a swing – just like Sam Spade would'. When arrested by the cops, Elliott Gould's shambling Philip Marlowe in Altman's transgressive version of Chandler's *The Long Goodbye* tauntingly points up the inexorable sway of cliché: 'This is where I say "What's this all about?" and you say "We ask the questions"' (actually a line from Chandler's original novel). At the end of the film, having shattered fundamental generic expectations by shooting down his unarmed opponent in cold blood, Marlowe capers off into the sunset to the strains of 'Hooray for Hollywood'.

'SAPPY ENDINGS'

The Long Goodbye's satirically reflexive, cheerfully amoral ending illustrates one of the most purposeful ways in which Hollywood Renaissance films modify classical narrative conventions. When the venal studio chief Griffin Mills in Altman's 1992 'comeback' film *The Player* (Avenue 1992) is asked what he looks for in deciding whether to develop a picture, he replies 'Suspense, laughter, violence, hope, heart, nudity, sex, happy endings . . . Mainly happy endings'. Renaissance films, on the contrary, tended to specialist in *un*happy endings. A good number close with their protagonists dead or dying: *Easy Rider, Butch Cassidy, The Wild Bunch, Midnight Cowboy, The Ballad of Cable Hogue* (Sam Peckinpah, WB 1970), *McCabe & Mrs. Miller, Last Tango in Paris* (Bernardo Bertolucci, US 1972), *The Parallax View, Pat Garrett and Billy the Kid, Thunderbolt and Lightfoot* (Michael Cimino, US 1973), *One Flew Over the Cuckoo's Nest, Night Moves*, to list only some of the most obvious. A still larger number of films leave their protagonists relatively intact but either defeated, stalled or – even if apparently successful – dissatisfied, conflicted or ambivalent: *Goodbye, Columbus, Alice's Restaurant, Little Big Man, Catch-22, Carnal Knowledge* (Embassy 1971), *The Last Picture Show, Deliverance, Serpico, The*

Long Goodbye, possibly *American Graffiti*, *Mean Streets*, *Chinatown*, *Shampoo*, *Dog Day Afternoon* (WB 1975), *Barry Lyndon* (WB 1975), *Network*, *Raging Bull* (UA 1980), *Heaven's Gate*, again to mention only a few.

Sometimes violence intrudes in unexpected, apparently arbitrary ways (for instance *The Sugarland Express*, *Electra Glide in Blue* (UA 1973), *Looking for Mr Goodbar* (Par 1977)) – though this arbitrariness is clearly intended to signal the intractably malign apparatus of contemporary American life, hence is not arbitrary at all: 'it's Chinatown'. The would-be ritual revenge startlingly meted out by minor mafioso Michael at the end of *Mean Streets* is bloody but inconclusive: all three of his targets stagger away from the scene in the film's closing shots, 'wounded, not even dead' as Bruce Springsteen put it (and a brief interpolated excerpt from a TV showing of Lang's *The Big Heat* reminds us that life lacks the melodramatic clarity of the big screen). Even Nixon-era 'Silent Majority' backlash movies such as *Dirty Harry* (WB 1971) tend to close on a note of ambivalence and resentful irresolution rather than rightist triumphalism. *The French Connection* closes with a barrage of offscreen gunshots as NY narc Popeye Doyle – having just accidentally shot an FBI agent in his no-holds-barred pursuit of the drugs kingpin Charnier – charges off after the fugitive object of his obsession; anticlimactic end-titles summarising the light sentences handed down to the criminals again point out that such outcomes rarely offer the satisfying definition of a Hollywood showdown.

Of course, some studio-era films had 'downbeat' endings too: but in general these were either institutionally mandated by the Production Code acting as social proxy – the capture or death of law-breakers (including those who fell into criminality through personal weakness or desire) illustrating the universal truth that crime does not pay – or acquired meaning and nobility through incorporation into a larger, moral or patriotic narrative: thus the obliteration of the platoon in *Bataan* (MGM 1943) or Marine Sergeant John Wayne's death in *The Sands of Iwo Jima* (Republic 1945) exemplified wartime duty and the lesson that the needs of the many outweighed those of the few. Death, even unmerited, could also be redeemed by a sense of tragedy, all the more if exquisitely sharpened by romantic love: Helen Hayes' death in Gary Cooper's arms as the bells of peace ring out the end of World War I in *A Farewell To Arms* (Par 1932) is a good example. Very much rarer was any suggestion that right thinking and acting was no guarantee of reward, let alone the opposite – that innocents might suffer while the undeserving profited. Once again, *noirs* such as *Force of Evil* offered a pessimistic counterpoint to the moral orderliness of the world as viewed from mainstream Hollywood; even here, though, we have at least the promise that evil will not go unavenged.

Scorsese's *New York, New York*, one of the most acutely reflexive of all Renaissance films, holds this entire tradition of wholesome narrative closure up to withering scrutiny in its 'Happy Endings' sequence. In this case, the film-within-the-film (an integrated musical within a backstage musical) all too obviously offers a wish-fulfilment fantasy version, or parodic metacommentary on the romance whose real unhappiness and unsustainability the rest of *New York, New York* has unfolded. In 'Happy Endings', musical star Francine Evans (Liza Minnelli) plays 'Peggy Smith', a film usherette who sadly sings that 'Happy endings, as far as I can see/Are only for the stars/Not in the stars for me' – only to have her disenchantment gloriously confounded. Later on, back in the 'real' world of *New York, New York*, Francine's definitively unromantic ex-husband Jimmy Doyle (Robert deNiro) teases her with what they both recognise is the disconnection of lived experience from what Jimmy derisively calls 'sappy endings'. Not content with this, Scorsese follows the happy ending of 'Happy Endings' with the *real* ending of *New York, New York* – in which Jimmy and Francine consider walking off together into the dusk of the film's MGM-style studio-lot streets, only to think better of it; this being, after all, real life, not the movies.

Robert Kolker points out that this ending in which Jimmy and Francine are not reunited, and do not live happily ever after, could in the light of the preceding two hours only strike us as an 'unhappy' ending if we insist on the comedic conventions of romantic union.[13] On any more realistic assessment, given what we know of the couple's fundamental incompatibility and the destructive strains in their relationship, their separation is clearly the happiest ending available. These two particular people are plainly just better off apart; unless, that is, we prefer the Hollywood dream-life over the lives that are actually given to us to lead. Yet as the film strongly suggests, the naïve belief in dreams coming true is what gets people into difficulties in the first place. The film thus functions as both an implicit rebuke to a formulaic cinema whose lessons are desperately, even dangerously, at odds with the awkward realities of modern relationships, and a warning to the audience – personified within the film by the credulous usherette Francine plays in 'Happy Endings' (but whose illusions she herself no longer shares) – of the necessity for separation from such redemptive fantasies.

In some of his other films, by allowing an antiheroic protagonist success (or the absence of defeat, which is not quite same thing), Scorsese contradicts audience desires and expectations and mobilises extra-textual irony at the expense of the convention of a 'happy ending'. *Taxi Driver* ends with the psychotic killer Travis Bickle apparently feted for his heroism; his cathartic violence seems to have purged his demons and as he drives down streets suddenly transformed from Expressionistic urban hell into oases of placid greenery, he is even able to rebuff gracefully the svelte campaign worker he had ineffectually stalked before. Sharp satire of a society so unbalanced it takes a maniac at his own estimation as a crusader? Or simply, as is also suggested, Travis's fantasy, the product of his final retreat into psychosis? A blink-and-you-miss-it final shot accompanied by a burst of discordant sound returns us to the urban inferno and suggests the entire cycle may be about to resume; or that it never really stopped. The reality of Rupert Pupkin's media apotheosis at the end of Scorsese's later *The King of Comedy* (Par 1982) seems less questionable, but once again how we are supposed to *feel* about it certainly is. These films join a small category of ironic endings including *Joe*, both *Godfather* films, *A Clockwork Orange*, *Cabaret* (Allied Artists 1972), and *Taxi Driver*.

Ambiguity and actual narrative irresolution pose even greater offence to Hollywood tradition – especially when they even obscure the outcome of a thriller, the most plot-driven of genres. At the end of *Cruising*, the undercover cop's ambiguous situation infects the narrative: after the killer has apparently been apprehended, the cop's gay neighbour is found murdered, mutilated in a similar fashion to the other victims. Suspicion falls on the neighbour's volatile lover, but it is implied to the audience that the cop himself may have committed this crime (and perhaps the others?). The question is left hanging and the film concludes on the charged and ambiguous image of the cop's girlfriend wearing his S/M regalia. The denouement of *The Parallax View* leaves unanswered, and probably unanswerable, questions dangling: at what point was the reporter's cover blown? How much of his investigation has Parallax stage-managed to manoeuvre him towards his doom? To what extent is Parallax itself simply a ruse to satisfy his (previously established) conspiratorial imagination?[14] The film reveals itself as conspiratorial in form as well as content, the object of its machinations the audience's narrative security. Walker (Lee Marvin), the implacable revenge hero of *Point Blank*, simply disappears in the final scene before the promised showdown can take place. (*Point Blank* also strongly suggests that its entire narrative – in which generic situations frequently take on a highly stylised, oneiric quality – is Walker's *Pincher Martin*-style revenge fantasy as he lies dying of the wounds inflicted in the opening sequence.)

A few films resist closure altogether – *Five Easy Pieces*, *Manhattan* (UA 1979), the dual endings of *Apocalypse Now*, *Cutter's Way* (UA 1981) – or like *Klute* tease the audience by concluding one (typically generic) storyline while leaving another (usually centred on character relations) unresolved. The conspiracy thriller *Three Days of the Condor*, playing off the decade's revelations about illegalities in the CIA, deflates its protagonist's moment of apparent triumph: as he heads to the *New York Times* armed with the proof of nefarious internecine activities whose publication will also save his life,[15] his CIA contact asks 'What if they don't publish them?' 'They will', he replies confidently, but his interlocutor will not let him (or us) off so easily: 'What if they don't?', he insists. Pressing home its theme of the faithlessness of trusted public institutions, the film closes on a freeze-frame of the hero's suddenly uncertain face.

'I BELIEVE IN AMERICA'

The narrative strategies of the Hollywood Renaissance implicated Hollywood itself, as an American institution and as a key vector of discredited values. Renaissance filmmakers turned their dissatisfaction on the procedures of their own predecessors, where it found expression by reworking those procedures. Form and narrative did not, however, exhaust the resources of seventies cinema for subjecting dominant ideology to sceptical, if not necessarily oppositional, scrutiny. In a number of Renaissance films, for example, a profuse display of 'Americana' – flags, parades, anthems, the regalia of disenchanted nationhood – is put to unmistakeably ironic and/or critical purpose.

The American flag is virtually ubiquitous in Renaissance films, starting with Wyatt's emblazoned petrol tank in *Easy Rider*. Traditionally, Hollywood had used the Stars and Stripes virtually without exception, and especially during and after World War II, in the straightforward patriotic spirit of Iwo Jima.[16] When on the other hand the flag provides the backdrop for the hackneyed, self-regarding tirade of a judge in Alan Arkin's film of Jules Feiffer's *Little Murders* (Fox 1971), the scene sums up the contrasting spirit of seventies Hollywood – accurately characterised by Pauline Kael as 'part of the new retroactive anti-Americanism'.[17] Hanging flaccid and defeated or flapping with ironic confidence, the flag lends a suggestion of political and social allegory or at least a wider frame of historical reference to films including *Alice's Restaurant*, *Joe*, both *Godfather* films, *Shampoo*, Michael Ritchie's 'American trilogy' of *The Candidate* (WB 1972), *Smile* (WB 1975) and *The Bad News Bears* (Par 1976), Altman's *Nashville* and *Buffalo Bill and the Indians*, and many others, including naturally *All the President's Men*. The iconoclastic trend runs the gamut from satiric diminution – the tiny flag planted on the indifferent desert soil of a distant planet that provokes Charlton Heston's caustic laughter in *Planet of the Apes* – to burlesque excess – the stories-high banner that corrupt patriarch John Huston rips apart as he tumbles to his death at the end of William Richert's anarchic conspiracy fantasy *Winter Kills* (Embassy 1979). *Nashville* famously concludes with an extended track back from another giant flag beneath which the film's fragmented communities briefly connect to sing along that, in the words of the film's me-generation idiots' anthem, 'It Don't Worry Me'. About the closest the Hollywood Renaissance gets to a traditionally affirmative flag-waving moment is the manifestly ambivalent (or ambiguous) symbolic presence of yet another outsize standard behind the eponymous Patton (George C. Scott) in the famous opening direct-to-camera address of Franklin J. Schaffner's 1970 Fox biopic.[18]

Many other pieces of quintessential Americana receive widespread ironic treatment: for example, the small-town parade. As a popular tradition, the parade traditionally declares not only civic pride but acts as a physical manifestation of the beloved community, and at least for the duration of the spectacle sublimates individual achievement in the performance of the larger whole. Once again, however, the parades of New Hollywood movies send a very different message. When Wyatt ('Captain America') and Billy in *Easy Rider* ride into the middle of a parade, the violently exclusionary principles of the majority culture it embodies are exposed. Although Wyatt and (especially) Billy seem genuinely torn between mockery and the simple desire to join in, they are thrown in jail for even venturing to suggest that dope-smoking long-hairs have any place in the parade's Norman Rockwell picture of American life. This provides the film's first suggestion that the counterculture's mere existence is an intolerable affront to straight America, and begins the coercive arc that follows a rising curve throughout the rest of the film until its inevitably bloody conclusion.

In this light, the carnage that tears apart the temperance parade at the start of *The Wild Bunch* might be seen as a kind of revenge-taking from a director of pronounced libertarian/countercultural leanings. But Peckinpah seems rather to want to suggest that these innocent prigs – massacred with equal disregard from both sides in the botched ambush, the outlaws who 'seldom see eye-to-eye with [their] Government' and the railroad posse that stands for power, if not the law – are actually the victims of an endemic and uncontainable violence in American society that makes a mockery of their appeals for 'temperance'. The slow-motion parade behind the opening credits of Ivan Passer's *Cutter's Way* is presented as a dream or a 'screen memory' of non-conflictual communal celebration swiftly and brutally belied by reality: the cheerleader who pirouettes gaily across the screen will shortly be found raped and murdered, her body stuffed into a trashcan. Furthermore the parade itself, at least as reconstructed in the paranoid but perspicuous perceptions of the mutilated Vietnam vet Cutter (John Heard), is revealed as a pageant not of popular will but of power. The pristinely beautiful white charger heading the parade was the steed of a secretive and powerful local businessman who may have been the killer. The riotous climax of *Animal House* simultaneously returns the parade to its distant historical origins in medieval carnival and – by demonstrating that this is only possible through a violent transgressive assault on authority (the Omega fraternity) by the excluded and reviled (the boys of Delta Tau Chi) – underlines the parade's modern appropriation as a vehicle for placing establishment power on display.

Nor do favourite American pastimes escape this kind of symbolic critique. Baseball in particular, whose centrality to the nostalgic American imaginary can hardly be overstated (and would be triumphantly reaffirmed in the 1980s in films such as *The Natural* (Tri-Star 1984) and *Field of Dreams* (U 1989)), receives satiric treatment at the expense of its (largely mythical) generosity and purity in *The Great Northfield, Minnesota Raid*, and *The Bad News Bears. Bang the Drum Slowly* (Par 1973) uses the terminal illness of a baseball pitcher as a thinly veiled eulogy for lost American innocence. Other sports receive comparable treatment, for instance motor racing: *The Last American Hero* (Fox 1971) relates the career of stock-car champion Junior Johnson as an emblematic tale of American corruption; conversely, in *Steelyard Blues* Donald Sutherland's enthusiasm for demolition derbies becomes the concrete manifestation of his character's rejection of the mainstream values incarnated in these rustbucket Fords and Chryslers.

On occasion, such iconoclasm is given a more explicitly political thrust. The famous opening line of *The Godfather* is 'I believe in America' – declared by an undertaker who then recants those convictions and seeks refuge and redress in the more primitive structures of loyalty and vengeance represented by the Mafia. Through the ensuing saga of the Corleone family between the turn of the century and the Eisenhower years, from Sicily via Ellis Island to Lake Tahoe, *The Godfather* and its first sequel develop one of the American cinema's most sustained and corrosive portrayals of the American Dream since von Stroheim's *Greed*, taking in detailed depictions of institutions and practices – the Mob, politics, neo-colonialism, immigrant communities – and reflection by the characters themselves about the nature of American identity and American success. Later in the decade, Michael Cimino controversially closed his Vietnam epic *The Deer Hunter* (U 1978) – a film of comparable epic ambition to Coppola's diptych – with a beleaguered round of 'America the Beautiful', a scene whose degree of ironisation or endorsement of its characters' naïve, battered patriotism provoked furious debate (surely intentionally) on both left and right.

Few of these films, any more than the decade's experiments in genre and narrative revisionism, directly addressed contemporary American politics. A partial exception to this rule was the cycle of conspiracy films that emerged at roughly the same time as the Watergate scandal was breaking. *Executive Action* and *All the President's Men* dramatise actual (real or posited) conspiracies; *Three Days of the Condor*, and *The Domino Principle* (Associated General 1977) take lightly disguised recent revelations about CIA malfeasance for their premises. Capitalising on Watergate and also the lingering trauma of the Kennedy and King assassinations (and the ensuing, widely discredited official inquiries), the conspiracy thriller quickly emerged as a thriving subgenre, a hybrid of the spy and the crime film in which the us-and-them moral certainties of the Cold War dissolved in the gangster mentality and corrosive cynicism of the Nixon years. Perhaps the most famous of this cycle, *The Parallax View*, is notable for finding a way to incorporate into its thriller narrative a fairly lengthy (eight minute) abstract film sequence in which the ideological mobilisation of 'American' signifiers is demonstrated in a strikingly direct way. Midway through the film, the investigative reporter who has (it appears) successfully infiltrated the shadowy Parallax Corporation is subjected by the organisation to an audio–visual aptitude test, a Rorschach for lone nuts (the monitored responses of the antisocial loners who interest Parallax determine whether they will be recruited as assassins – in fact, as fall guys). We share his point of view as, to begin with, tinkling muzak accompanies a slideshow of reassuring images of quintessential Americana: beneficent fathers and nurturing families, white picket fences, one-room schoolhouses, baseball and apple pie . . . But step by step these morph and darken into images of familial abuse, deprivation, militarism and the coercive state (Hitler, Selma, Daley cops, Vietnam). The opening vignettes of America, land of plenty, are replaced by orgiastic images of carnal and materialistic gratification culled from the pages of *Playboy* and *Fortune*. Through it all, assaulted now by a relentless, discordant electronic soundtrack, the viewer is reminded that he (this is a strongly gendered imaginary) is a victim, fallen from Eden, excluded from the feast, by an indistinct and inchoate (Nixon rubs shoulders with Mao), yet undoubtedly malign and powerful institutionalised authority.

Michael Ryan and Douglas Kellner suggest that the conspiracy genre, at once profoundly suspicious of establishment power and pessimistic about the prospects of overcoming it, reflects the early 1970s 'crisis of liberalism' induced by the twin failures of liberal policy at home (the Great Society) and abroad (the New Frontier).[19] Fredric Jameson, meanwhile, maintains that the significance of the genre is found in its political unconscious, namely its presentation of 'conspiracy as totality'. At a point in history when, Jameson argues, the spiralling complexity of geopolitical relationships, accelerated by information technology, renders untenable the lucidity, comparative simplicity and global comprehension of previous economic and political models, the frightening insistence on occult, amorphous and vastly powerful conspiratorial powers offers a paradoxical reassurance simply in providing *an explanation* and a totalising vision, however defeated and disempowered.[20]

'WE BLEW IT': THE EXPERIENCE OF DEFEAT

As the examples discussed in this chapter make clear, the cinema of the Hollywood Renaissance undertakes a performative critique of classic Hollywood's role in promoting what the MC5 called 'the American ruse'. A shared structure of feeling marks many Renaissance movies and connects them to the political climate of the time: that the values and institutions that had served America's postwar generation had become, or had always been, illusory, and that Hollywood cinema is culpable for persisting in and promulgating those values, and now shares in their bankruptcy. Without attempting (or having the tools or the inclination to attempt) a conventional or comprehensive political analysis of the reasons for America's crisis of political and economic legitimacy, the Hollywood Renaissance set about what could best be described as an immanent critique of the ideology of Hollywood cinema itself. Nathaniel West commented, in his 1933 novel *Miss Lonelyhearts*, that 'Men have always fought their misery with dreams. Although dreams were once powerful, they have been made puerile by the movies . . . Among many betrayals, this one is the worst.'[21] West's indictment is made visible in the many Renaissance films that parodically or polemically restage the dreams sold to Americans by Hollywood cinema, aiming to expose their bad faith, foolishness, naïveté or outright falsehood. The Renaissance filmmakers used their critical historical perspective on classic Hollywood as a weapon against the tradition their work at once invokes and rejects and carved out the space for a limited and often conflicted – yet in the context of Hollywood history nonetheless distinctive – critical position on dominant ideologies.

The degree and consistence of this oppositional dimension of Hollywood cinema in the 1970s should not be overstated; and it is not only with hindsight that some of its limitations are very apparent. Most Renaissance filmmakers were indifferent, at best, to the claims on representation of ethnic and racial minorities; while many films probed white masculinity, few engaged meaningfully with racial, let alone sexual, prejudice. Paul Schrader's union drama *Blue Collar* (U 1978) is a rarity not only in including two black actors (Richard Pryor and Yaphet Kotto) in leading roles, but in identifying the pernicious power of racism in inhibiting working-class solidarity. Realistically or sympathetically drawn gay characters are almost wholly absent from the films of this period (though the beloved Cheyenne community of Penn's *Little Big Man* includes an apparently transgendered character). Women were certainly visible, but almost as thoroughly subordinated by the masculinist bias of most Renaissance films; the principal, and almost the only, woman director of this period was Joan Micklin Silver (*Hester Street*, Midwest 1975). The moviegoing audience's bias towards young male experience also helped ensure that despite the decade's feminist consciousness-raising women's experience was central to only a few films including *Alice Doesn't Live Here Anymore*, John Cassavetes' independently produced *A Woman Under the Influence* (Faces International 1974) and Martin Ritt's *Norma Rae* (Fox 1979), alongside occasional traditional 'women's films' such as *The Turning Point* (Fox 1977). Robin Wood memorably characterised the seventies as the era of the 'incoherent text' – films often torn between progressive positions on public subjects such as Vietnam and Watergate (however these were allegorised) and conflicted or conservative social attitudes. (Though Wood does not cite it, a good example is *The Godfather*, which both condemns capitalism *and* valorises patriarchy.)[22]

In general, contemporary critics quickly identified the self-lacerating strain in the New Hollywood as crypto-politics and tended not to take it very seriously. In 1973, Pauline Kael argued that American films were implicated in, not commenting on, the zeitgeist of the Watergate era: 'Today, movies say that the system is corrupt, that the whole thing stinks . . . in the convictionless atmosphere, the absence of shared values, the brutalities taken for granted, the glorification of loser-heroes'. This Kael identified as itself a cynical and shallow move, a symptom not a diagnosis, less an authentic reaction of disgust at Vietnam and Watergate than the glib exploitation of those sentiments:

American movies didn't 'grow up'; they did a flipover from their prolonged age of innocence to this age of corruption. When Vietnam finished off the American hero as righter of wrongs, the movie industry embraced corruption greedily; formula movies could be energised by infusions of brutality, cynicism, and Naked Apism, which could all be explained by Vietnam and called realism.[23]

Kael was herself too glibly dismissive of the painful struggle evident in many films of this period to make sense of contradictory and turbulent times. Yet she was right about the fatally reactive nature of this project. Renaissance films are typified by the acute self-consciousness with which they regarded both their own antecedent tradition and Hollywood's historical role in the construction of a modern American social imaginary. The New Hollywood repeatedly expresses both its awareness of the affirmative ideologies promoted by Old Hollywood and its determination to distance itself from them. Yet this is a paradoxical project – to attack Hollywood using Hollywood's own devices – and it has an appropriately paradoxical outcome. The filmmakers of the French New Wave, to take one example, armed with a significantly more politically and theoretically elaborated understanding of Hollywood's cultural imperialism, operated both culturally and in terms of film form at one remove from the Hollywood norms they fondly invoked and polemically attacked. The commercial filmmakers of the American New Wave are denied this luxury of simultaneous investment and disassociation. *Easy Rider* and *The Godfather* are far closer to the classical Western and the gangster film, respectively, than Chabrol's *Les Bonnes Femmes* is to *Shadow of a Doubt*. The New Hollywood's critique of classical Hollywood is always constrained to be articulated in the very terms of the classical model itself. And this ultimately disables a coherent politics: Beatty's *Reds*, for instance, starts out as a counter-history of early twentieth-century America, touching on American socialism, feminism and literary bohemia, but the generic investment in the explanatory verities of the biopic encourages the film's subsidence into romantic melodrama. Ultimately, seventies filmmakers' inability to formulate their critique of classic Hollywood values outside the latter's own categories more or less guaranteed the success of the following decades' Hollywood counter-revolution.

NOTES

1. The focus of a *Business Week* article on the New Hollywood: 'New kind of movie shakes Hollywood', 3 January 1970, pp. 40–5.
2. Steve Neale, 'New Hollywood cinema', *Screen*, 1976; 17(2):117–22.
3. On the relationship between the BBS production unit at Columbia and the Movement, see Andrew Schroeder, 'The Movement inside: BBS Films and the cultural left in the New Hollywood', in Van Gosse and Richard Moser (eds), *The World the Sixties Made* (Philadelphia: Temple University Press, 2003).
4. John Morton Blum, *Years of discord: America 1961–1973* (New York: Norton, 1988).
5. Jack Nachbar, 'The Western: a century on the trail', *Journal of Popular Film and Television*, 2003; 30(4):179.
6. Joan Mellen, 'The Western', in Gary Crowdus (ed.), *The Political Companion to American Film* (Chicago: Lakeview Press, 1994), pp. 469–75.
7. Douglas Pye, 'Introduction: criticism and the Western', in Ian Cameron and Douglas Pye (eds), *The Movie Book of the Western* (London: Studio Vista, 1996), pp. 9–21.
8. Stephen Prince, *Savage Cinema: Sam Peckinpah and the Rise of Ultra-Violent Movies* (London: Athlone, 1998) is much the best the best of the numerous critical studies of Peckinpah.
9. Ralph Thomas modeled the massacre in *Soldier Blue* on photographs from My Lai.
10. See Jim Kitses, *Horizons West: The Western from John Ford to Clint Eastwood*, 2nd edn (London: BFI, 2007).
11. Noel Carroll, 'The future of allusion: Hollywood in the seventies (and beyond)', *October*, 1982; 20:51–81.
12. See Richard Slotkin, *Gunfighter Nation: The Myth of the Frontier in Twentieth-Century America* (Norman, OK: University of Oklahoma Press, 1998); also Tom Engelhardt, *The End of Victory Culture: Cold War America and the Disillusion of a Generation* (New York: Basic Books, 1995).
13. See Robert Kolker, *A Cinema of Loneliness: Penn, Stone, Kubrick, Scorsese, Spielberg, Altman*, 3rd edn (Oxford: Oxford University Press, 2000), p. 288.
14. *Arlington Road* (Sony 1998) has a broadly similar narrative, but minus the ambiguity.
15. An obvious allusion to the Pentagon Papers, a classified official history of America's involvement in Vietnam which made it clear the government had consistently lied to the American people about its intentions, methods and the prospects for victory, leaked to the *Times* and the *Washington Post* by Daniel Ellsberg and published in defiance of the Nixon administration's attempts to suppress them.
16. The Iwo Jima flagraising photo is discussed in relation to its re-enactment in the John Wayne film *The Sands of Iwo Jima* (1948) in Garry Wills, *John Wayne: The Politics of Celebrity* (London: Faber, 1999), pp. 152–9.
17. Pauline Kael, *Deeper Into Movies* (London: Calder & Boyars, 1975), p. 256.
18. Peter Lev, *American Films of the 70s: Conflicting Visions* (Austin: University of Texas Press, 2000), discusses the ambiguous address of the scene in detail, noting its very different receptions amongst elite critics – who found the flag scene clearly satirical, bordering on camp – and blue-collar 'silent majority' audiences, who gratefully received a reassuring confirmation of traditional American values.

19. See Douglas Kellner and Michael Ryan, *Camera Politica: The Politics and Ideology of Contemporary Hollywood Film* (Bloomington: Indiana University Press, 1988), pp. 95–105.
20. See Fredric Jameson, *The Geopolitical Aesthetic: Cinema and Space in the World System* (London: BFI, 1992), pp. 4–81.
21. Nathaniel West, *Miss Lonelyhearts* (New York: New Directions, 1969), p. 39.
22. Robin Wood, 'The incoherent text: narrative in the 70s', in *Hollywood from Vietnam to Reagan* (New York: Columbia University Press, 1986).
23. Pauline Kael, 'After innocence', *Reeling* (London: Marion Boyars, 1977), pp. 161–3.

PART III

New Hollywood 1982–2006

Introduction to Part III

In the late summer of 1985 one of the biggest hits of the previous year, Joe Dante's horror-comedy *Gremlins* (WB 1984), was given a limited re-release in markets including Columbus – perhaps to offer moviegoers a more acidic counterpoint to the affectionate spoof of suburban life in that season's all-conquering hit *Back to the Future*. In *Gremlins*, when the affectionate mogwai Gizmo (something like a cross between a koala bear and one of *Star Wars'* Ewoks) comes into contact with water, numerous smaller, and decidedly less benign, mogwais – the eponymous Gremlins – are parthogenetically gener-ated from his own squirming body. These small but vicious creatures proceed to put the film's perfectly confected small town (a briefly glimpsed TV clip invokes the Bedford Falls of Frank Capra's *It's a Wonderful Life*) to the sword. From the mid-1980s, motion picture exhibition in all its forms – theatrical and domestic – in Columbus, and in the US generally, was also a story of the rapid, and apparently endless, multiplication of small entities that seemed to find their way into every corner of a movie market itself growing rapidly in every direction. These new, fast-evolving market presences may not have launched the same cannibalistic assault as the Gremlins; their advent, nonetheless, spelled doom for at least some of their older competitors.

By Labor Day 1985, the twins and triples that sustained the market through its mid-seventies trough had given way to larger complexes. The two biggest, the Eastland Plaza 6 and the Westerville 6, both located at suburban shopping centres, were owned by American Multi-Cinemas (AMC), a Kansas City-based company which since the early 1960s had specialised in the construction of ever-larger multi-screen theatres, exclusively located in the large enclosed shopping malls that had transformed the American retail and leisure land-scape. In the early 1980s it was estimated that Americans were spending more time in shopping malls than anywhere else bar home and work, and movie theatres both added value to malls themselves and thrived on the endless consumer traffic. By the mid-1980s, Columbus's six-plexes were already at the smaller end of AMC's operations (the company had constructed its first eight-plex in Atlanta as long ago as 1974). Over the coming years, Columbus (thriving, unlike other, larger Ohio 'rustbelt' cities such as Cleveland because of its diversified economy, light on declining heavy industries and strong in the burgeoning information, technology and services sectors) would see the same relentless accumulation of screens as most other major markets. This expansion was driven by companies which – unlike the theatre chains formerly owned by the old Big Five, none of which remained extant by the 1980s – were nationwide rather than regionally focused, including AMC and the former drive-in chain General Cinema, which in late 1985 opened two new eight-screen cinemas at malls in the city's northern and western districts. In 1980, sixty-one screens had operated in the Columbus area. AMC's announcement in November 1986 of a planned ten-screen multiplex at yet another new mall – on the very same day it opened eight screens, seating some 2,000 patrons, on the east side of the city – took the number of screens in Columbus over 100 for the first time in its history.[1] This expansion was, of course, fuelled by the upswing in attendances dating back to the success of *Jaws* and *Star Wars* in the late 1970s. The Continent, a nine-screen theatre owned by the USA Cinemas chain, reported in 1985 that it had sold more than a million tickets for the first time that year.[2]

The new multiplexes expanded or replaced the sixties and seventies duplex and triplex cinemas, often located in older open-air shopping centres that were themselves falling victim to the newer mega-malls. The twin-screen Loew's Arlington, mentioned in the introduction to the previous section, closed its doors in early 1992, among several other similar theatres.[3] Their demise was rarely mourned as the disappearance of the old picture palaces had been (at least by cinephiles). Many of the sixties and seventies theatres had been shoddily constructed, cheerless environments, the proverbial shoebox theatres where carelessly projected films competed with the soundtrack from the next-door auditorium. The new multiplexes, although streamlined, functional and relentlessly commercial, were compelled by the increasingly competitive market (and the advent of DVD and high-quality 'home theatre' set-ups) to raise standards and offer an improved audio-visual experience, with more comfortable seats, steeply raked 'stadium seating' to improve eyelines, and multi-track Dolby or THX sound systems transforming the acoustic environment.

The expansionist drive seemed relentless, with regular announcements of new construction of ever larger multiplexes throughout the late 1980s and 1990s. The locations of these sites reflected development patterns, mostly centred on malls but also following on the heels of urban regeneration, such as AMC's construction in 1990 of a fourteen-screen complex in the newly

fashionable Brewery district south of downtown.[4] When in 1996, hard upon
the opening of its first 'mega-plex' in Columbus, the twenty-four-screen
Lennox Town Center, AMC announced further plans for two new twenty-
four- and thirty-screen megaplexes, it was estimated if all the announced
construction took place – and no existing theatres closed – by 2000 Columbus
might have an astonishing 217 screens, ninety-six of them owned by AMC.[5]
(In 1946, we may recall, with national admissions running at nearly four times
the 1990 yearly tally of just under 1.2 billion, Columbus had a total of forty-
nine first- and second-run theatres.)

Of course, in fact theatres did close. The multiplex boom finally put an end
to the remaining nabes, in whatever form they had struggled through the last
decades. (When Marty McFly finally returns from 1955 in *Back to the Future*,
we notice that one of the two movie theatres in downtown Hill Valley has
been converted into an evangelical church, while the other is a porno theatre.)
As the multiplex giants grew – and engaged in price-cutting wars with each
other[6] – smaller cinemas were inexorably squeezed. Excluded from the most
profitable sectors of the market, small theatre owners might choose to eke
out a living in the second-run 'dollar house business', showing major releases
weeks or months into their theatrical runs at discount prices; but with the
enormous marketing and publicity campaigns and media coverage that now
attended the opening weekends of 'must-see' movies (with box office grosses
widely reported in local and national media) and the ensuing concentration of
admissions (all but the most successful blockbusters had weak 'legs' and typically saw double-digit percentage week-on-week falls in attendance starting in
their second week of release), there was little business left to scoop up once the
chains finally released their blockbusters to second-run houses. The accelera-
tion of video release in the late 1980s – Warner Bros. released *Batman* to video
in November 1989, less than five months after its theatrical debut – further
compressed the theatrical release window at the expense of smaller theatres.
The advent of second-run multiplexes – the Texas-based Super Saver chain
opened an eight-screen theatre at the Scarborough Mall in Columbus in
summer 1989, undercutting the other second-run theatres with a $1.50 ticket
price – was a final nail in the coffin for many.[7] By 1995 there remained just one
neighbourhood second-run theatre in Columbus.

The closure of obsolete and uncompetitive theatres hardly put a dent in
the remorselessly ascending trend line. The number of screens hit historic
highs: the inauguration of the megaplex era in 1996 took the city's screens to
163. Part of this growth was accounted for by a rising population: by 2000,
Columbus had grown to over 700,000 inhabitants and was now the fifteenth
largest US city (partly as a result of the incorporation of outlying suburban
areas, another reason for the city's prosperity). Yet the rate of expansion outpaced not only population increase but, much more obviously, headline rates

of theatre admissions. In 2002 domestic admissions reached an annual postwar high of 1.6 billion (falling off slightly in the following years), but this was still much less than half the total for 1946. The number of screens nationwide that year, meanwhile, was almost double the postwar figure at 35,280.[8] (See Appendix: Figures 1, 2.) How are these figures to be reconciled? The answers include the concentration of theatres in profitable locations (and the consequent disappearance of most rural and neighbourhood theatres); ticket price rises that regularly outpaced inflation (in 1999 the US Consumer Price Index showed a rise of 2.2 per cent, while the cost of a movie ticket that year went up 8.3 per cent[9]); the changing economics of exhibition (with heavily automated projection and the elimination of ushers and other superfluous staff reducing overheads, multiple screens of varying sizes enabling greater flexibility and efficiency in programming, and the fact that popcorn and soda concessions generated far more revenue for exhibitors than ticket sales); and the concentration of profits in a small number of enormously successful films which earned the bulk of their grosses in their first few weeks of super-saturation release, a practice that became the norm in the 1980s and was predicated on the availability of an enormous number of screens for the all-important opening weekend. Then there was the simple fact that although the number of screens had multiplied, almost without exception the new auditoria were far smaller than those they replaced: the typical multiplex screen averaged between 200 and 300 seats, with only a tiny number over 500. Whereas the 17,689 indoor US theatres in 1946 had a seating capacity of 12 million, a rough rule-of-thumb calculation suggests that the 35,000-plus screens in 2002 could only seat around 9 million.[10]

One option for those exhibitors unable to compete with the chains was to enter the arthouse market, boosted in the late 1980s by the crossover success of films such as Miramax's cannily marketed *sex, lies and videotape*. With the adult film market now almost wholly converted to video (allowing pornography to be consumed privately), Columbus's Roxy – a skin-flick house since the late 1960s – returned to the mainstream market shortly after Labor Day 1985, refurbished as an art cinema. Columbus boasted America's largest university, Ohio State, and accordingly could support several arthouses to offer, according to the Roxy's manager, 'the discriminating moviegoer a choice between [i.e., other than] the hack-em-ups and the Rambos'.[11] Albeit on a smaller scale, this sector manifested the same trends as the mainstream multiplexes, with small chains and multi-screen cinemas becoming the norm here too. In Columbus, the longtime owner/manager of the Drexel, an arthouse cinema that had built a substantial reputation through adventurous programming of first-run art films alongside revivals backed up by canny marketing and promotion, acquired a second theatre midway through the 1980s, converted his original theatre into a triplex in 1991, and in 2001 took over the eight-screen

Arena Grand in the northern downtown area. Such theatres strove to maintain a cinephile ambience (espresso and wine rather than Diet Coke; piped jazz instead of thunderous rock; retro displays of film posters and lobby cards) distinct from the herd mentality of the multiplexes.[12]

More or less off the commercial spectrum altogether, but perhaps indicative of the medium's shifting cultural status, was the minor novelty, in Columbus as elsewhere, of a renewed 'heritage' interest in what remained of the old downtown picture palaces (part of a broader trend starting in the mid-1980s towards urban exploration and the tentative recolonising of depressed or derelict downtown areas). The Ohio and Palace began regular movie revival series, showing studio-era classics in conditions that evoked the glory of days gone by. Both the renovation and the ongoing closures of historic theatres like the Graceland and Majestic now also attracted nostalgic media attention – a sharp contrast to the almost entirely unremarked disappearance of the nabes *en masse* in the fifties and sixties (unsentimentally depicted in Peter Bogdanovich's *The Last Picture Show* (Col 1971)).[13]

In the real world of commercial first-run exhibition, in fact, in some ways surprisingly little had changed since the heyday of the downtown picture palaces now undergoing antiquarian reanimation. Independent exhibitors continued to complain at being effectively excluded from the market for first-run major studio releases. Although, in light of continuing antitrust concerns, this was now a matter of practice rather than corporate policy, the outcome was the same. Since small local theatre owners not backed by a chain could usually only offer distributors one or two venues, the studios found it far more efficient to place films in multiple locations at one swoop rather than deal with many small operators. In any case, the latter could rarely match the bids large chains put in for studio product: the chains' economies of scale and focus on concessions revenues meant they could afford to exhibit films on a high-volume, low-margin basis. Moreover, individual theatres were ill-adapted to super-saturation release strategies, with major blockbusters typically opening on 2,000 or (by 2005) even 4,000 screens nationwide. Although the major distributors no longer owned substantial theatre holdings, inevitably they formed preferential relationships with their biggest chain customers; chains in turn received 'clearances', the exclusive right to show a particular film in a specific region or municipality. The familiar features of studio-era exhibition practices had simply had a facelift.

In other and – to the moviegoer – more obvious ways, however, watching a movie in Columbus in 2006 was an incomparably different experience from 1946. Most moviegoers would drive, rather than walk, to theatres (inadequate parking was a frequently cited reason for the closure of theatres from the fifties onwards); they also had far fewer destinations to choose from. In place of the nearly fifty different theatre locations scattered around the (smaller) metropolitan region in 1946, the much greater number of movie *screens* in 2005 were clustered in just nineteen locations. Nor did the greater number of screens – justified by exhibitors in the name of consumer choice – in fact produce greater variety, at least compared to 1946. Altogether fifty-nine different films were available over the week beginning Friday, 26 August 2005 (all running through the week), compared to over 200 for the same week sixty years before. The biggest blockbusters might occupy several screens in the same complex simultaneously. In at least one regard things were pretty much the same: in all of Columbus the only language spoken in any of the films exhibited was English.

There was of course diversity in film consumption nonetheless, and on a scale inconceivable in the 1940s. The sixteen basic and five premium channels available on local cable systems in Columbus, in addition to the four network channels, three independent stations and single PBS affiliate, all included movies as part of their regular programming in various forms: edited, interrupted by advertising, and mostly older on the commercial broadcasters and most basic cable channels; a variety of more recent and classic films, all uncut, on the premium movie channels HBO (owned by Time Warner), Showtime, Cinemax, The Movie Channel and The Disney Channel. In addition, the area's two cable suppliers, Time Warner and Coax, ran pay-per-view services offering films from the previous twelve months, while countless channels were available to satellite subscribers. Beyond these was the vast panoply of DVDs of every vintage, genre and nationality, for purchase and rental, whether from one of Columbus's twenty-nine Blockbuster outlets or by mail from internet suppliers, both rental and retail. Finally, and (much to the fury of the MPAA) beyond the effective oversight or regulation of motion picture producers and distributors, was the virtually unbounded horizon of the internet, peer-to-peer sharing and downloading of theatrical films stored digitally in a variety of ways from off-air recording to obvious piracy.

In one last way, however, the moviegoing world in 2006 very much resembled that of 1946: from every one of these 'delivery systems' except the (extralegal) last, the media conglomerates that had absorbed the major Hollywood studios derived revenue. In addition to their traditional source of income from theatrical box office, revenues flowed to the studios from every home video transaction (sale and rental); directly (through licensing fees) or indirectly (for example, from advertising revenue) from the transmission of theatrical movies on the broadcast networks (all of which were owned by one of the majors) and basic and premium cable channels (of which most of the former and all of the latter were also owned by the majors). Indeed, the cable and satellite delivery systems themselves were also owned by the majors (not to mention Blockbuster, until 2004 a division of Paramount's parent company Viacom). How the majors achieved this full-spectrum dominance starting in the early

1980s, and what their strategies meant for Hollywood filmmaking, will be explored in the following chapters.

NOTES

1. '24 screens to sprout', *Columbus Dispatch*, 28 October 1984, p. 1B.
2. 'Box office business good locally', *Columbus Dispatch*, 10 January 1986, p. 7F.
3. 'Loew's Arlington closes', *Business First of Greater Columbus*, 20 January 1992, p. 2.
4. 'Movie screens popping up all over Columbus', *Columbus Dispatch*, 14 May 1990, p. 1A.
5. 'Industrial-strength multiplex', *Columbus Dispatch*, 18 December 1996, p. 1F.
6. 'Cut-rate tix latest volley in big screen war', *Business First of Greater Columbus*, 7 February 1994, p. 1.
7. 'Second-runs suffered summer of their discontent', *Columbus Dispatch*, 22 October 1989, p. 1G.
8. MPAA Theatrical Market Statistics 2008. (For 1946, the number of screens is assumed to be identical with the number of theatres – 19,000.)
9. *Ibid*.
10. Figures for 1946 from Stephen Prince, *A New Pot of Gold: Hollywood Under the Electronic Rainbow, 1980–1989* (Berkeley: University of California Press, 1997), p. 82; calculation assumes an average seating per-screen capacity in 2002 of 260.
11. 'Independent theater owners find market niche', *Business First of Greater Columbus*, 6 June 1987, p. 11.
12. 'The Drexel: making movies fun again', *Capital Magazine*, 13 May 1984, pp. 26–9; 'And then there were three', *Columbus Dispatch*, 3 March 1991, p. 1G; 'Growing pains: Arena Grand theater slowly catching on', *Business First of Greater Columbus*, 11 July 2003, p. 7.
13. 'Graceland's demise likely permanent, owners say', *Columbus Dispatch*, 10 April 1991, p. 7C; 'Historic theater's screen going dark', *Columbus Dispatch*, 27 June 1998, p. 1G; 'Southern Theatre reopening offers a glimpse of the past', *Columbus Dispatch*, 16 September 1998, p. 5G.

Marty McFly invents rock 'n' roll: *Back to the Future* (Universal 1985). Reproduced courtesy of The Kobal Collection

CHAPTER 7

Corporate Hollywood

I982 marked the end of an era for the film industry, in more ways than one. Coca-Cola's purchase of Columbia Pictures (which had narrowly escaped Kirk Kerkorian's fatal clutches[1]) for $692 million, following oil tycoon Marvin Davis's $725 million acquisition of Twentieth Century-Fox the previous year, saw the last of the old majors pass into corporate ownership. In the twenty years since MCA's takeover of Universal in 1962, all of the seven surviving members of the studio-era 'Big Eight' had been absorbed into larger conglomerate entities. Only Walt Disney Productions,[2] with its once unique (but soon to be widely emulated) business model in which filmed entertainment played a subordinate role (to theme parks and licensed merchandise), still retained its autonomy. However, in many ways both the Fox and Columbia deals looked backwards to an older business model – that of the mid-1960s – which by the early eighties was already fast being superseded by another. Davis's buyout of Fox, in particular, adding to his holdings in oil and gas, banking and real estate in the booming Sunbelt states, harked back to the concept of diversified conglomeration that informed the move into movies by Gulf + Western, Kinney (as was), and Transamerica. But in the 1980s and subsequently, the trend – discernible since Steve Ross remodelled Kinney into the more strongly media-focused Warner Communications in 1972 – was away from cross-industrial diversification and towards the concentration of business activity in related, complementary fields – or, to use the era's new buzzword, synergy.

The Davis/Fox and Coca-Cola/Columbia tie-ups at the start of the 1980s were old-fashioned because neither offered the kinds of synergistic business opportunities that became the industry's new Holy Grail. (Flush with the revenues from distributing the first two entries in the *Star Wars* franchise, Fox in the late 1970s had already diversified into unhelpful non-core areas like Colorado ski resorts, golf courses and soft-drink bottling, apparently under the spectacularly misguided impression that profitable investment opportunities were lacking in the entertainment market.[3]) Marvin Davis's industrial and commercial holdings only diluted the company's focus further and the oilman was disinclined to make the major investment necessary to increase Fox's media holdings. Similarly, at Columbia – which was largely undiversified, still relying on theatrical production for up to 60 per cent of its revenues as late as 1981 –the innate compatibility of soft-drink manufacturing and movies was never evident despite Coke's insistences to the contrary.[4] It was unsurprising, therefore, that before the decade was out both companies had changed hands again. In 1985 Davis sold Fox to Rupert Murdoch's NewsCorp for $575 million, and Japanese electronics manufacturer Sony bought Columbia from Coke for $3.4 billion in 1989.[5] Each new deal typified one variant of the new synergistic paradigm.

Murdoch had built up NewsCorp into a major multinational multimedia firm by relentless horizontal and vertical expansion, typically through the aggressive pursuit and acquisition of existing businesses in daring, often highly leveraged (that is, debt-fuelled) buyouts. NewsCorp's international media holdings now included publishing (newspapers, consumer magazines and books) and broadcasting, both terrestrial – also in 1985, NewsCorp bought stations in seven major US television markets, reaching 22 per cent of US homes (enough to attract national advertisers), and launched the Fox Network – and, before the decade's end, satellite. Fox overnight became a lynchpin of this immense media conglomerate, as it was able to supply copyrighted content which could then be fed to consumers through NewsCorp's multiple 'pipelines'. The Fox–NewsCorp deal thus embodied a content-centred synergistic model.[6]

Sony's acquisition of Columbia, by contrast, was motivated by the idea of creating synergies between software and hardware. Sony blamed the market failure of its Betamax home video system against JVC's technically inferior VHS on the shortfall of Hollywood film titles available for Beta, and by acquiring a major studio (a content supplier) intended to insure against similar problems in the future.[7] A similar logic informed another Japanese electronics giant, Matsushita's $6 billion purchase of MCA-Universal in 1990. Ultimately, however, neither of these two 'hardware–software' alliances delivered as the new owners had hoped. In 1994 Sony took a $3.2 billion loss on its motion picture business and announced it was writing down its studios (Columbia and Tri-Star, a joint venture with HBO and CBS launched in 1983) by $2.7 billion.[8] Matsushita sold MCA to Canadian liquor company Seagram in April 1995 for $7 billion. Although Sony have stayed the course, both ventures were compromised by the manufacturing-focused parent companies' failure to achieve the kind of horizontal integration epitomised by NewsCorp.

VERTICAL INTEGRATION: THE SEQUEL

The model and inspiration for the synergistic remodelling of the film industry in the eighties was Warner Communications' successful exploitation of the first two *Superman* films, each the second-highest domestic earner in its year of release (1978, 1981). Beyond the direct earnings of the films at home and overseas, WCI also profited from sales of both special editions and regular runs of *Superman* comic books published by DC (owned by Warner since 1971); nine different products, ranging from a novelisation to a *Superman* encyclopedia and calendar, published by Warner Books; dozens of new spin-off Superman toys, novelties and authorised by Warners' licensing division; a soundtrack album on Warner Records; and even an arcade pinball table from Warner-owned games manufacturer Atari. (*Star Wars* had of course opened the door to billion-dollar film-related merchandising, but by agreeing to assign merchandising rights to Lucasfilm, Fox infamously missed out on revenues ultimately greater even than the film's record-setting box office.)

Of all the major companies at the start of the 1980s, Warner's diversified media holdings made them best placed to exploit the synergistic dimensions of a blockbuster property such as *Superman*, 'a movie for adults that kids will want to see' (or so at least claimed director Richard Donner).[9] G + W/Paramount were close behind, but not until Charles Bluhdorn's successor Martin Davis[10] moved to divest G + W of most of its non-media interests did the company – renamed Paramount Communications in 1989 – become fully fit for purpose in the new Hollywood.[11] Disney had of course led the way in exploiting their animated characters as the basis for a huge leisure-time empire, but by the early 1980s had become a somewhat marginal player in the theatrical production/distribution arena where, as was now apparent, new 'brands' could most effectively be introduced.[12] Alone of all the studios, however, Disney had a clear and secure brand identity grounded in its identification with family entertainment. It took the new regime of Michael Eisner and Jeffrey Katzenberg, appointed to head the studio in 1984 following another string of box office failures, to renovate the company's film production (especially its hallmark yet moribund animation division), television (including the new pay-cable Disney Channel) and home video (repackaging classic Disney releases) arms, now reaching both the family and – under the new Touchstone marque – adult markets, and finally realising the company's unique capacity to exploit branded product. By the late 1980s Disney had for the first time in its history become a dominant force in Hollywood.

The industrial logic of the new Hollywood was relentlessly expansionist: as their new corporate parents brought Fox and Columbia to the top table, so the existing conglomerates looked to protect their own positions by further acquisitions and mergers. Lew Wasserman actively solicited Matsushita's takeover of MCA-Universal because he recognised that by 1990 his original 'octopus' had become almost a minnow in the media shark pool Wasserman had himself done so much to create.[13] As a result, to a far greater extent than in the sixties takeovers, the 1980s and 1990s saw the major studios swept up in a series of colossally expensive and often bewilderingly complex financial transactions. Some of these machinations – such as the ceaseless manoeuvrings of MGM owner Kirk Kerkorian, who at different times in the eighties was also involved as either a major stockholder or potential purchaser at Fox, Disney, Columbia, and (what remained of) UA – had very little to do with moviemaking and little direct impact upon the industry's direction of travel, beyond adding to the generally febrile atmosphere. Others provided dramatic evidence of the trend towards an ever greater concentration of cross-media ownership.[14]

Most eye-catching, perhaps, was the 1989 merger of Warner Communications with Time, Inc., which like the NewsCorp/Fox deal allied print and filmed entertainment interests. The new Time-Warner was at the time the world's largest communications company with assets of some $25 billion and estimated annual revenues of $7.5 billion. But it did not enjoy that status for long. 1994 saw Sumner Redstone's cable giant Viacom buy Paramount Communications for $9.5 billion, giving the latter a television arm for the first time with the launch of the UPN cable network. The integration of the film and television industries intensified in the second half of the decade. Disney's $19 billion acquisition of Capital Cities/ABC in 1995, by adding a broadcast network and several important cable stations to its existing filmed entertainment, licensing and merchandising and theme park operations, restored Disney's parity with its enhanced rivals. Not to be outdone, Viacom purchased CBS in 1999 for $35.6 billion. The last of the three terrestrial networks combined with a studio in 2003 when GE, owner of NBC, purchased 80 per cent of Universal Studios from Vivendi for an estimated $14 billion.[15] Yet another new chapter, the marriage of twentieth- and twenty-first-century media, opened in 2000 with the merger – easily the largest in US history – of Time-Warner and Internet service provider AOL, creating a company valued (briefly, before the late-1990s dot-com bubble burst) at $180 billion.

It is all too easy to discuss contemporary Hollywood simply in terms of this apparently endless parade of gargantuan deals. Yet there is more to this story than is revealed by merely listing such stupefying transactions – which are after all entirely characteristic of late capitalism as a whole. Such deals did clearly point up the very deep pockets now essential for taking full advantage of the new media landscape: only the very biggest (and most daring) players would henceforth be equipped for industry leadership. TV stations, cable networks and publishing divisions did not come cheap, and nor did the eye-wateringly expensive blockbuster productions on which Hollywood strategies increasingly came to centre. The days of the stand-alone major movie studio

were long past. Entry into the media market was restricted – at least as effectively as the old studio system's oligopolistic closed shop – to a small class of
transnational companies with the necessary enormous resources. The fates of
'mini-major' Orion in the 1980s and would-be integrated major DreamWorks
SKG from 1994 to 2005 each offer object lessons in these new facts of industry
life.

Orion was set up by Arthur Krim and Robert Benjamin following their
acrimonious departure from Transamerica-owned UA in 1979 and was in
this sense predicted on assumptions about the incompatibility of corporate
structures and the kind of filmmaker-centred culture Krim and Benjamin had
fostered in UA's glory days of the 1950s and 1960s. Yet of course Orion had
to swim in the same waters as any other producer and at different times its
principal backers included such major media companies as Warner, Viacom
and Metromedia. Orion expanded quickly in the early 1980s, acquiring a distribution network by buying Filmways (formerly AIP), and established itself
as a sympathetic home for auteurs such as Woody Allen and Milos Forman,
specialising in mid-range rather than blockbuster production. The studio had
its fair share of success, producing and/or distributing critical and commercial hits such as the Academy Award-winning *Amadeus* (1984), *Platoon* and
Hannah and her Sisters (both 1986) and *Dances With Wolves* (1990) as well as
audience-pleasers such as *10* (1980), *Arthur* (1981), *Back to School* (1986) and
Robocop (1987). But even with these successes the studio's resources were
inadequate to support the patchy, at best, performance of many of its other
releases, including expensive flops such as *The Cotton Club* (1984) and *The
Bounty* (1986). Orion was also slow to invest in its own video distribution arm,
its subsidiary Orion Home Entertainment coming onstream only in 1988;
in any case, the Filmways/AIP library was too weak to support continued
expansion. Orion's mostly mid-market productions were also lightweight in
ancillary markets like cable and video, yet the company lacked the capital to
compete in the blockbuster market.[16] Meanwhile the company increasingly
relied on mortgaging its assets and selling off foreign distribution (thereby
cutting out revenue streams) to pay for its forward programme. Orion had
its share of bad luck as well as misjudgements; having scored major hits with
two negative pickups,[17] *First Blood* (1982) and *The Terminator* (1984), it failed
to secure sequel rights for either. The heavily indebted company's financial
difficulties intensified, Orion became caught up in hostilities between its corporate backers, and in 1987 Metromedia acquired a controlling interest. The
company's last and biggest hits, *Dances With Wolves* and *The Silence of the
Lambs* (1991), were unable to retrieve its financial position and Orion entered
Chapter 11 bankruptcy protection (and exited active film production) in late
1991. Orion ultimately fell into the hands of Hollywood's junkyard dealer Kirk
Kerkorian, of whose MGM 'Orion' became a name-only subsidiary in 1997.[18]

If with hindsight Orion was clearly doomed by an obsolete business model, it seemed unlikely a similar fate would befall DreamWorks SKG, given the seminal part its eponymous owners – the SKG stood for Steven Spielberg, former Disney executive Jeffrey Katzenberg and recording mogul David Geffen – had played in shaping both the aesthetics and the business practices of the new media industries. Unlike Orion, an old-fashioned stand-alone producer-distributor, DreamWorks was launched amid enormous publicity in 1995 with the promise not only to produce and release both live-action and animated motion pictures but to exploit its properties across television, music and interactive media divisions. With a capitalisation announced at $2 billion and link-ups to ABC, Microsoft and other key media companies, plus the unparalleled expertise and inside knowledge of its power troika, DreamWorks seemed better placed than any new company since Columbia in 1924 to crack the Hollywood cartel. DreamWorks also had a vision: in keeping with Katzenberg's famous internal memo to Disney staff in 1989,[19] when he had argued for budgetary restraint and a return to narrative- and character-driven, rather than 'high concept', cinema, DreamWorks promised a return to the standards of the Golden Age quality picture.[20] Three consecutive Best Picture Academy Awards in 1999–2001 (for *American Beauty*, *Gladiator* and *A Beautiful Mind*) alongside other successful pictures including *Cast Away* (2000) and *Minority Report* (2002) suggested DreamWorks was making good on that promise. By 2005 the studio had distributed twelve films grossing over $100 million each, including *Saving Private Ryan* (1998, $217 million), *Gladiator* ($187m), and *Catch Me If You Can* ($165m). With *Shrek* (2001, $268 m) and *Shrek 2* (2004, $441m) as well as *Shark Tale* (2004, $161m), DreamWorks Animation not only delivered blockbuster hits but established a distinctive, hip style that contrasted effectively to its principal competitor and market leader, Disney/Pixar.

Yet ultimately DreamWorks went the same way, if not as fast or as catastrophically, as an earlier attempt to reinvent the old-style studio, Francis Ford Coppola's ill-fated and worse timed Zoetrope, in the early 1980s.[21] The studio had its share of expensive SF flops, including *A.I. Artificial Intelligence*, *Evolution* (both 2001), *The Time Machine* (2002), the animated *Sinbad: Legend of the Seven Seas* (2003) and *The Island* (2005). This record was not necessarily worse than other majors, but DreamWorks lacked the resources to sustain a losing streak. The music and television divisions never delivered and were closed down or sold off. The studio remained over-reliant on Spielberg's personal contribution and seemed oddly in thrall to his outmoded 'dream' (a word used frequently in DreamWorks corporate publicity) of an old-style Hollywood studio, wasting years planning a never-built state-of-the-art studio lot. In 1998, despite revenues of $1 billion, DreamWorks lost $200 million.[22] From 2000 almost all Dreamworks releases were co-financed with other studios, who got first call on the receipts of hits like *Cast Away* (2000, $234m), thus exacerbating DreamWorks' financial problems. In 2004 the animation division (which despite its successes had lost $350 million in the previous five years) was spun off into a separate, publicly traded company.[23] When DreamWorks' independence finally ended in 2005 with its acquisition by Viacom, the relatively low purchase price of $1.6 billion (some $850 million of which was the assumption of debt) testified to the company's problems.[24]

Among other difficulties, DreamWorks' library of just fifty-nine pictures at the time of the buyout was an inadequate asset to leverage the capital required for a full production slate, compared to the thousands of titles on the majors' books. Even the conglomerates cannot generate the money they need to sustain their global production and distribution operations internally. Since the 1980s, the majors have devised new ways of raising production capital. Between 1985 and 1990 Disney raised over $1 billion from small investors enabled to participate in film production through Silver Screen Partners I and II (even investment vehicles have sequels, and Hollywood glamour is as strong a draw for small investors today as it had been for G + W's Charlie Bluhdorn in the mid-1960s). The logos of larger equity partners such as New Regency, Spyglass and Village Roadshow (who co-financed *The Matrix*) have become almost as familiar at the start of blockbusters as those of the studios themselves. Its founding trio's track record enabled DreamWorks to access this kind of capital at start-up, drawing a $500 million investment from Microsoft's Paul Allen, but unlike its competitors the studio was unable to repeat the trick.

By 2000, therefore, it seemed certain that while external buyouts and mergers always remained a possibility, under whatever ownership the six companies (with MGM/UA a shrivelled spectral presence at the feast[25]) that dominated the entertainment market would continue to do so: Time-Warner, Viacom (Paramount), NewsCorp (Fox), Disney, Sony and NBC Universal. The concluding chapter will look in greater detail at the current holdings of these giant multimedia conglomerates. What is clear, however, is that since the 1980s these companies came to exercise near-monopolistic control, to a far greater degree than the old studios, over an industry which itself had expanded beyond all recognition.[26] Throughout the 1990s, the majors released less than half the total number of films annually distributed in the USA, but studio releases consistently accounted for some 95 per cent of domestic box office.[27] In 1979, dismissing a Justice Department antitrust suit against Kirk Kerkorian's (ultimately unsuccessful) takeover attempt on Columbia Pictures, the damning comment of a Federal judge sketched the industry in terms that would only become more accurate in the years ahead: 'How on earth the government can arrive at the thought that there will be a diminution of non-existent competition is beyond me'.[28] This remark testifies to changes in regulatory attitudes which would be formalised in the new laissez-faire economic environment fostered by the Reagan administration (1981–9) and largely maintained by its successors, of both political parties.

The Reagan Justice Department's acquiescence in the majors' re-entry into theatrical exhibition from 1986, in apparent contravention of the *Paramount* consent decrees, greenlighted a return to vertical integration, but on a vastly expanded and diversified scale of operations compared to the old studio system. The integration of the networks from the mid-1990s, similarly, was both enabled and necessitated by the FCC's retraction of its 1970 'Fin-Syn'[29] rules that prohibited networks from owning their own programming and forbade the cross-ownership of film studios and TV networks. In this new, diversified entertainment industry, theatrical exhibition held a strategically pivotal place, but in purely financial terms was far from the most important part of studio business.

Until the mid-1950s, when the majors began to sell or lease their films to broadcast television, a film's (and ultimately a studio's) profitability depended on box office performance. As we have seen in Chapter 4, revenues from network and syndicated TV sales quickly became sufficiently important to studio balances that when the networks, awash with product, temporarily froze purchases of theatrical films in 1968 this contributed meaningfully to the industry-wide financial crisis of 1969–70. The advent of Home Box Office (HBO) in 1975 introduced the new revenue stream of pay cable; yet as of 1980 these various modes of consuming theatrical motion pictures in the home remained clearly secondary to the theatrical box office: that year network and syndicated TV, pay cable and the nascent home video market altogether contributed less than 27 per cent of studio revenues, compared to nearly 30 per cent for domestic theatrical release and 23 per cent from overseas.

By the decade's end, this picture had been transformed. Overall industry revenues had increased hugely, from $4 billion in 1980 to $13.2 billion in 1990. Domestic theatrical revenues had risen to $2.1 billion, but after adjusting for inflation this represented only a fairly small increase. More importantly, worldwide theatrical box office now supplied just 25 per cent of Hollywood's income. Home viewing of various kinds (including overseas TV revenue) made up the remaining three-quarters. Within this sector, with new channels such as Cinemax and Showtime competing with market leader HBO, pay-cable revenues had soared – from $240 million to $1.1 billion – while the importance of network TV sales had shrunk dramatically, from nearly 11 per cent ($430 million) to less than 1 per cent ($100 million). There was no doubting the new king of the Hollywood hill: home video, which in 1980 contributed just $280 million (7 per cent), now comprised a $5.1 billion income stream and a whopping 38.6 percent of total revenues.[30]

This was a permanent shift in the industrial orientation of the film business: as Hollywood's revenues continued to grow throughout the 1990s, home video's pre-eminence was consolidated. Indeed, its value to the studios only grew as video itself changed from a predominantly rental market, which limited studios' profit participation (see below), to one geared primarily to sales, above all with the introduction of DVD in 1997. In 2000, Hollywood derived 37.5 per cent of its global revenues from the $12 billion home-video market.[31] The only major change was the growth in overseas revenues, which by 2000 almost matched domestic theatrical box office and as globalisation intensified would shortly outstrip it.[32]

The home video explosion flooded Hollywood with cash; and a good thing too, given the rampant inflation of production and marketing costs throughout this period – costs that, as in the roadshow era, could make it hard for even a hit film to show a return on theatrical release alone (*Alien*, for example, whose $16 million marketing budget dwarfed its $11 million production costs, took a year to turn any profit at all). Yet video itself was only part of the story. Starting in the 1980s, long-held assumptions and understandings about the nature of the film – or, as studio executives and industry commentators came increasingly to conceive it, the entertainment or even 'software' – business, and how to succeed in it, were fundamentally transformed. Put baldly, the theatrical release of a film ceased to be an end in itself: it became simply a means to a much larger end, the exploitation of the copyrighted intellectual property it represented across an expanding cascade of profit-taking opportunities, the overwhelming bulk of them centred not in theatres but in the home. To take full advantage of this transformation the Hollywood studios, in their turn, reconfigured themselves from companies which produced (or financed) and distributed movies, into much larger organisations which aimed to integrate the full diverse range of activities across which a modern media property, or 'brand', has opportunities to make money.

BRINGING IT ALL BACK HOME

Researchers at electronics companies such as RCA and Ampex had been developing magnetic videotape systems since the early 1950s. By the early 1960s VTR systems were being increasingly widely used in US television. The concept of home playback followed quickly: by 1970 several different videocassette, video cartridge, and vinyl-based and laserdisc systems were jostling for pole position in the (as yet non-existent) home video market.[33] At this stage, the consumer uses of home video were not yet clear: some influential early advocates of video hoped that the availability of alternatives to network programming would liberate viewers from the commercialised, formulaic 'vast wasteland' (in FCC chairman Newton Minow's famous words) of broadcast TV into a variegated viewing environment of educational, arts and other special-interest programming.[34] This vision would to some extent be realised, inasmuch as once the video market exploded the breadth of available choice for home viewing also mushroomed exponentially (though video utopians undoubtedly did not foresee the important role that hardcore pornography would play in driving takeup of video, and subsequently of other new media technologies, notably the internet). However, home video's success most of all benefited mainstream, rather than alternative, entertainment; by the end of the century this incorporated both network television programming and Hollywood film, since both were owned and controlled by the same giant media conglomerates.

Initially, Hollywood's response to home video was marked by the same schizophrenia that had characterised its first reactions to television. On the one hand, the studios were alert to video's commercial possibilities and between 1977 and 1981 all of the majors, starting with Fox, either entered into licensing agreements with video distributors or started their own home video divisions.[35] At the same time, however, Hollywood attempted to drive the nascent video industry's development in their own interests. These efforts reflected the studios' desire for ongoing control of the intellectual property – the copyright – represented by their films, and the profits of that control. In 1976, upon the introduction of the Betamax player-recorder in the US Universal and Disney sued Sony for copyright infringment. Sony had heavily promoted the VCR on the basis of its recording and 'time-shifting' capabilities (rather than as a playback unit for prerecorded entertainment) and both Universal (as a division of MCA, the largest producer of network television filmed entertainment) and Disney (who jealously guarded the value of their animated classics by cyclically withdrawing and re-releasing them in theatres to each new generation of child consumers) had powerful motivations for wanting to contain the potentially unsupervised and of course uncompensated reproduction and distribution of their product. The suit proceeded through the courts until 1984 when it was finally resolved by the Supreme Court in Sony's favour, ruling that home taping constituted 'fair use' under the US Copyright Act.

By this time, video distribution and sales were fast developing as an important new profit centre for Hollywood. VCR ownership was embarked on the steep upward curve that would make it the fastest-selling item of home technology in US history to date (until its takeup rate was in its turn surpassed by DVD in the late 1990s). (See Appendix: Figure 3.) However, thanks to the high initial price of prerecorded videocassettes ($70–$100), the market was at first dominated by rentals, not sales – to the dismay of the studios, who under US copyright law's 'first sale' doctrine[36] derived no income from rental transactions following the purchase of a videotape by a retailer. Attempts to introduce leasing, rather than outright sale, of tapes (on the model of theatrical distribution) were resisted by dealers (for whose businesses the resale value of a second-hand tape had a significant role), and revenue sharing (which would later be successfully introduced for DVD rentals) foundered owing to inadequate tracking technology.

The studios' concerns were understandable: this was precisely the moment when, with the emergence of new ancillary markets, the intensified control of intellectual property and through it access to expanding downstream revenues was crystallising as the new corporate Hollywood's core business. But home video threatened to evolve in ways that threatened those revenue streams. The studios responded to their reversal in the courts on home taping by lobbying Congress through the MPAA for tighter and more rigorously enforced anti-piracy and copyright violation controls, culminating in the Digital Millennium Copyright Act of 1998. Their response to the failure to gain control of video rentals was to promote a market for video sales to consumers. Starting with *Star Trek II: The Wrath of Khan* (1982), which Paramount priced at $39.95 and was rewarded with sales of 290,000 units, the studios pursued the 'sell-through' market for their most popular titles. *Top Gun* (1987), priced at $24.95 (with a further $5 rebate offer from Pepsi) earned $175 million for Paramount; the following year, *E.T.*'s debut on video at the same price-point (and also emulating Disney's strategy of a time-limited release window) earned MCA-Universal some $225 million;[37] and the Time-Warner merger in 1989 was sealed with $400 million from video sales of *Batman*.

Although the rentals market continued to outstrip sales throughout the rest of the videocassette era – in 1993, rental spending had reached $7.3 billion, against $5.2 billion for sales[38] – as far as the studios were concerned the shift to sell-through was decisive in the composition of the industry's new 'filmed entertainment' economy. As noted above, by 1990 worldwide video revenues were outstripping theatrical box office by a considerable margin, and the revenue from video sales meant that an ever larger share of that money was being returned to distributors. With the introduction of DVD in 1997 the shift towards sales became irreversible. DVD was priced as a sell-through medium from the start, and this plus its clear advantages as a playback medium over VHS videotape – much better image quality, non-linear navigability, and the inclusion of supplementary materials (optional filmmakers' commentaries, 'making of' featurettes, deleted scenes, etc.) – sealed the demise of VHS. DVD adoption outpaced both television and the VCR before it to become the fastest-selling item in the history of US consumer electronics: by 2005 DVD players were to be found in more than three-quarters of TV households (it had taken the VCR almost twenty years to achieve the same penetration: see Appendix, Figure 3).[39] DVDs' attractiveness as consumer products sparked off a new culture of collecting and library-building: an unexpected bonus for the studios was the appeal of boxed sets of TV series (many of them produced by the majors' TV and cable divisions, like Time Warner's HBO). The success of the DVD revolution saw the value of the studios' libraries soar; according to one insider, for example, Time Warner's library had appreciated by an estimated $7 billion since the advent of DVD.[40]

The effect of the home video revolution on studio practices was profound and enduring. But it was far from simply the case that theatrical distribution was displaced by home consumption (which also of course included pay and broadcast television). Theatrical release retained pride of place, if only because it was in the theatrical market – and through the high-visibility, multi-million-dollar publicity campaign that attended it – that a picture established the profile that would help sell it in its subsequent release windows and platforms. By 1987, as the studios' sell-through policy was being consolidated, VCR penetration in US TV households passed the 50 per cent mark. From this point, the new life cycle of Hollywood films took the shape which it has largely retained since: a series of release 'windows' into successively lower-margin (though not necessarily less profitable, for a variety of reasons) media formats. (As David Waterman points out, this tiered release system effectively modernised the old studio 'run clearance' model from downtown first-run to subsequent-run and outlying theatres, with some obvious differences – for example, the film's indefinite ongoing availability, once released, in home video.[41]) Following a film's theatrical run, its domestic video release follows between four and six months later. About forty-five days later the film debuts on pay-per-view cable, and four to six months later – that is, about a year after opening in theatres – it moves to premium cable channels (HBO, Showtime, etc.). The film's network premiere – a devalued currency now compared to the 'Saturday Night at the Movies' days of the 1960s – follows another year or more later, and the final stop is syndication to local TV stations and cable systems. In all of the windows downstream from theatrical distribution, the film's performance in that first, traditional market is crucially important. Theatrical release has effectively become a 'loss leader', a glamorous (and hugely expensive) shop window to establish brand awareness and hence create value for subsequent platforms. In David Geffen's words, 'The initial theatrical release is the locomotive that determines the film's value'.[42]

As noted, these release windows offer successively lower margins per transaction – that is, of every dollar spent on buying a ticket to see a film in a multiplex cinema a higher proportion is returned to the distributor than with a video/DVD sale. Moreover, the huge costs of producing and marketing a major studio picture make it difficult, if not impossible, to turn a profit on domestic box office receipts alone. However, in many cases a film's costs can be effectively amortised during its theatrical release, meaning that subsequent revenues are relatively far more lucrative, if not indeed pure profit for the distributor. The ancillary revenues from video and other modes of home consumption of theatrical motion pictures have not come at the cost of shrinking theatrical revenues: on the contrary, apart from a slight dip from 1985 to 1988 when attendances dropped close to mid-1970s levels (perhaps reflecting video's attritional initial impact), annual US theatre admissions climbed steadily throughout the 1990s, by 1999 reaching nearly 1.5 billion – the highest level since the late fifties. Where a film underperforms in theatres, as frequently happens – filmmaking after all remains an inexact science (but see below) – the promise of income from its subsequent release platforms means that in many cases losses can at least be recouped. Notably, marketing costs for home video release are generally negligible – the heavy lifting has all been done by the film's theatrical publicity.

The extension of the revenue 'chain' means that it has become much harder for all but the most spectacularly ill-conceived projects to make an enormous loss. This in turn of course encourages rising negative and marketing costs, bolstered by the assumption that ancillary revenues will at least pick up the pieces. The old logic of 'making them big and selling them big' never made more (business) sense. Certainly, neither *Heaven's Gate* at the start of the 1980s nor Jeffrey Katzenberg's famous memo towards the end of that decade had any impact on the inexorably rising trend in production costs, which by 1990 had risen (by some six times the rate of inflation) to an average of more than $26 million, by 1995 reached $36 million and by 2000 $55 million. (See Appendix: Figure 4.) Marketing (in industry jargon, 'print and advertising' or P&A) costs kept pace, rising to $18 million in 1995 and over $27 million in 2000 – approximately half the negative cost, in other words. In 2003, the studios spent a combined $3.4 billion on television advertising alone.[43]

By 2005, therefore, the total *average* cost of producing and distributing a major Hollywood motion picture approached $100 million (and the most expensive blockbusters often cost much more). In 2004, the combined negative costs of the top-grossing films released by each of the six majors plus DreamWorks reached $900 million; add in marketing costs and these seven films alone represented an investment of between $1.5 and $2 billion – roughly the same amount they took at the domestic box office. Some industry observers questioned the sustainability of this level of expenditure, and indeed there were some indications that production costs might have hit a ceiling some of kind, stabilising around the $60 million mark in the early 2000s (P&A costs initially continued to rise before falling back somewhat).[44] Yet there was little real incentive for cost-cutting: those 2004 releases included *Harry Potter and the Prisoner of Azkaban*, the third in Warner's key franchise of that decade, which having covered its negative ($130 million) and marketing costs with its $250 million domestic gross, proceeded to rake in a further $546 million at the international box office.[45]

Enormous hits such as *Harry Potter* – and its peers in 2004, films such as Sony's *Spider-Man 2*, Disney/Pixar's *The Incredibles* and Fox's *The Day After Tomorrow* – were known in the industry as 'tentpoles', releases whose success across all media could prop up an entire year's production slate. Saturation booking strategies became the norm for most studio pictures from the early eighties: by mid-decade, the biggest 'tentpole' releases were receiving 'super-saturation' bookings of 3,000, or by the mid-2000s even 4,000 screens. (At $1,500 per print, this of course contributes towards spiralling P&A costs: in 2003, print costs for the six majors and their subsidiaries came to $540 million for the USA alone.[46])

Primed by high-impact trailers, starting with 'teasers' a full year ahead of release, and a rising crescendo of media coverage in 'infotainment' vehicles such as *Entertainment Tonight* on (studio-owned) networks and cable channels, such films became almost literally inescapable. This contributed to a fixation on opening-weekend performance, now widely reported in mainstream media as a new kind of spectator sport: record-breaking openings, proudly flagged by distributors in full-page *Variety* ads (where they would impress video retailers and other downstream revenue sources), became an almost annual event – predictably, as ticket prices also rose throughout this period. However, another notable aspect of the blockbuster era was that such mammoth openings were often followed by a sharp tail-off in attendances and receipts. Given the intense pressure on available screening slots during the peak summer release months between Memorial Day and Labor Day, as one would-be blockbuster followed another into theatres, only the rare true breakaway hits (for example, *Independence Day* (Fox 1996; $306 million gross) or *Titanic* (Par/Fox 1997; $600m)) were able to hold off the competition.

For example, the heavily publicised TV spin-off *Mission: Impossible* (Par 1996), pre-sold on nostalgia for the gimmicky NBC series (1968–70) and its memorable Lalo Schiffrin theme tune, starring Tom Cruise as CIA super-agent Ethan Hunt, opened in May 1996 on over 3,000 screens, with an impressive opening-weekend gross of $45.5 million – approaching *Jurassic Park*'s record $50 million opening weekend the previous year – propelling a first-week total of over $67 million. But in its second week *M:I*'s takings dropped a startling 55 per cent to $30.6 million. The next nine weeks each saw further successive falls of between 25 and 52 per cent: by its tenth week *M:I*, steamrollered like all the other competition that summer by *Independence Day*, had scaled down to 511 theatres (still more, that is, than *Jaws*' famous 'saturation' opening in 1975), and was earning barely $1,200 at each engagement. When the film was finally pulled from theatres just before Christmas it had grossed a total of $180.1 million and placed third in the year-end box office rankings – a substantial if not a breakout hit, enough to merit two sequels (2000, 2007), and in line with industry orthodoxy that a film's final tally will generally be 2½–3 times its opening-week gross.[47]

It remained possible for a film to build an audience through more traditional strategies such as platforming (a limited initial release in key markets, building to wider distribution as the picture gathered momentum and good word of mouth) and to demonstrate 'playability': also in 1996, for example, Fine Line (the arthouse division of Time Warner subsidiary New Line Cinema) gradually built *Shine*, the inspiring true story of troubled pianist David Helfgott, from a barely visible opening in just seven theatres soon after Thanksgiving – where, however, its per-screen average was a very high $37,934 (almost twice that of *M:I* at its peak) – widening to 207 screens in its sixth week, when the lack of competition in the January doldrums and the film's appearance in critics' year-end top-ten lists boosted interest. Thirteen weeks into its run, Geoffrey Rush's Best Actor Academy Award prompted a wide release to 850, and a fortnight later 1,050 screens. *Shine* never placed higher than eighth in the weekly *Variety* rankings; but when it completed its twenty-six-week run it had grossed a total of $36 million – placing it just fortieth for the year, but marking a very good return on its $5 million negative cost.[48] But such strategies were ill suited to major studio blockbusters, which relied not on 'playability' but on 'marketability'. By the late 1990s, with the independent sector also increasingly co-opted by the majors (see below), wide release had become the absolute norm for all but a tiny handful of pictures deemed to have 'challenging' subject matter: from 2000 to 2005, just ten films in the six years' combined top thirty grossers were released on fewer than 1,700 screens, including *Traffic* (USA Films 2000; a multi-strand narrative dealing with the 'war on drugs'), *A Beautiful Mind* (U/DreamWorks 2001; schizophrenia), *Million Dollar Baby* (WB 2004; euthanasia), and *Brokeback Mountain* (Focus 2005; gay cowboys).[49] (All of these were also multiple Academy Award nominees/winners, another notable early twenty-first-century trend.)

The drastically reduced numbers of films now distributed by the majors – between ten and twenty each year, compared to around forty in the mid-1940s – mean that each film carries enormous hopes and expectations. It comes as no surprise that although *Cleopatra* still tops an inflation-adjusted list of the most expensive films ever made, the remainder of the top ten were all made since 1995. This supports the argument – which for a variety of reasons, studios and producers like to maintain – that the film business is hugely risky, trading as it does on the vicissitudes of public taste. Indeed, six out of every ten pictures fail to return their costs. But as we have seen, the movie business is no longer just about movies. The new business model in which ancillary sales – at worst – backstop theatrical performance significantly reduced the level of risk in the film industry, as an analysis of the perceived disappointments on the most-expensive list reveals. Everyone knows that *Titanic* justified its estimated $247 million cost. But everyone also knows that the (then) third costliest film ever made, Kevin Costner's *Waterworld* (U 1995) was a notorious disaster (in fact, domestically the film grossed just short of $100 million – the post-*Batman* threshold for a major hit). So it is salutary to note that in overseas theatrical release *Waterworld* accrued a further $230 million. Add in home video, cable and TV sales and the film may even have turned a profit.

SHOWMANSHIP, NOT GENIUS

Of course the new economics of movies affected the kinds of films the majors increasingly made. As seen in Chapter 4, the studios' blockbuster trajectory was already well underway in the wake of *Jaws* and *Star Wars* – that is, before the video age really dawned (indeed, as Chapter 1 showed this course was partly set by the mid-fifties). Video and the other new ancillary revenue streams therefore confirmed and consolidated, rather than set, industry trends. Throughout the video era, theatrical performance has remained an excellent barometer of a film's prospects in the purely lucrative home video market. 'Event pictures' are events whether in theatres or in video retailers. Despite numerous examples of lower budget films capturing a larger than expected market share on video through positive word-of-mouth, and box office flops which partly redeem themselves by finding a home audience, almost without exception the same films that dominate annual box office rankings also clean up on video. With the growth in high-end 'home theatres', the home viewing experience of the large-scale effects-driven spectacles that have become Hollywood's stock-in-trade can rival or even surpass that of the multiplex. The major studios therefore have every incentive to continue to concentrate on proven and profitable blockbuster production.

The attractions of the 'pre-sold' property as a means of hedging against the inevitable variables of non-repeatable production have grown throughout the blockbuster era. In 1981, three of the top thirty films were sequels or entries in a series (and one more, *Raiders*, would generate a franchise); in 2004 there were eight. In 1981, surprisingly, just three films were adapted from books (and one, *Superman II*, from a comic book), whereas in 2004 eight were (with a further two comic book/graphic novel adaptations). In addition, in 2004 there were two remakes (one of a Japanese horror film, Sony's *The Grudge*, another – Warner's *Ocean's Twelve* – actually a sequel to a remake) and also two big-screen adaptations of television shows, both categories unknown in 1981. This left just twelve slots for films from original screenplays, only one – Disney/Pixar's *The Incredibles* – in the top five. (As usual, one should not overstate the degree of novelty; just outside the top thirty was Fox's *Alien vs. Predator*, a film which combined two of the studio's successful monster franchises, recalling the Universal monster match-ups of the 1940s such as *Frankenstein Meets the Wolf Man*).

For the studios, a home-run is a film from which a multimedia 'franchise' can be generated; the colossally expensive creation of cross-media conglomerates predicated on synergistic rewards provides an obvious imperative to develop such products. UA's James Bond series (twenty-three films, 1962–) served in many ways as the prototype for the lavish, shallow, crowd-pleasing, action-packed repeatable entertainments in which Hollywood traded increasingly heavily after *Star Wars*. Major franchises of the 1980s and 1990s included *Rocky* (five films, 1976–90), Paramount's *Star Trek* (ten films, 1979–2002), Fox's *Alien* (four films, 1979–96), Warner's *Superman* (four films, 1979–90), *Batman* (four films, 1989–97) and *Lethal Weapon* (four films, 1987–98).[50] SF-fantasy and superhero franchises, replete with eye-catching artefacts (monsters, spaceships, light sabres, 'technical manuals', and the like) are of course especially suitable for tie-in promotions and licensing activities targeted at children (toys, costumes, memorabilia, etc.) and also circulate within a pre-existing fan subculture receptive to memorabilia, collectibles and the like. The rise of SF and fantasy moreover offers an obvious showcase for spectacular state-of-the-art technologies of visual, sound and above all special-effects design, the key attractions that provide a summer release with crucial market leverage. The genre is well suited to the construction of simplified, action-oriented narratives with accordingly enhanced worldwide audience appeal, potential for the facile generation of profitable sequels (often, as with the two *Jurassic Park* sequels (U 1997, 1999), virtual reprises), and ready adaptability into profitable tributary media such as computer games and rides at studio-owned amusement parks. Of course, not every film is sufficiently 'toyetic' to generate such merchandising opportunities; but their importance was 'a fact of life', according to a Disney executive. A notoriously blatant example was Warner's *Space Jam*, a combined live action-animation that linked up NBA star Michael Jordan with Warner's stable of Looney Tunes cartoon characters and was actually originated by a TV commercial. *Space Jam*, said Time Warner chairman Gerald Levin candidly, 'isn't a movie. It's a marketing event'.[51]

The dictates of the market propelled to the fore a new generation of directors, replacing the mavericks and auteurs of the Hollywood Renaissance. Many of the latter found the 1980s especially testing; alongside Cimino, who never really recovered from *Heaven's Gate*, the careers of Friedkin, Bogdanovich, Rafelson, Coppola and others went into long-term decline. Of the two most distinctive and individualistic Renaissance auteurs, Martin Scorsese endured rather than thrived in the eighties, turning to independent production with *After Hours* (Geffen 1985) before his workmanlike handling of the profitable *The Color of Money* (Touchstone 1986) restored his industry bankability;

Robert Altman meanwhile forsook mainstream filmmaking altogether for a series of low-budget independent stage adaptations (*Come Back to the Five and Dime, Jimmy Dean, Jimmy Dean*, 1983; *Streamers*, 1983; *Fool for Love*, 1984). Both directors would re-emerge at the start of the 1990s with major critical successes (Altman's *Short Cuts*, Scorsese's *GoodFellas* (WB 1989)); thereafter they secured a privileged status as revered auteurs, though arguably at the price of much of their creative energy of the 1970s. In their stead emerged – alongside Spielberg and Lucas, who as producers both presided over numerous successful fantasy blockbusters in addition to the films they directed[52] – a generation of directors prized less for their personal vision than for their ability to rise to the massive logistical and technical challenge of delivering – on time if not on budget – a 'tentpole' film, often involving a lengthy and complex post-production, for the crucial summer release date targeted through months of pre-release publicity. The motto on RKO's letterhead after the studio had cancelled Orson Welles's contract following *The Magnificent Ambersons* – 'showmanship, not genius' – could equally have served as the strap-line for the new corporate Hollywood.

Some of the principal new director-technicians were Robert Zemeckis (*Back to the Future*, three films, U 1985–90; *Who Framed Roger Rabbit?*, Disney 1988; *Forrest Gump*, Par 1994; *Contact*, WB 1997, etc.), James Cameron (*The Terminator*, Hemdale 1984; *Aliens*, Fox 1986; *The Terminator, Part II: Judgement Day*, Carolco 1991; *True Lies*, Fox 1994; *Titanic*, Par/Fox 1997), John McTiernan (*Die Hard*, Fox 1986; *The Hunt for Red October*, 1990; *Die Hard: With a Vengeance*, Fox 1995), gigantism specialist Roland Emmerich (*Independence Day*; *Godzilla*, Sony 1998; *The Day After Tomorrow*, Fox 2004) and the more sober Ron Howard (*Backdraft*, U 1991; *Apollo 13*, U 1995; *The Da Vinci Code*, Col 2006). Those few blockbuster directors – notably the Scott brothers, Ridley (*Gladiator*; *Black Hawk Down*, Sony 2001) and Tony (*Crimson Tide*, Touchstone 1995; *Enemy of the State*, 1998), John Woo (*Face/Off*, Par 1997; *Mission: Impossible 2*, Par 2000), and Michael Bay (*Bad Boys*, 1995; *The Rock*, 1996; *Armageddon*, 1998; *Pearl Harbour*, 2001: all Touchstone) – who could claim a signature style adopted a high-impact, high-gloss advertising/music video aesthetic rather than the *caméra stylo*.

Spielberg and perhaps a handful of others, including the Gothic fantasist Tim Burton (*Batman*; *Batman Returns*, WB 1992; *Planet of the Apes*, Fox 2001), could lay claim to auteur status; but the real auteurs of the blockbuster were not directors but producers such as Joel Silver, who commanded (it seems the right word) the hugely lucrative *Lethal Weapon*, *Die Hard* and *Matrix* (three films, WB 1999–2004) franchises, all bearing his trademarks of stylised violence, lovingly photographed military hardware (assault weapons, helicopters, etc.), large-scale destruction of property and accelerating bouts of ever-more-intense violence building up to a pyrotechnical climax. Equally successful and influential was the partnership of Don Simpson and Jerry Bruckheimer, whose films – typically slightly less thick-eared than Silver's – included *Beverly Hills Cop* and *Beverly Hills Cop* 2 (Par 1984, 1987), *Top Gun*, *Bad Boys* and *The Rock*. Following Simpson's death in 1996, Bruckheimer maintained the pair's trademark style but continued to reach out to female and younger audiences with *Armageddon* and the record-breaking *Pirates of the Caribbean* franchise (Disney, three films, 2003–7).[53]

Also much more important than their directors were the small group of (exclusively male) stars who could reliably 'open' a film – that is, guarantee a weekend opening in line with expectations. In the 1980s and early 1990s these included Arnold Schwarzenegger, Harrison Ford, Sylvester Stallone, Bruce Willis, Tom Cruise, Mel Gibson, and Tom Hanks; later Nicolas Cage, Russell Crowe, Jim Carrey, Johnny Depp and Brad Pitt could be added to this select group. Black stars Eddie Murphy in the 1980s and Will Smith and (perhaps) Denzel Washington from the mid-1990s leavened this overwhelmingly white cadre. The limited number of such surefire marquee names, and the insurance they were perceived to offer, bid up the prices they – or rather, their agents at William Morris, ICM or CAA, whose Michael Ovitz rivalled any studio head or producer in both visibility and clout (in 1990 Ovitz topped *Premiere* magazine's 'Power List' of Hollywood's 100 most influential players) – could ask, and get. The $1 million Marlon Brando reputedly demanded for his cameo as Jor-El in *Superman* was quickly dwarfed by the eight-figure sums top stars received from the mid-1980s.

It also seems likely that, as a domestic medium, the primacy of home video has propelled the softening of Hollywood content. A glance at the top ten sell-through home video titles from any of the last twenty years indicates that family entertainment in most cases predominates: relatively few R-rated pictures makes these lists. Additionally, the shift since 2000 away from specialist video dealers towards general retailers as the principal outlet for video sales, above all Wal-Mart – whose market share for DVD sales was by 2002 over 25 per cent, and who refuse to stock any titles carrying parental advisory warnings – must have encouraged 'family-friendly' production policies. The introduction of the new PG-13 rating in 1984 – to accommodate *Indiana Jones and the Temple of Doom*, which had been threatened with a potentially disastrous R – allowed filmmakers a little more leeway with 'adult' material, and the great majority of each year's top-grossing films were rated either PG or PG-13. Valuable potential commercial partners – merchandisers and candidates for tie-ins and product placement – are also mindful of elements (sex, violence, moral or political controversy) that might detract from their corporate images.

DEGREES OF INDEPENDENCE

Of course, even studio pictures are not all blockbusters, and fewer than half the films distributed in the US annually are released through the majors (the proportion declined steadily throughout the 1990s, and in 1999 stood at less than four in every ten releases).[54] In the late 1980s and early 1990s, in fact, not even every blockbuster was a studio picture. One unexpected outcome of the video boom was a proliferation of independent production companies eager to capitalise on the new market's hunger for product and make good the shortfall left by the majors' concentration on a limited number of high-budget productions. Companies such as Carolco, Morgan's Creek and Castle Rock, while not aspiring like Orion to 'mini-major' status, positioned themselves firmly at the top end of the market, like Selznick and the other old top-line independents of the studio era, and produced a small volume of high-budget 'event' action blockbusters with major stars, often financed by pre-selling distribution and ancillary rights. In this way Carolco delivered a stream of major hits including the Rambo franchise (*First Blood*; *Rambo: First Blood Part II*, 1985; *Rambo III*, 1989), *Total Recall* (1990), *Terminator 2: Judgment Day*, and *Basic Instinct* (1992).[55]

In addition to Carolco at the top end, several other independent companies focused on lower budgeted productions entered the theatrical market in the mid-1980s, including Cannon, Dino de Laurentiis's DEG, Vestron, Island and others, resulting in a 50 per cent rise in independent production over the decade (from 206 releases in 1983 to 316 in 1988).[56] Many adopted Carolco's creative financing practices, and often offset genre and borderline exploitation projects with more adventurous and unclassifiable works (for example, in the same season (1987) Cannon produced the ludicrous Stallone arm-wrestling melodrama *Over the Top* and, extraordinarily, Jean-Luc Godard's deconstructive *King Lear*, while DEG's releases included David Lynch's landmark *Blue Velvet*). Yet ultimately all – including Carolco – fell victim to the non-negotiable logic of the conglomerate era. As Orion was simultaneously discovering with its less than world-beating library of old AIP films, the video market was hit-driven: the audience for low-budget genre films without major marquee names was too small to sustain any meaningful volume of production. Carolco's strategy of course recognised this, but like the smaller companies its margins were tight and its room for manoeuvre limited; the ancillary pre-sales that offset production costs also effectively closed out key markets and, lacking the immense assets against which the majors secured their credit lines, the independents were always effectively collateralising the very films they were looking to fund. Thus, while on the one hand the independents attempted to break into the only game in town by bidding up salaries for key talent (Carolco in particular paid astronomical sums to Arnold Schwarzenegger – $10 million for *Total Recall* and $14 million for *T2*), on the other a single box office failure could still threaten the whole enterprise. The independents were also mostly reliant on the majors for distribution (Carolco released its blockbusters through Tri-Star), which also ate into the bottom line; but if, like DEG, they acquired their own distribution arm they took on both debt and overheads they could hardly support.

None of the independent companies discussed above, or others that attempted to take on the studios on their own turf, survived long into the 1990s. Two companies that fared better, New Line and Miramax, took a different strategy, identifying niche markets not addressed by the majors and targeting them intensively with creative marketing. Both, not coincidentally, first succeeded as distribution rather than production companies and benefited from both the profitability of this activity (New Line, for example, distributed Carolco's non-blockbuster productions) and the edge it gave them in market knowledge and insight. New Line established itself in the 1980s as a success-ful purveyor of low-end high-concept genre franchises with the *Nightmare on Elm Street* (six films, 1985–91) and *Teenage Mutant Ninja Turtles* (three films, 1990–3) series. New Line's success with these and its other horror-fantasy productions enabled it to establish its art-cinema subsidiary Fine Line, which offered Robert Altman his path back into mainstream theatrical production with *The Player* (1988) and *Short Cuts* (1991). The market savvy and self-professed 'guerrilla marketing' of the Weinstein brothers (Harvey and Bob) at Miramax brought them success from the mid-1980s as distributors of mostly imported arthouse films. The breakout success of Steven Soderbergh's *sex, lies and videotape* in 1989 simultaneously established a new image of edgy, offbeat independent film (with Robert Redford's Sundance Institute and its associ-ated Film Festival – where *sex, lies . . .* won the 1989 Audience Award – as a central focus) and firmly identified Miramax – who now moved into produc-tion as well as distribution – at its leading edge.[57] The Weinsteins' keen eye for the controversial and marketable end of contemporary art cinema was evident throughout the early 1990s with such left-field hits as Peter Greenaway's NC-17-rated *The Cook, the Thief, His Wife and Her Lover* (1989), Neil Jordan's transsexual IRA thriller-melodrama *The Crying Game* (grossing $63 million in 1992), and the director with whom both Miramax and the new 'indie' film became indelibly associated, Quentin Tarantino, whose *Pulp Fiction* became the tenth-ranked box office film of 1994 with $108 million.

Miramax and New Line succeeded by investing in subject matter that lay outside the majors' orbit, at levels beneath the majors' usual threshold. The enormous return on investment generated by their most successful projects – *sex, lies and videotape*, made for $1.2 million, picked up for $1 million by Miramax who invested another $1 million marketing the film, eventually grossed $25 million domestically – proved this was a sector worth paying attention to. Sundance (soon joined by other high-profile independent film markets like the Los Angeles and Tribeca film festivals) evolved from a slightly worthy summer-camp atmosphere to an annual orgy of networking and deal-making, with the majors increasingly prominent alongside not only Miramax but also proliferating new distributors spawned by the burgeoning indie market. As for Miramax and New Line, their ambiguous if perhaps inevitable reward was to be drawn directly into the majors' orbit; in 1993 Miramax was bought out by Disney and New Line was acquired by Ted Turner (who bought Castle Rock at the same time). When Turner Broadcasting in turn merged with Time-Warner in 1996, New Line also became a what Justin Wyatt calls a 'major independent' – arthouse producer-distributors who can call on the resources of a media conglomerate.[58] The value of such operations to the majors was quickly apparent in smash hits like Miramax's *Pulp Fiction* and New Line's $120 million-grossing *The Mask*. In the subsequent decade, independent production companies would change hands repeatedly as the majors reorganised and reprioritised their operations.

Self-generated 'major independents' or 'specialty' divisions such as Sony Pictures Classics (established 1994), Fox Searchlight (1994), Paramount Classics (1998), (Universal) Focus Features (2002), Warner Independent (2003),[59] etc., appeared at all of the majors, all acting as producer-financiers as well as distributors, creating a new and dominant hybrid 'Indiewood' sector. These divisions operating with varying degrees of creative autonomy from their parent corporations, producing films that combined (some, also very variable) departure from the stylistic and narrative (more rarely, ideological) norms of the studio blockbuster to target a crossover arthouse/mainstream market. The upshot of this 'institutionalisation of American independent cinema', as Yannis Tzioumakis calls it, was the reassertion of conglomerate hegemony, at least at the level of financing and distribution of 'independent' film. Led by Miramax with such hits as *The English Patient* (1996) and *Shakespeare in Love* (1998), 'Indiewood' increasingly offered a home to largely conventional mid-dlebrow entertainments indistinguishable from the 'prestige' releases of the old studio era. 'Genuine' independent production, meanwhile, persisted at the margins of the industry, empowered by new, cheaper technologies of digital production and distribution.[60]

NOTES

1. 'Columbia, after Kerkorian, is free to move', *Business Week*, 8 June 1981, pp. 70–1.
2. The company changed its name to The Walt Disney Company in 1986.
3. '*Star Wars* lights Fox's future', *Business Week*, 23 January 1978, pp. 106–8; according to a Fox V-P, 'Five years ago we thought in terms of entertainment acquisitions. But the entertainment ballpark isn't very big'.

4. See 'Columbia Pictures: are things really better with Coke?', *Business Week*, 14 April 1986, pp. 79–80.
5. The markdown on Davis's 1981 purchase price reflected his sell-off of major assets to address the $400 million he inherited; the enormous price-tag paid by Sony, by contrast, testifies to the massive expansion of entertainment revenues in the latter half of the decade. See 'Why Sony is plugging into Columbia', *Business Week*, 16 October 1989, pp. 33–4.
6. 'Rupert Murdoch's big move', *Business Week*, 20 May 1985, pp. 70–4 [cover story].
7. That VHS machines were manufactured and retailed in greater numbers – because JVC, with its limited manufacturing capacity, licensed manufacturing rights to a larger number of companies whereas Sony proposed to manufacture most Beta VCRs itself – was just as significant, maybe more so. See Paul McDonald, *Video and DVD Industries* (London: BFI, 2007), pp. 35–6.
8. Tino Balio, '"A major presence in all of the world's important markets": the globalization of Hollywood in the 1990s', in Steve Neale and Murray Smith (eds), *Contemporary Hollywood Cinema* (London: Routledge, 1997), p. 69.
9. 'Hoping to soar with Superman', *Business Week*, 11 December 1978, pp. 149–51.
10. Bluhdorn died unexpectedly in 1983.
11. 'The big sell-off', *Time*, 29 August 1983, p. 45.
12. 'What is dimming the magic of Disney?', *Business Week*, 9 November 1981, p. 25.
13. The deal was brokered by *über*-agent Michael Ovitz of CAA.
14. 'The studio snatchers', *Business Week*, 16 October 1989, pp. 20–2.
15. Matsushita sold 80 per cent of MCA to Seagram in 1995 for $5.7 billion. Seagram was itself acquired by French holding company Vivendi for $34 billion in 2000, creating Vivendi Universal.
16. 'Why Orion Pictures' star isn't rising', *Business Week*, 27 August 1984, pp. 60–1.
17. Negative pickup: an already-completed independently produced film acquired for distribution.
18. The history of Orion is discussed in detail in Yannis Tzioumakis, *American Independent Cinema* (Edinburgh: Edinburgh University Press, 2005), pp. 225–39.
19. Leaked and published in *Variety* as 'The thoughts of Chairman Jeffrey'.
20. 'Hey, let's put on a show!', *Time*, 27 March 1995 [cover story], pp. 54–60.
21. The story of Zoetrope is told and analysed in Jon Lewis, *Whom God Wishes to Destroy . . . Francis Coppola and the New Hollywood* (London: Athlone, 1995).
22. 'Reality is, DreamWorks never needed a studio', *Los Angeles Times*, 30 July 1999, p. C7.
23. 'Waking from the dream', *Time*, 2 August 2004, pp. 56–7.
24. The full story of DreamWorks through its acquisition by Viacom is recounted in Daniel L. Kimmel, *The Dream Team: The Rise and Fall of DreamWorks: Lessons from the New Hollywood* (Chicago: Ivan R. Dee, 2006).
25. MGM's reacquisition of a distribution arm with its $380 million purchase of UA from Transamerica in 1981 (following the *Heaven's Gate* debacle) was part of an attempt to revive its fortunes having all but withdrawn from film activity in the late 1970s. A string of box office failures, however, immediately put the heavily indebted studio under renewed pressure; the result was that MGM became further embroiled in Kerkorian's relentless wheeler-dealing, being largely dismembered in a series of deals in mid-decade. As an active film studio, MGM was a questionable asset; its real value lay in its invaluable film library, which included not only MGM's own classic back catalogue but the RKO, UA and pre-1950 Warner libraries; the MGM portion (but not the rest) was acquired by Ted Turner in 1986. Kerkorian finally offloaded what remained of MGM to

Italian financier Giancarlo Parretti in 1990, but when financial crisis and scandal engulfed Parretti the following year, MGM was taken over by one of his creditors, French bank Crédit Lyonnais. Tragedy turned farcical when in 1996 the bank sold the studio back to Kerkorian. Through all this MGM remained active – barely – in production and distribution, but it was an eccentric, almost random presence in the industry. Only with MGM's purchase by Sony in 2004 did the prospect of stability materialise and Leo the Lion reappeared, appropriately enough, in front of the James Bond 'reboot' *Casino Royale* (MGM 2006). Whether MGM is really more than a famous logo remains to be seen.

26. See 'Return of the Magnificent Seven', *Business Week*, 28 March 1988, p. 29.
27. Michael Pokorny, 'Hollywood and the risk environment of movie production in the 1990s', in John Sedgwick and Michael Pokorny (eds), *An Economic History of Film* (London: Routledge, 2005), p. 280. This figure includes DreamWorks SKG and Miramax (owned by Disney since 1993).
28. Quoted in Jon Lewis, 'Money matters: Hollywood in the corporate era', in Jon Lewis (ed.), *The New American Cinema* (Durham, NC: Duke University Press, 1998), p. 95.
29. Financial Interest and Syndication.
30. Statistics from Harold Vogel, *Entertainment Industry Economics* (New York: Cambridge University Press, 1990), p. 52. Not mentioned here is a significant revenue stream – 17.5 per cent in 1980 and 15.2 per cent in 1990 – from made-for-TV films, which have been included in the overall percentage figure for home media.
31. Statistics from Harold Vogel, *Entertainment Industry Economics*, 4th edn (New York: Cambridge University Press, 2001), p. 62.
32. See Conclusion for a discussion of Hollywood and globalisation.
33. The history of video's development, exploitation and reception is covered exhaustively in Frederick Wasser, *Veni, Vidi, Video: The Hollywood Empire and the VCR* (Austin: University of Texas Press, 2001).
34. 'Video cartridges: a promise of future shock', *Time*, 10 August 1970, pp. 40–1.
35. See Wasser, *Veni, Vidi, Video*, pp. 95–8.
36. Which entitled the original owner ('first user') of a copyrighted product to transfer or dispose of it subsequently as they wished. Hence, having purchased a prerecorded tape from a wholesaler, a video retailer/renter (or 'rentailer') was under no obligation to make further payments to the copyright owner (i.e. the distributor) no matter how many times that tape was subsequently rented out.
37. Figure estimated by McDonald, *Video and DVD Industries*, p. 135.
38. Statistics from McDonald, *Video and DVD Industries*, p. 123.
39. McDonald, *Video and DVD Industries*, p. 143.
40. Edward Jay Epstein, *The Big Picture: Money and Power in Hollywood* (New York: Random House, 2005), p. 218.
41. David Waterman, *Hollywood's Road to Riches* (Cambridge, MA: Harvard University Press, 2005), pp. 65–72.
42. Quoted in Kimmel, *The Dream Team*, p. 149.
43. Source: US Entertainment Industry, MPA Market Statistics 2003, pp. 20–2.
44. Source: MPAA Theatrical Market Statistics, 2003, 2005; figures not adjusted for inflation.
45. Sources: *Variety*; www.boxofficemojo.com/intl/yearly; imdb.com.
46. Epstein, *Big Picture*, p. 117.
47. Source: *Variety*.
48. Source: *Variety*.

49. This number excludes Michael Moore's *Fahrenheit 9/11* (LionsGate 2004), whose controversial political content (provoking a row between the film's original producer-distributor Miramax and its parent company Disney, which refused to release it) certainly limited its initial release to 868 screens. Disney's animated features invariably debut in just one or two showcase theatres before 'going wide'.

50. The 'rebooting' of the *Batman*, *Superman* and *Star Trek* franchises is discussed in the Conclusion.

51. '101 movie tie-ins', *Time*, 2 December 1996, pp. 74–5.

52. Lucas produced 'Episodes V–VI' (i.e., the second and third pictures) of *Star Wars* in 1980 and 1983 but returned to directing 'Episodes I–III' from 1999 to 2004. Lucas produced the three Spielberg-directed *Indiana Jones* films in the 1980s (and a fourth film in 2008). Spielberg produced, or sponsored as executive producer, numerous films including the *Back to the Future* trilogy, *InnerSpace*, *The Goonies* and *Poltergeist*.

53. See Warren Buckland, 'The role of the auteur in the age of the blockbuster', in Julian Stringer (ed.), *Movie Blockbusters* (London: Routledge, 2003), pp. 84–98.

54. Pokorny, 'Risk environment of movie production', p. 280.

55. Carolco is analysed in detail in Justin Wyatt, 'Independents, packaging, and inflationary pressure in 1980s Hollywood', in Stephen Prince, *A New Pot of Gold: American Cinema in the Eighties* (Berkeley: University of California Press, 1989), pp. 143–9.

56. Wyatt, 'Independents', p. 149.

57. For a discussion of the stylistic attributes of contemporary independent film, see Chapter 9.

58. 'The formation of the 'major independent': Miramax, New Line and the New Hollywood', in Neale and Smith, *Contemporary Hollywood Cinema*, pp. 74–90.

59. Warner Independent ceased operations in October 2008.

60. 'Truly independent cinema', *Time*, 26 October 1998, p. 86.

The Biggest, the Best: 1985

Best Picture: *Out of Africa* (Mirage/Technovision)
D, P: Sydney Pollack; **W:** Kurt Luedke (from the writings of Karen Blixen)
Box Office No. 1: *Back to the Future* (Universal/Amblin)
D: Robert Zemeckis; **P:** Bob Gale and Neil Canton; **W:** Robert Zemeckie and Bob Gale

Upon its release in the summer of 1985, *Back to the Future* met with the kind of grudging critical approval such an obviously crowd-pleasing popcorn picture might expect: recognition of what were received as the essentially functional virtues of a tightly constructed and expertly assembled entertainment machine, combined with reserve at what were seen, even then, as its conformist or even potentially reactionary politics. (The film also broke Robert Zemeckis into the big time, building on the success of the previous year's *Romancing the Stone* (Fox 1984). Remarkably, of Zemeckis's ten films since *Back to the Future* only one has failed to gross $100 million domestically (*Death Becomes Her*, U 1992); three have grossed over $200 million, making the Spielberg protégé among the most plausible candidates for his mentor's crown.) Critical enthusiasm that year was reserved instead for Sydney Pollack's portrait of the early life of Karen Blixen (the writer Isak Dinesen), a handsomely mounted period romance lushly filmed on location in Kenya with star turns from Robert Redford and Meryl Streep. It was *Out of Africa* which dominated at that year's Oscars, collecting Best Picture, Director, Cinematography and four other awards (*Back to the Future* was nominated for its screenplay and title song, but won neither).

Yet from twenty-five years later it is the apparently disposable *Back to the Future* that has endured while the well-crafted *Out of Africa* is largely forgotten. In fact, Pollack's film, very much a classic Hollywood 'prestige' picture, was already old-fashioned – perhaps proudly so – when it was released and an endangered species. The early 1980s had seen success for films boasting similar traditional attributes – period settings in exotic and picturesque locations, a prestigious literary or historical source, and leading roles calibrated to award-winning actors in a similar vein – such as *The French Lieutenant's Woman* (MGM 1981), *Gandhi* (Col 1982), *Sophie's Choice* (U 1982, for which Streep won her first Oscar), *Yentl* (MGM 1983) and *Amadeus* (Orion 1984). Although *Out of Africa* was joined in the year's top five films by the comparable *The Color Purple* (WB), over the next decade fewer and fewer films of this kind, which represented a considerable investment for uncertain rewards in the multiplex market, would appear; some of the more successful examples included *Driving Miss Daisy* (WB 1989), *Dances With Wolves* (Orion 1990), *Far and Away* (U 1992), *The Bridges of Madison County* (WB 1995). In the late 1990s Miramax, following its acquisition as Disney's speciality division, started to corner the remaining market for such upscale romantic attractions with pictures like *The English Patient* (1996) and *Cold Mountain* (2002).

Back to the Future, meanwhile, enjoys a rather special status as a film that seems to epitomise with remarkable precision both its own historical moment – Michael Hammond suggests that it could stand as 'the representative film of the 1980s'[1] – and Hollywood's future direction of travel, which would leave films like *Out of Africa* trailing in its wake like Marty McFly's DeLorean speeding out of the quaintly ossified 1950s. The appositeness of the title has been often noted, in an era when President Ronald Reagan was urging a return to the alleged verities of Eisenhower-era America: Marty McFly has to travel thirty years into his family's and America's past not simply to restore the present but to rectify its manifold failings. In the film's present-day opening, the dysfunctions of Marty's family – his alcoholic, disenchanted mother, burger-flipping brother and wallflower sister – are attributed to his 'slack' father George's lack of virility and assertiveness. Marty's intervention in the past – when he inadvertently prevents his parents from meeting as teenagers and so has to rearrange their, and his, posterity over a series of farcical, fast-paced and often very witty events (including the Oedipal nightmare/fantasy of his own future mother's attraction to him) – ends with teenage George discovering the backbone that in Marty's 'original' future he never had; so that upon his return Marty finds his family transformed through this now historical act of phallic assertion into a high-achieving yuppie fantasy. Rather like George Lucas's *American Graffiti*, of which it might be seen as a fantasy cousin, in its quest for a prelapsarian American identity *Back to the Future* simply elides the 1960s and 1970s – understood as decades of trauma, rupture and loss – in favour of a restorative dose of the all-American fifties.[2]

Critics have also noted the ways in which the thoroughly whitebread Marty's project of restitution apparently extends to appropriating African-American history, with both the civil rights movement (in 1955, Marty inspires black soda jerk Goldie Wilson to imagine himself as the town mayor whose re-election posters, sure enough, we have already glimpsed in 1985) and rock 'n' roll (Marty's abominable Van Halen-style massacre of 'Johnny B. Goode' prompts a member of the backing band to call his cousin Chuck [Berry] so he can hear 'that sound you've been looking for'). (Here too there is an echo of *American Graffiti*'s use of predominantly black R&B performers as a soundtrack for white suburban teen anomie.) Where the intervening decades of progressive social change cannot be ignored or rolled back, it appears, a renascent majority white culture can at least take credit for them.

In fact, *Back to the Future* is far too hip and self-aware *merely* to transcribe conservative nostalgia onto the screen. The casting of Michael J. Fox as hero Marty McFly,[3] for example, is ingeniously intertextual, since Fox's mid-1980s reputation rested on his portrayal of Alex Keaton, the Reaganite yuppie son to ex-hippie parents in the long-running NBC series *Family Ties*. Nor does Marty especially enjoy the fifties (unlike Reese Witherspoon as the promiscuous teenage sister in Garry Marshall's *Pleasantville* (New Line 1998), who finds the fantasy world of the TV fifties so much more fulfilling than contemporary American reality that she decides to stay there.) The film's effectiveness as a 'ride' (it was of course subsequently transformed into a successful attraction at Universal Studios theme parks in California and Florida) relies on assuring its audience that the advantages of the present (designer underwear, sugar-free Pepsi) can, indeed, be seamlessly blended with those of the past.

Notes
1. Michael Hammond, *'Back to the Future'*, in Linda Ruth Williams and Michael Hammond (eds), *Contemporary American Cinema* (Maidenhead: McGraw-Hill, 2005), pp. 272–4.

2. *American Graffiti* is in fact set in 1962, which is presented in the film as a last moment of American innocence before (presumably) JFK's assassination inaugurates the long nightmare of the sixties 'proper'. See Barry Langford, '*American Graffiti*', in Mandy Merck (ed.), *America First: Naming the Nation in American Film* (London: Routledge, 2005), pp. 157–76.

3. Eric Stoltz was originally cast in the role but replaced soon after shooting began.

CHAPTER 8

Culture Wars

'The imaginary relationship of individuals to lived historical reality' was Marxist political philosopher Louis Althusser's description of ideology in general. It also seems apposite to the specific case of the politics of Hollywood cinema since the 1980s. Overall this was a period typified by a retreat from the kinds of critical – if often confused and ambivalent – engagement with social and political issues that characterised the Hollywood Renaissance of the late 1960s and 1970s. As a suitable emblem of this transition, consider how *Chinatown*'s Watergate-era account of Los Angeles history was rewritten as animated comedy in *Who Framed Roger Rabbit?* (Disney 1988). The notion of imaginary, or fantasy, resolutions to concrete problems and debates has a particular relevance to the upsurge of science fiction and fantasy cinema from *Star Wars* to the *Lord of the Rings* (New Line, 2001–3) and *Pirates of the Caribbean* (Disney, 2003–7) trilogies. While sometimes, as in Ridley Scott's *Alien* and *Blade Runner* (WB 1982) or, more loosely, Andy and Larry Wachowski's *The Matrix* (WB 1999), these films built on the seventies tradition of dystopian SF satire (*Soylent Green*, MGM 1973; *Rollerball*, UA 1975), more often they followed George Lucas's lead to 'a galaxy far, far away' where contemporary concerns, at least ostensibly, were absent. One might suggest that these journeys to a fantasy elsewhere were impelled by a desire for other-worldly redemption from the disenchanted present, or even a retreat from the concerns of adult social life altogether. The close alliances forged against established (adult) authority between childlike aliens and human children (or childlike adults) in such post-*Close Encounters* SF films as *E.T.*, *Starman* (Col 1984) and *Flight of the Navigator* (Disney 1986) seemed to be motivated by the desire to escape the complexities of contemporary family and professional life to a numinous enchantment strongly identified with pre-adult perspectives.[1] (A context that perhaps explains the box office failure of John Carpenter's remake of *The Thing* (U 1982), which both offered

Making his mark on history: *Forrest Gump* (Paramount 1994). Reproduced courtesy of The Kobal Collection

a horrifically un-benevolent alien and depicted social bonds disintegrating, rather than strengthening, under stress.)

In Chapter 7 we have seen how these particular generic strains were promoted by industrial conditions. But nostalgia for an earlier era (in the case of *Star Wars*, Universal's 1930s 'space opera' serials) when American science fiction film abjured social speculation also caught the political tide. In the era of Ronald Reagan, elected to the White House in 1980 on a platform of conservative populism and homely patriotic platitudes encouraging a wilful disengagement from the late-1970s 'malaise' of social and political complexities in favour of the appealing simplicities of a fantasy past, the pursuit of enchantment in these 'regressive texts' was anything but apolitical. Their distinctive contribution was to stake out a terrain of cultural politics around the politics of private life, family, gender and (to a lesser degree) sexuality that marked a clear break with the public-policy preoccupations of their seventies precursors. (Later in this period, *Contact* (1997) and the second *Star Wars* trilogy presented cosmic family romances that explored similar territory, while the sequels to *Alien* – especially *Aliens* (Fox 1986) and *Alien: Resurrection* (Fox 1994) also replaced the original's unsettling, very 1970s combination of corporate critique and body-horror with a focus on the family.) To the extent that Hollywood films during his presidency adopted Reaganism, they mostly did so less in terms of explicit New Right ideology (with the partial exception of foreign policy) than through a similar reliance on streamlined, affirmative and restorative fictions, deploying both renovated and new generic forms to do so. Coincidentally or not, the two most popular films of Reagan's first year in office were Paramount's *Raiders of the Lost Ark* and ITC's *On Golden Pond* – the former a knowingly retro reinvention (of course on a far larger scale) of the 'simple' pleasures of the juvenile action serials of the 1930s, the latter a traditional domestic melodrama that equally self-consciously staged a high-profile generational rapprochement (between old-style Hollywood liberal icon Henry Fonda and sometime radical daughter 'Hanoi' Jane) that promised to assuage the festering wounds of the American sixties.

The films of the period, in other words, were far from apolitical. Such in fact is the very nature of ideology: it is to be found not only in party political programmes or debates around public policy, but also – perhaps even more – sedimented in the textures of daily life, majoritarian social and cultural attitudes, the unexamined 'common knowledge' through which we make sense of the enormous complexities of modern society. The just-folks simplicity of Ronald Reagan's bromides in the 1980s or George W. Bush's cowboy style twenty years later, soliciting assent to conservative orthodoxies about small government, national defence and traditional morality in the name of 'ordinary Americans', show just how deeply political 'common sense' can be. In fact, the late twentieth-century presidencies, very much including the Democrat Bill

Clinton (1993–2001), as much as the New Right/neoconservative administrations that preceded and followed him,[2] were characterised discursively by a turning away from the language of traditional politics – economic management, the application of professional political judgment to complex policy challenges, the inevitable compromises entailed in foreign relations – towards an affective rhetoric of values, and a cultural politics in which the image played an ever greater role.

This in turn meant that Hollywood was squarely in the centre of political culture in this period. Of course, as ever, we cannot simply 'read off' changes in national political culture – such as the clear hegemony (in both political office and cultural agenda-setting) of the right from the late 1970s – on to cultural products such as movies. However carefully one mediates such readings (say, by looking for implied and symbolic, rather than explicit or programmatic, political positions) they are always likely to beg more questions then they answer about the precise mechanisms whereby commercial entertainment, produced collaboratively over months or years, interacts with its social and political contexts. So, tempting as it might be to take the image of Christopher Reeve holding aloft the Stars and Stripes at the end of *Superman II* in 1981 as a symbolic conservative rebuttal of the previous decade's critical appropriation of American iconographies,[3] such an interpretation needs to be handled carefully; not only because this particular poster image of comic-book patriotic restitution (Superman is restoring Old Glory to the White House lawn having defeated the vaguely totalitarian Kryptonian renegades who demeaned and humiliated the President) is self-conscious and tongue-in-cheek to the point of camp; nor because – to take just the eighties, and to confine discussion only to openly political films, as ever a small minority of Hollywood films – alongside unabashed Reaganite fantasies such as *Red Dawn* (MGM/UA 1984), the *Rambo/ First Blood* trilogy, *Missing in Action*, *Invasion USA* (both Cannon 1985), and *Iron Eagle* (Tri-Star 1986), the mid-eighties saw other releases (mostly independently produced) that were unequivocally critical of aspects of New Right foreign or economic policy, including *Under Fire* (Orion 1983), *Salvador* (Hemdale 1985), *Platoon* and *Wall Street* (American Entertainment 1988). As several analyses of eighties and nineties films have established, Hollywood's politics remained heterogeneous, though of course within clearly defined parameters.[4] In some regards these parameters seemed to shift rightwards during the period, but plotting these co-ordinates on a film-by-film basis can only go part of the way to explaining the politics of contemporary Hollywood cinema. This is because the ideology of corporate Hollywood found expression (and perhaps refuge) in a 'deep politics' of form as much as, or more than, manifest content.

It was not merely a neat historical irony that saw former Warner contract player Reagan in the White House: Reagan was the prototypical proponent of the politics of the image, whose feel-good soundbites – 'It's Morning in America', the theme for his landslide re-election in 1984 – neatly bound up, assuaged and wholly mystified issues of declining national economic competitiveness, the painful transition to a post-industrial economy and the paradoxical impotence of a nuclear superpower. Later, similarly if more aggressively and controversially, George W. Bush's 'good guys and bad guys' approach to international relations sidestepped complex questions of global security in a multipolar world multiply divided by power, economics and faith. In between, Clinton's empathetic politics of the self (particularly following the collapse of his major first-term policy initiatives) furthered the shift of political discourse towards an impressionistic, identificatory mode and away from reasoned argument and nuance. This was a period of 'identity politics', in which many Americans preferred to see their interests in terms of immediate affinity groups – those with whom they shared a common culture grounded in race, ethnicity, sexuality or faith – and pursued an emotive politics of injury and victimhood (real or perceived), complaint and – typically symbolic – restitution. Mythical GIs held hostage by fanatical Vietnamese Communists; criminalising flag burning; the entitlement of gays to serve in the US military or to enter same-sex marriages recognised by the state; a fictional TV newscaster's single parenthood;[5] the ethics of adulterous oral sex in the Oval Office; the sexual proclivities of a Supreme Court nominee; abortion rights; the teaching of creationist doctrines in public school science classes: these were the kinds of issues that suddenly seemed to dominate political life. Many of the most intense controversies in more conventionally political contexts – such as the ongoing racial division, the legacy of slavery, that continued to fracture American society more than any other developed nation – also found expression in overdetermined conflicts where the problems identified and solutions proposed were as powerfully symbolic as they were substantive, such as school busing, affirmative action and the drug culture. Just as symbolic was the militaristic rhetoric that infected so many areas of policy, from the 'war on drugs' to the equally open-ended and attritional 'war on terror'. Of course these issues and the debates they ignited related to issues of profound importance for American society. But the specific *forms* they took often seemed to divert energy and activism towards eye-catching epiphenomena rather than the causes that underlay them.

All of which suggests the ways in which we might interrogate the relationship of Hollywood cinema to its political and social contexts in these years. This was a period in which, more than ever before, Hollywood's stock-in-trade – both new technologies of disseminating information and generating images, and old techniques of narrativising, making sense of the world through stories – came to dominate political culture too. The Reagan and Clinton White Houses each saw an unprecedented mingling of Washington and

Hollywood in both personnel and style (Bill and Hilary Clinton in particular seemed as much, or more, at home in the company of LA power players such as David Geffen and Barbra Streisand as on Capitol Hill). The uncannily timely satire *Wag the Dog* (New Line 1997) – in which a Hollywood mogul and a Washington fixer join forces to 'produce' an overseas war to distract attention from a domestic sexual scandal, and whose release coincided with the Monica Lewinsky episode and NATO intervention in Kosovo – skewered this connection adroitly. But the affinity of Hollywood and the new politics went deeper. The emergent postmodern politics was about stories, spectacle, symbolism and emotional catharsis: Hollywood's meat and drink. Movies could not turn their back on politics even if they tried.

Phenomena such as the 'triumph of representation', the cultivation of style over substance, the politics of the image and the fragmentation of larger social totalities and collectivities into a bricolage of localised interests and affinities also raise the vexed question of Hollywood's relationship to postmodernism. A critical consensus on this has proved elusive, perhaps because postmodernism itself is a notoriously slippery concept and accordingly there are numerous overlapping frameworks through which this relationship can be conceived or contested. On the one hand, as culture industry products circulating in a globalised economy where narratives themselves become commodified and synergistically reconstituted across a series of iterations (as sequels, videos, 'special editions', computer games, comic books or graphic novels, spin-off merchandise, etc.), Hollywood movies are exemplary postmodern artefacts. On the other hand, while films such as *Batman* and *Jurassic Park* seem almost to celebrate the seamless interpenetration of their textual, inter-textual and extra-textual aspects, others such as *Blade Runner*, *The Matrix* and *The Truman Show* (Par 1998) appear to thematise and elaborate postmodern concepts (*The Matrix* actually cites the French postmodern theorist Jean Baudrillard) in ways that strongly suggest a critical purchase on the process they themselves help constitute.

Postmodernism is also often characterised as heterogeneous, suspicious of larger categories and conclusions, and in political terms somewhat two-faced: differentiated from a more aggressively parodic, subversive and contestatory modernism by its tendency simultaneously to deconstruct and reinscribe mainstream practices, ending up, it would seem, very much where it started from. All of which makes generalisations about ideological direction problematic and probably futile. In contemporary Hollywood there are no formal structures, such as the Production Code, through which the regulation of content is explicitly propounded (although downwards pressure on ratings for commercial reasons can certainly play a part).[6] Production cycles and generic trends, however, continue to offer a means to map trends, at least provisionally. Prior to the occupation of Iraq, at least, Hollywood cinema engaged with political subject matter most obviously in the cycle of films that dealt retrospectively with the Vietnam War and with its contemporary legacies (a cycle that began in the 1970s but which crystallised as a genre in the Reagan years). This chapter begins with a discussion of these films and a related set of films that addressed the legacy of the sixties more generally, before going on to look at ways in which themes and motifs from these cycles, which had largely run their course by the early nineties, were adapted by the action blockbusters that came to typify studio production in this period. As previously noted, not all Hollywood films are blockbusters even today, and accordingly the chapter concludes with a consideration of the ways in which independent and off-Hollywood or 'Indiewood' productions challenge hegemonic positions, and the limits to such challenges.

VIETNAM: 'DO WE GET TO WIN THIS TIME?'

Vietnam was the most glaring unfinished business confronting America as it entered the 1980s. Redressing the wounds of the war upon the social body and redeeming the experience of defeat emerged as an important dimension of New Right ideology. Hollywood Vietnam films participated prominently in this process.

The history of 'Hollywood's Vietnam' is well known: absent, with the notorious (but dismayingly popular) exception of John Wayne's *The Green Berets*, from US screens during the war itself, the Vietnam combat film emerged shortly after the end of the conflict in several diverse forms.[7] The first of these were independent productions including *Go Tell the Spartans* and *The Boys in Company C* (both 1978), hewing closely to the standard World War II model whose popularity with audiences had faded in the Vietnam era itself, and failing to renovate the genre successfully for the more recent conflict. Major Hollywood Renaissance statements such as *The Deer Hunter* and *Apocalypse Now* started to establish a new – more visceral, more paranoid, and in Coppola's case decidedly trippier – visual lexicon for the portrayal of the war. The Vietnam combat film peaked in the mid-1980s with *Platoon*, *Hamburger Hill* (Par 1987), *Casualties of War* (Col 1989) and the independent *84 Charlie Mopic* (1989), among others; these also adopted the 'embattled platoon' variant familiar from World War II combat films such as *Bataan*, but combined this familiar generic syntax with novel semantic elements such as napalm, drug abuse, 'fragging', rock music soundtracks, graphic, visceral violence and a novel and memorable jargon ('grunts', 'gooks', 'clicks', 'on point' and so on) to establish a distinctive and briefly popular generic strain.[8] The tone of most of these films was bleak to the point of masochism, emphasising the attritional, disorienting nature of jungle combat (lacking the clear territorial and by extension ideological co-ordinates of traditional warfare) and the confusion and terror of conscript infantrymen (there were few Air Force Vietnam films, such as *Bat 21* (Tri-Star 1989), and no Navy ones).

A distinct strain of revisionist Vietnam films lightly disguised as heroic rescue missions acknowledged the despair of these mainstream 'Nam' movies, only to subsume and triumphantly redeem it. These included *Uncommon Valour* (Par 1983) and *Missing In Action*, but by far the most successful – and one of the iconic films of the 1980s – was *Rambo: First Blood Part II* (Carolco 1985). Their shared premise was the New Right shibboleth that American POWs remained captive in Vietnamese camps a decade after the war's end, and the 'rescue fantasy' of their narratives offered audiences symbolic restitution of a variety of real or perceived injuries, foremost among them the opportunity to rewind the war itself and fight it over again, employing different strategies and of course with a different outcome.[9] When the eponymous hero John Rambo (Sylvester Stallone) is offered the chance to return to Vietnam, he frames the film's ensuing GI Joe-style fantasy with the question 'Do we get to win this time?' The rescue films replayed the captivity narratives that have been a fixture of American popular culture from colonial times through the nineteenth-century Indian Wars and thence the Western, with the added twist that the objects of savage captivity here are US soldiers, rather than (as in *The Searchers*) white women. The captives are victims twice over, brutalised by their captors and betrayed by an indifferent, incapable, cowardly or actually treacherous civilian government bureaucracy (Rambo's mission is supposed to be just a public-relations exercise – his determination to bring the men home meets with outraged opposition from his government sponsors). Rambo accomplishes the 'recovery' of the POWs in more than just the physical sense: as the men are roused from passive despair to play an active role in their own liberation, and help Rambo defeat not only the Vietnamese but their Soviet advisors (who are modelled after the Japanese and Nazis, respectively, of World War II combat films), they enact a symbolic return of American strength and self-confidence to the untroubled climate of 1945.

The POW captivity narratives redeem not only a lost war but the stereotypical image of the Vietnam veteran as a borderline psychotic and a danger to society. Even while Vietnam itself remained offscreen in the seventies, deranged vets started to abound. Ex-Marine Travis Bickle in *Taxi Driver* (which, given its allusions to *The Searchers*, might also be seen as an early Vietnam rescue film) is the most famous of these, but in 1977 *Rolling Thunder* (AIP), *Black Sunday* (Par) and, rather more lightheartedly, *Heroes* (U) all featured manic veterans, followed in 1978 by *Who'll Stop the Rain?*. That same year Hal Ashby's *Coming Home* (UA) offered a canonical depiction of post-traumatic stress syndrome driving the vet to violence and/or suicidal despair (alongside the kind of sympathetic portrayal of antiwar activism that would largely vanish from eighties films). By the mid-eighties, Vietnam combat experience had become a ubiquitous backstory for male characters in a wide variety of genres, whose usually unspecified but universally understood wartime trauma motivated unhinged behaviour. Such films partly followed the lead of late-forties *noirs* that presented inadequately resocialised veterans as threats to the social order. Other films, starting with *Coming Home*, followed the tradition of films such as *The Best Years of Our Lives* and sympathetically explored veterans' problems of reintegration, including *Jacknife* (Vestron 1988), *In Country* (WB 1989) and the second of Oliver Stone's Vietnam 'trilogy', *Born on the Fourth of July* (Par 1989).

Rambo himself, as introduced in 1982's *First Blood*, links the negative/phobic and empathetic versions of the vet. Through the child-man Rambo, the vet – notwithstanding the hyper-masculinity of his pumped-up body – is presented as a lost child whose violence reflects his confusion and rage at his abandonment by his symbolic 'parents', the nation; his ill treatment in the film represents an extreme version of widespread cultural myths around the victimisation and rejection of returning Vietnam veterans.[10] At the end of the film, *First Blood*, the besieged Rambo explains to his former CO and surrogate father Colonel Trautmann that 'we [i.e., Vietnam vets] just want our country to love us as much as we love it'. At the same time, as several commentators have noted, both here and in the first sequel Rambo appropriates several tropes of the antiwar counterculture (long hair, anti-modernism, guerrilla fighting style that turns the Viet Cong's tactics against themselves, and so on: his scapegoating by narrow-minded small-town 'straights' in *First Blood* echoes the victimisation of Wyatt and Billy in *Easy Rider*) – offering a Right libertarian position that mirrors the Left libertarianism of some strains of the counterculture, hence working to anneal the wounds of the sixties.

Thus, surprisingly, at the start of the eighties, both *First Blood* and *On Golden Pond* proved to be connected to the larger question of – as the title of a successful public television documentary series had it – 'Making Sense of the Sixties', a problem that would continue to preoccupy American public life during the Reagan era (which was partly predicated on repealing the social, political and cultural legacy of those years) and into the ascendancy of the Baby Boomers themselves in the Clinton and George W. Bush years, throughout which election campaigns continued to be haunted by charges and counter-charges about draft-dodging and/or past associations with the antiwar Left.[11] In films such as *The Big Chill* (Col 1983), *Running on Empty* (WB 1988), *Field of Dreams* (U 1989) and *Flashback* (Par 1990) the 1960s are figured as a period of trauma and schism in American life whose reparation is the primary duty of the present. The films of Oliver Stone from the mid-eighties to the mid-nineties – including his Vietnam 'trilogy', his two meditations on sixties presidents *JFK* (WB 1991) and *Nixon* (Entertainment 1995) and also the self-indulgent *The Doors* (Guild 1991) – obsessively reworked and re-examined the decade's key events and their influence on, and meanings in, the present.

Stone was unusual if not unique in stressing – sometimes (notably in *Nixon*) through a striking, fragmented montage approach to narrative and visual style – the aliveness of the past and its inevitable susceptibility to ideological appropriation. Most other films 'about' the sixties either contented themselves with the nostalgic accretion of period detail, like *1969* (Entertainment 1988), or aligned themselves with one of the ideological axes around which the sixties were 'made sense of'. John Sayles's unapologetically progressive micro-budget independent production *Return of the Secaucus Seven* was a surprise minor hit in 1980, but given the dominant political paradigms of the period it was unsurprising that conservative paradigms predominated. The Vietnam combat film itself reflects the intense and ongoing politicisation of the war and the fallout from modern America's first experience of defeat.[12] Revisionist Vietnam films such as *Rambo* openly acted out the conservative orthodoxies that had developed since the mid-1970s to make sense of the war, in particular the 'stab in the back' fantasy according to which valiant US forces had been compromised by un-American protestors and pusillanimous civilian authorities who denied the troops the tools to finish the job. But even less gung-ho Vietnam films frequently relied on very conventional, and in that sense conservative, narrative paradigms for interpreting the war. And they were almost invariably focused on American experience in ways that seemed to exclude Vietnamese land and culture, still less the 2 million Vietnamese dead (compared to 57,000 US casualties), as anything other than a stage for the enactment of an 'American tragedy'. In fact, 'Hollywood's Vietnam' is a mythic landscape across which symbolic narratives of American male selfhood are enacted. *Platoon*, a fable of an American Everyman's passage to disenchanted manhood and lost innocence via the symbolic intercession of 'good and bad fathers' in the shape of his platoon's two – saintly and demonic – sergeants, is the best example. The half-glimpsed Vietnamese are little more than functions of what remains a private American agony. (Stone's third and final Vietnam film, *Heaven and Earth* (WB 1993), based on Le Ly Hayslip's account of her own wartime and postwar experiences, seems partly intended to act as recompense.)

Such ideas were central to Robert Zemeckis's *Forrest Gump*, the top-grossing film as well as the Academy's Best Picture of 1994, which brought both the Vietnam film and the sixties cycle to a culmination of sorts. Forrest (Tom Hanks) progresses, Candide-like, through what are presented as two decades (the sixties and the seventies) of disenchantments and moral disorientation – taking in the war, at home and in-country, the counterculture, and the permissive society – from the wreckage of which only his simplicity allows him to emerge untouched. Meanwhile, the film ingeniously both acknowledged and neutralised the reflexive critiques of meaning-production of the Oliver Stone cycle by its use of then-novel digital post-production technology to paint Forrest into or alongside the era's key events and personalities – or rather, to incorporate their real histories to Forrest's imagined one. Whereas *Zelig* (Orion 1984), Woody Allen's typically modernist thesis about the urban 'Man Without Qualities', explored the individual's desire to leave a mark on the historical record, Forrest by contrast communicates his own vacancy to history itself. His obliviously pivotal intervention in historical events denies the spectator's assumptions about the course and meanings of such events without offering any alternatives: indeed, the film's message time and again is that any attempt to take hold or make sense of history, still less to do so under the motivation of a political cause, is futile and delusory. And by its adroit manipulation of historical footage to introduce Forrest to JFK, LBJ, John Lennon, *et al.*, *Forrest Gump* extends this evacuation of historical content to a principle of narrative organisation. The material of history itself is effortlessly reshaped and can presumably be reshaped as many times again. If Stone's biopics *Born on the Fourth of July* and *Nixon* still fell prey, almost despite themselves, to the valorisation of personality that has always guided Hollywood's treatment of history as individualised narrative, in *Gump* material history collapses into the black hole of a subjectivity that itself barely flickers into independent life. It was perhaps unsurprising that in the years between *Gump* and the US-led attack on Iraq in 2003, which ultimately provoked a measurable return of critical political consciousness to Hollywood films, Stone's political cinema seemed to lose its way after *Nixon* while other would-be radical attempts at counter-histories to the now hegemonic conservative narrative, such as *Panther* (Polygram 1995) and *Dead Presidents* (Hollywood 1994), failed to clear a path through historical and generic confusion.

Ultimately, the cinematic legacy of the Vietnam film was indirect. While the genre certainly helped produce a thriving discourse about the war, given the intensely conflicted historical situation of their own production Vietnam movies could probably never have been realistically expected to produce insight rather than catharsis. Indeed they illustrate as well as anything the ways in which Hollywood's engagements with history quickly sediment into the genre conventions out of which they are already partly shaped (both the Vietnam combat film itself and its conditions of production were sharply satirised, well after the fact, in *Tropic Thunder* (DreamWorks 2008)). What the Vietnam film bequeathed to the largely ahistorical and apolitical action films that succeeded it was, above all, a thematics of male identity formation through combat and male bonding. Given the terms in which US intervention in Indochina had been conceived historically, it was perhaps inevitable that the (re-)construction of masculine identity would emerge as a central focus once the conflict was accommodated to Hollywood's narrative demands. Lyndon

Johnson repeatedly justified his obsessive commitment to the war as phallic competition – a 'pissing contest' between himself and North Vietnamese leader Ho Chi Minh. Johnson's successor Nixon warned that defeat in Vietnam risked diminishing the US in world eyes to a 'pitiful, helpless giant'. Unsurprisingly, therefore, in this climate of urgent phallic anxiety the New Right's principal foreign policy project became what Susan Jeffords calls 'the remasculinisation of America'.[13] Vietnam films, both combat and home front, were highly receptive to this cultural discourse around masculinity: sexual dysfunction as a result of war wounds is the dramatic focus of both *Coming Home* and *Born on the Fourth of July*; the Vietnam veteran antihero of *Rolling Thunder*, a survivor of Viet Cong torture, suffers a symbolic emasculation by having his hand forced into a waste disposal unit; and a GI is actually castrated by the North Vietnamese Army in *Dead Presidents*.

'I FEEL YOUR PAIN': THE ACTION MELODRAMA

Alongside the Vietnam film in the 1980s evolved the form that would outlast it, to become the paradigmatic mode of contemporary Hollywood production, the action blockbuster. Although the action blockbuster was generically syncretic, subsuming older, more semantically consistent genres like science fiction (*Star Wars*), the crime thriller (*Lethal Weapon*) and the exotic adventure film (*Indiana Jones*), it also worked through in a more obvious fantasy register many of the same concerns – particularly around masculinity – as the Vietnam film. In fact, allusions to Vietnam abounded (often as personal or familial backstory motivating characters such as Riggs, the loose-cannon cop played by Mel Gibson in the *Lethal Weapon* series, or Maverick, the fighter pilot impersonated by Tom Cruise in *Top Gun* who has to live up to the memory of his father, also a fighter ace shot down over – as it transpires – Cambodia). The action film, however, was distinguished by the way in which such issues were detached from the specific historical and political contexts that the Vietnam film (however inexactly) was compelled to address, and resituated in genres where their socially symbolic functions become, paradoxically, both even more apparent and less directly topical.

I have argued elsewhere that the post-*Star Wars* action film diverged into two distinct melodramatic strains: one more juvenile, rollicking, overtly fantastic and often nostalgic in either setting or (like *Stars Wars* itself) tone, including the Lucas/Spielberg collaboration *Raiders of the Lost Ark* and more recently the *Mummy* franchise (U 1999, 2001, 2008) and *Journey to the Center of the Earth* (WB 2008); the other taking its cue from the seventies vigilante cycle and centring on lone, or more often paired, male adventurers in contemporary urban and warzone settings, highlighting massive and spectacular destructive of person and property often accompanied by extreme and graphic violence. Starting with late-eighties 'male rampage' films like *Die Hard* and *Lethal Weapon*, this form of action film thrived into the new century, primed by an ever more stylised and propulsive visual style. Whereas the first category solicited a family audience, the second was more likely to win an R rating and primarily courted a young male audience. I also argued that 'whereas the action-fantasy cycle solicited a pre-Oedipal wonder, the "hard" action films' emphasised 'reasserted masculinity and male bonding' at the expense of a marginalised domestic-feminine sphere.[14]

However, the differences between these strains, though real, can easily be overstated. From the late 1990s, the growing commercial priority of the family audience ensured that an ever larger proportion of big-budget action blockbusters avoided the kinds of excessive violence, sex (mostly a minority concern in the genre anyway) and language that would earn an R and accordingly reduce their potential market. Apart from Stallone's *Rocky* and *Rambo* vehicles, most of the R-rated 'hard body' action films of the 1980s and their muscle-bound stars – including Arnold Schwarzenegger, at least until the very end of that decade – occupied a lower rung on the Hollywood ladder than the 'tentpole' releases, many of which were SF-fantasy spectacles, including the *Ghostbusters* (Col 1984, 1989), *Indiana Jones*, *Star Trek*, *Back to the Future* and *Batman* franchises. On the other hand, Schwarzenegger, Jean-Claude van Damme and their like delivered impressive results in the expanding overseas and home video markets. Accordingly, as these sectors grew in importance on Hollywood's economic calculus, action films and action stars became more central to studio production strategies. And in turn the enhanced status and budgets of action blockbusters encouraged some softening of the often brutal tenor of the genre in the 1980s, in pursuit of the PG-13 rating that would deliver a wider audience. With a corresponding attempt to differentiate some fantasy action films from a revitalised children's sector now dominated by animated features (for example, by stressing 'darker' aspects in the second *Star Wars* trilogy and attaching auteur directors such as Alfonso Cuarón to the later instalments of the *Harry Potter* series), the two modes of action film increasingly came to occupy common and recognisably melodramatic terrain dominated by questions of family and of masculine identity, which in turn were partly inherited and adapted from the Vietnam film.

In its eighties form, the action film's Vietnam legacy was particularly visible in those productions that seemed to embody in barely coded form certain Reaganite political orthodoxies, such as rampant individualism, hostility to 'Big Government' and the valorization of 'traditional values'. Rambo and other eighties action heroes like Schwarzenegger's *Commando* (Fox 1985) and Stallone's *Cobra* (WB 1986) tended to be isolated figures such as Clint Eastwood's seminal 'Dirty Harry' Callahan (who also had two final outings in the decade), though a sidekick, often a woman or a person of colour (Rambo's doomed Vietnamese ally is both), might offer support while helpfully expanding the film's demographic appeal. Their loneliness was intensified not only by the massiveness of the forces of evil arrayed against them but also by endemic flaws in American social and political structures that critically impeded their heroic efforts. In an era when politicians competed with one another to establish their 'outsider' credentials as the best route to electoral popularity, federal government agencies are unsurprisingly often portrayed as ineffective or actually corrupt. Rambo's betrayal and abandonment by the craven CIA operative in *Rambo* is a paradigmatic example – again traceable back to Harry Callahan's outrage at the 'liberal' *Miranda* doctrine protecting suspects' rights that allows a serial killer to walk free in *Dirty Harry*. Smugness and incompetence, rather than treachery, characterise the LAPD and the FBI in *Die Hard*, but the antiterrorist team in *Die Harder* (Fox 1990) turn out to be in league with the drug-running terrorists; meanwhile political infighting and sclerotic bureaucracy imperil heroic US special forces in *Clear and Present Danger* (Par 1994).

In the absence of real wars in which to enact the revitalised masculinity of the eighties, the hypertrophic violence of some eighties action films might be seen as an attempt to generate enemies of sufficient stature to justify an overwhelmingly violent response. (Rather as the Reagan years saw the first in a series of ludicrous attempts to 'sex up' the threat posed by various wildly outgunned developing world adversaries, from the Sandinistas in Nicaragua, the Marxist government in tiny Grenada – whose overthrow is bombastically depicted as an exorcism of Vietnam in *Heartbreak Ridge* (WB 1986) – and the regime of Manuel Noriega in Panama, culminating in Saddam Hussein in Iraq and the conveniently global and Hydra-headed Al-Qaeda.) Having largely disappeared from US screens during the years of détente, Soviet armed forces supplied the opposition for Rambo and for indigenous US partisans in the invasion fantasies *Red Dawn* and *Invasion USA*. The MiGs against whom Maverick tests his mettle in the climax of *Top Gun* are unidentified (and incidentally flying over international waters) but presumably Russian. Following the collapse of the USSR, revanchist Stalinist diehards appeared, trying to restore Communism in *The Package* (Orion 1989), *Crimson Tide* (Hollywood 1995), *Air Force One* (Sony 1997) and *The Sum of All Fears* (Par 2002). International drug cartels featured in *Lethal Weapon*, *Die Harder*, *Licence to Kill* (MGM/UA 1991), *Bad Boys* (Col 1995) and countless others.

The villain of choice, however, was the 'international terrorist', often associated with the newly designated 'rogue states' that challenged American hegemony in the Middle East. Libyan terrorists feature in *Back to the Future* and the *Top Gun* derivative *Iron Eagle*; generic Arab terrorists, first featured in *Black Sunday* (allied with a psychotic Vietnam vet prior to the vet's cinematic rehabilitation), were the antagonists in *True Lies* and *The Siege* (Fox 1998), but *Patriot Games* and *Blown Away* (MGM 1994) feature Irish Republican extremists. A Bosnian inflamed by the US failure to intervene in the Yugoslav war attempts to set off a portable nuclear device in New York in *The Peacemaker* (DreamWorks 1997). It was not entirely clear who paid the way of the international assassins featured in *The Jackal* (U 1997) and *Face/Off*. Rarely, if ever, were these antagonists permitted to articulate their own motivation or ideology, or even to suggest that one might exist (parodying the whole idea of political commitment, the Armani-clad former terrorist turned master-thief in *Die Hard* demands the release of obscure political prisoners culled from the pages of *Time* magazine as a cover for his heist). Overall, most Hollywood pictures painted a picture of an outside world that was as obscurely yet endemically hostile as the alien invaders who are finally defeated by US forces (led by a president who is, inevitably, a former Vietnam fighter pilot) in *Independence Day*. When George W. Bush expressed the insight in the aftermath of the attacks of 11 September 2001 that Al-Qaeda were simply 'bad folks', it appeared that – like Reagan before him when he adopted *Star Wars* terminology to designate the Soviet Union an 'evil empire' – Hollywood did not so much reflect a prevailing worldview as shape it. The return to real contemporary events in *Black Hawk Down* (Col 2001), portraying the ill-fated US intervention in Somalia in 1996, showed no greater insight or interest in those who mysteriously choose to oppose American good intentions. (Released the same month as the 11 September attacks, the film was pressed into service as an early declaration of the 'war on terror'.)

During the 1990s, however, it was increasingly the subtextual spine of the Vietnam film – the politics of masculinity – rather than these more obviously ideological stances, that linked it to the worlds of fantasy action-adventure. Susan Jeffords suggests that the violence of 1980s action films served to reassert masculine power as a figure of national identity. In these films, the muscular 'hard body' heroes (and through them the audience) often endure, but survive, sado-masochistic ordeals of physical and mental torture at the hands of their enemies. Rambo is crucified by sadistic Russians and Vietnamese; John McClane in *Die Hard* is forced to run barefoot across an office floor strewn with broken glass; Murphy and Riggs in *Lethal Weapon II* are subjected to prolonged electric-shock torture; even Rocky Balboa suffers ritual poundings at the hands of mouthy ghetto trash (*Rocky III*, MGM/UA1982) and Soviet supermen (*Rocky IV*, MGM/UA 1985). Such sequences – and the vengeful 'male rampages' that invariably followed them – both literalised the white male pathos and sense of beleaguerment and injury (visible in movies at least as far back as *Rocky*) on which New Right social policies preyed and demonstrated a renewed capacity (contrasted to the emasculated passivity of the post-Vietnam period) to take enormous punishment and come out not just standing but fighting.[15]

Thereafter, with patriarchal confidence restored, the male action hero could afford to relax somewhat from his adamantine isolation, and less aggressively one-dimensional stars like Harrison Ford, Bruce Willis, Michael Douglas, Tom Cruise, Mel Gibson, Nicolas Cage, Russell Crowe, the rejuvenated John Travolta, the boyish Leonardo DiCaprio and even the African American Will Smith could take the place of eighties icons like Stallone, many of whose careers declined sharply. Arnold Schwarzenegger's box office dominance throughout the 1990s was sustained by a careful adjustment and softening of his star persona to accommodate gentler, comic, and, most importantly of all, domestic/familial elements. This was a period in which action films used the more flexible personae of the new stars to render male identity in more complex ways than simple demonstrations of military prowess.

Through a sustained emphasis on marriage, the family and/or parent–child relationships, action blockbusters from the early 1990s shifted the genre's focus from the concretely historical (like Vietnam). Films as different as *Terminator 2: Judgment Day*, *True Lies* (Fox 1993), *Jurassic Park* (U 1993), *Face/Off* (Par 1997), *Armageddon* (Touchstone 1998), *Gladiator* and *Spider-Man* (Sony 2002) grounded their spectacular sequences of combat and destruction in melodramatic narratives of male crisis and recovery. (Male stars in the 1990s and 2000s were also likely to vary and extend their star images by alternating popcorn blockbusters with more character-driven pictures, many of which also revolved around crises of masculinity and confirmed the centrality of this motif in contemporary American culture: for example, Nicolas Cage in the independent *Leaving Las Vegas* (1995), Tom Cruise in *Eyes Wide Shut* (WB 1999), Tom Hanks in *Cast Away*.) This complex, its relationship to male violence and the fantasy relations it sustained were satirised in *Fight Club* (Fox 1999).

The advent of new digital technologies in the 1990s, ubiquitous by the end of the century, moved the action film on in both obvious and not-so-obvious ways. The most apparent, of course, was the capacity via computer-generated imagery (CGI) to deliver spectacle on a scale unknown since the fifties wide-screen era and with a degree of verisimilitude never approached before. A bifurcation started to emerge within the blockbuster. On the one hand, large-scale fantasy adventures, such as *The Matrix*, *Lord of the Rings*, *X-Men* and *Pirates of the Caribbean* trilogies, as well as monster movies, including *Independence Day*, *Godzilla* (Sony 1998) and *King Kong* (U 2005), heavily marketed to youthful audiences, moved away from any visible connection to social or personal relations beyond a sort of residual nod to heterosexual romance. Other films meanwhile, especially a series of increasingly colossally scaled natural disaster movies including *Twister* (WB 1996, tornadoes), 1997's twin volcano adventures *Dante's Peak* (U) and *Volcano* (Fox), 1998's double asteroid collisions *Armageddon* and *Deep Impact* (DreamWorks), *The Core* (Par

2003, geophysical derangement) and in *The Day After Tomorrow* (Fox 2004, catastrophic climate change), along with some comic-book superhero adaptations such as the *Spider-Man* trilogy, *Hulk* (U 2003) and above all the *Harry Potter* franchise, all return insistently and almost obsessively to themes around parents and children. Both options might be thought to reflect the increasing importance of the family (meaning child) audience/market to the blockbuster as an industrial product. In terms of ideology, the increasingly virtual green-screen environments in which these narratives take place tend to abstract them from any evident social relation – which of course may partly be the point. Banally, perhaps, but undeniably, many commentators have pointed out that the computerised protagonists of Pixar films such as *Toy Story* and *The Incredibles* (2004) seem not only more 'human' but more alert to social and cultural context and nuance than their live-action counterparts.[16]

OTHER VOICES

Of course, not every production in this period was an action blockbuster. Comedy, for example, thrived in a variety of forms; as well as idealised romantic comedies typified by *Notting Hill* (Polygram 1999), comedies centred on excess, either in star performance – notably Jim Carrey, whose unique brand of physical and verbal comedy made him box office gold in the mid-nineties – or in subject matter, with the Farrelly Brothers (*There's Something About Mary*, 1998) leading the way. Outside mainstream genre pathways, too, the Hollywood film industry continued to offer some room for filmmakers to explore more unconventional, personal and politicised visions. Although, as discussed in the previous chapter, by the mid-nineties the absorption of the independent production/distribution sector by the majors was well underway, the 'major independents' (both the merged companies and the studios' own bespoke speciality divisions) continued to enjoy a (varying) measure of functional autonomy that allowed them to green-light less mainstream, commercially surefire material. The production of smaller-scale, riskier projects alongside 'tentpole' movies plays an important part in the complex politics of the industry: A-list talent may desire artistic challenges that go beyond the popcorn blockbusters (and win peer recognition in the shape of awards), and have the clout to persuade studios to back their smaller or riskier ventures; for their part, in gratifying such requests and thus keeping key talent onside, studio executives are also keen to enhance their own reputations as enablers of artistic creativity and freedom, and to bask in the reflected glory of an award-winning production. These industry dynamics ensure that the picture of contemporary Hollywood output remains more volatile and multi-dimensional than an unremitting emphasis on the blockbuster might suggest.

In the late 1980s and early 1990s, alongside but distinct from the 'indie' boom kicked off by *sex, lies and videotape*, emerged cinematic movements that explicitly aimed to articulate subject positions marginalised by dominant US culture and Hollywood cinema alike. Both New Black Cinema and New Queer Cinema had some impact on the Hollywood mainstream, but both also ran up against institutional resistances that ultimately limited that impact. Following Spike Lee's success and media prominence following *She's Gotta Have It* (1986) and the Universal release *Do the Right Thing* (1989), several younger African American directors contributed to a cycle of films, some with major studio distribution, that vividly depicted the lives of inner-city black youth, including *Boyz n the Hood* (John Singleton, Col 1991), *Straight Out of Brooklyn* (Matty Rich, Artificial Eye 1991), *Juice* (Ernest Dickerson, Par 1992), *Menace II Society* (Albert and Allen Hughes, New Line 1993). While documenting contemporary black experience with an authenticity previously unseen in mainstream US cinema, these films were also criticised from within the black community for pathologising young black males and repeating dominant clichés of black culture as dominated by violence and drugs. Such objections were raised even more vociferously to a cycle of 'gangsta' movies inaugurated by *New Jack City* (Mario van Peebles, WB 1991) in which the line between the documentation and glorification of gang lifestyles seemed increasingly blurred. Such debates not only suggested that, notwithstanding the measurably increased contribution of black talent, the ghost of blaxploitation had not yet been completely laid to rest, but also echoed very similar controversies around ethnicity and the very first cycle of violent urban gangster films at the start of the sound era. As Spike Lee and other directors moved away from solely black-identified subjects in the late 1990s and early 2000s (for example, Lee's *25th Hour* (Touchstone 2002) and the clever but conventional heist thriller *Inside Man* (Touchstone 2005)), it was unclear whether a distinctly black experience was bankable in contemporary Hollywood, or if so what form it might take.[17]

Perhaps because, unlike the New Black Cinema, the filmmakers of the more diffuse New Queer Cinema of the early 1990s set out to destabilise power as grounded in gender and sexuality as well as (or, some would say, more than) economics, their films were more formally inventive and non-conformist, abjuring, for example, the kinds of clear genre affiliations and linear, individual-centred narratives that typify many New Black Cinema films (although not Spike Lee's) and favouring a high degree of reflexivity and intertextuality. In other words, it is not merely by incorporating unconventional content but through critiquing dominant means of representation that subtend normative ideologies that these films 'queer' cinematic conventions. Thus Rose Troche's lesbian romance *Go Fish* (Mainline 1994) not only pastiches the conventions of 'straight' romantic comedy but deliberately confuses eyeline matches in shot-reverse-shot sequences. Such non-conformist practices ensured New Queer Cinema made fewer inroads into mainstream production financing and distribution than more readily marketable New Black counterpart. Todd Haynes, however, whose *Poison* (1991) helped put the New Queer Cinema on the map, established himself in the 'Indiewood' sector and continued in films such as the Douglas Sirk pastiche *Far From Heaven* (Focus 2002) to maintain a clear continuity in both style and content with the movement in which he began.[18]

Few films outside these relatively short-lived, if at times highly visible, insurgent cinemas attempted in this period to combine formal and political challenges to the mainstream. Without overstating the extent to which (some) sixties and seventies films contested dominant ideologies, as we have seen in Chapters 5 and 6 there was a sufficiently consistent strategy of stylistic and generic innovation to create a genuine sense of challenge across the period as a whole that added up to more than the sum total of the films grouped loosely together as the Hollywood Renaissance. The opposite is true of the films of the conglomerate era. Numerous individual films, including films made entirely or mostly within the major studios such as Oliver Stone's Vietnam and sixties films and also his *Natural Born Killers* (WB 1994), Warren Beatty's *Bulworth* (Fox 1998), David O. Russell's *Three Kings* (WB 1999) and David Fincher's *Fight Club* (Fox 1999), combined sometimes quite radical departures from mainstream style with an explicitly oppositional political stance. It was also the case that subject positions ignored or even suppressed during the Renaissance found some articulation in this later period. Women directors, for example, were more in evidence than ever before, and not only in 'softer' genres like romantic comedy (where Nora Ephron (*You've Got Mail*, WB 1998) and Nicole Holofcener (*Lovely and Amazing*, Good Machine 2001) were noted exponents); Kathryn Bigelow (*Blue Steel*, Vestron 1990; *Point Break*, Fox 1991; *Strange Days*, UIP 1995) was one of the period's most distinctive action directors. Gay men and women also finally emerged from the margins, although the fact that the Best Screenplay Oscar for the melodramatic *Milk* (Focus 2007) was celebrated as a 'breakthrough' for gay representation as late as 2008 suggested that there remained a fair way to go.

The liberal or, more rarely, radical perspectives of these films and others like them in any event never succeeded in setting the tone of the industry as a whole in the way their Renaissance predecessors had done. They remained exceptions to a general rule that the ongoing process of reinventing and updating genres and film style was divorced from any particular critical project. Many films supported by the studios' speciality divisions, such as Roman Polanski's *The Pianist* (Focus 2002) or Fernando Meirelles' *The Constant Gardener* (Focus 2005) seemed to be distinguished from their parent companies' other releases, if at all, only by their (smaller) budgets, their somewhat more unconventional subject matter, and perhaps a certain unspecifiable veneer of 'classiness'. Films whose style or narrative structure were more obviously unconventional, such as *The Hours* (Miramax 2002) or *Eternal Sunshine of the Spotless Mind* (Momentum 2004), nonetheless generally lacked any discernibly critical perspective on fairly conventional narrative material. The Academy's surprise choice as Best Picture of 2005, the multi-stranded racial drama *Crash* (Lionsgate 2005), revealed both the extent and the tightly defined limits of social awareness and stylistic challenge in modern Indiewood.[19]

Various reasons might be suggested for this beyond studio executives' obvious reluctance to court political controversy. One might be that whereas, as we have seen, the Hollywood Renaissance was enabled by circumstances including the industry's severe financial crisis of 1969–72, no comparable industry-wide malaise afflicted Hollywood in the 1990s. On the contrary, notwithstanding periodic bouts of introspection and anxiety about increasing costs and formulaic blockbuster production such as those expressed in Jeffrey Katzenberg's 1989 memo, this was a period of rising revenues and expanding markets. If the apple cart was not upset, in the eyes of the studios there was no justification for radical departures from convention. By the same token, it could be argued that notwithstanding increasingly bitter political partisanship (a notable feature of America politics from congressional Republicans' attempt to impeach Bill Clinton in 1997–8), the socio-historical context lacked the 'critical mass' of protest, war, violence and governmental malfeasance that drove politics on to American screens in the 1970s. America's problems at the turn of the millennium seemed (prior to 9/11, Iraq and the crash of 2008) chronic rather than acute and consequently both hard to dramatise (well illustrated by Beatty's *Bulworth*) and apparently lacking in urgency.[20] While Iraq did eventually generate a number of films dealing with both combat experience, such as *Jarhead* (U 2005, set during the First Gulf War) and with the larger ethical swamp of the 'war on terror' (including *Rendition*, *Lions for Lambs*) – and including a remake (MGM 2006) of Mark Robson's post-World War II social problem film *Home of the Brave* (UA 1949) – these showed little sign of learning from the limitations of the Vietnam cycle: the same inability to represent the 'enemy' and male melodramas abounded.

Beyond these contextual factors we can understand the general absence of a critical politics in nineties Hollywood in terms of the 'postmodern' sensibility sketched at the start of this chapter. The appearance of the occasional non-hegemonic film such as *Three Kings*, presented as evidence of a studio's commitment to freedom of creative expression (regardless of how problematic this might have been in practice), typifies the pervasive recursion to individualist and relativist perspectives in this period. Politics, when present in these isolated and exceptional forms, thus inevitably becomes as much, or more, a statement of personal style as a genuine intervention. For its own part, in an era of superficially proliferating stylistic diversity the elaboration of a personal style became largely an end in itself, divorced from any critical relationship to dominant conventions, as the next chapter will show.

NOTES

1. The 'childlike gaze' in the films of Steven Spielberg is considered in more detail in the following chapter.
2. The administration of the traditional, non-'movement' conservative George H. W. Bush (1989–93) was something of an exception to this rule.
3. As discussed in Chapter 6.
4. Excellent examples include Stephen Prince, *Visions of Empire: Political Imagery in Contemporary American Film* (New York: Praeger, 1992) and Alan Nadel, *Flatlining on the Field of Dreams: Cultural Narratives in the Films of President Reagan's America* (New Brunswick, NJ: Rutgers University Press, 1997). See also Further Reading.
5. Murphy Brown, played by Candice Bergen in the CBS series of the same name from 1988 to 1998.
6. See Kevin Sandler, 'Movie ratings as genre: the incontestable "R"', in Steve Neale (ed.), *Genre and Contemporary Hollywood* (London: BFI, 2002), pp. 201–17.
7. US ground troops were engaged in Vietnam from 1965 to 1973; South Vietnam finally fell to the Communist North in 1975.
8. See Gilbert Adair, *Hollywood's Vietnam* (London: Heinemann, 1989). See also Further Reading.
9. See Robert Burgoyne, 'National identity, gender identity, and the "rescue fantasy" in *Born on the Fourth of July*', *Screen* 1994; 35(3):211–34.
10. See Jerry Lembcke, *The Spitting Image: Myth, Memory and the Legacy of Vietnam* (New York: New York University Press, 1998).
11. George H. W. Bush's vice-presidential pick Dan Quayle, who had avoided the draft, was the first candidate for national office to have his Vietnam-era record scrutinised. Subsequently Democrats Bill Clinton in 1992 and 1996 (who also avoided service) and 2004 presidential candidate John Kerry (who was a decorated veteran but who had publicly opposed the war on his return) were viciously excoriated by conservative commentators for their alleged cowardice and/or unpatriotic attitudes. Ironically enough, though both Bush, Sr, and 1996 Republican candidate Bob Dole were decorated veterans of World War II, the most bellicose members of the second Bush administration – Bush himself, vice-president Dick Cheney and Defense Secretary Donald Rumsfeld – had all avoided combat in Vietnam.
12. See Michael Klein, 'Beyond the American Dream: film and the experience of defeat', in Michael Klein (ed.), *An American Half-Century: Postwar Culture and Politics in the U.S.A.* (London: Pluto, 1994).
13. Susan Jeffords, *The Remasculinization of America: Gender and the Vietnam War* (Bloomington: Indiana University Press, 1989).
14. See Barry Langford, *Film Genre: Hollywood and Beyond* (Edinburgh: Edinburgh University Press, 2005), pp. 246–51.
15. See Fred Pfeil, 'From pillar to postmodern: race, class, and gender in the male rampage film', in Jon Lewis (ed.), *The New American Cinema* (Durham, NC: Duke University Press, 1998), pp. 146–86.
16. On Pixar, see 'The Biggest, the Best: 1995'.

17. On New Black Cinema, see Further Reading.
18. On New Queer Cinema, see Further Reading.
19. On *Crash*, see 'The Biggest, the Best: 2005'.
20. On *Bulworth*, see Dana Polan, 'The confusions of Warren Beatty', in Jon Lewis (ed.), *The End of Cinema As We Know It* (London: Pluto, 2001), pp. 141–9.

The Biggest, the Best: 1995

Braveheart (Twentieth Century-Fox/Icon/Ladd)
D: Mel Gibson; **P:** Mel Gibson, Alan Ladd, Jr, Bruce Davey; **W:** Randall Wallace
Toy Story (Pixar/Walt Disney)
D: John Lasseter; **P:** Ralph Guggenheim, Bonnie Arnold; **W:** Joss Wheedon, Andrew Stanton, Joel Cohen, Alex Sokolow

Entertainment Weekly critic Owen Gleiberman's paradoxical (one imagines intentionally so) description of *Toy Story* as 'magically witty and humane' epitomises the response provoked by Pixar's first digitally animated feature, and indeed to most of its astonishingly successful successors (rating *Toy Story 2* (1998) even higher than the original, Linda Ruth Williams invokes *The Godfather, Part II* for comparison[1]). The film earned director and Pixar co-founder John Lasseter a 'Special Achievement' Academy Award but the film was otherwise mystifyingly passed over at the Oscars, earning just two nominations for screenplay and song; Mel Gibson's *Braveheart*, an earnest mangling of British medieval history, took home the Best Picture and Director awards.[2]

Toy Story launched Pixar on an unprecedentedly successful ascent. Releasing a film approximately every two years, the studio has never had a flop: its lowest-grossing film, *A Bug's Life* (1998), took $168 million on domestic theatrical gross alone, while its most successful, *Finding Nemo*, grossed $865 million worldwide and also set new records in DVD sales. (Like Disney's own animated films, Pixar's catalogue can be endlessly re-released on both theatrical and domestic platforms to new generations of children.) Pixar's unique brand recognition and commercial success bought the company leverage within Disney that, for example, Harvey Weinstein, head of another 1990s Disney acquisition Miramax, could only envy: having provided Disney with more than half the entire income of its film divisions from 1995 to 1999, Pixar was able to negotiate a reduction in Disney's distribution charge from 33 per cent to just 12 per cent.[3] In 2006 John Lasseter was appointed 'Chief Creative Officer' at Disney.

Like many earlier Disney classics, *Toy Story* taps into a simple and universal idea: in this case, the idea that inanimate objects, like toys, modelled after sentient creatures might actually have a hidden internal life. Unlike *Pinocchio*, however, with which it has some thematic resonances, or the fairy tales of E. T. A. Hoffman, *Toy Story* dispenses with the uncanny or menacing dimensions of this fantasy, apart from the initial scenes in Sid's bedroom with the Dr Moreau-like mutant toys (who are, however, quickly revealed to be benign). This might be regarded as a defensive gesture – given the widespread and deep-reaching fears of Frankenstein technology (which would receive a cyber-boost from *The Matrix* in 1999), a wholly computer-generated film might well prefer not to dwell too long on the scary aspects of artificial consciousnesses. It finds depth and resonance instead in a much more contemporary problematic of the quest for identity and authenticity in a denatured world. As Bill Brown notes, one of the film's many ironies is that Andy's world of naïve preadolescent physical play, and the sunny idealised suburbia in which it happily unfolds, is in millennial reality threatened with obsolescence by the very digital technologies of which *Toy Story* is such a sensational avatar (including, of course, Disney Interactive's *Toy Story* computer game).[4]

In a different sense, uncanniness nonetheless remains an important part of the success of this and subsequent Pixar films. Few commentators on *Toy Story* have been able to resist quoting Marx's famous account of the commodity in *Capital* in which he comments on how 'relations between people assume the fantastic form of relations between things . . . the products of the human brain appear as autonomous figures endowed with a life of their own, which enter into relations both with each other and with the human race'.[5] This genuinely uncanny animation (in all senses) of the material world here extends to the virtual one, and is reflected in the frequently expressed view that Pixar's films are more authentically 'human' than most of their live-action competitors.

Toy Story certainly inaugurates a Pixar tradition of addressing powerful themes in subtle, unexpected and often touching ways, and without losing its audience. (In this sense, *Toy Story 2* is 'about' accepting mortality; *Finding Nemo* is an allegory of Holocaust survivor guilt; *Wall-E* confronts the consequences of environmental devastation for the planet and for human identity; and so on.) The film mobilises issues of personal and national identity in complex ways. Woody the vintage wooden cowboy (an unlikely toy to be found in a modern child's collection, voiced by all-American Tom Hanks) of course represents one form of traditional American masculinity. Woody's initial antagonism to, and ultimate alliance with, the astronaut Buzz symbolises the negotiation of tradition and technological modernity invoked by *Star Trek*'s 'space: the final frontier' (itself consciously echoing John Kennedy's 'New Frontier') or Sam Shepherd's impersonation of Westerner/space pioneer Chuck Yeager in Philip Kaufman's complex and unjustly overlooked *The Right Stuff* (WB 1983). There is an obviously cinematically reflexive dimension to their relationship too – science fiction having long displaced the Western post-*Star Wars* from its role as the key vector of American ideology. But just as NASA astronauts – carefully selected, trained and publicised agents of a massive military–industrial–governmental complex – are problematic bearers of the pioneer tradition, so Buzz is also an ambivalent figure: the label on his arm – the signifier that confirms his 'real' identity – reads 'Made in Taiwan'. American heroism in the 1990s, it appears, is no longer self-generating. Perhaps Buzz's embrace of his diminished status – his surrender into 'falling with style', since he can't fly – might be seen as an invitation to the nation to do the same?

Notes

1. Linda Ruth Williams, '*Toy Story*', in Linda Ruth Williams and Michael Hammond (eds), *Contemporary American Cinema* (Maidenhead: McGraw-Hill, 2005), pp. 370–2.
2. John Lasseter had previously won a Short Subject Oscar in 1988 for *Tin Toy*, a digitally animated short that previewed the *Toy Story* concept and is included on the 'Special Edition' DVD.
3. Edward Jay Epstein, *The Big Picture: Money and Power in Hollywood* (New York: Random House, 2005), pp. 123–4; based on a 2002 Morgan Stanley Equity Research report on Disney.

4. Bill Brown, 'How to do things with things: a toy story', *Critical Inquiry* Summer 1998; 24(4):935–64.
5. Karl Marx, *Capital*, Vol. 1, trans. Ben Fowkes (London: Penguin, 1976), pp. 163–5.

'Welcome to Jurassic Park!' The digital sublime in *Jurassic Park* (Universal 1993). Reproduced courtesy of The Kobal Collection

CHAPTER 9

Post-Classical Style?

With that first shot [of *Star Wars*], new cinematic technologies redefined space, displaced narrative, and moved cinema into a revived realm of spectacular excess . . . *Star Wars* exploded the frame of narrative cinema, referring back to early cinematic and precinematic spectacles.[1]

Here, Scott Bukatman argues that the special effects-driven science fiction films of contemporary Hollywood are the leading edge of a shift away from the traditionally narrative-focused models of classic Hollywood and towards an immersive hyper-textuality in which the film as such is merely one part of a seamless mesh of 'collective, immersive experiences' including theme park rides and virtual reality programmes, in all of which narrative codes are 'swept away in an aural and visual crescendo'.[2] Science fiction itself surrenders its traditional role as the proponent of rationalist, technological solutions to new and initially terrifying situations (in which regard it contrasts to the irrationalist frenzy of the Gothic tradition represented in movies by the horror film[3]) in favour of a hyperbolic visual excess that pushes towards a postmodern delirium. To the extent that narrative remains part of this new (and New) Hollywood dispensation – which Bukatman does not fail to relate to the evolving corporate entertainment environment of exploiting properties on cross-media platforms, and which extends, he suggests, beyond the generic bounds of SF to constitute a new industrial dominant in contemporary Hollywood – it paradoxically testifies to the possibility, or likelihood, of its own possible supersession by an anxiously *over*-emphatic storytelling, using the tools of the classical narrative cinema in a way that suggests a lack of confidence and sophistication in its own capacity to communicate story information, or the audience's ability to process it.

Bukatman's 1998 essay is itself, one might say, an intensified iteration of other analyses during the 1990s of contemporary Hollywood film that analysed the seeming fragmentation and attenuation of character-centred narrative in favour of a self-advertising visual style, divorced from both narrative content and – in significant contrast to the New Wave styles of the Hollywood Renaissance – any critical purchase on the conventions it assaulted. In several cases this appeared to have its origins, appropriately enough, in the career trajectory that saw high-profile eighties/early nineties directors such as Alan Parker, Ridley and Tony Scott and Adrian Lyne begin their careers in British television advertising. According to Justin Wyatt, the high-gloss, ultra-commercial aesthetic such directors brought to films like *Fame* (MGM 1980, Alan Parker), *Flashdance* (Par 1983, Adrian Lyne), and *Top Gun* (Tony Scott) wedded itself perfectly to the cross-media (videos, soundtracks, fashion) marketing strategies of producers like Don Simpson and Jerry Bruckheimer. The 'high concept' film that emerged subordinated plot and character to striking but superficial imagery: the story was not told, rather the film was sold.[4] The devaluation of movies' traditional narrative currency was driven not by any consciously revisionist project, but arose from the combination of directors' relentless pursuit of eye-catching stylistic novelty and a new ultra-commodified industrial practice.

These analyses possess some of the suasive qualities – a striking, singular point, vividly expressed – of the style they describe (and largely deplore). However, as several writers have pointed out, there are difficulties with such accounts. One obvious problem is that a small number of films are often required to do a lot of work. Bukatman's essay cites only a small number of films, mostly from the 1980s – including *Blade Runner*, *The Right Stuff*, *Brainstorm* (MGM 1983) and *Batman* – but on them rest large claims for the emergence of a new stylistic (and economic/ideological) dispensation in the American commercial cinema. Wyatt similarly seems to generalise about Hollywood cinema in general from a limited sample of (different) films. David Bordwell points out that in the 1980s such 'stylistically unprepossessing' films as *Stir Crazy* (Col 1980) and *Terms of Endearment* (Par 1983) fared as well or better at the box office as either the high-style films Wyatt analyses or the postmodern SF on which Bukatman focuses, and there were many more of them. At the textual level, Geoff King, Murray Smith, Warren Buckland, Kristin Thompson and others have produced close analyses of contemporary Hollywood blockbuster films and have found a good deal more attention to narrative structure, character arcs, and other parts of the traditional architecture of Hollywood film than such arguments suggest.[5] Bordwell meanwhile notes that regardless of the hyper-kinetic, disorienting montage techniques that characterise some action set-pieces, the quieter scenes that inevitably still predominate even in the films of 'frame-fucking' state-of-the-art directors like Michael Bay are managed according to the broad principles of continuity editing established in the American cinema eighty years ago. While acknowledging the more emphatic visual style (accelerated cutting rates, more extensive use of close-ups, push-ins, reaction shots and other devices all used in studio-era films, but more discerningly), instead of Bukatman's rhapsodic postmodernism he suggests a range of traceable influences from industry practice and institutions (the influence and example of the Hollywood Renaissance, changing orthodoxies promulgated in film schools and training manuals, the impact of television, music video and new editing techniques, etc.) that account for this regime of 'intensified continuity'. He proposes a historical model of continuous evolution and diversification rather than decisive rupture: not only are post-1980s movies 'sixties movies, only more so', but the further 'intensifications of an intensified style' visible in early twenty-first-century films build in turn on the experience of the past two decades: 'perhaps the movies of the 2000s are the movies of the 1980s, only more so'.[6]

Debates around 'post-classical style' in contemporary Hollywood have two principal axes. The first concerns the emergence of forms of visual spectacle that appear to mark a pronounced shift away from character-centred linear narrative; in their most extreme forms, offering audiences a disconnected series of ever more massively scaled set pieces which are to all intents and purposes autonomous, modular and exchangeable elements with little or no relation to plot or character. The second addresses aspects of the heightened, sometimes frenetic – but also extremely diverse – visual style that Bordwell calls 'intensified continuity'. We will consider these in the same order.

EMPIRE OF THE GAZE, OR, NARRATIVE VS. SPECTACLE – THE SEQUEL

Concluding his 1986 pioneering essay on early cinema, 'An aesthetic of astonishment', Tom Gunning suggests that the contemporary action blockbuster film might constitute a renovated form of the pre-classical 'cinema of attractions'.[7] By de-emphasising characterisation and narrative in favour of overwhelming spectacle, such films seemingly reversed the evolutionary trend which by the end of cinema's first decade had established narrative as the senior partner in the narrative-spectacle relationship. The 'hyperstimulus' identified as a novel aspect of the modern urban environment by early twentieth-century commentators and theorists – a barrage of sights, sounds and textualities of which early cinema actively partook[8] – also finds its modern-day avatars in the amped-up action spectacles of Simpson/Bruckheimer and Joel Silver. Such propositions – in Gunning's case thrown out almost as an afterthought at the very end of his essay – have been enthusiastically received by some theorists, who see in such recursions the (market-driven) temporal regression and aesthetic cannibalism typical of postmodernism generally.

According to Fred Pfeil, for example, writing with specific reference to the 'male rampage' action films of the late 1980s (*Die Hard, Lethal Weapon,* etc.), 'an older model of plot development, moving from an initial, relatively tranquil state through destabilization and development to a new and more fully resolved stasis, is largely superseded . . . by the amnesiac succession of self-contained bits and spectacular bursts'.[9] 'Spectacle' here, and in other analyses in the same vein, means several things beyond the familiar vistas of colossal, exotic sets and casts of thousands – which, having become economically unfeasible and culturally unfashionable once the roadshow era crashed and burned in the 1960s, do make a comeback in the early 2000s in films such as *Troy* (WB 2004) and *The Return of the King* (New Line 2003), digitally expedited and enhanced following the success of *Titanic* and *Gladiator*. In contemporary Hollywood, these traditional spectacular elements are wedded to the eye-popping special (and latterly visual/digital) effects that first emerged as an attraction for audiences with *2001: A Space Odyssey* but took on their more emphatic, overpowering form with *Star Wars*.[10] Finally, the large-scale stunts and action sequences that punctuate blockbuster narratives (themselves extensively and increasingly reliant on special effects, both 'real' and virtual) also come into the category of spectacular attractions. All these instances of spectacle are often contrasted to an apparently beleaguered tradition of linear, character-centred narrative that they increasingly overwhelm; the result is that movies have fragmented into a more or less disconnected series of ever-bigger, but also emptier, set pieces that are not *told*, but presented to (or flung at) the spectator.

For writers such as Bukatman, the opening shot of *Star Wars* – the vast bulk of the Imperial star cruiser grinding (and growling, in Dolby surround sound) endlessly, crushingly overhead – has become the foundational moment of a new audio-visual regime. *Star Wars* is widely held to have relegitimated the spectacular, after the relative restraint of (some) Hollywood Renaissance films. It is less George Lucas himself, however (who after *Star Wars* shifts from directing to the roles of producer, entrepreneur and technological impresario until *The Phantom Menace* in 1999), than his *Indiana Jones* collaborator Steven Spielberg with whom the subsequent elaboration of this form of spectacle is most closely identified. In fact, much of Spielberg's earlier career (until 1993) seems dedicated to working through and enforcing upon the spectator a new aesthetic economy centred on the awestruck submission to physically and emotionally overpowering sights. The famous climax of *Close Encounters of the Third Kind* atop Devil's Tower in Wyoming is an extended festival of this kind of looking, with Spielberg's characters – pre-eminently his child–man protagonist Roy Neary – gazing reverently up at the alien mother ship in attitudes of awe, wonderment and speechless acceptance which Spielberg's colossal *mise en scène* demands the spectator also adopt.

Critics have not been slow to identify this literally monstrous (from *monstrare*, to show) extended sound-and-light show reflexively with *Close Encounters* itself as an overwhelming audio-visual experience, and with the consolidation more generally of a kind of technological sublime. Roy Neary's regressive trajectory in *Close Encounters* – retreating from adulthood, with all its unwelcome complexities (work, a shrewish wife, kids who don't like Walt Disney, and so on), through a period of infantile play (making mud pies in the front room), until his final absorption into the community of diminutive, apparently sexless aliens (they lack external genitalia) inside the aptly named 'mother ship' – diminishes him to a condition of helpless, child-like subjection even as the vast panoply of Douglas Trumbull's effects work dwarfs the human figures in the widescreen frame. Spielberg's own screenplay[11] strongly valorises this capacity in Roy for a particular kind of naïve, uncritical looking: it is no accident that in a kind of symbolic exchange at the film's climax he swaps places inside the mother ship with the gurgling, wide-eyed toddler Barry (Spielberg has misled us to expect a romantic encounter between Roy and with Barry's mother Gillian when in fact Roy proves not her lover but her surrogate child).

As spectators, in order to participate fully in the climax of *Close Encounters* we need to identify with Roy and effectively to adopt the qualities of his gaze: this is very clear. Some writers, however, have discerned in the spectacular *mise en scène* of Spielberg and his epigones a disturbingly coercive dimension. One of Spielberg's fiercest critics, Robert Kolker, argues that his powerfully affective cinema recalls the 'fascist aesthetics' of Leni Riefenstahl. As ever, form and ideological content are indissociable, since as Kolker succinctly observes of Riefenstahl's *Triumph of the Will* (Germ 1934), 'formally it not only points the way to the ideology, it is ideology in action'. According to Kolker, *Close Encounters* too offers 'a fascinating example of a kind of quasi-fascist form'.[12] Notwithstanding the film's ostensible reversal of the xenophobic hostility of the alien-invasion movies of the 1950s, and the post-Watergate critique of conspiratorial government in the large-scale military cover-up orchestrated to exclude ordinary American citizens from the alien rendezvous, still just as the protagonist Roy Neary surrenders his own agency throughout the film to the overriding imperative of the extra-terrestrials' telepathic suggestion, the film is also – formally – predicated on denying the viewer free will. (Roy ultimately, of course, also accepts a role within the military–scientific complex.) The climax of *Close Encounters*, Kolker argues, confronts the spectator with a visual spectacle so overwhelming that it courts no response beyond awestruck submission. 'The film provides no place to move emotionally and no place to think . . . the viewer, like the characters in the film, has no choice but to yield'.[13] Thus for Kolker, watching this film seals the viewer into an enforced passivity: the spectator is not only invited but effectively directed to abdicate (critical, intellectual, political) responsibility in favour of the numinously super-human. In *Star Wars*, similarly, the *narrative* significance of the enormous mass of the Imperial star cruiser in the opening (it embodies the military might of the fascist Empire against which the courageous partisan heroes are fighting) is contradicted, and perhaps overcome, by the *image's* authoritarian domination of the spectator, who masochistically relishes his or her own subordination to technological overkill.[14] (The film's coda, in which the victorious heroes – who owe their triumph to a mystical, anti-rational 'Force' upheld by an elite warrior cadre – are honoured in a sequence blatantly modelled on *Triumph of the Will*, does not help matters.)

This analysis of the formal politics of fantasy spectacle, while not directly concerned with the alleged attenuation of narrative and the 'postmodern sublime', could lend these claims a more specific ideological valence: the reduction of character complexity to two dimensions (to which interpretations of *Star Wars* in terms of Jungian archetypes also unwittingly testify), and the disempowerment of narrative in favour of an essentially static posture of acquiescent submission, are not simply the concomitant outcomes of an ever-greater reliance on spectacle, but its very *point*. Over the two decades following *Close Encounters*, Spielberg continued to construct increasingly didactic frameworks in which his protagonists can learn to see properly, and by seeing them seeing, the spectator can see like them, culminating in the first appearance of the digitally generated dinosaurs in *Jurassic Park* (U 1993). Here a virtual taxonomy of gazes – a series of close-ups of the various characters pantomiming their slack-jawed stupefaction – works to validate some ways of looking (the palaeontologist protagonists' giddy rapture, childishly uncritical, literally wide-eyed – they both take off their sunglasses) and devalue others (the exploitative and doubly charmless – neither charming nor charmed – gaze of the corporate lawyer; more complexly, the justifiable scepticism of Jeff Goldblum's 'chaotician'). Again, it is the professional adult whose scientific training washes away in a flood of child-like jubilation – he capers, staggers, stammers, giggles, holds his head in his hands, buckles at the knees – with whom we are invited to identify. The film also seems to confess its own formal and industrial procedures in an unusually frank way: 'Welcome to Jurassic Park!' declares the entrepreneur/impresario John Hammond at the end of this scene, ostensibly to the other characters, but in fact very obviously – as he advances away from them towards the camera, and makes his announcement positioned frontally – to the audience, for whom *Jurassic Park* could be said to really begin only now, when the much promoted, but carefully withheld, digital dinosaurs finally make their entrance. Hammond – a figure identified in the film with illusion-based popular entertainment (he began his career, we are told, running a fairground flea circus) – also takes charge of ending the movie, or rather (because nothing is resolved) pausing it before the inevitable sequel/

reprise (*Jurassic Park: The Lost World*, U 1997): 'it's over!' he cries, and it is – the film's last dialogue. Finally, there is the famous track through the Jurassic Park gift shop selling *Jurassic Park*'s own logo-bearing merchandise, fusing the intra- and extra-textual dimensions of the blockbuster not as narrative but as product and intellectual property.

These analyses offer a powerful account of the workings of the contemporary blockbuster. However, their force is at least partly dissipated if the blockbuster spectacle can be shown to be less novel, or its consequences for narrative less apocalyptic, than has been claimed; and a good deal of sceptical scholarship has set out to prove exactly that. One immediate difficulty is how far they seem to rely on an outright opposition of narrative and spectacle which, as we have already seen, is not borne out by the history of Hollywood cinema. Spectacular elements, often highly intrusive and in strictly narrative terms excessive if not superfluous – like extravagant musical numbers or panoramic views of casts of thousands – have co-existed with more straightforward storytelling throughout much of Hollywood history. The historically exceptional sobriety of the immediately preceding Hollywood Renaissance – a stylistic shift driven, as we have seen, by industrial and institutional factors – threw the re-emergence of spectacle into high relief and made it seem more novel than it might have done otherwise. So we surely do not have to rewind film history all the way back to Griffith and beyond to find sources for the kinds of dominating visuals associated with contemporary blockbusters.

The exploration of historical precedents for the contemporary action spectacle may also ask some questions about the ways in which it interpellates its spectator. For example, one argument advanced in support of the dissolution-of-classical-narrative thesis has been that classical Hollywood film drew spectators smoothly and seamlessly into the story by inviting identification with characters accessed through the unremarked agency of the camera. By contrast, the ride-like address of films such as *Jurassic Park* or *Armageddon* – simultaneously immersive yet non-identificatory – has a somatic (rather than emotional) orientation that produces 'embodied' spectators, recalling them to their physical presence in the auditorium, like tourists on a theme park attraction – or indeed like the distracted, thoroughly socialised audiences of early cinema.[15] This leads ineluctably, and by corporate design, to the elision of the distinction between movies as rides, and rides as, or licensed from movies in actual theme parks: as the Universal Studios Hollywood tour guide has it, promoting the *Terminator 2: 3D* ride, 'a multi-dimensional adventure so real you can't tell what is film and what is live action'.

Yet in Chapter 3, we have identified ways in which, as far back as the early widescreen era, changes to film style and exhibition practices foregrounded the act of spectatorship, whose self-conscious participation (including an ability to compare competing cinema technologies like CinemaScope and 3-D, as well as to compare film generally with television) was expressly solicited. More recently – yet still before the advent of the postmodern action blockbuster, by most accounts – in 1974 MCA-Universal publicised its new Sensurround process by claiming that 'the audience [of *Earthquake*] will actually be partici-pating in the film. The torso will vibrate. So will the diaphragm. Flesh and auditory nerves will receive the sensations one might feel while experiencing the event depicted on the screen'.[16] These examples might of course all be located within an ascendant curve of post-classical style that acquires critical mass in the 1980s. But if such attraction-like qualities are to be found in the otherwise quite different dispensations of Hollywood cinema in the fifties, the seventies and the eighties and after – as well, of course, as in early cinema itself – then perhaps it is classic Hollywood's own normative claims which demand interrogation.

The embodied, distracted, alert spectatorship proposed in these examples is also hard to square with the infantilised subject of ideology in Kolker's analysis. Michelle Pierson has noted the detached, connoisseur-like dimension of science fiction fandom, where obvious enthusiasm and enjoyment co-exists unproblematically with critical scrutiny of effects technologies, narrative strat-egies, and the like.[17] This attitude can be seen to be present as well in general audiences; when I attended a packed showing of *Jurassic Park* at Manhattan's Ziegfeld Theater (one of the last extant picture palaces) at the start of its record-breaking opening weekend in 1993, the dinosaurs' first appearance provoked universal and spontaneous audience applause. This applause was in important ways unlike the familiar whoops and cheers that often greet the protagonist's moment of triumph in popcorn blockbusters (especially if accompanied by a crowd-pleasing zinger – Ripley's 'Get away from her you *bitch*!' as she prepares to do battle with the Alien Queen in *Aliens* (Fox 1986), for instance). Occurring just twenty minutes into the film, it seemed to express, neither a traditional identifactory, nor yet a fascistically subjugated, relationship to the image. Rather, the response – expressing the audience's pleasure that the film's effects technologies indeed lived up to their publicity – was semi-detached, 'cool' rather than 'hot'. Geoff King comments that such sequences involve 'a version of the dynamic that operates more generally in film viewing: a shift between the states of being 'taken into' the fictional world and of remaining self-consciously aware of ourselves as watching a technically and technologically well-rendered construct'.[18] The 'wow' factor, it seems, can entail measured approbation as well as uncritical acquiescence.

A number of writers have argued that in any event the reports of the demise of classical narrative have been considerably exaggerated. Both the extent to which narrative conventions have been jettisoned, and whether this tendency, insofar as it does exist in effects-led action blockbusters, can be said to typify contemporary Hollywood as a whole, have been strenuously contested. In a number of books and articles, Geoff King has argued that, on the contrary, the modern high-impact action blockbuster – however spectacular – cannot to any meaningful degree be said to dispense with or even significantly to discount narrative and character. 'These films retain significant investments in narrative structure, in terms of both story construction and underlying dynamics'; spectacle itself, he adds, 'is in almost every instance narratively situated'.[19] Sampling blockbuster films including *Titanic, Jurassic Park, The Rock* and the Spielberg-produced *Twister* (WB/U/Amblin 1996), King finds them motivated by such classical narrative structures as the heterosexual couple (*Titanic*), the nuclear family (most of Spielberg's films – where it tends to displace the heterosexual romance – and *The Long Kiss Goodnight*, New Line 1996), and the nation (*The Rock, Armageddon, Saving Private Ryan*). David Bordwell suggests that notwithstanding the excessiveness of some action sequences such as the Humvee chase through the streets of San Francisco in *The Rock* (directed by Michael Bay, among the prime suspects in the 'death of narrative' inquiry), far from abandoning narrative structure, 'most American pictures are more tightly woven than they need to be'.[20] Far beyond the action blockbuster, over the past decade a number of films deployed ostentatiously complex, even transgressive narrative structures, ranging from the Altmanesque multi-strand narratives of *Magnolia, Crash* and others to 'puzzle films' such as *The Usual Suspects* (Polygram 1995), *Fight Club, Memento* (Pathé 2000), and *Synecdoche, New York* (Sony Classics 2008).[21] However unconventional these are, collectively they appear to testify to the ongoing importance of narrative as a vector of audience involvement, not to its supersession.

Do these counter-readings risk over-compensating? For it certainly seems as if 'action' in its more traditional sense as the outcome of visible and comprehensible choices made by or imposed on characters in defined narrative situations – for example, Pike Bishop's moment of silent decision in the Mexican brothel prior to the final massacre in *The Wild Bunch* – has been mostly displaced by spectacular 'event'. But if by these standards Michael Bay's *The Island* (DreamWorks 2003) fails to deliver, and one notes the utter lack of any meaningful development or even discernible reaction on the part of the 'characters' impersonated by Ewan McGregor and Scarlett Johanssen to the (presumably traumatic, but predictably spectacular) episodes through which the film manoeuvres them; this may all simply be to say that narrative and character are handled in a slapdash and contemptuous way, rather than that they are absent.

All in all, it makes sense to be careful. When Murray Smith claims that 'in action films the plot advances *through* spectacle; the spectacular elements are, generally speaking, as "narrativised" as are the less ostentatious spaces of other genres', this may overlook the extent to which narrative is conceived in such cases as a kind of conduit, a channel or service tunnel (the sort of thing one finds the heroes of *Aliens* and *Jurassic Park* crawling along as they seek to elude the monsters) through which to access the spectacular elements which are, commercially speaking, the film's *raison d'être*. It is also reasonable to assume that films adapted from video games (*Resident Evil*, Screen Gems 2002), theme park rides (*Pirates of the Caribbean*), toys (*Transformers*, DreamWorks 2007), or even, with staggering circularity, from movie-derived comic books (*Alien vs. Predator*, Fox 2005) are liable to have less than fully fleshed out characters if our point of comparison is *The Best Years of Our Lives* or *Five Easy Pieces*. Spectacle can only be encountered in and through narrative; yet that does mean that narrative ever takes full possession of the spectacular? Perhaps the contemporary action spectacle is less a cinema of attractions than a cinema of contradictions.

STYLISTIC HETERODOXY

In any event, to acknowledge the ongoing importance of narrative does not exhaust the ways in which contemporary Hollywood film style may have adapted or even abandoned classical practices. As noted in an earlier chapter, 'narrative' is such an expansive concept that its persistence cannot in itself reasonably be used as a criterion for judging the post-classical, 'hyperclassical' (Bordwell), or 'classical-plus' (Larry Knapp) formations of contemporary Hollywood cinema. Movie narratives have to be organised, conceptualised and visualised in order to be told at all. And at this textual level many departures (but also of many different kinds) from the conventions of previous periods – the studio era, obviously, but the more expressive films of the Hollywood Renaissance too – are readily apparent. These include editing, bravura camerawork and other self-advertising visual techniques, altered sonic regimes, a simultaneous intensification and dilution of the Renaissance practice of allusion and a different (less integrative) relationship to both historical and contemporary avant-garde and experimental film.

Perhaps the most obvious change in the visual field of Hollywood cinema, apparent even to casual viewers (especially when an early twenty-first-century film like *Pirates of the Caribbean* is viewed alongside a comparable film from the 1940s or 1950s – *The Pirate* (MGM 1948), say, or *The Crimson Pirate* (WB 1952)) is the quickened pace achieved through a faster succession of shorter, punchier scenes, cutting rates that have continued to accelerate since the late 1960s, the intensified destabilisation of scenic space and a constantly moving camera. By the mid-2000s, a handful of films each year were cut at rates of less than 2 seconds per shot. Predictably, these tended to be propulsive high-style action vehicles like *Miami Vice* (U 2006, ASL 1.9 seconds) or *The Bourne Ultimatum* (U 2007, 1.7 seconds). It was not the rapid succession of shots alone, but movement within the frame and movement of the frame itself that made these films so exhausting to watch. Action scenes were no longer composed of static setups, however rapidly alternated or intercut. While the ASLs of some of the principal action sequences in Michael Bay's *Transformers* (Par/DreamWorks 2007) – the assault on the military base, the desert compound battle and the downtown finale – are actually a good deal slower, at around 2 seconds, than Peckinpah's montage in *The Wild Bunch*, the camera is in almost constant, and fast, movement: rapid tracks and Steadicam glides, whip pans, rack focus shifts all give such sequences a relentless propulsive quality. Shots from different angles and focal lengths are cut together in ways that deny the viewer spatial security at any point in the sequence (a major difference from Peckinpah, where the Aqua Verde hacienda setting is carefully established and explored in a number of scenes prior to being demolished in the final battle). Interpolated images from other media – monitors, night-vision goggles, computerised read-outs representing the robots' 'point of view' – are thrown into the mix. Objects are often flung out towards the screen or past the camera at high velocity – what Geoff King calls the 'impact aesthetic'.[22] In these sequences, at least, continuity principles are not so much violated as wholly irrelevant. An impressionistic account of combat or flight is thrust at us, and we can only hang on for dear life.

In the context of action films – where they also constitute another form of spectacle – such sequences are designed to hammer the audience into a state of dazed battle fatigue. Of course, not every film batters its spectators this way; but even less frenziedly kinetic genes such as romantic comedies now deliver more visual information far more quickly than in the 1960s, let alone before. From the early 1970s to the early 2000s, the range of typical ASLs shortened from 6 to 9 seconds to between 3 and 5 seconds. (For example, Bordwell records that *Love, Actually* (U 2003) clocks in at an ASL of 3.8 seconds, *not* including its concluding quickfire montage.[23]) More rarely, such information overload is turned to critical uses. Oliver Stone's films of the mid-1990s – notably *Natural Born Killers* and *Nixon* – deploy a radical mix-up technique, intercutting scenes, alternating different film stocks, live action and animation, using double exposures and non-synchronous sound overlays both to express the trash-media-saturated, amphetamine consciousness of his serial killer protagonists and to activate the spectator by compelling him or her to sort through the barrage of images and effects and make, rather than merely receive, meaning.

What accounts for this hyperstimulated style, spectacular surely but in very different ways from, for example, the contemplative spectatorship encouraged in the early widescreen era? As ever, Hollywood was alert and open to outside influences (on its own terms, as Charles Foster Kane might say). The influx of British advertising directors in the 1980s and their contribution to the high-gloss look of films such as *Top Gun* has already been mentioned. Hollywood filmmakers could also take inspiration from a new generation of ultra-stylish European directors like Jean-Jacques Beneix (*Diva*, Fr 1981), Luc Besson (*Subway*, Fr 1985), and Jean-Pierre Jeunet (*Delicatessen*, Fr 1990) who would presently bring their flashy '*cinéma du look*' aesthetic to Hollywood in films such as Jeunet's *Alien: Resurrection* (Fox 1994) and Besson's *The Fifth Element* (Col 1997). In the globalised film economy of the 1990s, the super-stylised Hong Kong action cinema of directors like John Woo (*Bullet in the Head*, Hong Kong 1990) was also added to Hollywood's toolbox (*Face/Off*, Touchstone 1997). This process of globalised stylistic transfusion continues up to the present with the arrival in Hollywood of filmmakers such as the Brazilian director of the fearsomely amped-up *City of God* (2002), Fernando Meirelles, (*The Constant Gardener*, Focus 2002) and the *outré* Russian action director Timur Bekmambetov (*Wanted*, U 2008).

Closer to home, a major influence on Hollywood style since the 1980s has been music video. The advent of MTV in 1981 transformed the pop promo, a longstanding small-scale music industry tool to get performers into chart shows in minor or faraway markets. Almost overnight, MTV created both a massive expansion of demand for promos to supply its 24-7 schedule and a heightened visibility of the videos themselves. As MTV, quickly joined by other dedicated video channels, became a mainstay of the music industry, the production values and artistic ambition of videos also grew. By 1990, the simple skits, visual puns and performance recordings of the early years had given way to dynamic three- and four-minute short films whose per-minute cost could, in the case of the biggest artists, approach that of a Hollywood feature. Music videos found ways to cram narratives of ever greater scope and scale into their miniature formats. Around the same time, MTV began crediting video directors in the play-in and play-out titles and videos became 'calling cards' for directors fresh from film school.

By the mid-1980s, the impact of 'music video aesthetics' on mainstream Hollywood was already obvious and widespread. Jerry Simpson and Don Bruckheimer's high-concept, high-style action films heavily promoted soft-rock songs like Giorgio Moroder's 'Take My Breath Away' (rendering love scenes, in particular, all but indistinguishable from any number of female vocalist videos) and incorporated redundant hardware-driven sequences (the fighter training duels in *Top Gun*, the racing-circuit routines in *Days of Thunder*) which are held together only by the screeching rock soundtrack. Their rapid, impressionistic editing, multiple camera angles and reliance on stylised photographic effects, largely achieved with long lenses (heat hazes, silhouettes against sunsets and so on), are a virtual lexicon of high-end mid-eighties rock video/advertising technique. As more music video directors graduated to features – David Fincher (*Alien3*, Fox 1991; *Se7en*, New Line

1995), Brett Ratner (*Rush Hour*, New Line 1998), Spike Jonze (*Being John Malkovich*, U 1999), McG (*Charlie's Angels*, Col 2000), Michel Gondry (*Eternal Sunshine of the Spotless Mind*, Focus 2004) – while simultaneously established Hollywood directors like Brian De Palma (Bruce Springsteen's *Dancing in the Dark*, 1985), Martin Scorsese (Michael Jackson's *Bad*, 1991) and Spike Lee (Michael Jackson's *They Don't Care About Us*, 1996) commuted lucratively in the other direction, the stylistic crossover also grew.

Music video's novel interactions of sound and image not only contributed to, but also partly reflected one of post-studio-era Hollywood's most striking and wide-ranging stylistic innovations, the transformation of the soundtrack. The use of pop and rock songs in early Renaissance films like *The Graduate* and *Easy Rider*, where they bind together montage sequences (Ben Braddock 'drifting', Billy and Wyatt enjoying the freedoms of life on the road), comment or ironically counterpoint the inner lives of characters, and also supply an extra-textual connection to contemporary youth culture, established possibilities of using pre-recorded popular music that ran counter to classical Hollywood scoring conventions.

Composite pop soundtracks differed from both the Romantically styled 'through-scoring' of great studio-era composers such as Max Steiner, Erich Korngold or Miklos Rosza and the more aggressively modern compositions and sound experiments of Bernard Herrman, especially in scores for Alfred Hitchcock's films of the late fifties and sixties, notably *Vertigo*, *Psycho* and *The Birds*. One of the most emphatically modernist scores was composed for Altman's *The Long Goodbye*, ironically by John Williams – whose symphonic scores for *Star Wars* and the films of Steven Spielberg would come to epitomise the retreat from the stylistic experimentation of the 1970s. Williams's score consists entirely of one tune, which over the course of the film is played as lounge music, a torch song, even a marimba number. The endless recycling of material – like the imitations of Old Hollywood stars such as Jimmy Stewart with which Elliott Gould's Marlowe is greeted by a car-park attendant – confirms the film's cynical attitude towards a culture starved of originality or authenticity, in which social and personal relations are drained of meaning.

The Long Goodbye is an unusual example of the way in which both classic and modernist Hollywood scores generally were woven into the textual fabric of the film – regardless of whether they worked to estrange or to suture the spectator. Rock soundtracks, by contrast, were transferable in ways that proved both creatively and financially profitable, as two very different films of 1973 illustrated. In *Mean Streets*, Scorsese used an inspired mixture of new and vintage pop and rock – along with snippets of opera – to layer and deepen both the social and the inner worlds of his characters. Music could be directly expressive ('Jumpin' Jack Flash' as Johnny Boy makes his slow-motion entrance, bathed in hellish red light), evocative ('Be My Baby' behind the opening credits), or speedy and bugged-out ('Please Mr Postman' accompanying the pool-hall 'mook' brawl). This dense textuality continued to be a notable feature of Scorsese's subsequent soundscapes, notably in *GoodFellas* (the series of mob hits scored to the plangent playout from 'Layla') and *Casino*, and clearly influenced Quentin Tarantino's quotational scoring for *Pulp Fiction* and *Kill Bill*. Back in 1973, meanwhile, *American Graffiti*'s forty-two rock 'n' roll and doo-wop numbers, artfully integrated into the world of the film by Walter Murch's much praised sound design (thus foreclosing on the expressivity achieved by Scorsese's associative soundtrack selections), could also be separately packaged into a chart-topping soundtrack album, confirming the precedent of *Easy Rider*. The advent of Dolby Stereo sound in theatres in 1977 not only enabled the enveloping sonic environments of *Star Wars*, *Close Encounters* and subsequent blockbusters, but empowered a new cycle of rock musicals including *Saturday Night Fever* (Par 1977) and *Grease* (Par 1978) whose stylish musical sequences drove triple-platinum sales of soundtrack albums. MTV's debut in 1981 thus coincided with an already reinvigorated relationship of music and movies, which the music video boom then intensified.

In light of the subsequent canonisation of the 1970s as a last hurrah for a human-scale, socially relevant American cinema, it is ironic that many of the new MTV-generation directors found inspiration in the Hollywood Renaissance's own often overlooked displays of stylistic excess. Given the constraints of the form, ostentatious visuals were the obvious means for ambitious young music video directors to get themselves noticed; and the originators of the trend towards ostentatious visual style were directors like Scorsese (the bravura following shots in *Mean Streets*, the energised big-band jazz numbers in *New York, New York*), Coppola (the combination of The Doors and hallucinogenic imagery in *Apocalypse Now* and the Expressionist stylings of *Rumblefish* (U 1983)) and De Palma (whose *Phantom of the Paradise* (Fox 1974) previews many aspects of music video style). Like their predecessors, numerous music video directors also put their film school education to good effect: in their case, not to put on display and interrogate classic Hollywood conventions, but to pillage the archives of film style in search of eye-catching effects, not least the avant-garde European silent cinema of the 1920s (German Expressionism, Soviet montage). Older pop promos, especially in the psychedelic sixties (such as The Beatles' *Strawberry Fields Forever* promo in 1967) had also displayed influences from contemporary experimental art. In the eighties, this relationship became a house style (fuelled by the simultaneous commodification of the contemporary art world). As E. Ann Kaplan noted in an early study of MTV, this enthusiastic – indeed indiscriminate – raiding of cinematic esoterica, and the unabashed co-optation and commodification of such styles (many of them originally predicated on a critical, even hostile, stance to capitalist modernity) in the service of what were after all essentially advertisements were among music video's most distinctively 'postmodern' attributes.[24]

Allusionism thus became another Renaissance-era tactic repurposed for the 1990s. A culture of referencing older films remains very much part of contemporary Hollywood, but both the film-historical co-ordinates and the intention of these allusions have changed. With the effective demise of the Western, for example, allusions to Ford, Hawks and Boetticher are less generally legible, and no longer have the same iconic function, that they did for Peckinpah, Altman, Bogdanovich or Penn. In the sealed film-world of Quentin Tarantino's *Kill Bill*, their place has been taken by a new pulp canon: meticulous, recondite allusions to the parodic sixties spaghetti Westerns of Leone and Corbucci, seventies Shaw Brothers kung-fu movies, and obscure blaxploitation potboilers. Art cinema references such as Godard (but not Bergman or Fellini anymore) rub shoulders indiscriminately with this universe of cultish junk, in impeccably postmodern fashion. All are intended to be discovered, circulated and hotly debated on internet fan forums. But once identified, there is nothing much else to say: the critical stance that informed the allusionism and genre revisionism of the 1970s and linked them back to their social contexts has been supplanted by a hermetic, pure textuality with no 'larger' agenda. It is tempting to see Spielberg's citation of the Paramount mountain at the start of (Paramount's) *Raiders of the Lost Ark* – which is then 'quoted' in its turn in *Indiana Jones and the Last Crusade*; and once again, now an expected pleasure, after a twenty-year gap in *Indiana Jones and the Kingdom of the Crystal Skull* (Paramount 2008) – as emblematic of this trend. Pastiche, the 'blank parody' famously claimed by Fredric Jameson to typify postmodernism's evacuation of affect and critique, rears its head in Tarantino's recreation of blaxploitation in *Jackie Brown* (Miramax 1997).

A well-known early nineties example of all these trends is David Fincher's video for Madonna's *Express Yourself* (1990). The elaborate *mise en scène* of the large-scale fantasy setting announces Fincher's film literacy by explicitly mimicking Fritz Lang's *Metropolis*, as does the fairly nugatory narrative, depicting the sybaritic sky-city dweller Madonna's passion for a predictably buff labourer in the subterranean industrial zones. The ostentatious following shots and dollies, along with the Stygian industrial underworld and the chiaroscuro effects, establish a striking visual style Fincher would maintain into his first features, *Alien3* and *Se7en*. In both of these films, in fact, a foregrounded visual style competes with the narrative for the viewer's attention. Such commodified Gothic forms, run riot in music video, became a recognisable stylistic reference point for films such as *The Matrix* and *Underworld* (Screen Gems 2003). As Fincher moves further into the mainstream, his self-advertising style accompanies him: the camera digitally 'dollies' through the handle of a coffee pot in *Panic Room* (Col 2002).

Another early nineties Fincher video, *Janie's Got a Gun* by Aerosmith, typifies music video's condensation of complex narrative information into extraordinarily abbreviated, often symbolic, forms. Intercut with Aerosmith performance footage, the song's account of child abuse and revenge is elaborated via a series of elliptical *noir*-ish vignettes into a story of a wealthy financier father whose repeated abuse of his teenage daughter provokes her to kill him. The girl then flees the scene of the crime, only to be tracked down by a sympathetic cop. The video lasts a total of four and a half minutes; once the performance sequences are subtracted, the whole rape–revenge–redemption narrative is carried through in just 170 seconds of screen time.

Narrative ellipsis, look-at-me visuals and the mainstreaming of formerly avant-garde or underground styles all became familiar features of Hollywood cinema in the 1990s as the full impact of music video made itself felt. Critics were quick to attribute the emergence of impressionistically rapid editing – what one writer memorably calls the 'hysterical blenderisation of visuals' in films such as *Nixon* and *Leaving Las Vegas* – to MTV's influence.[25] 'If viewers can now process cuts as brief as two frames, the equivalent of one twelfth of a second', suggests another observer, 'it's because MTV and its surrounding advertising-marketing context have finely tuned our optic nerves, both promoting and portraying a more accelerated pace of daily life and, consequently, a new rhetoric of emotional and psychological fragmentation and disorder'.[26] If anything, this (written in 2000, eons ago in the evolutionary history of contemporary media forms) underestimates the impact of music video by suggesting that such high-intensity editing is compositionally motivated (that is, it is used to reflect agitated, febrile states of mind). Larry Knapp makes a persuasive case that the frenzied time-schemes and barrage of visual devices in Tony Scott's *Man on Fire* (Fox 2004) and *Domino* (New Line 2005) indeed partly enact the subjective crises of their protagonists.[27] Yet David Bordwell notes the general climate of agitation and activity that now characterises the presentation of even quite simple dialogue scenes – so (unless we take it that contemporary life as such is pervasively hysterical or manic, which may indeed be the case) the style has exceeded the bounds of narrative accountability. Indeed, the studios' appetite for such hyper-stylised filmmaking became a source of grievance on the part of directors who wished to establish higher-minded auteurist credentials: Billy Bob Thornton, complaining about studio pressure to abandon his long-take final scene in *All the Pretty Horses* (Col 2000), lamented that 'these days, they want to cut everything like a rock video'.[28]

If music video and advertising helped accustom directors, producers and audiences to processing visual information in ever faster, more compressed bursts, there also seems little doubt that new editing technologies – specifically, the introduction of first video, and in the early 1990s non-linear, digital packages like Avid – made faster cutting far easier and less risky and time-consuming. Near-subliminal edits of a few frames, if desired, became effortlessly straightforward to undertake (and, if unsuccessful, to undo). 'Where classical film editing melds transition into seamless, gliding passages', notes Maria Demopoulos, 'New School editing slams images together in head-on collision'.[29]

Echoing many others, Wheeler Winston Dixon complains that such stylistic overkill has desensitised viewers to longer takes and subtler approaches, 'thrust[ing] new images – *any* image – at the viewer to prevent him/her from becoming even momentarily bored'.[30] David Bordwell has argued that the unmistakeable and seemingly irreversible trend to faster cutting and the much more extensive use of close-ups, compared to the late studio era, paradoxically *reduces* directors' options. Not only are certain traditional starting points (notably the *plan américain*) all but ruled out by the new directorial orthodoxies but, he argues, the compulsion to supply visual interest and variety at every juncture perversely makes it harder to achieve the impact on the spectator that under a more conservative visual regime could be realised by the sharp contrast between, say, a medium-length two-shot and a rare (hence emphasised) close-up at a moment of particular emotional intensity or dramatic tension.[31] A different, less judgmental (of filmmakers *and*, implicitly, audiences) take on this might simply say that changing assumptions about audience preferences and capabilities have been a necessary part of Hollywood practice since before the shift to features. Given that films are now more likely to be consumed on home video than in cinemas, directors may elect to give audiences more than they can handle at one viewing in the knowledge that there can always be a second, and third, aided if needs be with the pause/frame advance button to catch the fleeting or suggestive detail. Of course, Hollywood has often misunderstood or underestimated its public, but so have cultural commentators: in light of assertions about the cinema of postmodern attractions, it's also worth noting that early cinema provoked somewhat similar jeremiads from contemporaries whose class or cultural location predisposed them to disapprove of the new medium. 'Dulled senses demand powerful stimuli; exhaustion of the vital forces leads to a desire for crude, for violent excitation', fretted one middle-class observer of the nickelodeons in 1909.[32] Still, it can seem as if some films in the MTV mode are impatient with, or afraid of, accomplishing even the most straightforward piece of business in anything less than high style: so Kiefer Sutherland leaves his dorm room each morning in Joel Schumacher's *Flatliners* by abseiling down the outside wall; in Michael Bay's *Armageddon*, the roughnecks' recall from vacation to save the world is staged as a series of high velocity chases and round-ups. It's certainly all a long way from *Marty*; but then so was *Around the World in Eighty Days*, which won the Best Picture Oscar the following year.

TO THE POST-CLASSICAL — AND BEYOND

As already noted, one of the difficulties in these debates is establishing how far any given example is representative of Hollywood cinema as a whole – if, indeed, such a totalising vantage point is either possible or necessary. Box office popularity on its own seems unlikely to resolve the issue; the highest-grossing films each year may well be varieties of action spectacle, but (just as with Bordwell's counter-examples to eighties high-concept), they are usually closely followed by films that offer very different kinds of pleasure – verbal and performative as well as visual. In 1999, for example, the runaway box office number one was, predictably, *Star Wars Episode 1* (Lucasfilm/Fox), but number two was *The Sixth Sense*, a film famous for, precisely, its narrative structure and one that is also notable for its reliance on relatively long takes. *Spider-Man*, action-packed and kinetic to the max, headed the list in 2002, but at five and six, respectively, were the breakout independent ethnic comedy *My Big Fat Greek Wedding* (IFC) and another fairly sombre paranormal effort from *Sixth Sense* writer–director M. Night Shyamalian, *Signs* (Touchstone).

In fact, beyond the general climate of visual activism – quite unlike the restraint and transparency aimed for and achieved by a majority of studio-era films – the contemporary Hollywood cinema is typified by a proliferation of approaches to narrative form and visual style, running from the self-conscious stylisation of the Coen Bothers (*O Brother Where Art Thou?*, U 2000) and Wes Anderson (*The Darjeeling Limited*, Fox Searchlight 2008) to the restraint of Ang Lee (*Brokeback Mountain*, Entertainment 2005). Yet even at the individual level generalisations are precarious: the Coens delivered the understated, reflective *No Country for Old Men* (Paramount Vantage/Miramax 2007) – and won a clutch of Oscars in the process – while Lee created the fantasy martial arts crossover hit *Crouching Tiger, Hidden Dragon* (Col 2000) – the highest-grossing foreign-language film ever at the US box office – and followed that with the world's first arthouse comic-book movie, *Hulk* (U 2003). Might this very heterogeneity, which makes it impossible to speak in anything but the most general terms of a 'contemporary Hollywood style' to set against the classical style, be considered its most unclassical aspect?

Or might it be rather that to speak of 'Hollywood *cinema*' at all begs a major question? For over twenty years, filmmakers have been mindful that their work is most likely to be consumed on the small, not the big screen. In fact, as previous chapters have shown, the past seven decades have seen Hollywood orient its activities ever more clearly towards the home, rather than theatrical markets. This book has tried to demonstrate that questions of film form cannot be considered in isolation from either their industrial or their social contexts. And so it is with contemporary Hollywood: since the advent of home video, filmmakers have been unable to ignore the commercial imperative to compose for the small screen, aided by technologies such as the video assist. This has ensured that as varied as they have become, stylistic options have nonetheless been contained – quite literally, within the 'safe space' marked out by the video assist, the zone where action will play safely on the home screen. The advent of DVD and widescreen, higher-definition televisions may have eliminated the horrors of eighties-style pan-and-scan, but 'composing for television' – a smaller screen, a 'distracted' spectator, the deconstructable (paused, rewound, switched off) text – is widely held to have promoted some of the dominant practices of contemporary Hollywood style (such as the more extensive use of close-ups and faster cutting rates, as a means of enhancing visual interest). Perhaps then post-classical style consists in this consciousness – present and visible at every stage of the conceptualisation, production, distribution and exhibition of a Hollywood film – that is the world beyond film that in fact defines it.

NOTES

1. Scott Bukatman, 'Zooming out: the end of offscreen space', in Jon Lewis (ed.), *The New American Cinema* (Durham, NC: Duke University Press, 1998), pp. 248–72.
2. Bukatman, 'Offscreen space', p. 261.
3. On the relationship between science-fiction and horror, see Barry Langford, *Film Genre: Hollywood and Beyond* (Edinburgh: Edinburgh University Press, 2005), pp. 185–6.
4. Justin Wyatt, *High Concept: Movies and Marketing in Hollywood* (Austin: University of Texas Press, 1994).
5. See Geoff King, *Spectacular Narratives: Hollywood in the Age of the Blockbuster* (London: I. B. Tauris, 2000); Murray Smith, 'Theses on the philosophy of Hollywood history', and Warren Buckland, 'A close encounter with *Raiders of the Lost Ark*: notes on narrative aspects of the New Hollywood blockbuster', both in Steve Neale and Murray Smith (eds), *Contemporary Hollywood Cinema* (London: Routledge, 1997); Kristin Thompson, *Storytelling in the New Hollywood: Analyzing Classical Narrative Technique* (Cambridge, MA: Harvard University Press, 1999).
6. David Bordwell, *The Way Hollywood Tells It* (Berkeley: University of California Press, 2005), pp. 147, 179.
7. See Chapter 3.
8. See Ben Singer, 'Modernity, hyperstimulus and the rise of popular sensationalism', in Leo Charney and Vanessa Schwartz (eds), *Cinema and the Invention of Modern Life* (Berkeley: University of California Press, 1998), pp. 72–99.
9. See Fred Pfeil, 'From pillar to postmodern: race, class, and gender in the male rampage film', in Jon Lewis (ed.), *The New American Cinema* (Durham, NC: Duke University Press, 1998), p. 147.
10. Traditionally, 'special effects' referred to 'pro-filmic' objects or events recorded by the camera – miniatures, models, pyrotechnics, etc. – while 'visual effects' denoted optical effects achieved by manipulation of the image track itself (mattes, 'trick' photography, etc.). The advent of digital effects obviously renders this distinction largely moot.

11. Spielberg's unusual decision to take a solo screenplay credit himself might be seen as testifying to the significance *Close Encounters* held for him personally.

12. Robert Kolker, *A Cinema of Loneliness: Penn, Stone, Kubrick, Scorsese, Spielberg, Altman*, 3rd edn (Oxford: Oxford University Press, 2000), p. 141.

13. Kolker, *op cit.*, p. 142.

14. *Ibid.*

15. On early cinema audiences, see Miriam Hansen, *Babel and Babylon: Spectatorship in American Silent Film* (Cambridge, MA: Harvard University Press, 1997), pp. 60–126.

16. MCA Universal 'Sensurround Handbook'(1974). Online: http://www.in70mm.com/newsletter/2004/69/sensurround/index.htm

17. See Michelle Pierson, *Special Effects: Still In Search of Wonder* (New York: Columbia University Press, 2002).

18. King, *Spectacular Narratives*, p. 39.

19. King, *Spectacular Narratives*, p. 2. King's analysis is presented in updated form in 'Spectacle and narrative in the contemporary blockbuster', in Linda Ruth Williams and Michael Hammond (eds), *Contemporary American Cinema* (Maidenhead: McGraw-Hill, 2005), pp. 334–52.

20. Bordwell, *The Way Hollywood Tells It*, p. 105.

21. On *Crash* and 'network narratives', see 'The Biggest, the Best: 2005'.

22. Geoff King, *New Hollywood Cinema: An Introduction* (London: I. B. Tauris, 2001), p. 246.

23. Bordwell, *The Way Hollywood Tells It*, pp 121–3.

24. E. Ann Kaplan, *Rocking Around the Clock: Music Television, Postmodernism, and Consumer Culture* (London: Routledge, 1987), pp. 33–48.

25. Wheeler Winston Dixon, 'Twenty-five reasons why it's all over', in Jon Lewis (ed.), *The End of Cinema As We Know It* (London: Pluto, 2001), p. 360.

26. Maria Demopoulos, 'Blink of an eye: filmmaking in the age of bullet time', *Film Comment* 2000; 36(3):34–9.

27. Larry Knapp, 'Tony Scott and *Domino* – Say hello (and goodbye) to the postclassical', *Jump Cut* 2008; 50(Spring). Online: http://www.ejumpcut.org/archive/jc50.2008/DominoKnapp/index.html

28. Quoted in Bordwell, *The Way Hollywood Tells It*, p. 140.

29. Demopoulos, 'Blink of an eye', p. 38.

30. Dixon, 'Twenty-five reasons', p. 360.

31. Bordwell, *The Way Hollywood Tells It*, pp. 184–5.

32. Elizabeth Beardsley Butler, 'Women and the trades: Pittsburgh 1907–1908', quoted in Garth Jowett, *Film: The Democratic Art* (Boston: Little, Brown, 1976), pp. 38–9.

The Biggest, the Best: 2005

Best Picture: *Crash* (Lionsgate)
D: Paul Haggis; **P:** Cathy Schulman, Don Cheadle; **W:** Paul Haggis, Bobby Moresco
Box Office No. 1: *Star Wars Episode III: Revenge of the Sith* (Lucasfilm/Fox)
D, W: George Lucas; **P:** Rick McCallum

When the independently produced *Crash* won the 2006 Best Picture Oscar, it confirmed a trend over the course of the decade distinguishing those films Hollywood enjoyed publicly congratulating itself for making, from the pictures that paid the studios' bills. Since 1970, the top-grossing film had also been judged the year's best on only seven occasions, most recently *The Return of the King* in 2003; but in only eleven years had the Best Picture failed to make the year's top ten, and only twice the top twenty – Bernardo Bertolucci's *The Last Emperor* (Col 1987) and the previous year's pick, Clint Eastwood's *Million Dollar Baby* (WB 2004). Its Oscar notwithstanding, *Crash* placed forty-ninth among 2005 releases. Its $55 million domestic gross represented an excellent return on the $3.3 million that independent distributor Lionsgate had gambled on the US distribution rights when 'no-one else seemed to want it', but it did not come close to emulating *Platoon*, the last wholly non-studio-financed (though not distributed) Best Picture and the third most popular film of 1986.[1] *Crash*'s earnings, like its $6.5 million budget, were small change by the standards of 2005's runaway top film, a very different kind of independent production – Lucasfilm's *Revenge of the Sith* (Fox), the final instalment in the *Star Wars* prequel trilogy showing Anakin Skywalker's transformation into Darth Vader. Budgeted at $180 million, *Revenge of the Sith* grossed $380 million domestically and a further $453 million (61 per cent of total earnings) overseas. With *Crash* began a period of 'Indiewood' domination at the Oscars in the late 2000s, interrupted only by Martin Scorsese's *The Departed* (WB 2006) the following year (arguably the low-budget, downbeat *Million Dollar Baby*, produced by Eastwood's Malpaso which since the early 1970s has had a distribution deal with Warner, also belongs in this category). The 2007 award went to Indiewood stalwarts, the Coen Brothers' *No Country For Old Men* (Miramax 2006) and 2008 honoured Fox Searchlight's British import *Slumdog Millionaire*, both successful films (especially *Millionaire*, which grossed over $140 million) that never threatened the majors' 'tent-pole' releases. Effectively, the 'best' and the 'biggest' – never synonymous, even in the 1940s – now seemed to inhabit increasingly separate worlds, or perhaps galaxies.

Crash is a quintessential Indiewood film, as representative of its moment in industrial and social history as *The Best Years of Our Lives* or *Back to the Future* were of theirs. Like most Indiewood productions, *Crash* adopts a strategy of carefully calibrated difference that allows it to challenge (or seem to challenge) some aspects of mainstream Hollywood while remaining conventional enough to attract a large audience, if not on the scale of the popcorn blockbusters. In the case of *Crash*, the deviations from convention occur partly at the level of narrative structure, but primarily in terms of content.

Crash (Lionsgate 2005). Reproduced courtesy of The Kobal Collection

Crash belongs to a sub-genre of multi-strand films depicting characters straddling various class and racial divides in contemporary Los Angeles, including Lawrence Kasdan's *Grand Canyon* (Fox 1991), Paul Thomas Anderson's *Magnolia* (New Line 1999), and pre-eminently Robert Altman's *Short Cuts* (Avenue 1991). All of these films (like Michael Mann's *Collateral* (DreamWorks 2004)) play off Los Angeles's received image as decentred, denatured and socially fragmented – the opening lines of *Crash* programmatically invoke this city of freeways and disconnection where everyone is 'always behind this metal and glass' and so yearns for human contact that they will seek it out even in conflict. In this deracinated environment, the possibility of connection arises only through chance and coincidence – so in all of these films, over a tightly delimited period of time (a single night, a weekend), separate and mutually oblivious, but thematically paralleled, storylines and characters intersect occasionally, but fatefully. In *Crash*, these encounters are so overdetermined and frequent over the twenty-four hours the film covers that, as several reviewers commented, the supposedly atomised megalopolis feels more like a small town. Less glib than Kasdan, less self-consciously 'arty' than Anderson, and a good deal more redemptively inclined than Altman, writer–director Paul Haggis adroitly triangulates his film in the contest of a market where the appearance of a radical edge is likely to sell a lot better than the real thing.

Crash's principal, in fact virtually its sole, subject is race, a field that not only defines the plot but which all the characters discuss to the exclusion of almost anything else. As in the other LA films as well as other examples of multi-strand 'network narratives' in this period (including *Pulp Fiction* and Alejandro Iñárritu's *21 Grams* (Icon 2003) and *Babel* (UIP 2006)), the inevitably flattened characterisations and arcs – as well as the visual devices (especially match cuts on movement and wipes) used to link scenes, locations and characters – make the filmmaker highly visible as an organising force. The mostly conflictual, often ironic, repeated encounters between Haggis's carefully racially variegated characters are stage-managed in ways that topple the social and institutional issues around race back into the personal and melodramatic mode – most notably in the two encounters between a rich African American woman (Thandie Newton) and the racist cop (Matt Dillon) who first sexually molests her, then later saves her from a burning car in a mist of redemptive tears. But such melodramatic devices – and the upscale cast, also including such name actors as Sandra Bullock, Terence Howard and Don Cheadle – are precisely the means whereby *Crash* flatters its audience with a small measure of challenge while finally remaining firmly within the circles of convention.

For both Haggis and Lionsgate, the success of *Crash* secured a place at Hollywood's top table. Haggis quickly carved out a highly marketable niche as a writer able to add literary qualities to mainstream historical (*Flags of our Fathers*, WB 2006) or action (*Casino Royale*, Sony 2006) material. Armed with their Oscar, meanwhile, Lionsgate established themselves as the leading non-studio-affiliated independent, leavening a lucrative stream of high-concept, low-budget horror franchises like *Saw* (five pictures starting in 2004) and *Hostel* (2005, 2007) with upscale projects chosen with an eye to profitable controversy such as *Away From Her* (2007) and Oliver Stone's *W* (2008). In autumn 2007 Lionsgate was number one at the domestic box office. By 2008 the company was publicly traded, had successfully diversified into television production (including the Emmy-winning *Mad Men*) and music publishing, and entered into partnerships with various of the majors on pay-TV and other projects. Lionsgate has also acquired a video library of over 8,000 titles that, perhaps symbolically, includes titles from such 1980s would-be majors as Vestron and Carolco.[2] The ghosts of such companies and countless others, great and small, who have tried and failed to break into the Hollywood oligopoly are cautionary spectres at Lionsgate's feast, but the cannily managed company seems as well placed as any, and better than most, to crack it.

Notes
1. 'Is little Lionsgate set to roar?', *Business Week*, 2 March 2006, p. 21.
2. Online: http://corporate.lionsgate.com/Division.asp

Hollywood's nightmare: pirated DVDs seized by police. Reproduced courtesy of The Kobal Collection

Conclusion: 'Hollywood' Now

This book began by noting that the identification of the American commercial film industry with 'Hollywood' has always been a convenient shorthand masking a complex network of institutions, practices and conventions. As we have seen in subsequent chapters, that network has changed radically over the past seven decades. So it might be helpful to conclude this study by asking what 'Hollywood' means today.

There is a temptation to say that, if the confusion of 'Hollywood' with the American film industry as a whole has always been simplistic, today it is plain wrong. If only as a provocation, one might come up with the following propositions:

1. There is no Hollywood;
2. it isn't American; and
3. it isn't a film industry.

Such claims would likely be as misleading and over-simplifying as whatever they replace. Yet they at least indicate, in ways that the continued unexamined usage of terms like 'Hollywood' or 'the Hollywood studios' do not, that the object of contemporary 'Hollywood studies' is indeed something fundamentally different from that of historical 'film studies' (a term that begs a number of important questions). So let us take these provocations as a starting point for our concluding discussion.

DOES HOLLYWOOD EXIST?

Commentators have been writing Hollywood's obituary, alongside that of the film industry, since the early 1950s. The rise of television, the shift

towards independent and runaway production, the layoffs of contact personnel and shrinking of the old studio lots, the absorption of the studios themselves into larger conglomerates, have all provoked premature declarations of
Tinseltown's demise. Yet Hollywood has not died, but evolved; as an industry,
an image, and even as a physical location Hollywood remains a tangible reality,
albeit a very different one from what it was sixty-five years ago.

In some ways Hollywood today is a mirror image of the industry in the
1940s. Seventy years ago the *production* of motion pictures was confined to
the West Coast studio lots while corporate decision-making was centred on
the head offices in New York. Today Hollywood is the location of the corporate offices of the filmed entertainment divisions of the enormous media
conglomerates, while the production process itself is widely dispersed across
a huge range of territories and specialist service providers located not just in
the US but globally. *The Lord of the Rings*, financed by New Line, a division
of Time Warner, but almost entirely created on the opposite side of the globe
in New Zealand – that is, not only principal photography but the whole vast
panoply of design and post-production elements from which Middle-earth
was fabricated – is only the most famous example. The two *Matrix* sequels
were largely filmed at the Fox Australia studios in Melbourne. US states and
foreign countries compete to provide attractive alternatives (including a less
heavily regulated and unionised labour environment) to Southern California
for production companies through subsidies, tax incentives and local government support. (Malta, for example, has attracted over seventy productions by
offering tax subsidies.[1])

Thus in certain ways 'Hollywood' is less a metonym for the film industry
than it was before. As part of the general retrenchment of the early 1970s,
several of the majors closed their New York offices and moved operations to
California, with the result that for the first time the distribution and (what
remained of) production arms were housed in the same place. Hollywood,
the place, remains very much a locus of industry power: ask any screenwriter
aiming to 'pitch' an idea to one or other division of the studios, who still has to
travel to Los Angeles and take meetings with studio executives in their palatial
offices on studio lots. (US screenwriting magazines urge beginning writers to
relocate to the West Coast as soon as practically possible.) The networking that
sustains the industry still centres on the season's fashionable LA restaurants,
hotels and clubs. The *Los Angeles Times* covers the entertainment industry
extensively as a local story; despite the growth of the West Coast financial
services sector since the 1980s (its importance enhanced by its easier connec-
tions to the surging Pacific Tiger economies), Los Angeles remains at heart a
one-industry town.

Beyond the art of the deal, which took on such importance in Hollywood
from the 1950s with the shift to independent production and the rising power of

agents, a good deal of physical space in the Hollywood and greater Los Angeles areas is still devoted to film production and services. The major studios sold off much of their acreage – the studio lots and ranches – in the 1960s and 1970s, either to raise cash to ward off financial crisis or simply to cash in on the booming Californian real estate market (perhaps the best-known example is Fox's sale of 260 acres of back lot in 1960 for $43 million, eventually developed as the Century City office complex – which in 1986 featured prominently as the 'Nakatomi Tower' in Fox's *Die Hard*). But they retain ownership of soundstages and post-production facilities and continue to compete with independent suppliers to rent soundstage space and supply the range of auxiliary services needed to bring a modern motion picture to release. These include (roughly in order of use during production) set design and construction, prop houses, photographic processing laboratories, screening and editing rooms, sound studios, and specialist producers of 'coming attractions' trailers. The creation and delivery of digital visual effects, meanwhile, has attained the status of an industry in its own right. While contemporary communications technology and location-based shooting means that few of these facilities need to be located in California, in practice almost three-quarters of them are.[2] A few of these are giants in their own right – notably George Lucas's Industrial Light & Magic, based in the beautiful Marin County north of San Francisco – but most are smaller companies that compete intensively with one another for studio business. A major 'studio' production often involves a congeries of such specialists, as revealed by a glance at the several different companies contributing digital effects to a CGI-driven blockbuster like *Watchmen* (WB/Par 2009), for instance.

All of these satellite and service operations, however, are reliant on the majors for the large contracts that keep them in business. As ever in Hollywood, follow the money and you arrive soon enough back at the studio gates. Since *Paramount* the studios have kept a careful eye on possible antitrust violations, and have become much more authentically competitive than before – but collusive practices and partnerships between ostensible rivals remain very much a part of industry life. For example, to ensure that major studio releases secure their all-important preferred opening dates for their 'tentpole' releases and do not dilute the impact of their marketing campaigns by competing with each other for the same demographic at the same time (say, by releasing two high-octane action blockbusters on the same weekend), the studios – who cannot legally simply coordinate their activities to avoid competition – all subscribe to the same market research company whose results, circulated to all the studios, alert management to potential clashes.[3] Many of the studios also have either formal or informal partnerships and alliances in various aspects of technology and sales.

The majors' various subsidiaries, including the former independents they have acquired, like New Line, Miramax and DreamWorks, enjoy or endure

varying degrees of autonomy, subject to their performance, their own executives' reputation and clout (hence DreamWorks retained a high degree of
functional autonomy following its acquisition by Paramount), corporate
reorganisation, changing business models or executive whim. In 2008, for
example, New Line lost its independent status with the Time Warner empire
and became a unit of Warner Bros. On occasion the power struggle between
a subsidiary and its parent emerges into the public domain, as in 2003 when
Disney refused to distribute Michael Moore's incendiary *Fahrenheit 9/11*,
produced by its Miramax subsidiary, through Buena Vista. Operations may
have become dispersed in contemporary Hollywood; power is as concentrated
as it has ever been, possibly more so.

IS IT AMERICAN?

The answer perhaps depends on where you are standing when you ask the
question. Like most other American industries, in the past quarter-century
Hollywood has been subject to investment and takeovers from overseas. Five
of the six majors are currently in American hands – though this has changed,
may change in the future, and is in any case more complicated than that simple
statement suggests. In addition to Japanese-owned Sony Pictures (incorporating Columbia Tri-Star and MGM), one-fifth of Universal NBC is still
controlled by its former owners, French holding company Vivendi, while
the parent company of Twentieth Century-Fox, NewsCorp International, is
– notwithstanding the company moving its base of operations to the USA in
2004 – basically Australian.

The extent to which the conglomerates develop globalised – that is, non-
US-based, rather than simply export – businesses varies. Sony, for example,
hindered in the US market by FCC rules prohibiting foreigners owning US
television stations (which Rupert Murdoch circumvented by naturalising as a
US citizen in 1986), has recently unified its US production and international
television divisions 'to take strategic advantage of the globalization of the
television market'. Sony Pictures Television now feeds Sony movies and TV
shows through a global channel network including 114 channel feeds in 130
countries.[4] Disney have acquired a majority stake in Mumbai-based production company UTV.

Of all the studios, NewsCorp/Fox is the most thoroughly 'borderless'.
Murdoch's acquisition of DirecTV's satellite stations in 2003 – adding to his
Sky and Star satellites in Britain and Asia – enabled the distribution of Fox-
generated content (and premium, subscription-generating sports events like
English Premier League football, for the rights to which Murdoch companies
paid astronomical sums) direct to paying audiences worldwide.[5] NewsCorp

describes itself as 'a diversified global media company' and its principal holdings at the end of 2008, in the US mostly gathered under the Fox brand, included Fox Filmed Entertainment – Twentieth Century Fox, Fox 2000, Fox Searchlight, Fox Home Video, Fox Licensing and Merchandising, and Fox Television; Fox Broadcasting, MyNetwork TV and 24 US television stations; the Star television network in South-East Asia; Fox US cable channels including Fox News, numerous sports channels and a majority share in National Geographic; Sky broadcast satellites in Britain, Italy, Germany, Asia and Australia; the multi-national book publisher HarperCollins; Fox Interactive Media, including MySpace and the film review website RottenTomatoes; and newspapers and magazines across the USA, UK, Asia and Australasia including the *Wall Street Journal*, *New York Post*, (London) *Times* and *Sunday Times*, and Murdoch's original Australian newspaper empire. With holdings (albeit small ones) in India, Polynesia and Latin America, NewsCorp is the most extensively and diversely internationalised of the 'Big Six' conglomerates.

At the level of the 'mini-majors', one tier down from the conglomerates, things are just as complicated. Excluding the 'major independents' acquired by the studios in the 1990s, important players in this market include the French Pathé and the originally Canadian Lionsgate, now operating out of Santa Monica. Over the last decade, the Australian film-finance and production company Village Roadshow has established itself as a frequent partner on blockbusters including *The Matrix* and *Ocean's Eleven* trilogies and *I Am Legend* (WB 2007). At DreamWorks, remaining founding partner Steven Spielberg exercised his three-year buy-back option included in the studio's 2005 purchase by Viacom, and in summer 2008 announced a $600 million tie-up with Indian entertainment giant Reliance: the first major incursion into Hollywood by an Indian company but, given the scale of the Bollywood film industry (in global terms, second only to Hollywood itself), unlikely to be the last.

Viewed from overseas, Hollywood's American-ness is indisputable and indeed a cause for concern. The majors all but monopolise overseas markets. In 1950, Hollywood films' share of the box office in Europe and Japan was 30 per cent; by 1990 it had grown to 80 per cent. While that earlier figure may have been artificially depressed by postwar protectionism in the shape of tariffs and quotas,[6] the liberalisation of world trade since the 1980s has seen most of the remaining barriers to Hollywood's penetration and domination of world markets fall. Over the last two decades France has successfully led a loose coalition of nations at GATT[7] and its successor, the World Trade Organisation, arguing for a 'cultural exception' to protect French-produced films against the Hollywood onslaught. (Predictably, the MPAA has strenuously opposed this at every opportunity.) Nonetheless, even with the 'cultural exception' US films still accounted for 49 per cent of French moviegoing in 2007.[8]

Overseas markets have, of course, always had a significant part to play in Hollywood's business. But the contemporary globalised economy has hugely ramped up the studios' revenues from abroad. The marketisation of the former Communist economies of central and eastern Europe from 1989 opened up territories that had been inaccessible to Hollywood product since before World War II, or, in the case of the former Soviet Union, that had never before been penetrated. Concurrently, the rapid development of the economies of South-East Asia, mainland China, and South Asia, successively, from the 1980s onwards in turn created new demand for studio-produced entertainment among the vast populations of those nations. Although these have also been the parts of the world where piracy has most seriously cut into studio revenues, this has not prevented them returning enormous amounts of money to the media conglomerates. Overseas grosses started to outstrip domestic sales in the late 1970s, and by 2008 contributed 65 per cent ($18.3 billion) of total box-office.[9] A 2008 report estimated that the Indian theatrical market alone would be worth $4 billion annually to Hollywood.[10]

Like so many changes in the movie industry since World War II, globalisation is perceived by the studios as both a boon and a travail, problem and opportunity. For example, no sooner had the DVD explosion sent studio revenues soaring than the unexpected emergence of 'grey' transnational markets with the growth of internet shopping in the late 1990s potentially undermined the studios' sequenced release strategies, which operated internationally as well as within countries (that is, films were usually released in foreign theatrical markets after their domestic first-run – thus saving on print costs, already sky-high in the era of saturation releasing) by enabling consumers to buy DVDs in countries where the DVD, or even the films, had not yet been released. The studios' response was to raise the threat of digital piracy to protect their business model, successfully lobbying Congress through the MPAA to incorporate a provision in the 2000 Digital Millennium Copyright Act that made adapting a DVD player to play multi-region discs a criminal offence under US law (a futile gesture, since the market for imported DVDs in the US is tiny, whereas countless owners and retailers in Europe and Asia routinely 'chip' machines for multi-region playback).

The rise and rise of a global market for Hollywood product, as well as concomitant anxieties about piracy, have encouraged the studios to abandon their normal phased international release for some of their most important 'tentpole' pictures and instead stage spectacular simultaneous international openings, 'opening wide' on the biggest possible – literally global – scale. In November 2003, Warner opened the third and final film in the *Matrix* trilogy, *The Matrix Revolutions*, in over sixty countries simultaneously.

One should not overstate the novelty of all this (as some wide-eyed accounts of globalisation in many different contexts tend to do). Walt Disney's biographer tells us that before World War II, Mickey Mouse (renamed Miki Kuchi) was the second-most popular figure in Japan, after the Emperor.[11] Universal and Paramount have jointly operated the largest overseas distributor of Hollywood films, United International Pictures (UIP), since 1970.[12] Today, UIP handles these studios' releases and also those of major independents such as DreamWorks and Lionsgate. The conduct of business is continuous with Hollywood traditions in other ways too: because US antitrust laws do not apply overseas, the studios can continue to use domestically-outlawed block-booking and other sharp practices to force their pictures into foreign theatres at the expense of indigenously produced films.

IS IT A FILM INDUSTRY?

None of the modern media conglomerates describe themselves as film studios, because that is not what they are. The corporate publicity that articulates these companies' image to the world is remarkably homogeneous, and none of them give film as such pride of place. Viacom (parent of Paramount), for example, is 'a leading global entertainment company' whose 'brands engage, empower and connect across every platform'. Now the smallest of the major conglomerates after Sumner Redstone's parent corporation National Amusements separated out its broadcast division CBS in 2005, Viacom's principal holdings now include Paramount (Paramount Pictures, Vantage and Classics), the MTV music video networks, BET (Black Entertainment Television), Nickelodeon children's channels, and a thriving interactive games division including the *Rock Band* franchise. Viacom 'connects with our diverse audiences everywhere they are' and 'proudly delivers' what those audiences want through 'television, motion pictures and a wide range of digital media'.[13]

Time Warner is 'a global leader in media and entertainment with business in television networks, filmed entertainment, publishing and interactive services . . . deliver[ing] high-quality content worldwide through multiple distribution platforms'. Its principal businesses include Warner Bros., which produces films for theatrical release, direct-to-DVD productions, television programming and animated television including the Looney Tunes characters; New Line; the Turner cable networks; premium pay-TV channels, principally HBO (also now a major producer of original drama); the internet service provider AOL; and the Time, Inc. magazine publishing empire.[14]

Minor differences in corporate publicity reflect companies' historical culture as well as the current market positioning: hence The Walt Disney Company emphasises 'The Disney Difference – a value-creation dynamic based on high standards of quality and recognition that set Disney apart from our competitors'. The company stresses its family orientation – 'a leading diversified international family entertainment and media enterprise' whose 'business segments' are 'media networks, parks and resorts, studio entertainment and consumer products' (with movies ranking third).[15] Disney's businesses include Walt Disney Studios, Disney-Pixar and Miramax; Disneyland parks and resorts; a worldwide retail network of Disney Stores; the ABC television network; and cable channels including the Disney channels and sports broadcaster ESPN. Disney's aim is 'to create exceptional content, experiences and products that are embraced by consumers around the world' through an 'integrated set of creative assets and businesses'.[16]

The other two major conglomerates, both industrial manufacturers, have rather different profiles. In addition to its electronics business, Sony owns Sony Pictures, Sony Pictures Classics and MGM, and also has extensive music industry holdings. NBC Universal is the smallest of the giant conglomerate GE's divisions, which include construction, transport, retail and investment banking and healthcare; as well as Universal Pictures and the French film company Canal+, NBC Universal's holdings include the NBC broadcast network, cable networks including MSNBC, USA, the Spanish-language Telemundo and an extensive music business.

The financial data in corporate annual financial reports give some indication of the part played by theatrical motion pictures, in their various different formats and platforms, in the totality of their parent companies' diverse and dispersed activities. The picture, however, is less than crystal clear because the conglomerates tend to include a number of different revenue streams in the amounts they attribute, variously, to 'Filmed Entertainment' (Fox and Time Warner), 'Pictures' (Sony), 'Studio Entertainment' (Disney) or simply 'Entertainment' (Viacom).[17] Which revenues are embraced by these categories also vary, and might or might not include television (broadcasting and/or production), movie theatres, licensing, theme parks, and music publishing. Edward Jay Epstein has suggested that this confusion of categories and terminologies between and within companies is entirely intentional, and is designed to conceal from potential participants in (or claimants on) studio revenues – equity partners, talent, and so on – the full nature and extent of those revenues. In Epstein's account, this reflects the nature of the contemporary Hollywood studio: not a producer or even a vendor of 'products' in the traditional sense, but 'clearinghouses' across whose books flows a constant stream of revenues to and from a variegated and ramified series of activities, partners and personnel. The studios naturally wish to control this money as much, or failing that as long (so while on their books it can accrue interest and boost their working capital), as possible.[18]

What we do know is that, for example, revenues from filmed entertainment 'content' for Time Warner in 2008 totalled $11 billion, of which 'theatrical product' – including theatrical box office, home video, electronic delivery and television sales – contributed almost $7 billion to total corporate revenues of just under $47 billion, or around 15 per cent.[19] But this only takes us so far in trying to calculate the value of motion pictures to the company: for example, it does not take into account the extent to which theatrical films produced by Warner Bros. and its various subsidiaries and affiliates, such as New Line and Castle Rock, drive subscriptions to Time Warner's premium cable services HBO and Cinemax (as they are certainly intended to). Nor are the revenues generated by motion picture-related merchandise and other media products calculable in this way. For instance, *The Dark Knight*, which earned a staggering $533 million at the domestic box office in 2008, was also a major earner across various iterations in Warner's comic book and licensing divisions. At Sony, where 'pictures' remain a junior partner in the electronic giant's portfolio, the segment's $7.9 billion revenues made up just 9 per cent of total revenues – but again the intellectual property vested in the year's 'locomotive' feature releases like the James Bond film *Quantum of Solace* drove profits in other sectors, such as the quickly growing market for high-definition Blu-Ray players and discs.[20] That same year, revenue from 'studio entertainment' at Disney was $7.3 billion, supplying some 20 per cent of the total (and in dollar terms ranking well behind 'media networks' and just ahead of theme parks).[21] The lower headline figure of just under $6 billion for feature films' contribution to the balance sheet at the less diversified Viacom – who also had blockbuster successes in 2008 with *Iron Man* and *Indiana Jones and the Kingdom of the Crystal Skull*, tied on $318 million each – nonetheless comprised a much larger overall proportion (almost 40 per cent) of revenues.[22]

All of these figures need to be placed in the historical context explored in the preceding chapters: namely that, even though the studios partly renewed their exhibition holdings in the deregulated 1980s (and had never surrendered them overseas), and continue to produce a minority of films in-house, their principal business today is not film production nor exhibition, but financing, distribution and marketing. In reality, this has largely been the case since the shift to independent production in the post-*Paramount* period; today, however, the full industrial logic of that shift has, one might say, been realised. In particular, modern movie marketing recognises, in ways that the studios failed to do in the fifties and sixties, the need to manufacture an audience for each and every film they release, and moreover that that audience will be different from one release to the next. Over the past sixty years the movie audience has not only shrunk and become demographically narrower (increasingly heavily tilted towards young people), but is subject to demographic variation from film to film. So today the studios make full and intensive use of the panoply of modern marketing techniques – from identifying target audiences at the early development stage of a project to the use of audience surveys, focus groups, test screenings and a carefully sequenced marketing campaign from the earliest awareness-building teaser trailers months before release to the immediate pre-release advertising blitzkrieg. The intensive use of television spot advertising (which exploits the studio-owned networks' and cable stations' own extensive research to target both the mass audiences the major networks can still command and particular audience niches such as teens or black viewers) reflects the contemporary realities of audience-capturing.

As we have already seen, in modern movie economics theatrical release plays a crucial but limited role, as the trailblazer or shop window for the far more lucrative chain of downstream revenue-taking opportunities. The family audience – strictly speaking, children (and their parents) and teenagers – is the most important market. Ever since the teenage Luke Skywalker was introduced to audiences in *Star Wars* playing with a toy starfighter, the 'family film' has moved inexorably from an industrially marginal position to a central one. Of the top twenty highest-grossing films in 2008, only three were rated R. Five were animated features, three based on comic books, four were child- or teen-friendly fantasies, three action spectacles with strong child and youth appeal, and two were family comedies.

In 1934, when Walt Disney announced the production of the world's first animated feature, *Snow White and the Seven Dwarfs*, his decision was widely derided as folly. *Snow White and the Seven Dwarfs* became the first film to gross over $100 million. Could Disney have realised the full extent of the windfall profits – in licensed merchandise and repeat business, for starters – that the children's market would offer? Unlikely, given that much of this business would require the transformed consumer market that has unfolded since the 1950s: the world of theme parks (which are closed environments in which every attraction, every concession and every expensive souvenir and item of merchandise promotes and cross-promotes the company brand and delivers revenue for the company), home entertainment – including television, video, computer games – and modern parenting culture, which caters to children's fads and preferences in everything from toys to clothing, food and entertainment on an unprecedented scale. Regardless, today all of the studios produce films which can be intensively marketed to youngsters in all of these forms, most of them directly controlled by the studios themselves.

In some measure, perverse as it sounds, even exhibitors' primary concern is no longer with showing movies as such. Particularly given the extremely favourable terms demanded by distributors in the early, and invariably most lucrative, weeks of a film's release (typically 70:30 or higher in the distributor's favour, including the 'house nut'[23]), for theatre owners a blockbuster movie is above all a means to draw moviegoers to the high-volume, high-margin concession stands (fizzy drinks and popcorn – preferably salty popcorn, as this encourages the purchase of more drinks) where they make their profits. The ways some exhibitors cut corners (and costs) in the projection room – failing to replace fading projector bulbs, automating projection (thus reducing projectionists' oversight), leading to darker and out-of-focus movies – underline that the audience's experience watching the film is not their principal concern. To this extent, Martin Scorsese's recollection – speaking for the whole 'auteur generation' – that he knew the era of personal filmmaking was doomed when the mainstream press started printing weekend grosses in the late 1970s, missed the point. In the studio era, the public obsession with Hollywood production helpfully obscured the mundane businesses of distribution and exhibition which alone justified the expense and trouble of making films in the first place. Today, oddly parallel, the ballyhooed, much-dissected weekend grosses are just vivid ornaments on the real business of making money through video discs and super-size carbonated sugar-water.

In another, even more fundamental sense, to speak of the 'film industry' is, if not yet a misnomer, then heading in that direction: for the role of film itself – the chemically-treated strip of celluloid emulsion which receives light through the camera lens – continues to dwindle in the contemporary entertainment industry. Virtually every picture, of course, makes at least some use of digital effects, if only to 'paint out' extraneous elements (shadows, anachronisms) from the frame. Most major blockbusters are almost wholly reliant on CGI for their major action set pieces, which even if they do not involve actual fantasy elements typically depict stunts and spectacles too dangerous and gargantuan to be performed in 'real life'. All films are now edited digitally, with consequences for pacing and style discussed in the last chapter. A growing number of films are shot mostly or entirely with digital cameras, including the last two episodes of the second *Star Wars* trilogy (LucasFilm 2002, 2004) and Michael Mann's *Collateral* (DreamWorks 2004). For such films – and of course digital animated features, whose 'cameras' are entirely virtual[24] – the final conversion to a film negative for printing is a retrograde step. Before too long, however, this too may become a minority practice: MPAA statistics record that the number of digital screens had grown to comprise 14 per cent of all US screens by 2008 (up nearly a fifth on the previous year).[25]

It is not invariably the case that new technology, as one might assume, enhances technical quality. Colour balancing, for example, a time-consuming and complex yet vital final stage in the preparation of the answer print,[26] is now accomplished by converting the entire film into an easily manipulated and adjusted 'digital intermediate' – notwithstanding that this convenience actually entails some minor degradation in image quality. More abstractly, cinephiles and film theorists continue to debate the philosophical implications of the incipient abandonment of film's (and photography's) 'indexical contract' – the guarantee that what appears onscreen records a place, object or organism that in fact existed, sharing a time and space with the camera, the passage of light through whose 'eye' (the lens) is in fact the physical transcription of that object's then-presence.

Movies, however – film or digital – still matter in Hollywood, notwithstanding all the challenges to their pre-eminence. Notwithstanding the relatively minor role of movies within Sony's business, the 40 per cent second-weekend drop-off in *Spider-Man* 3's US box office prompted a $1.41 drop in Sony's share price in one day. This has as much to do with industry traditions and status as with cold hard cash. Unsentimental as they are, studio bosses today still like to see themselves as the heirs to the moguls who founded the companies whose names today's media conglomerates mostly still bear. Directors feel at least as strongly attached to film in the traditional sense: when Steven Soderbegh's independently financed, digitally filmed murder-mystery *Bubble* was released simultaneously in theatres and on pay-cable in 2006, digital download and DVD, Tim Burton worried this would destroy film as an art form and M. Night Shyamalan declared he would rather stop making movies than see DVDs compete with theatrical releases.[27]

RISKY BUSINESS?

Investing tens or even hundreds of millions of dollars in a given film remains a risky proposition, given all the variables affecting that film's chances of success. Viacom's 2008 annual report declares, typically, that 'the production and distribution of programming, motion pictures, games and other entertainment content are inherently risky business because the revenues we derive from various sources depend primarily on our content's acceptance by the public, which is difficult to predict'.[28] Shifting audience tastes, market competition and economic circumstances all have an impact on profitability. Hollywood consistently portrays its business in such terms as a venturesome and perilous one: doing so enhances, among other things, its chances of a receptive hearing when lobbying legislators and governments to pass laws criminalising de-encryption of DVDs or satellite signals, or reproduction of copyright content – all of course protecting the studios' profits. At the same time, however, the analysis of the ways the film industry has evolved since World War II has shown how the proliferating domain of supplementary ancillary markets, starting in the mid-1950s with telefilm production and network TV broadcasts of theatrical pictures and expanding continuously to the present, and production trends adjusted accordingly towards films that can support such activities – to say nothing of the enormous resources and reserves of their corporate parents – have all largely hedged the studios against the kind of catastrophic losses that almost sank Fox and Columbia in the early 1970s.

This does not, however, mean that making movies is a license to print money, even for the majors. In November 2007 the alarming findings of a confidential advisory report produced by Wall Street bank Merrill Lynch and intended for potential investors were widely circulated in the trade and mainstream press. The report predicted a combined loss for the six majors of nearly $2 billion on their 2006 release slate, with earnings slumping by 5 per cent while costs spiked by more than 13 per cent. The report's author, industry insider Roger Smith, blamed a variety of factors for this anticipated downturn, but his core argument was that complacency induced by the DVD-driven boom of the early 2000s had led to unrealistic earnings and consequent fiscal irresponsibility. The universal assumption of guaranteed downstream earnings had allowed stars to demand, and get, stratospheric gross participation deals that earn them tens of millions of dollars even on loss-making pictures: Disney's costs on such deals rose from $154 million in 2002 to $554 million in 2006. Marketing costs were spiralling out of control: the report cited figures such as a $53.3 million marketing spend on Disney/Pixar's *Cars* and $45.5 million on Warner's *Superman Returns*. These astronomical sums were sustained only by a flow of outside money from hedge funds which itself had inflationary consequences. But Smith identified declining revenues across all of Hollywood's principal profit centres: domestic and overseas box office, television revenues and above all DVD, where sales flatlined as consumers' appetite for replacing their video collections eased off. The increasing fragmentation of the entertainment market, with domestic electronic and online options in particular proliferating and taking more of consumers' leisure time, were also likely threats.

Of course, any attempts to estimate the actual, let alone, the projected profitability of one particular segment of the operations of any of the major conglomerates – such as theatrical box office – are doomed both by the seamless nature of the modern media business, in which the same or related products (a film in theatrical release, the same film – and perhaps later a 'director's cut' or 'expanded edition' – on DVD and various television outlets, publishing spin-offs and tie-ins, film-related merchandise, and so on) circulate through all of a company's various divisions, and by the film industry's notoriously arcane and opaque accounting procedures. And the next season's figures, with theatrical revenues bouncing back strongly, seemed to bear out the studio bosses who dismissed Smith's predictions as speculative and unduly pessimistic.

But the global economic downturn of 2007, followed by the financial crisis and recession of 2008, hit Hollywood just as previous downturns had done. And just as in the mid-1960s, the boom in blockbuster production seemed to have peaked as more ultra-high-budget productions failed to meet inflated expectations. US DVD sales did indeed slide, down more than 7 per cent from 2007 to 2008.[29] The banking crisis saw large banks withdraw as much as $12 billion from the industry. Francis Ford Coppola, who had weathered enough industrial and personal meltdowns to speak with some authority, warned that 'the cinema as we know it is falling apart', and predicted that major Hollywood studios could go under.[30]

The majors' responses were touted as unprecedented in the business press: Disney and Fox announced layoffs and slates of lower-budget productions (in Fox's case by setting up a new youth-oriented division, Fox Atomic). But a longer historical view could see echoes of the early 1950s, when the postwar downturn prompted similar announcements.[31] (Disney's announcement that as of 2008 all its new animated features would be released theatrically in 3-D also echoed Spyros Skouras's declaration in 1953 that all future Fox releases would be in 'Scope.) Meanwhile, even as DVD sales fell away, sales of Blu-Ray discs (which carry premium prices despite almost identical manufacturing costs, and so are more profitable for the studios) began to rise sharply. Tech-savvy creative entrepreneurs like director James Cameron continued to push at the formal (as opposed to the – highly porous – industrial) boundaries dividing traditional moviemaking from computer gaming with projects to develop multimedia texts that would unfold simultaneously on theatrical screens and in online multiplayer games.[32] Marvel Comics' clever financing arrangements to produce the well-received *Iron Man* (2008, distributed by Paramount) and other superhero films itself proved that the industry could still be energised by infusions of new ideas; while Disney's acquisition of Marvel shortly before this book went to press in summer 2009 indicated in turn that the majors would be, as ever, quick to adapt such innovations to their own needs.[33]

This is not to say that the challenges the majors faced at the end of the first decade of the twentieth century were not real and severe. But over the seven decades since the end of World War II, the Hollywood film industry has had to reinvent itself several times, institutionally, aesthetically and ideologically: partnering with television in response to the *Paramount* decision and the postwar drop in attendances; discovering new audiences and conjuring the new, convention-busting filmmaking styles of the Hollywood Renaissance from the wreckage of the roadshow era; and evolving in the deregulated, globalised media environments since the 1980s into today's diversified multi-national media conglomerates. Although some of these companies still bear the names of men like William Fox, Jack Warner and Louis B. Mayer, their sophisticated yet essentially straightforward studio-era business of earning money by distributing the films made by (and at) the studios themselves to theatres owned by themselves and others has been transformed beyond their imaginings. It should not be forgotten, however, that 'classical Hollywood cinema' was, when these men created it, not 'classical' at all, but an entirely new way of creating and delivering mass entertainment. By the same token, there seems little reason to doubt that what the world still knows as 'Hollywood' will continue to reinvent itself for the as-yet-unforeseeable entertainment worlds of the next fifty years. Above and beyond any defined or definable set of stylistic parameters or industrial practices, this ongoing reinvention may be the most classical of all Hollywood's enduring traditions.

NOTES

1. Edward Jay Epstein, *The Big Picture: Money and Power in Hollywood* (New York: Random House, 2005), p. 160.
2. Allen J. Scott, *On Hollywood: The Place, the Industry* (Princeton: Princeton University Press, 2005).
3. Epstein, *Big Picture*, pp. 96–7.
4. Sony Annual Report 2009, p. 28.
5. 'Rupert's World' [cover story], *Business Week*, 19 January 2004, pp. 26–9.
6. See Chapter 1.
7. General Agreement on Trade and Tariffs.
8. Source: www.cineuropa.org . Online: http://cineuropa.org/cfocus.aspx?lang=en&documentID=89394&treeID=1618
9. Source: MPAA Theatrical Market Statistics 2008.
10. 'Hollywood meets Bollywood as India's movies go global', *Business Week*, 23 February 2009, p. 18.
11. Richard Schickel, *The Disney Version: The Life, Times, Art and Commerce of Walt Disney* (London: Michael Joseph, 1986), p. 167.
12. With MGM/UA as a third partner from 1981 to 1999.
13. Online: http://www.viacom.com/aboutviacom/Pages/default.aspx
14. Online: http://www.timewarner.com/corp/aboutus/our_company.html
15. Online: http://corporate.disney.go.com/corporate/overview.html
16. The Walt Disney Company *Annual Report 2008*, p. 8.
17. The different segments (film and television) of NBC Universal, which is a subsidiary of the giant industrial conglomerate GE, are not separated out in GE's annual reports.
18. Epstein, *Big Picture*, pp. 111–12.
19. Time Warner *Annual Report 2008*, p. 53.
20. Sony, Inc. *Annual Report 2009*, p. 4. The Japanese fiscal year is reckoned differently from the USA so the periods covered by these reports are not directly comparable, but much of US fiscal 2008 is covered in Sony's 2009 filing.
21. The Walt Disney Company *Annual Report 2008*, p. 1.
22. Viacom, Inc. *Annual Report 2008*, p. 46.
23. The flat-rate fee paid by exhibitors before the division of box office returns.
24. An early Pixar trademark in *Toy Story*, *Monsters, Inc.*, and *Toy Story 2* was the inclusion of 'bloopers' (fluffed 'takes', etc.) in the end credits as a reflexive technological joke.
25. Source: MPAA Theatrical Market Statistics 2008.
26. Colour balancing: adjusting the intensity of colours during film processing. Answer Print: the first positive, fully synched print following colour correction.
27. 'Will bubble burst a Hollywood dogma?', *Business Week*, 24 January 2006, p. 55.
28. Viacom, Inc. *Annual Report 2008*, p. 22.
29. 'Resuscitating the DVD', *The Economist*, 11 July 2009, pp. 63–4.

30. 'Dark future as cash-hit Hollywood slashes new films', *The Guardian*, 19 October 2009, p. 23.
31. 'Disney and Fox narrow their focus', *Business Week*, 23 August 2006, p. 23.
32. 'James Cameron's game theory', *Business Week*, 13 February 2006, p. 40.
33. 'A secret identity for Marvel', *Business Week*, 19 May 2008, p. 34.

Appendix

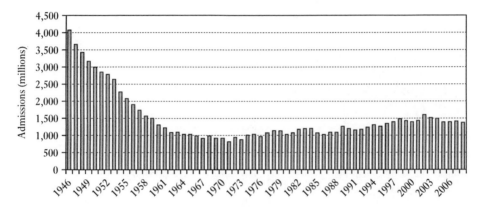

Figure 1 Domestic US cinema attendances 1946–2008.

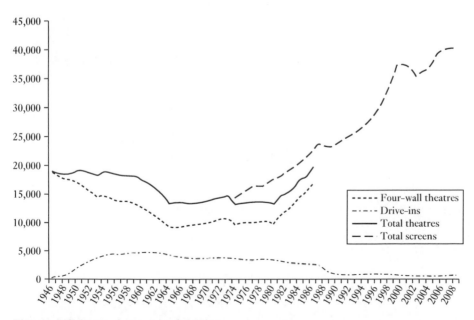

Figure 2 US theatres/screens 1946–2008.

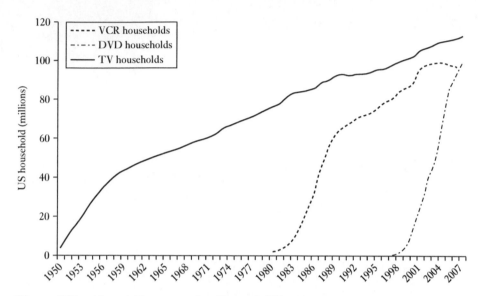

Figure 3 TV and home video penetration, Domestic US 1950–2007.

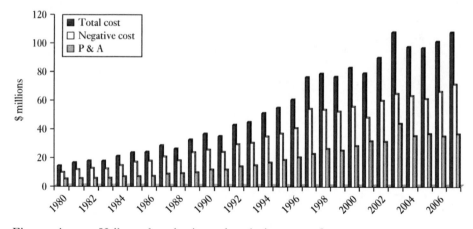

Figure 4 Average Hollywood production and marketing costs 1980–2007.

Further Reading

GENERAL WORKS

Belton, John (2004), *American Cinema/American Culture*, 3rd edn, New York: McGraw-Hill.
Bordwell, David, Janet Staiger and Kristin Thompson (1985), *The Classical Hollywood Cinema: Film Style and Mode of Production to 1960*, London: Routledge.
Cripps, Thomas (1997), *Hollywood's High Noon: Moviemaking and Society before Television*, Baltimore: Johns Hopkins University Press.
Gomery, Douglas (2005), *The Hollywood Studio System: A History*, London: BFI.
Finler, Joel (2003), *The Hollywood Story*, revised edn, London: Wallflower.
Jewell, Richard B. (2007), *The Golden Age of Cinema: Hollywood 1929-1945*, Oxford: Blackwell.
Jowett, Garth (1976), *Film: The Democratic Art*, Boston: Little, Brown.
Langford, Barry (2005), *Film Genre: Hollywood and Beyond*, Edinburgh: Edinburgh University Press.
Lewis, Jon (2007), *American Film*, New York: Norton.
Maltby, Richard (2003), *Hollywood Cinema*, 2nd edn, Oxford: Blackwell.
Neale, Steve (2000), *Genre and Hollywood*, London: Routledge.
Schatz, Thomas (1988), *The Genius of the System: Hollywood Filmmaking in the Studio Era*, New York: Henry Holt.
Williams, Linda Ruth and Michael Hammond (eds) (2005), *Contemporary American Cinema*, Maidenhead: McGraw-Hill.

PART I: HOLLYWOOD IN TRANSITION 1945–65

Chapter 1: The Autumn of the Patriarchs

Anderson, Christopher (1994), *Hollywood TV: The Studio System in the Fifties*, Austin: University of Texas Press.
Balio, Tino (1987), *United Artists: The Company That Changed the Film Industry*, Madison: University of Wisconsin Press.

Biskind, Peter (1983), *Seeing Is Believing: How Hollywood Taught Us to Stop Worrying and Love the Fifties*, New York: Pantheon.

Casper, Drew (2007), *Postwar Hollywood, 1946–1962*, Oxford: Blackwell.

Dixon, Wheeler Winston (ed.) (2006), *American Cinema of the 1940s: Themes and Variations*, Oxford: Berg.

Horne, Gerald (2001), *Class Struggle in Hollywood, 1930–1950: Moguls, Mobsters, Stars, Reds, and Trade Unionists*, Austin: University of Texas Press.

Kashner, Sam and Jennifer MacNair (2003), *The Bad and the Beautiful: Hollywood in the Fifties*, London: Time Warner.

Lev, Peter (2003), *The Fifties: Transforming the Screen, 1950–1959*, Berkeley: University of California Press.

McDougal, Dennis (1988), *The Last Mogul: Lew Wasserman, MCA, and the Hidden History of Hollywood*, New York: Crown.

Mann, Denise (2008), *Hollywood Independents: The Postwar Talent Takeover*, Minnesota: University of Minneapolis Press.

Pomerance, Murray (ed.) (2006), *American Cinema of the 1950s: Themes and Variations*, Oxford: Berg.

Schatz, Thomas (1997), *Boom and Bust: American Cinema in the 1940s*, Berkeley: University of California Press.

Wilinsky, Barbara (2001), *Sure Seaters: The Emergence of Art House Cinema*, Minneapolis: University of Minnesota Press.

Chapter 2: The Communication of Ideas

Ceplair, Larry and Steven Englund (1983), *The Inquisition in Hollywood: Politics in the Film Community, 1930–1960*, Berkeley: University of California Press.

Cohan, Steven (1997), *Masked Men: Masculinity and Movies in the Fifties*, Bloomington: Indiana University Press.

Doherty, Thomas (2007), *Hollywood's Censor: Joseph L. Breen and the Production Code Administration*, New York: Columbia University Press.

Film Noir

Bould, Mark (2005), *Film Noir: From Berlin to Sin City*, London: Wallflower.

Cameron, Ian (ed.) (2003), *The Movie Book of Film Noir*, London: Studio Vista.

Chopra-Gant, Mike (2005), *Hollywood Genres and Postwar America: Masculinity, Family and Nation in Popular Movies and Film*, London: I. B. Tauris.

Dimendberg, Edward (2004), *Film Noir and the Spaces of Modernity*, Cambridge, MA: Harvard University Press.

Kaplan, E. Ann (1998), *Women in Film Noir*, 2nd edn, London: BFI.

Krutnik, Frank (1991), *In a Lonely Street: Film Noir, Genre, Masculinity*, London: Routledge.

Naremore, James (1998), *More Than Night: Film Noir in its Contexts*, Berkeley: University of California Press.

Polan, Dana (1986), *Power and Paranoia: History, Narrative, and the American Cinema, 1940–1950*, New York: Columbia University Press.

Spicer, Andrew (2002), *Film Noir*, London: Arnold.

Chapter 3: Modernising Hollywood

Belton, John (1992), *Widescreen Cinema*, Cambridge, MA: Harvard University Press.

Bordwell, David (2008), 'CinemaScope: the modern miracle you see without glasses', in *Poetics of Cinema*, New York: Routledge, pp. 281–325.

Cowie, Elizabeth (1998), 'Storytelling: classical Hollywood cinema and classical narration', in Steve Neale and Murray Smith (eds), *Contemporary Hollywood Cinema*, London: Routledge, pp. 178–90.

Hansen, Miriam (1999), 'The mass production of the senses: classical cinema as vernacular modernism', *Modernism/Modernity*, 6 (2):59–77.

Kindem, Gorham (1982), 'Hollywood's conversion to color: the technical, economic and aesthetic factors', in Gorham Kindem (ed.), *The American Movie Industry: The Business of Motion Pictures*, Carbondale, IL: Southern Illinois University Press, pp. 146–58.

Neale, Steve (1985), *Cinema and Technology: Image, Sound, Colour*, London: Macmillan Education.

Salt, Barry (1992), *Film Style and Technology: History and Analysis*, London: Starword.

PART II: CRISIS AND RENAISSANCE 1966–81

Chapter 4: The Changing of the Guard

Bach, Steven (1985), *Final Cut: Dreams and Disaster in the Making of* Heaven's Gate, New York: William Morrow.

Balio, Tino (ed.) (1990), *Hollywood in the Age of Television*, Boston: Unwin Hyman.

Bart, Peter (1990), *Fade Out: The Calamitous Final Days of MGM*, New York: William Morrow.

Biskind, Peter (1998), *Easy Riders, Raging Bulls: How the Sex'n'Drugs'n'Rock'n'Roll Generation Changed Hollywood*, London: Bloomsbury.

Bodroghkozy, Aniko (2002), 'Reel revolutionaries: an examination of Hollywood's cycle of 1960s youth rebellion films', *Cinema Journal*, 41 (3):38–58.

Cook, David A. (1998), 'Auteur cinema and the "Film Generation" in 1970s Hollywood', in Jon Lewis (ed.), *The New American Cinema*, Durham: Duke University Press, pp. 11–37.

Cook, David A. (2000), *Lost Illusions: American Cinema in the Shadow of Watergate and Vietnam*, Berkeley: University of California Press.

Corrigan, Timothy (1998), 'Auteurs in the New Hollywood', in Jon Lewis (ed.), *The New American Cinema*, Durham: Duke University Press, pp. 38–63.

Corrigan, Timothy (1991), *A Cinema Without Walls: Movies and Culture After Vietnam*, New Brunswick, NJ: Rutgers University Press.

Dick, Bernard F. (2001), *Engulfed: The Death of Paramount Pictures and the Birth of Corporate Hollywood*, Lexington: University Press of Kentucky.

Elsaesser, Thomas and Andrew Horwath (eds) (2004), *The Last Great American Picture Show: The New Hollywood of the 1970s*, Amsterdam: Amsterdam University Press.

Friedman, Lester D, (ed.) (2007), *American Cinema of the 1970s: Themes and Variations*, Oxford: Berg.

Grant, Barry Keith (ed.) (2008), *American Cinema of the 1970s: Themes and Variations*, New Brunswick, NJ: Rutgers University Press.

Grant, William R. (2004), 'The Political Economy of Blaxploitation', in William R. Grant (ed.), *Post-soul Black Cinema: Discontinuities, Innovations, and Breakpoints, 1970–1995*, New York: Routledge, pp. 27–49.

Gustafson, Robert (1985), 'What's Happening to Our Pix Biz? From Warner Bros, to Warner Communications, Inc.', in Tino Balio (ed.), *The American Film Industry*, 2nd edn, Madison: Wisconsin University Press, pp. 574–86.

King, Geoff (2001), *New Hollywood Cinema: An Introduction*, London: I. B. Tauris.

Kolker, Robert Philip (2001), *A Cinema of Loneliness: Penn, Stone, Kubrick, Scorsese, Spielberg, Altman*, 3rd edn, New York: Oxford University Press.

Krämer, Peter (2005), *The New Hollywood: From* Bonnie and Clyde *to* Star Wars, London: Wallflower.

Lev, Peter (2000), *American Films of the 1970s: Conflicting Visions*, Austin: University of Texas Press.

Lewis, Jon (2000), *Hollywood v. Hard Core: How the Struggle Over Censorship Saved the Modern Film Industry*, New York: New York University Press.

Lewis, Jon (1995), *Whom God Wishes to Destroy . . .: Francis Coppola and the New Hollywood*, London: Athlone.

Monaco, Paul (2001), *The Sixties, 1960–1969*, Berkeley: University of California Press.

Neale, Steve (2005), '"The Last Good Time We Ever Had?": revising the Hollywood Renaissance', in Linda Ruth Williams and Michael Hammond (eds) (2005), *Contemporary American Cinema*, Maidenhead: McGraw-Hill, pp. 90–108.

Schatz, Thomas (1993), 'The new Hollywood', in Jim Collins, Hilary Radner and Ava Preacher Collins (eds), *Film Theory Goes to the Movies*, London: Routledge, pp. 8–36.

Chapter 5: New Wave Hollywood

Carroll, Noel (1982), 'The future of an allusion: Hollywood in the seventies (and beyond)', *October*, 20: 51–81.

Krämer, Peter (1998), 'Post-classical Hollywood', in John Hill and Pamela Church Gibson (eds), *The Oxford Guide to Film Studies*, Oxford: Oxford University Press, pp. 289–309.

Prince, Stephen (1998), *Savage Cinema: Sam Peckinpah and the Rise of Ultra-Violent Movies*, London: Athlone.

Ray, Robert B. (1985), *A Certain Tendency of the Hollywood Cinema, 1930–1980*, Princeton: Princeton University Press.

Sarris, Andrew (1985), *The American Cinema: Directors and Directions, 1929–1968*, Chicago: University of Chicago Press.

Schaefer, Dennis and Larry Salvato (eds) (1984), *Masters of Light: Conversations with Contemporary Cinematographers*, Berkeley: University of California Press.

Chapter 6: Who Lost the Picture Show?

Berliner, Todd (2001), 'The genre film as booby trap: 1970s genre bending and *The French Connection*', *Cinema Journal*, 40 (3): 25–46.

Elsaesser, Thomas (2004), 'The pathos of failure: American films in the 1970s: notes on the unmotivated hero', in Thomas Elsaesser and Andrew Horwath (eds), *The Last Great American Picture Show: The New Hollywood of the 1970s*, Amsterdam: Amsterdam University Press, pp. 279–92.

Heffernan, Kevin (2002), 'Inner-city exhibition and the genre film: distributing *Night of the Living Dead* (1968)', *Cinema Journal*, 41 (3): 59–77.

Jameson, Fredric (1992), *The Geopolitical Aesthetic: Cinema and Space in the World System*, London: BFI.

Neale, Steve (1976), 'New Hollywood cinema', *Screen*, 17 (2): 117–22.

Ryan, Michael and Douglas Kellner (1998), *Camera Politica: The Politics and Ideology of Contemporary Hollywood Film*, Bloomington: Indiana University Press.

Schroeder, Andrew (2003), 'The Movement Inside: BBS Films and the Cultural Left in the New Hollywood', in Van Gosse and Richard Moser (eds), *The World the Sixties Made*, Philadelphia: Temple University Press, pp. 101–20.

Wood, Robin (1986), *Hollywood from Vietnam to Reagan*, New York: Columbia University Press.

The Western

Cameron, Ian and Douglas Pye (eds) (1996), *The Movie Book of the Western*, London: Studio Vista.

Kitses, Jim (2007), *Horizons West: The Western from John Ford to Clint Eastwood*, 2nd edn, London: BFI.

PART III: NEW HOLLYWOOD 1982–2006

Chapter 7: Corporate Hollywood

Balio, Tino (1998), '"A major presence in all of the world's important markets": the globalization of Hollywood in the 1990s', in Steve Neal and Murray Smith (eds), *Contemporary Hollywood Cinema*, London: Routledge, pp. 58–73.

Buckland, Warren (2003), 'The role of the auteur in the age of the blockbuster', in Julian Stringer (ed.), *Movie Blockbusters*, London: Routledge, pp. 84–98.

Hall, Sheldon (2002), 'Tall revenue features: the genealogy of the modern blockbuster', in Steve Neale (ed.), *Genre and Contemporary Hollywood*, London: BFI, pp. 11–26.

Lewis, Jon (1998), 'Money matters: Hollywood in the corporate era', in Jon Lewis (ed.), *The New American Cinema*, Durham: Duke University Press, pp. 87–124.

Lewis, Jon (ed.) (2001), *The End of Cinema As We Know It: American Film in the Nineties*, London: Pluto.

Lewis, Jon (ed.) (2001), *The New American Cinema*, Durham: Duke University Press.

Kimmel, Daniel L. (2006), *The Dream Team: The Rise and Fall of DreamWorks: Lessons from the New Hollywood*, Chicago: Ivan R. Dee.

Neale, Steve and Murray Smith (eds) (1998), *Contemporary Hollywood Cinema*, London: Routledge.

McDonald, Paul (2007), *Video and DVD Industries*, London: BFI.

Pokorny, Michael (2005), 'Hollywood and the risk environment of movie production in the 1990s', in John Sedgwick and Michael Pokorny (eds), *An Economic History of Film*, London: Routledge, pp. 277–311.

Prince, Stephen (2000), *A New Pot of Gold: Hollywood Under the Electronic Rainbow, 1980–1990*, Berkeley: University of California Press.

Sedgwick, John and Michael Pokorny (eds) (2005), *An Economic History of Film*, London: Routledge.

Vogel, Harold (2001), *Entertainment Industry Economics*, 4th edn, New York: Cambridge University Press.

Wasko, Janet (1995), *Hollywood in the Information Age: Beyond the Silver Screen*, Austin: University of Texas Press.

Wasser, Frederick (2001), *Veni, Vidi, Video: The Hollywood Empire and the VCR*, Austin: University of Texas Press.

Wyatt, Justin (1994), *High Concept: Movies and Marketing in Hollywood*, Austin: University of Texas Press.

Independent and Indiewood film

Andrew, Geoff (1998), *Stranger Than Paradise: Maverick Filmmakers in Recent American Cinema*, London: Prion.

Biskind, Peter (2004), *Down and Dirty Pictures: Miramax, Sundance, and the Rise of Independent Film*, New York: Simon & Schuster.

Hillier, Jim (ed.) (2001), *American Independent Cinema: A Sight and Sound Reader*, London: BFI.

King, Geoff (2009), *American Independent Cinema*, London: I. B. Tauris.

King, Geoff (2009), *Indiewood, USA*, London: I. B. Tauris.

Kleinhans, Chuck (1998), 'Independent features: hopes and dreams', in Jon Lewis (ed.), *The New American Cinema*, Durham: Duke University Press, pp. 307–27.

Levy, Emmanuel (1999), *Cinema of Outsiders: The Rise of American Independent Film*, New York: New York University Press.

MacDonald, Scott (ed.) (1992), *A Critical Cinema 2: Interviews with Independent Filmmakers*, Berkeley: University of California Press.

MacDonald, Scott (1998), *A Critical Cinema 3: Interviews with Independent Filmmakers*, Berkeley: University of California Press.

Perren, A. (2001–2), 'Sex, lies and marketing: Miramax and the development of the quality Indie blockbuster', *Film Quarterly*, 55 (2): 30–9.

Pribram, Deidre (ed.) (2002), *Cinema and Culture: Independent Film in the United States, 1980–2001*, New York: Peter Lang.

Sconce, Jeffrey (2002), 'Irony, nihilism and the new American "smart" film', *Screen*, 43 (4): 349–69.

Tziuomakis, Yannis (2005), *American Independent Cinema: An Introduction*, Edinburgh: Edinburgh University Press.

Waterman, David (2005), *Hollywood's Road to Riches*, Cambridge, MA: Harvard University Press.

Wyatt, Justin (1998), 'The formation of the "major independent": Miramax, New Line and the New Hollywood', in Steve Neal and Murray Smith (eds), *Contemporary Hollywood Cinema*, London: Routledge, pp. 74–90.

Wyatt, Justin (2000), 'Independents, packaging, and inflationary pressure in 1980s Hollywood', in Stephen Prince, *A New Pot of Gold: Hollywood Under the Electronic Rainbow, 1980–1990*, Berkeley: University of California Press, pp. 142–60.

Chapter 8: Culture Wars

Aaron, Michelle (2004), *New Queer Cinema: A Critical Reader*, Edinburgh: Edinburgh University Press.

Adair, Gilbert (1989), *Hollywood's Vietnam*, London: Heinemann.

Anderegg, Michael (ed.) (1991), *Inventing Vietnam: The War in Film and Television*, Philadelphia: Temple University Press.

Arroyo, Jose (ed.) (2000), *Action/Spectacle Cinema*, London: BFI.

Diawara, Manthia (ed.) (1993), *Black American Cinema*, London: Routledge.

Dixon, Wheeler Winston (ed.) (2000), *Film Genre 2000: New Critical Essays*, Albany: State University of New York Press.

Jeffords, Susan (1989), *The Remasculinization of America: Gender and the Vietnam War*, Bloomington: Indiana University Press.

Jeffords, Susan (1994), *Hard Bodies: Hollywood Masculinity in the Reagan Era*, New Brunswick, NJ: Rutgers University Press.

Klein, Michael (1994), 'Beyond the American dream: film and the experience of defeat', in Michael Klein (ed.), *An American Half-Century: Postwar Culture and Politics in the U.S.A.*, London: Pluto.

Nadel, Alan (1997), *Flatlining on the Field of Dreams: Cultural Narratives in the Films of President Reagan's America*, New Brunswick, NJ: Rutgers University Press.

Neale, Steve (ed.) (2002), *Genre and Contemporary Hollywood*, London: BFI.

Pfeil, Fred (1998), 'From pillar to postmodern: race, class, and gender in the male rampage film', in Jon Lewis (ed.), *The New American Cinema*, Durham: Duke University Press, pp. 146–86.

Prince, Stephen (1992), *Visions of Empire: Political Imagery in Contemporary American Film*, New York: Praeger.

Tasker, Yvonne (ed.) (2004) *Action and Adventure Cinema*, London: Routledge.

Chapter 9: Post-Classical Style?

Bukatman, Scott (1998), 'Zooming out: the end of offscreen space', in Jon Lewis (ed.), *The New American Cinema*, Durham: Duke University Press, pp. 248–72.

Bordwell, David (2005), *The Way Hollywood Tells It: Story and Style in Modern Movies*, Berkeley: University of California Press.

Buckland, Warren (1998), 'A close encounter with *Raiders of the Lost Ark*: notes on narrative aspects of the new Hollywood blockbuster', in Steve Neale and Murray Smith (eds), *Contemporary Hollywood Cinema*, London: Routledge, pp. 166–77.

Elsaesser, Thomas and Warren Buckland (2002), *Studying Contemporary American Film: A Guide to Movie Analysis*, London: Arnold.

King, Geoff (2000), *Spectacular Narratives: Hollywood in the Age of the Blockbuster*, London: I. B. Tauris.

King, Geoff (2005), 'Spectacle and narrative in the contemporary blockbuster', in Linda Ruth Williams and Michael Hammond (eds), *Contemporary American Cinema*, Maidenhead: McGraw-Hill, pp. 334–52.

Knapp, Larry (2008), 'Tony Scott and *Domino* – Say hello (and goodbye) to the postclassical', *Jump Cut* 2008; 50(Spring). Online: http://ejumpcut.org/archive/jc50.2008/DominoKnapp/index.html

Murray Smith (1998), 'Theses on the philosophy of Hollywood history', in Steve Neale and Murray Smith (eds), *Contemporary Hollywood Cinema*, London: Routledge, pp. 3–20.

Pierson, Michelle (2002), *Special Effects: Still In Search of Wonder*, New York: Columbia University Press.

Stringer, Julian (ed.) (2003), *Movie Blockbusters*, London: Routledge.

Thompson, Kristin (1999), *Storytelling in the New Hollywood: Analyzing Classical Narrative Technique*, Cambridge, MA: Harvard University Press.

Conclusion: 'Hollywood' Now

Epstein, Edward Jay (2005), *The Big Picture: Money and Power in Hollywood*, New York: Random House.

Grainge, Paul (2008), *Brand Hollywood: Selling Entertainment in a Global Media Age*, London: Routledge.

Miller, Toby, Nitin Govil, John McMurria, Richard Maxwell and Ting Wang (2005), *Global Hollywood 2*, London: BFI.

Scott, Allen J. (2005), *On Hollywood: The Place, the Industry*, Princeton: Princeton University Press.

Wasko, Janet (2003), *How Hollywood Works*, London: Sage.

Wasko, Janet and Paul McDonald (eds) (2007), *The Contemporary American Film Industry*, Oxford: Blackwell.

Index

Academy of Motion Pictures Arts and Sciences, 76–7
'Academy ratio', 82, 85, 86, 94 n.18
Academy Awards, 159, 195, 196, 205, 228, 237, 238, 261
Ace in the Hole (1950), 53
action films, 230–5, 247–8, 254
adult theatres, 99–100
African-Americans in movies, 43 n.2, 50, 217; *see also* blaxploitation
After Hours (1985), 207
AIP (American International Pictures), 127, 160, 162, 195, 210
Airport (1970), 116, 125, 134
Alice Doesn't Live Here Anymore (1974), 168, 177
Alien (1979), 199, 207, 219, 221
Aliens (1986), 221, 252, 254
Alien vs. Predator (2004), 206–7, 254
All That Jazz (1980), 127
All the Pretty Horses (2000), 260
Allen, Dede, 142
Allen, Robert C., 74
Allen, Woody, 117, 119, 195, 229
Allied Artists, 33
Althusser, Louis, 219
Altman, Robert, 117, 118, 152, 162–3, 165–6, 169, 208, 259
allusionism, 167–9, 258–9
American in Paris, An (1951), 58, 69
American Graffiti (1973), 154, 170, 217, 218 n.2, 258
American Multi-Cinemas (AMC), 124, 183

American Zoetrope, 229
Animal House (1978), 126–7, 174
Apocalypse Now (1979), 127, 143, 172, 225, 258
Arbuckle, Roscoe ('Fatty'), 49
Ardrey, Robert, 64, 118
Around the World in Eighty Days (1956), 87, 261
arthouse cinemas, 99–100, 138, 186–7
Ashley, Ted, 113
ASLs, 83–4, 141–2, 254–5
Aubrey, James, 112–13

BBS, 118, 161
B-films, 4, 33
Back to the Future (1985), 183, 185, *190*, 216–17, 231, 232, 265
Barry Lyndon (1975), 149, 170
Bataan (1943), 225
Batman (1989), 185, 201, 207, 224, 231, 246
Bay, Michael, 208, 246, 253, 255
Bazin, André, xii–xiii, 42, 83
Beatty, Warren, 119
Ben-Hur (1959), 9, 34, 43, 69
Benjamin, Robert, 25–6, 38 n.31, 70, 110, 112, 195
Bergman, Ingmar, 150, 259
Berkeley, Busby, 79, 81, 89, 93 n.11
Best Years of Our Lives, The (1946), xii, *12*, 24, 41–4, 52, 53, 78, 87, 227, 254, 265
Beyond a Reasonable Doubt (1955), 92
'Big Five', 3, 16, 19–20, 24, 79, 184
Big Sleep, The (1945), 80

Billy Jack (1971), 123, 130 n.32
Birth of a Nation, The (1915), 48, 74, 75, 89, 121
Black Hawk Down (2001), 233
Blackboard Jungle, The (1955), 88
blacklist, 55–7
Blade Runner (1982), 219, 224, 246
blaxploitation, 121, 122–3, 160, 259
blockbusters, 32–6, 206–10, 230–5, 246, 247–54
Blow-Up (1966), 135
Blue Collar (1978), 177
Bluhdorn, Charles, 110–11, 112, 113, 197
Bogdanovich, Peter, 117, 118, 119, 162, 168–9, 207, 259
Bonnie and Clyde (1967), 115, 134, 142, 143, 147, 160
Bordwell, David, xii–xiii, 77, 80, 81, 83–4, 87, 134, 135–6, 141, 148, 150, 246–7, 253, 254, 255, 261
Born on the Fourth of July (1989), 227, 229, 230
Braveheart (1995), 241
Brecht, Bertolt, 67 n.12, 78, 93 n.10
Breen, Joseph, 13, 49, 50, 64–5
Bride of Frankenstein (1935), 79
Bridge on the River Kwai, The (1957), 35, 57, 69
Brokeback Mountain (2005), 205, 262
Bruckheimer, Jerry, 209, 246, 247, 256
Bukatman, Scott, 245–7, 248
Bulworth (1998), 237, 238
Butch Cassidy and the Sundance Kid (1969), 136, 164, 169
Burstyn v. Wilson see Miracle judgment
Burton, Tim, 208, 280
Bush, George W., 221, 223, 227, 233
Bwana Devil (1952), 83

cable television, 102–3, 188, 198
Cagney, James, 15, 24, 70
Cameron, James, 208, 282
Capra, Frank, 15, 25, 41, 50, 51, 183
Carolco, 210–11, 267
Carrey, Jim, 235
Carroll, Noel, 167
Casablanca (1943), 78, 150
Chaplin, Charles, 50–1, 56
Chapman, Michael, 146
Chinatown (1974), 141, 167, 170, 219

Chrétien, Henri, 82, 83
'cinema of attractions', 88–9,
Cimino, Michael, 117, 127–8
Cinerama, 34, 72, 81, 82–3, 88
CinemaScope, 6, 34, 81, 83–8, 94 n.15, n.21, 251
Citizen Kane (1941), 42, 81, 148
Classical Hollywood Cinema, The, xii–xiv, xv, 80, 135–6, 147, 151
classical Hollywood style, 282
Clear and Present Danger (1994), 232
Cleopatra (1963), 36, 87, 108, 116,
Clinton, Bill, 221–2, 223, 224, 227, 238
Clockwork Orange, A (1971), 121, 143, 149, 172
Close Encounters of the Third Kind (1977), 126, 248–50
Coca-Cola, 191–2
Coen Brothers, 262, 265
Cohn, Harry, 37 n.2
Collateral (2004), 266, 279
Color of Money, The (1986), 207
Columbia Pictures, 15, 30, 37 n.2, n.3, 108, 109, 191–2; *see also* Screen Gems; Coca-Cola; Sony
colour, 90–1, 95 n.35
Columbus, OH, xvi, 3–9, 64, 99–103, 138, 183–9
Coming Home (1978), 226–7
computer-generated imagery (CGI), 234–5
conspiracy films, 162, 175–6
Constant Gardener, The (2002), 237, 256
contract system, 14–15, 23–4
continuity system, 75–6, 80
Conversation, The (1974), 135–6, 143
Cook, David A., 49
Coppola, Francis Ford, 117–18, 119, 127, 196, 207, 258, 282
Corman, Roger, 119, 162
Crash (2005), 238, 253, 265–7
Crossfire (1947), 52, 53
Cruising (1980), 144, 172
Cukor, George, 87, 118
Cutter's Way (1981), 172, 174

Dark Knight, The (2008), xii, 277
Davis, Martin, 112, 193
Davis, Marvin, 191–2, 213 n.5
Dead Presidents (1994), 229, 230
Deer Hunter, The (1978), 175, 225

DEG, 210
DeMille, Cecil B., 34, 36, 43, 55, 78, 90
Demopoulos, Maria, 261
dePalma, Brian, 161, 257, 258
Devil Is a Woman, The (1935), 79, 81
Die Hard (1986), 208, 231, 232, 233, 271
Die Harder (1990), 232
digital cinema, 207, 279–80
Digital Millennium Copyright Act 2000, 274
Diller, Barry, 127
'Direct Cinema', 145
Dirty Dozen, The (1967), 159
Dirty Harry (1971), 160, 170, 232
Dixon, Wheeler Winston, 261
Douglas, Kirk, 36, 56, 70
drive-ins, 7–8, 61, 122
Disney, Walt, 14, 27, 31–2, 49, 55, 109, 275, 278; *see also* Walt Disney Company
Disneyland (TV show), 31–2
DreamWorks SKG, 196–7, 271, 273, 275
DVD, 188, 199, 201–2, 263, *268*, 274, 281, 282; *see also* video

Earthquake (1974), 252
EastmanColor, 90
Eastwood, Clint, 119, 231–2
Easy Rider (1969), 115, 141, 146, 147, 148, 160, 169, 173, 174, 178, 227, 257, 258
Ebert, Roger, 151
editing, 260–1; *see also* continuity system
Eisenhower, Dwight D., 45–6
Eisner, Michael, 193
Elmer Gantry (1960), 9, 66
Emmerich, Roland, 208
epics, 34, 248
E.T. (1982), 137, 201, 219
Evans, Robert, 113, 117
Exorcist, The (1973), 121, 123, 124

Fail-Safe (1964), 92
family audience, 235
Farewell to Arms, A (1932), 170
'fascist aesthetics', 249–50
Federal Communications Commission (FCC), 10 n.13, 29, 198, 199
Fight Club (1999), 234, 237, 253
film festivals, 139, 212
film noir, 52–4, 57, 81, 148
film schools, 119, 138–9
film stock, 77, 90

Fincher, David, 256, 259–60
Fine Line, 205
Five Easy Pieces (1970), 144, 150, 151, 172, 254
First Blood (1982), 227
Force of Evil (1948), 53, 170
Ford, John, 58, 78, 92, 118, 163, 165–6, 168, 259
Forman, Milos, 119, 154, 195
Forrest Gump (1994), 220, 228–9
Frankenheimer, John, 92, 118
French Connection, The (1971), 160, 170
Friedkin, William, 117, 118, 127, 207
Fuller, Sam, 86, 92
Funny Girl (1968), 116, 134, 159

Geffen, David, 196, 202, 224
General Cinema, 124, 184
genre, xv, 162
Gentleman's Agreement (1947), 42, 52
Getaway, The (1972), 117, 137–8, 142–3
Girl Can't Help It, The (1958), 87
globalisation, 270, 272–5
Go Fish (1994), 236
Godard, Jean-Luc, 136, 139, 150, 151, 153 n.24, 259
Godfather, The (1972), 111, 117–18, 124, 125, 143, 146, 172, 175, 177, 178
Godfather, Part II, The (1974), 149
Goldwyn, Samuel, 3, 15, 16, 41, 43 n.3, 77
Gone With the Wind (1939), 80, 89, 141
Graduate, The (1967), *108*, 115, 133–4, 147, 160, 257
Grease (1979), 126, 258
Greatest Show on Earth, The (1952), 156
Greatest Story Ever Told, The (1965), 102
Green Berets, The (1968), 159, 225
Gremlins (1984), 183
Griffith, D. W., 74, 75, 251
Gulf + Western, 110–11, 191, 193
Gunning, Tom, 88–9, 247

Haggis, Paul, 266–7
Hammond, Michael, 216
Harry Potter and the Prisoner of Azkaban (2004), 203
Haynes, Todd, 237
Hays Code *see* Production Code Administration
HBO, 188, 198

Head (1968), 141, 145
Heartbreak Ridge (1986), 232
Heaven's Gate (1980), 127–8, 166, 170, 203, 207
Hecht-Hill-Lancaster, 26, 47, 69–70
Herrmann, Bernard, 257
Hill, The (1965), 92
Hiller, Jim, xiv
High Noon (1952), 56, 58, 165
Hitchcock, Alfred, 91–2, 118
Hollywood Renaissance, xiv, 79, 118, 125–7, 134–52, 154–5, 161–79, 207–8, 219–21, 225, 237, 238, 246, 247, 251, 254, 258, 282
'Hollywood Ten', 46, 55, 56
Hopper, Dennis, 119, 127
horror film, 121
Howard, Ron, 208
HUAC (House UnAmerican Activities Committee), 35, 43, 47, 54–7, 63, 110
Hunt's Cinestage (theatre), 8, 98
Hughes, Howard, 20, 31, 110
Hunting Party, The (1971), 137

In the Heat of the Night (1968), 159
Incredibles, The (2004), 204, 206
Independence Day (1996), 204, 233, 234
India, 273, 274
independent production, 3–4, 16, 24–7, 35–6, 139, 210–12, 235–6, 270–1
'Indiewood', 212, 225, 265
Intolerance (1917), 89, 149
Invasion of the Body Snatchers (1955), 60–2
Iraq war (2003), 232, 238
Iron Man (2008), 277, 282
Island, The (2005), 253

Jackie Brown (1997), 259
Jaffe, Leo, 124
Jaffe, Sam, 113, 117
Jameson, Fredric, 176, 259
Jaws (1975), 71 n.2, 122, 124, 125, 150, 154–6, 204
Jazz Singer, The (1927), 86
Jeffords, Susan, 230, 233
Johnson, Lyndon Baines, 157, 229–30
Johnston, Eric, 55, 66 n.6, 150
Journey to the Center of the Earth (2008), 230
Jowett, Garth, 48
Jules et Jim (1963), 136

Jurassic Park (1993), 207, 224, 234, 244, 250–1, 252, 253, 254

Kael, Pauline, 151, 173, 177
Kaplan, E. Ann, 258–9
Karloff, Boris, 162
Katzenberg, Jeffrey, 193, 196, 203, 238
Kazan, Elia, 54, 56, 65, 67 n.13, 69
Kennedy, Robert F., 158–9
Kent State University, 159
Kerkorian, Kirk, 112–13, 128, 194, 195, 197–8, 213 n.25
Kesey, Ken, 154, 155
Kill Bill (2004), 258, 259
King, Geoff, xiv, 151, 153 n.24, 252–3, 255
King Kong (1933), 80
King, Martin Luther, Jr., 157–8
King of Comedy, The (1982), 172
Kinney National Services, 111, 112; *see also* Warner Bros.; Warner Communications
Kinsey, Alfred, 64
Kitses, Jim, 166
Knapp, Larry, 254, 260
Kolker, Robert, 137, 155, 171, 249, 252
Krämer, Peter, xiv, 116, 121
Kramer, Stanley, 25, 36, 38 n.31, 47, 52, 53, 57, 58, 59, 118
Krim, Arthur, 25–6, 38 n.31, 70, 110, 112, 195
Kubrick, Stanley, 58, 66, 86, 92, 149

Ladd, Alan Jr., 129
Lang, Fritz, 92, 259
Lasseter, John, 241
Last Movie, The (1971), 127, 134
Last Picture Show, The (1971), 134, 138, 168–9, 187
Leaving Las Vegas (199x), xxx, 260
Lee, Ang, 262
Lee, Spike, 236, 257
Legion of Decency, 49, 63, 64–6
Leone, Sergio, 86, 259
Lethal Weapon (1986), 207, 208, 230, 231, 233
Lev, Peter, 58
Levin, Gerald, 207
Lewis, Jon, 48
Lionsgate, 265–6, 273, 275
Little Big Man (1970), 164–5, 169, 177
'Little Three', 3, 24
Loew's Broad (theatre), 4, 6, 85, 99

Loew's Ohio (theatre), 85, 99, 187
Loew's-MGM *see* MGM
Logan, Joshua, 87
Long Goodbye, The (1973), 147, 169, 170, 257
Lord of the Rings trilogy (2001–2003), 270
Love, Actually (2005), 255
Love Bug, The (1969), 116
Love Story (1970), 116, 124, 125
Lucas, George, 117, 119, 154, 208, 215 n.52, 217, 248, 271
Lumet, Sidney, 92, 118

McCabe & Mrs. Miller (1971), *158*, 165–6, 169
MacCabe, Colin, 136
McTiernan, John, 208
Maltby, Richard, 82, 91, 118
Man On Fire (2004), 260
Man Who Shot Liberty Valance, The (1962), 92
Manchurian Candidate, The (1962), 92
marketing, 155–6, 199, 203, 277–8
Marnie (1964), 92
Marty (1955), 69–71, 261
Marx, Karl, 242
Matrix, The (1999), 208, 219, 224, 234, 241, 259, 270, 273, 274
Matsushita, 192, 193–4
MCA, 8, 26–7, 30, 109; *see also* MCA-Universal
MCA-Universal, 110, 115, 191, 192, 193–4, 252
Mean Streets (1973), 137, 143, 147, 170, 257, 258
Meirelles, Fernando, 237, 256
Mellen, Joan, 163
MGM (Metro-Goldwyn-Mayer), 3, 6, 16, 20, 24, 29, 31, 34, 47, 77, 78, 81, 82, 102, 109, 112–13, 128, 197, 213 n.25
Mickey One (1965), 92–3
Midnight Cowboy (1969), 103, 115, 169
Mills, C. Wright, 61
Mildred Pierce (1945), 53
Milk (2007), 237
Million Dollar Baby (2004), 205, 265
Miramax, 186, 211–12, 215 n.49, 216, 241, 271, 272
Miracle judgment, 63
Missing In Action (1985), 222, 226
Mission: Impossible (1996): 204–5

Moore, Michael, 215 n.49
Motion Picture Alliance, 55
MPAA, 55, 64, 116, 201, 273
MPPDA, 51, 57; *see also* MPAA
MPEA, 51, 57
MTV *see* music video
Mutiny on the Bounty (1962), 102
multiplex cinemas, 102, 124, 183–6
Mummy, The (1998), 230
Murdoch, Rupert, 192; *see also* NewsCorp
music video, 247, 256–60
Mutual v. Ohio, 47–9, 63
My Darling Clementine (1946), 165–6

nabes, 4–5, 6–7, 99–100
Nachbar, Jack, 163
narrative, 73–5, 89, 147–50, 169–72, 246, 247–54, 261, 266–7
Nashville (1976), 152, 173
Natural Born Killers (1994), 237, 255
NBC Universal 272, 276
Neale, Steve, 116, 161
Network (1976), 154
New Black Cinema, 230
New Left, 161, 227
New Line, 211–12, 271, 272
New Queer Cinema, 236–7
New Waves, 84, 93, 107, 119, 134, 136, 139–40, 178
New York, New York (1977), 78, 127, *132*, 167–8, 170–1, 258
NewsCorp, 192, 272–3; *see also* Twentieth Century-Fox
Nichols, Mike, *108*, 117
Night Moves (1975), 144–5, 147, 169
Nixon (1995), 227, 228, 255, 260
Nixon, Richard, 159, 170, 230
No Country for Old Men (2006), 262, 265

Oboler, Arch, 82–3
Obsession (1974), 147
Oliver! (1968), 116
On Golden Pond (1981), 221, 227
On Her Majesty's Secret Service (1969), 136
On the Town (1948), 168
On the Waterfront (1954), 56, 69
One Flew Over the Cuckoo's Nest (1975), 125, 154–6, 169
Orion, 112, 195–6
Othello (1951), 141, 152 n.13

Out of Africa (1985), 216
overseas distribution, 21, 35
Ovitz, Michael, 209
OWI, 51

Pabst, G. W., 77
Pakula, Alan J., 117
Panic Room (2002), 259
Parallax View, The (1974), 145, 147, 169,
    172, 175–6
Paramount Communications, Inc., 193, 194,
    275
Paramount decision, xiv, 6, 10 n.8, 17–21,
    22–3, 28, 31, 32, 37, 56, 61, 65, 90, 107,
    117, 123, 198, 271, 277, 282
Paramount Pictures, 14, 16, 24, 36, 77, 86,
    110–11, 113, 127, 129 n.6; *see also* Gulf +
    Western; Paramount Communications
Pat Garrett and Billy the Kid (1973), 113,
    120, 148, 150, 163, 169
Patton (1970), 173
Pawnbroker, The (1965), 66, 92, 138
pay-per-view, 102
Peckinpah, Sam, 107, 113, 117, 118, 119,
    137–8, 141, 142–3, 162–4, 166, 174, 259
Peacemaker, The (1997), 233
Penn, Arthur, 93, 115, 144–5, 162–3, 164–5,
    169, 259
Pentagon Papers, 179 n.15
Pfeil, Fred, 248
Phantom of the Paradise (1974), 258
Pierson, Michelle, 252
Pirates of the Caribbean (2003), 209, 234, 254
Pixar, 241–3, 276, 283 n.24
Platoon (1986), 222, 225, 228, 265
Play It Again, Sam (1972), 169
Player, The (1992), 169, 211
Pleasantville (1998), 217
Point Blank (1967), 151, 172
Polanski, Roman, 119
Pollack, Sydney, 216
Polonsky, Abraham, 53, 57
postmodernism, 224
'pre-sold' movies, 155–6, 206–7
Preminger, Otto, 36, 57, 64, 65, 70
producer-unit system, 76, 93 n.4
Production Code Administration (PCA), 13,
    47, 49–51, 62–6, 113, 115, 170, 224; *see also*
    ratings system
production costs, 21–2, 42, 202–4

Psycho (1960), 66, 91–2, 95 n.37, 95 n.39, 119
Pulp Fiction (1994), 152, 211, 258, 266
Pye, Douglas, 164

Quigley, Martin, 51

Raiders of the Lost Ark (1981), 125, 128, 206,
    221, 230, 259
Rambo: First Blood Part II (1985), 210, 222,
    226, 227, 232, 233
ratings system, 100, 113–14, 129 n.14, 209,
    231, 278
Ray, Nicholas, 54, 58, 88, 90, 91–2
Reagan, Ronald, 198, 221–3, 227
Reap the Wild Wind (1944), 90
Rear Window (1952), 91
Rebel Without a Cause (1955), 88, 90
Red River (1948), 169
Reds (1981), 128, 178
Redstone, Sumner, 36, 194, 275
release windows, 202–3, 278
Renegades (1946), 85
Republic, 4, 31
Resnais, Alan, 140–1
Return of the Secaucus Seven (1980), 228
Revue Productions, 8, 30, 95 n.39; *see also*
    MCA
Riefenstahl, Leni, 249
Riesman, David, 61
Right Stuff, The (1983), 242, 246
Rivette, Jacques, 84
RKO (Radio-Keith-Orpheum), 3–4, 6, 16,
    20, 31, 78, 208
RKO Grand (theatre), 3, 6, 99
RKO Palace (theatre), 3–4, 6, 24, 99, 187
Road to Utopia (1945), 80
roadshows, 101, 105, 116–17, 248
Robe, The (1953), 34, 83, 85–6, 88
Rock, The (1996), 208, 209
Rocky (1976), 70, 207, 233
Rolling Thunder (1977), 226, 230
Ross, Steven, 111, 112, 191
Rumblefish (1983), 258
run-clearance system, 4–5, 38 n.14, 202
runaway production, 35, 40 n.53, 121

Salt, Barry, 141
Salt of the Earth (1953), 67 n.15
Salvador (1984), 222
Samson and Delilah (1949), 34, 36

Sarris, Andrew, 139
saturation opening, 122–3, 155–6, 186
Saturday Night Fever (1977), 126, 258
Sayles, John, 228
Schary, Dore, 64
Schenck, Joe, 16
Schenck, Nick, 16, 18, 20, 112
Schneider, Bert, 161
Schwarzenegger, Arnold, 210–11, 231, 234
Scorsese, Martin, 78, 119, 144, 167–8, 170–2, 207, 257–8, 279
Scott, Ridley, 208, 246
Scott, Tony, 208, 246, 260
Screen Gems, 30, 31, 109
Searchers, The (1955), 92, 226
Selznick, David O., 3, 16, 24–5, 37 n.7, 41, 89
Seventh Seal, The (1956), 150
sex, lies and videotape (1989), 186, 211, 236
science-fiction film, 33, 58–62, 207, 219–21, 230, 245
Shiel, Mark, 154
Shine (1996), 205
Shock Corridor (1963), 92
Shootist, The (1976), 166
shopping malls, 61, 100, 183–4
Short Cuts (1993), 208, 211, 266
Shurlock, Geoffrey, 65–6
Silk Stockings (1957), 87
Silver, Joel, 208–9, 247
Silver Screen Partners, 197
Simpson, Don, 209, 246, 247, 256
Singin' in the Rain (1952), 80
Sirk, Douglas, 79, 90
Sixth Sense, The (1999), 262
Skouras, Spyros, 10 n.8, 20, 83, 109, 129 n.4, 282
Smith, Murray, 246, 253
Snow White and the Seven Dwarfs (1935), 278
social problem film, 51–2, 57–8
Soldier Blue (1970), 165
Sony, 192, 200, 213 n.25, 272, 276, 277; *see also* Columbia Pictures
Sound of Music, The (1965), 100, 104–6
Space Jam (1997), 207
Spider-Man (2002), 262
spectacle, 80, 88–90, 247–54
Spielberg, Steven, 117, 119, 154–6, 196–7, 208, 248–51, 253, 259, 269 n.11, 273
Steadicam, 146

Stallone, Sylvester, 23
Star Trek (franchise), 207, 242
Star Trek: The Motion Picture (1979), 118, 128
Star Trek II: The Wrath of Khan (1982), 201
Star Wars (1977), 102, 124, 125, 126, 128, 191, 193, 207, 221, 230, 245, 247, 250, 262, 278
Star Wars Episode III: Revenge of the Sith (2005), 265
Starman (1984), 219
Steelyard Blues (1973), 175
stereophonic sound, 94 n.15, 258
Stewart, James, 27, 92
Sting, The (1973), 167
Stone, Oliver, 227–8, 229, 237, 255, 267
Streisand, Barbra, 120, 224
suburbia, 60–1, 62
Sullivan's Travels (1941), 49
Sundance Film Festival, 212
Superman (1979), 125, 128, 193, 207
Superman II (1981), 222

talent agencies, 26–7, 271; *see also* MCA; Wasserman, Lew
Tarantino, Quentin, 211, 258, 259
Taxi Driver (1976), 144, 153 n.24, 171–2, 226
Technicolor, 90
television, 8, 27–32, 62, 100, 108–9, 113, 139, 188, 275–6, 281
'tentpole' releases, 204, 208, 235, 265, 271
Terminator 2: Judgment Day (1991), 210, 211
Thalberg, Irving, 50, 78
They Shoot Horses Don't They? (1969), 148
Thing, The (1981), 219–21
Thornton, Billy Bob, 260
3-D, 81, 82, 85, 251
Three Days of the Condor (1975), 172, 175
Three Kings (1999), 237, 238
Time-Warner, 194, 201, 202, 207, 212, 275, 276–7
Titanic (1997), 204, 205–6, 253
Todd-AO, 87, 88
Toland, Gregg, 42, 43 n.3, 77
Top Gun (1986), 201, 230, 232, 246, 256
Total Recall (1990), 211
Toy Story (1995), 241–3, 283 n.24
Transamerica Corporation, 112
Transformers (2007), 255
Triumph of the Will (1934), 249, 250

Tropic Thunder (2008), 229
Truffaut, François, 136, 139
Truman, Harry S., 45, 54
Truman Show, The (1998), 224
Trumbo, Dalton, 55, 57
Twelve Angry Men (1957), 32, 69
Twentieth Century-Fox, 4, 6, 16, 31, 81, 83,
    104–5, 108, 109, 129 n.4, 191–2, 200, 270,
    271, 272–3, 282; *see also* David, Marvin;
    NewsCorp
2001: A Space Odyssey (1968), 86, 116, 149,
    160, 248

UFA, 77
'Ufa shots', 77
United Artists, 25–6, 38 n.31, 39 n.42, 47, 51,
    69–70, 104, 108, 110, 112, 128
United International Pictures (UIP), 275
Universal Pictures, 4, 10 n.3, 21, 27, 30,
    33, 39 n.49, 109, 129 n.1, 156, 194, 200,
    221, 275; *see also* MCA-Universal; NBC
    Universal
Universal Studios Hollywood (theme park),
    106, 251

Valenti, Jack, 113–14
Viacom, 36, 188, 194, 197, 273, 275, 277, 280
Vera Cruz (1954), 142
vertical integration, 3–4, 6, 14, 198–9
Vertigo (1958), 91
video, 112, 185, 198–202, 213 n.7, 262–3; *see
    also* DVD
Vidor, King, 78
Vietnam War, 113, 121, 157–9, 178, 225–30,
    231–2, 233–4, 239 n.7, n.11
Village Roadshow, 197, 273
VistaVision, 6, 34, 81, 86–7, 88, 94 n.32,
von Sternberg, Josef, 79, 81
von Stroheim, Erich, 78, 81

Wag the Dog (1997), 224
Wall Street (1988), 222
Waller, Fred, 82
Wal-Mart, 209
Walt Disney Company, The, 107, 108, 110,
    115, 191, 193, 194, 197, 200, 212, 215 n.49,
    241–2, 272

Wanger, Walter, 49
war/combat film, 51, 126, 226–8
Warner Bros., 16, 23, 27, 81, 93 n.8, 111, 274,
    275, 281; *see also* Warner Communications
    International; Time-Warner
Warner Communications International
    (WCI), 102–3, 112, 191, 193, 194; *see also*
    Kinney Services International; Warner
    Bros.; Time-Warner
Warner, Jack, 34, 50, 55, 109
Wasserman, Lew, 26–7, 71 n.2, 109, 110,
    112, 155–6, 193–4
Watchmen (2009), 271
Watergate, 162, 175, 178, 249
Waterworld (1995), 206
Wayne, John, 159, 166
Weinstein, Harvey, 211, 241
Welles, Orson, 54, 77, 78, 81, 152 n.13, 208
West, Nathaniel, 177
Westerns, 58, 81, 121, 163–6, 168–9
Wexler, Haskell, 146, 161
Who Framed Roger Rabbit? (1988), 219
Whyte, William, 61
Wild Bunch, The (1969), 119, 142, 163–4,
    166, 174, 253, 255 275–6, 277, 281, 282
Wilder, Billy, 54, 62, 70, 102
Williams, John, 257
Williams, Linda, 91
Willis, Gordon, 146
Wilson, Michael, 57, 67 n.15
Wizard of Oz, The (1939), 90, 168
Woo, John, 208, 256
Wood, Robin, 177
Woodstock (1970), 120
World Trade Organization (WTO), 273
Wuthering Heights (1939), 77
Wyatt, Justin, xiv, 129, 212, 246
Wyler, William, 12, 25, 41–3, 53, 55, 57,
    118

youth-oriented films, 160–1

Zanuck, Darryl, 50, 102, 110
Zanuck, Richard, 102–3, 113
Zelig (1984), 229
Zemeckis, Robert, 208, 216–17
Zukor, Adolph, 14, 18, 74